Apropos of Something

Apropos of Something

A History of Irrelevance and Relevance

ELISA TAMARKIN

The University of Chicago Press
Chicago and London

The University of Chicago Press, Chicago 60637
The University of Chicago Press, Ltd., London

Published 2022
Printed in Canada

31 30 29 28 27 26 25 24 23 22   1 2 3 4 5

ISBN-13: 978-0-226-45309-5 (cloth)
ISBN-13: 978-0-226-45312-5 (paper)
ISBN-13: 978-0-226-45326-2 (e-book)
DOI: https://doi.org/10.7208/chicago/9780226453262.001.0001

Library of Congress Cataloging-in-Publication Data

Names: Tamarkin, Elisa, author.
Title: Apropos of something : a history of irrelevance and relevance / Elisa Tamarkin.
Description: Chicago : University of Chicago Press, 2022. | Includes bibliographical references and index.
Identifiers: LCCN 2021047952 | ISBN 9780226453095 (cloth) | ISBN 9780226453125 (paperback) | ISBN 9780226453262 (e-book)
Subjects: LCSH: Relevance (Philosophy) | Meaning (Philosophy)
Classification: LCC B105.R3 T36 2022 | DDC 111—dc23
LC record available at https://lccn.loc.gov/2021047952

The University of Chicago Press gratefully acknowledges the generous support of the Andrew W. Mellon Foundation and the Division of Arts and Humanities at the University of California, Berkeley, toward the publication of this book.

⊗ This paper meets the requirements of ANSI/NISO Z39.48-1992 (Permanence of Paper).

Shipwrecks are *apropos* of nothing.

STEPHEN CRANE

Contents

Figures

1

Introduction

Accidentals

"Shipwrecks," writes Stephen Crane, "are *apropos* of nothing." They are nothing we can figure on. The line comes from his story "The Open Boat" and tells what it was like for a newspaper correspondent to be stranded at sea off the coast of Florida and the feeling, in a dinghy far from any lifesaving station, that "the whole affair is absurd." Accidents always feel inconsequent. Likewise, the signals the men in the boat try to make out from the shore "don't mean anything." That person on the beach twirling his coat around his head was not signaling to them at all, but just playing with his coat and an "idiot."[1] You would think, the correspondent says, that fate could do better.

The story, first published in 1897, is based on Crane's own adventure when, as a correspondent on his way to cover the Cuban War for Independence, his ship hit a sandbar and later sank. He rowed his way to shore in an open boat with the captain, a cook, and an oiler, but the oiler, named Billie Higgins, died when the boat overturned in the surf. Crane gave his account of the shipwreck in a newspaper right away and only then in "The Open Boat," a tale, that, according to its subtitle, is "intended to be after the fact" being "the experience of four men from the sunk steamer." In the tale, the correspondent insists that even at the time he knew it was "the best experience of his life."[2]

He tells us that there was a quality in it that was heartfelt in how the men on the dinghy were friends and were devoted to the work they were doing together and to their captain who continued to command while lying hurt in the bow. There is a body of scholarship that insists on what seems to be Crane's own strategy: the extraction of some valuable experience out of the shipwreck in a story that works to give it this transcendent quality after the fact.[3] But this is not enough for me. I want to know exactly what it means to say that the "best experience" of a life turns out to be a shipwreck and, even more, to understand this experience as the plainly ludicrous admission of something that was apropos of nothing.

Crane's tale is about how things that "don't mean anything" come to matter in the way that for thirty hours in a dinghy off the Florida coast you discover that behind every wave there is another wave that becomes "just as important." For the correspondent at the oars, each wave was so real it seemed like "the last effort of the grim water," and the result was to solidify the perception so that each wave appears like an immense "wall of water" that "shut all else" from view. "The waves," we are told, again, "were important." Now you would think it would be obvious that men in a boat rowing for their lives would not see, for example, the color of the sky at daybreak as Crane describes it except for its effect on the color of the waves. They might not see the lighthouse behind them when the waves are in front of them or the horizon very well except as it rises and dips between the monumental waves that "thrust up in points." Clearly on an open boat the waves are the point. Still, the narrator keeps insisting that the waves are *important* in a way "that is not probable to the average experience, which is never at sea in a dingey." He makes us overconscious of the fact that the men are not rowing "for sport" and that the other little boat that finally hits Billie Higgins in the head and drowns him is *important*, too, because "an overturned boat in the surf is not a plaything to a swimming man."[4] The idea seems to be that the waves take on an emphasis out of all proportion to their supposed significance if you measure them by ordinary standards, and while this should go without saying in the case of the waves, it is less apparently true of other things that become "important" to the correspondent as he rows.

In the story, it is always the expression of importance that is primary, and in every instance it depends on an attention to objects that at other times might "shade off variously into a vast penumbra of vague, unfigured things, a setting which is taken for granted" and also on a shutting out for the time being of less immediate things as the wall of water shuts out the view. Here John Dewey, drawing on William James's idea of "selective attention" from the 1890s, describes how at moments of great stress, these once "unfigured things" can become "momentarily focal," much as Crane's waves leap out against the background of the gray sky or the little dinghy comes to the surface in the current in the end.[5] An overturned boat in the surf is not interesting to most anybody, but it is immensely important to a swimming man. To him it is not a "plaything" but a part of his reality; it is, in fact, enormously real because of how in this decisive moment it gains some unexpected relation to himself. For the narrator to bring up the boat in the surf as something other than a plaything is to suggest, with William James, that wherever we feel the urgency or "excitement of reality," there "*is* 'importance' in the only real and positive sense in which importance ever anywhere can be."[6] We become conscious of the value of the same things that seemed negligible or insignificant before. The appropriateness of the kind of attention they now demand means the end of impertinence, but the value they gain depends entirely on our attitude toward them and on the way they come to impinge on each one of our lives at a particular time.

Naturally for a man at sea, the sea is shot through with meanings. In the last line of Crane's story, the narrator says that the rescued men "felt that they could then be interpreters" in much the way that the narrator has been telling us all along how some surroundings that were taken for granted come to stand out as significant. I think this is always, for Crane, the last effort of fiction—of bothering, in other words, to give a fictionalized account after a journalistic one in which something as apropos of nothing as a shipwreck becomes interpretable. The question of the setting seems key to me. From a "bit of scenery" in the story certain things take on a distinctive shape and become thematic. Out from the background or the back of consciousness, they emerge, Crane writes, as a "personification," or a living thing, like the waves the rowers had never really noticed but that now "growl" at their crests as they roll forward.[7] Once unfigured things become part of a figured framework that lifts certain aspects of an environment into importance while others sink into unimportance. The fact that the real importance of waves to people at risk of drowning is so obvious that it should but does not go without saying means that for Crane even "importance" is a matter of insistence that needs interpreters.

In 1915 Henry James wrote to H. G. Wells, "It is art that *makes* life, makes interest, makes importance." I see this book in many ways as a gloss on James's line, and the lines that precede it, in which he claims that any type of art, including literature or painting, is exactly as much "for use" as any other and, now quoting from more of James's letter,

> so far from that of literature being irrelevant to the literary report upon life, and to its being made as interesting as possible, I regard it as relevant in a degree that leaves everything else behind. It is art that *makes* life, makes interest, makes importance, for our consideration and application of these things, and I know of no substitute whatever for the force and beauty of its process.[8]

Here, briefly, is what seems distinctive in James's letter. Importance is *made*. No particular type of principle or belief exhausts the whole meaning of importance. Importance follows from "interest." It defines how an aspect of life, inviting our attention like never before, comes to mean something to us and to matter. Importance is importance *to* someone. "Our consciousness," Dewey writes in 1887, "is not indifferent or colorless, but it is regarded as having importance, having value, having *interest*. It is this peculiar fact of *interest* which constitutes the emotional side of consciousness, and it signifies that the idea which has this interest has some unique connection with the self."[9] Most deeply for James, art is exceptionally suited to raising this kind of consciousness—to bringing, that is, life *to* consciousness by making aspects of the world by which we had been unaffected as interesting and important as possible. Art is a vital business for exactly the way it compels us to take an interest and care, and it is the beauty of that process that makes James regard art "as relevant in a degree that leaves everything else behind."

Is this what being relevant is? Coming to consciousness as "having importance, having value, having *interest*?" Dewey and James offer one statement of the theme, and I will return to them but say for now that by the time James writes to Wells that art is "relevant in a degree that leaves everything else behind," people had already been thinking very hard about what it means to raise consciousness and about the force of the process by which we become conscious of things that never appeared to matter before. In other words, how the things we take in *take on* importance, value, and interest at one time or another was both a philosophical and psychological question about the "use" and "application" (in Dewey's words) of our objects of attention and the needs they meet the moment we find them worthwhile. Around 1890 William James defined consciousness as the way new feelings of "relevancy" and "practical interest" enlarge the scope and scale of our experience. From a constant stream of impressions and sensations, whenever we attend to certain elements and exclude others—whenever an object is welcomed and lingered over, emerging where it had been negligible or else arousing aversion and turning us toward a new object—we are widening our sense of "experience." More of the vast world becomes part of our intelligible world. Central to the pragmatism of James and Dewey—and later to Alfred North Whitehead, who admired them both—was understanding the sort of ideas we attend to and the sort of ideas we push into the background each time, encountering a problem or sensing a discrepancy, we quicken into awareness. What feels important is simply what we happen to select from the possibilities of a particular moment to address the needs of that moment and to cope with its contingencies—what, in recent pragmatist Robert Brandom's words, we let "pop to the surface and float in a sea of random variability."[10] What pops to the surface, in other words, becomes "relevant" to that moment, and James, Dewey, and others, including Alain Locke, dedicated themselves to understanding just how certain ideas and things happen to come up or get raised when they do. And so did their colleague, the British pragmatist F. C. S. Schiller, whom Dewey in a eulogy credits with the philosophy and "principle of relevancy."[11]

No one thought about relevance and irrelevance before the nineteenth century aside from their limited use in Scottish law for determining evidence or pleading a case. The "great discovery," in Schiller's words, of the concept of relevance was so slow that in an essay called "Relevance" for the journal *Mind* in 1912, he claimed that its "indispensability" was still "so little grasped." The *Oxford English Dictionary* traces the word *relevant* to 1560 in the context of law, but *relevance* does not occur until 1733; *irrelevant* is attributed first to Edmund Burke in 1786 and *irrelevancy* to Jeremy Bentham in 1802. Schiller finds it interesting that *irrelevant* should be centuries younger than *relevant.*

Schiller also finds that by the turn of the twentieth century, the expression of *relevance* and its opposite, *irrelevance,* were unique to the English language with nothing nearly equivalent in Greek or Latin and nothing in French, German, or Italian either. "The whole vocabulary is untranslatable," Schiller writes, because relevance is an Anglo-American idea that nevertheless took English speakers across the Atlantic centuries to appreciate where all sorts of approximations—including "it is not to the purpose" and "it doesn't matter" and "it is unessential"—simply could not fill the "lacunae in language" that *relevance* did. So while for Schiller, writing in 1930, the theory of relevance was "still rudimentary" and "entirely foreign to any philosophic language," the sense of it was "too valuable not to be in constant use under a variety of names, English being the only language equipped with a complete and adequate vocabulary for it." The best French translation around the time was something like *pertinent* or *à propos*, but these terms do not conceptually work the way *relevant* works, which is why French ultimately imports the word *relevante* as a loanword from English. In German, *Relevanz* is borrowed from English too.[12]

The difficulty of finding a good translation for a word that is English in its use and currency—a translation that honors its debts and inscribes in another language the most "relevant" or right equivalent for the original—makes the French word *relevante*, for Jacques Derrida, an epitome of the challenges of translation itself. "Well," he says, "this word 'relevant' carries in its body an ongoing process of translation . . . ; as a translative body, it endures or exhibits translation as the memory or stigmata or suffering [*passion*] or, hovering above it, as an aura or halo."[13] Derrida's essay, "What Is a 'Relevant' Translation," defines translation *as* an operation of relevance—that of finding the most adequate, the most appropriate or fitting, words we can—while the word *relevance* proves that even a smart translation has the stigma of being adequate at best. Derrida's efforts to find a relevant translation for *relevance* in German and French—a translation that at least has an *aura* of relevance—tells us a lot about the origins and philosophy of relevance and how it operates. His essay will come up again.

The word *relevant* derives from the verb "to relevate" which has dropped out of use but whose meaning is to bring up or to lift (as in "to elevate"). So to make something relevant is to raise it. When the subject or idea that is raised is fitting or apropos to the moment that it arises—when it has some bearing on that moment—then we say that *this* object or idea is relevant and, of course, when it has no bearing at all and does not seem well suited, then we say that it is irrelevant. To relevate, then, is to take something up; but, actually, to re-levate, with its prefix (*re-*) meaning *again*, is to take it up again, on another occasion. So some subject—let's say a nineteenth-century story of a shipwreck—will be raised in another context on another occasion (let's say our contemporary context), and if it is fitting to this new context, then it is relevant, and if it is not fitting, then it is irrelevant.

I thought it would be interesting to understand how these efforts to raise something, or make it relevant, came to be seen as the ethical imperative that defines both our adequacy as critics and the worth of those subjects that either will or will not stand up to our unprecedented demands on them. After all, whatever our potential as writers or scholars might be, I doubt we ever would choose to be irrelevant—although we often make the case in the humanities for the value of the trivial, the inappreciable, the details and gestures, the everyday, the momentary, the neglected and forgotten, and also for the use of the useless along the lines of Abraham Flexner's classic book, *The Usefulness of Useless Knowledge*. We mean to draw out and realize these nonapparent things. To make visible, in Wallace Stevens's words, the "seemings" of things "intenser than any actual life could be" as a legitimate and perceptible part of life.[14] We want them to rise up like a tidal wave on an open boat and be important and not subside. But when we bring something to attention, we have to show what we mean by its mattering even if the use of the useless only comes in its refusal of other instrumentalities, applications, and monetized gains. We try to show why it is worth noticing even if the answer comes only in the way that it withstands the managerial language of "deliverables" and "takeaways." Some of my colleagues believe that the humanities should be recognized for the intrinsic value they have and that our interest in them should be devoid of any interest in what they can or must do or in what we can do with them. But faith in the intrinsic value of the humanities at a time when universities are asked to make a calculable impact on society, the economy, and the larger public stills puts stock in a measure of their doing and our taking away. What they can do may in fact be to serve our need for immediate or enhancing experiences beyond a specialized function and its metrics of success, but it seems useless to deny a use altogether or to say that intrinsic value is somehow opposed to utility. Ends and imperatives will always drive a sense of importance and never go away so long as we continue to act with purpose and try to be more conscious and aware than we are now. For the humanities to remain *interesting*, for example, would be very much to the point.

The question of relevance was always a response to a "problem" or a "crisis" in the university or art world. It was about making things that did not seem to matter matter against the pull of oblivion. But the people who first defined relevance insisted that you had to know first what the matter is. We rarely rethink the value of anything when nothing is wrong. Value is a pragmatic idea arising out of a nineteenth-century moment that had abandoned the search for enduring truth and replaced it with the search for enduring relevance—with the study of how things evolve to stay interesting, paramount, critical, and most of all meaningful for coming to terms with the predicaments we are in. I wanted to find out how relevance itself came to matter—what its own historical evolution reveals about the situations in which it continues to count as a value and redeeming principle—that the point of its persisting might be rescued from oblivion too.

Relevant. Originally from the Latin *relevāns*, meaning "to lift up again" and, also, "to give relief." From a phenomenal stream of thoughts and perceptions, what had seemed remote or inessential is thrown into relief. Now it is of the essence. It looms remarkably large. The apparent change in the scale of the thing does not make me believe that I am focusing on something new but on something old from a different angle. Its value lies in its adequacy to the moment in which it surfaces and in how much it satisfies the needs of the occasion. It also lies in my belief in how satisfying it can be. Relevance, Schiller writes, "implies a relation to a human purpose by its very etymology. The 'relevant' is that which *helps* by affording us *relief*."[15] From a stock of knowledge and perceptions we only become conscious of those objects that have practical importance. What stands out finally is a relief. Some objects help, but never at all times, and when we are not using them, they "will be practically irrelevant," William James writes,

> and had better remain latent. Yet since almost any object may some day become temporarily important, the advantage of having a general stock of *extra* truths, of ideas that shall be true of merely possible situations, is obvious. We store such extra truths away in our memories, and with the overflow we fill our books of reference. Whenever such an extra truth becomes practically relevant to one of our emergencies, it passes from cold-storage to do work in the world and our belief in it grows active.[16]

That inconsequential thing we buried somewhere or never even knew was there is just the thing we need right now. Maybe we saw or heard it a while ago or maybe it was that "extra truth" in a bundle of perceptions whose own practical importance we never could have realized at the time. A fact, a saying, a look, a feeling, a song, a picture, the story of an open boat, the color of the sky at daybreak. We never knew we would need it. But just when it might help us make sense of a situation, it comes to us. It lights out from the background ("cold-storage"). For William James, it becomes "relevant." Our faith that it can work by offering some kind of relief and satisfaction at the moment it reappears makes it temporarily important. For the time being it becomes part of our reality.

Again, the nineteenth century was interested in the way certain things get raised while others fall into obscurity. Since most of the perceived world is immaterial to us most of the time, how do particular objects or qualities come to matter? It became one task of philosophy to understand the "acts of attention" by which things that had been ignored or dismissed gain interest and answer to a heartfelt need, by which something that was apropos of nothing is brought into an intimate, coordinated relation to oneself. There is always a moment of recognition: the awareness of the object in question's plausibility for the occasion on which it comes into focus and demands attention after being so trivial and how fitting it seems for bringing that occasion into focus. There is even a sense that this moment never would have come together or meant much at all except for the way that that object that had once seemed negligible is now the missing piece. It happens a lot in Henry James's fiction. In *The Golden Bowl,* in ways we'll see, everything depends on a cracked bowl from an antiquarian's back shop that Maggie Verver buys with "strange inconsequence." She loiters on her way home, buying the bowl *by the way,* and eventually mounting it on her mantelpiece. How this bit of scenery is thrown into relief, how it reappears later with intensified interest, so that with "a sudden large apprehension" the worthless bowl is of the utmost relevance for solving Maggie's problem and bringing clarity and also for readjusting the picture of who matters to whom and how (it is just what she needed)—all this, for James, suggests the operation called consciousness, which is the process (or processing) by which something yet ignored or unrealized can be taken in and come to matter and bear with all its weight for us right now. Maggie brings home the bowl, and then the bowl is brought home to her as having meaning and value. She admits what it suggests (namely, that Prince Amerigo and Charlotte had known each other before), and then everything else she knows falls into place in light of it. When James tells the aspiring writer to "try to be one of the people on whom nothing is lost," it is because one never knows specifically which impressions, cast into time for future moments and selves, might all at once "become interesting" and meaningful. The concept of how we might start to count a bowl—or any object, sight, story, novel, especially one of his novels—as of interest or importance to us is fundamental to what James hopes literature can be responsive to and show. While for his brother, William James, "the whole function of philosophy ought to be to find out what definite difference" some concrete experience "will make to you and me, at definite instants of our life."[17]

Stephen Crane's story is also about "the question of the importances" as Henry James calls it, and the way things come alive for us—or become vital—as they loom into focus and demand attention. We recognize "an attached importance," James says, whenever our "consciousness bristle[s] with the notes" of "re-perusal"—that is, not simply of the memories of experiences stored away but their active transformation or "reconstruction" into useful terms for coming to terms with other experiences.[18] Life is filled with these sorts of realizations at the moments of crisis that bring them to mind.

And so, on an open boat surrounded by sharks at night off the coast of Florida, a poem "mysteriously entered the correspondent's head." It is about a soldier in the Foreign Legion dying on the sands of Algiers.

> But a comrade stood beside him, and he took that
>   comrade's hand,
> And he said: "I never more shall see my own, my
>   native land."

The correspondent had learned the poem in school but had been "perfectly indifferent" to it and "had never considered it his affair that a soldier of the Legion lay dying in Algiers." He "had never regarded it as important." In fact "he had even forgotten that he had forgotten this verse, but it suddenly was in his mind."[19]

Now, on the open boat, the poem that meant nothing to him and that he simply had forgotten he had forgotten "came to him as a human, living thing" so that he could see the solider laid out on the sand with his hand on his chest and blood oozing around his fingers. On the boat on which he cannot see a lighthouse beyond the waves, the correspondent can see a low city in the far Algerian distance set against a sky that was faint with the last colors of sunset and, as he rows, the movement of the oars keeps time with the slow and slower movement of the lips of the soldier as he takes his comrade's hand. And now the poem that mysteriously entered his head moved him to "a profound and perfectly impersonal comprehension," and he "was sorry for the soldier of the Legion who lay dying in Algiers." The poem is "no longer merely a picture of a few throes in the breast of a poet, meanwhile drinking tea" but has become part of the correspondent's reality, a "living thing," no less so than the waves that "suddenly raged out like a mountain-cat." Its power was to come to him with sudden intelligibility, demanding his full attention that night in the boat and becoming the object of his thoughts and feelings like never before. It "was an actuality—stern, mournful, and fine."[20] In the way that the poem materializes for the correspondent that night as a touchstone of his understanding, it comes to matter after all that time.

The poem had nothing to do with him, but that night on the dinghy the correspondent finds correspondences between his situation and the soldier's in Algiers. His new consciousness of the poem involves the rise into importance of something that was already there. It came to mind of all the countless things that could. Out on the boat, the poem is relevant. It has, in Whitehead's words, a "perfection of importance for that occasion," which is only to say that a poem the correspondent had so utterly disregarded that he did not even know he had disregarded it was suddenly of great interest to him.[21] For some mysterious reason, in mortal danger at sea he takes an interest in a poem he learned in school (by Caroline Sarah Elizabeth Norton, though he doesn't know her name) and in the dying soldier in the desert who seems to speak to him and who moves him toward a "profound and perfectly impersonal comprehension."

Consciousness, Dewey writes, is the "organ of adjustment in difficult situations." The difficult situation is that the correspondent knows he might drown and that "nature does not regard him as important" or care about "disposing of him." The world is indifferent to him. But then the poem that comes to mind at the moment of despair and to which he had been "perfectly indifferent" concerns him now, and so does the dying soldier in it for whom he feels sorry.[22] Something that meant nothing now bears on him greatly as an object of concern.

Who cares about rediscovering a poem in the perilous aftermath of a shipwreck? The correspondent does. How could an "unimportant" poem possibly feel important to the correspondent as he rows (like the waves or like an overturned boat to a swimming man)? Shipwrecks are apropos of nothing, but the correspondent keeps looking for meaning and sense. In the poem he finds something that satisfies this need for "comprehension"—in the felt intensity of a shared reality or maybe in the way that he and the soldier in Algiers are, so to speak, "in the same boat." The poem the correspondent learned as a child and that never interested him invites this connection, and the more it interests him and comes to life for him, the more the picture it presents becomes a part of his reality ("an actuality"). And the excitement of this realization—of realizing, that is (or actualizing for him), something he had always discounted—means that he overcomes indifference.

Well then, could there be anything *more* important for an exhausted man whose life depends on rowing through the night?

"Events," Dewey writes, "that have no attributed meanings are accidents and if they are big enough are catastrophes." But events that stand out from what went before and came after, so as to express some pervading or consummatory quality, become for Dewey "*an* experience and [reveal] a dimension of the meaning of the human encounter of the world." It is fair to say that the correspondent on the boat is trying to avert catastrophe. He does this not by asking the point of the shipwreck (since shipwrecks are apropos of nothing) but by seeing what purpose he can give it. I think this is what the story means when it says that the correspondent knew even at the time that it was "the best experience of his life," a line all the more surprising for suggesting that the shipwreck remained the best experience of his life even "after the fact" when the oiler had drowned. The story is out to show how the shipwreck emerged for him as an experience that came to matter or that clarified what matters by making him conscious of a pervasive human quality that he never would have noticed otherwise. It took a crisis, but what was lost or mere wreckage is brought within the range of appreciation. So for the poem in the story as for the story of the shipwreck written after the fact, the correspondent pulls these things out from the abyss and holds them up for consideration. He feels then that he could be an "interpreter."[23] Finding value where he had missed it before—expanding the sense of what might count as appreciable to him and worth reflecting on within a changing field of consciousness—he enlarges his understanding too. Seeing a wreck as relevant—something that raises consciousness so as to reveal "a dimension of the meaning of the human encounter of the world"—is practically how the correspondent overcomes indifference and gets on with his task, whether it's rowing all night in a dinghy or readjusting to the circumstances of his life after a shipwreck in which a friend has drowned.

Laurence Buermeyer, a philosopher, critic, and friend of Dewey, writes of a trainwreck instead of a shipwreck:

> To take a trip in a train is usually no more a single "experience" than to sit reading in a room for an afternoon. It becomes such, it becomes an "adventure," if the train is wrecked. . . . In general, the stream of events which flows by us unnoticed takes on order, and its parts become distinct and clearly interrelated, the moment our feelings are strongly touched and our resulting actions modify the matter under way. Even if what is impressive or momentous is merely observed and not participated in, its parts take shape and stand out from the background of what is observed vaguely or

> not at all. They do so because our spontaneous interests furnish a criterion of momentousness and a rule of relevance.

How does an accident become an "experience?" Against the stream of events that flows by us unnoticed, this event, inciting an immediate and emotional response, stands out. It takes on a distinctive shape against the background of all the events that are observed vaguely every day or not at all. One decisive moment extricated from the perceptual field and made momentous because it violates expectations and routine. Not all train rides capture our attention, but a disturbing one does. It becomes, in Dewey's terms, "a conscious fact." It acquires importance. Relative to everything else happening at this time, it is phenomenally salient. We attempt to make it out and make sense of it. Our spontaneous interest in it, Buermeyer says, furnishes "a rule of relevance."[24]

Relevance makes it possible to think about the unthinkable; Buermeyer, in other words, is trying to understand how the noncognitive becomes a special object of attention and thought. Psychologies of relevance set out to understand the selectivity of consciousness and emphasis—why we turn to *this* and not to *that* out of a world of possible objects. "Any perception itself involves the problem of choice," writes Alfred Schutz in his study "Preliminary Notes on the Problem of Relevance," inspired by William James.[25] Buermeyer uses the example of a trainwreck because it is obvious why a trainwreck would create a sudden "problem" in consciousness and excite our interest enough to turn to it. So Buermeyer chooses a trainwreck to show the vivid emergence of something that is apropos of nothing *as* paramount, but he might as well have chosen a poem that leaps to mind in the midst of a trainwreck, because his concern is with the ways in which an unexpected or puzzling perception may lead to a meaningful "experience." His concern is with the suddenly real particularities of a created consciousness rising from the dead or from obscurity, from out of the wreck and into relief so that we pick up on them while also picking them up or *taking them up* as a spontaneous matter of interest. The rule of relevance suggests that they will amount to something. That they will have value in this context. But our "experience," for Buermeyer—or our "adventure"—implies that they are only of value insofar as they happen to you or me. Whitehead, writing in *Process and Reality* about what relevance entails, sees it as the process by which exposure to new or unfamiliar things takes on value and importance; like Buermeyer, he defines relevance as an "adventure": every "flash of novelty," he suggests "is an adventure in the clarification of thought." Dewey also describes relevance as an "adventure," and so does Isabelle Stengers in reference to Whitehead. The sociologist Martin Savransky calls his great book about relevance in the social sciences *The Adventure of Relevance*.[26] For all of them, finding relevance is in the nature of what it means to have an experience.

Buermeyer writes about the experience of a trainwreck in his book *Aesthetic Experience*, so I mean it when I say that the trainwreck might as well be a poem. His trainwreck is a model for the ways in which an object commands our attention and interest, making us turn to it and then, in turning it over, discovering we care. How can a trainwreck be like an artwork? Because, Buermeyer would say, we are mostly unaware, so "what we notice, among the innumerable things and events to which our senses testify, is primarily what bears upon our conduct, what serves as a guide to what we are to do."[27] Art, in other words, is phenomenally good at making us aware of things we never would bother to notice otherwise. It makes us look and take an interest right where we are ordinarily oblivious. It holds out something unapparent for particular accentuation and manifests it concretely, like the soldier in Algiers for the correspondent in the boat. A poem, in other words, can work to enlarge our understanding of what counts as important—to admit things that had been immaterial or lost to us, or wholly alien to us, into a significant relationship to ourselves. And, in bringing us to acknowledge so much more than we had before by bringing these things up at a problematic moment or under circumstances in which they would seem to be apropos of nothing, we "furnish a criterion of momentousness and a rule of relevance." There can be value beyond where we had imagined it to be. I think this is what Crane is after when he suggests that an "unimportant" poem by Caroline Sarah Elizabeth Norton might acquire importance and become the touchstone of the best experience of a life. Or what anyone would be after in suggesting that a story by Stephen Crane about a nineteenth-century shipwreck might be relevant today.

Stephen Crane gives us only a glimpse of the framework for recovering what relevance is and why people keep insisting that art or literature should have it even if they are insisting for the wrong reasons. I hope that the history of relevance will come together eventually in these pages and feel valuable, even as relevance emerged in the nineteenth century as the phenomenology and psychology of "mattering for oneself and for others." Relevance is always at its core a struggle for "perceptual recognition," which is the term Alain Locke uses to describe how the redistribution of attention that art demands can change our perception of importance so that what is unperceived in the background comes to the foreground and takes on substance instead. For Locke, these revelations are gestalt shifts and have enormous social and ethical consequences. William James, in an essay titled "What Makes a Life Significant," writes that the work of looking for significance has "the most tremendous practical importance," being the "basis of all our tolerance, social, religious, and political."[28] It is a statement that I will need to explain as I go, but for James, the *practical importance* of critical recognition is not so dissimilar from the way that coming to terms with a poem about a soldier in Algiers helps a correspondent save himself and some friends on a boat.

Nowadays questions of relevance are most often associated with the ongoing crisis in the humanities at a time when university funding increasingly depends on external measures of utility and social consequence. We have gotten in the habit of insisting on the "practical importance" of what we do. We justify our labor as scholars in ways that confirm our worth to the public. We calculate the employment outcomes, financial benefits, and profitability of a liberal arts education in the past and as a predictor of its future. Or we argue for the relevance of the humanities to other distant fields and domains of knowledge, from economics to the sciences and technology, whose social impacts are more measurable. Sometimes, in claiming that the humanities sharpen our moral perception or our critical understanding of complexity and difference, we aspire to the civic goals that Martha Nussbaum, Geoffrey Harpham, and others describe as "the fashioning of an informed citizenry."[29] That is, in teaching us to think critically, the arts and humanities prepare us to participate in a democracy.

We say that the humanities have value for the wider world or else we object, like Stanley Fish, and say that the humanities have value for their own sake and "cannot be justified except in relation to the pleasure they give" (though the pleasure, for Fish, is worth subsidizing). Still others reject the notion of value altogether as the measure of an "audit culture" focused on market-driven aims and productivity and on justifying the humanities as a personal investment—in future happiness or earning power, take your pick. They speak instead of meaning in the humanities that is of the essence and not fungible or manipulable toward payoffs elsewhere. They would say that the humanities are fundamentally against value, since value is complicit with the neoliberal systems of accountability that define the institutions that fund them and does not acknowledge experiences of significance and even insignificance that may be *invaluable*. Reading a poem can be wonderful perhaps but also largely unproductive by any measure of social or economic ends that in turn fail to evaluate adequately what is so wonderful about a poem that eludes every system of value. It is what Maurice Blanchot means when he writes, "In this sense, criticism—literature—seems to me to be associated with one of the most difficult, but important, tasks of our time, played out in a necessarily vague movement: the task of preserving and of liberating thought from the notion of value."[30] And so around we go, identifying some quality that is relevant or corresponds to contemporary society or else some quality (aesthetic, spiritual, intellectual, pleasurable) that is valuable in itself. Or we propose that the value of the humanities and arts is in their irrelevance, being the experience of nonattachment and nonparticipation in an abstracted, instrumentalizing world of costs and profit margins. But the moment we make a case for the importance of the humanities—the moment we ask ourselves why in the world a poem should ever matter to us or to anyone else in the midst of a crisis or what kind of problems or needs it might address or why a poem justifies the attention we seem to be giving it anyway—we are making value judgments, not only judgments of relevance but judgments that a poem is interesting and worth pursuing. We are suggesting that the humanities are not being ignored because they are irrelevant but irrelevant because they are being ignored. We are taking a pragmatic approach to what we do.

The pragmatists who first defined relevance as a concept were unapologetic about their aestheticism and love of the arts. They were influenced by earlier nineteenth-century writers and thinkers—including logicians, philosophers, psychologists, and scientists—who, also believing that the arts have practical importance, kept them steadily in focus. The pragmatists influenced Whitehead, Schutz, and other philosophers in turn but also, more or less directly, a range of figures in the fields of sociology, logic, linguistics, cognitive science, and communications theory—including the first authors of "relevance theory" in the 1980s—who, at various times, placed literary or visual art at the center of their investigations into how human minds are so organized as to seek and find relevance whenever they are exposed to something new.

So I came to realize that to write a history of relevance across these fields—and as the point, I think, at which they converge—put me easily in the position of writing criticism too. Criticism itself emerges from a philosophy and "logic of values," the logic being that each poem or painting might be considered a proposition for getting hold of something and then raising it in a particular way. Each just might, through some process of appreciation, arrive at a moment of real clarity—a crystallization—or what Schiller, in speaking of relevance, likes to describe as the sudden large awareness of having gathered loose ends and gotten to "the point." In other words, it became clear to me that the concept of finding relevance was from the start linked to questions of art's *point* and worth in human affairs and also that art appeared to be a form that essentially demonstrated the perceptual and attentional process of taking something up as valuable that relevance implied. Not only is the idea of *relevance* not opposed to art and artistic pursuits but the function of art, in raising and accentuating "what is characteristically valuable in things of everyday enjoyment" is, these thinkers suggested, the epitome of what relevance can be. So while they might not have gone so far as the poetry critic Laurence Perrine as to say that "total relevance is the condition to which all art aspires" (in a line I promise to explain), they certainly thought that poems or paintings were consummate acts of taking up unexpected, unregarded, and insignificant objects and making them serve the needs of the occasion, making them, in fact, utterly important to the experience the occasion demands.[31] When it works, art instantiates relevance as a value.

It may not be the case, as Schutz writes, with Thomas Luckmann, that "the relevance problem" is "the most important and at the same time the most difficult problem that the description of the life-world has to solve." And yet when so much depends for continuance on claims of relevance—when the ubiquitous demand to *be* relevant has become a referendum on the future of literary studies especially, whose "death" (as a primarily literary concern) appears to be its only hope—it might help to understand what relevance as a practical problem entails and the value it promises when we choose to pursue it. I keep returning to Henry James's belief that "literature is relevant in a degree that leaves everything else behind" as reason to have faith, too, before we leave anything else behind as irrelevant to institutions of knowledge that demand constant novelty and shifting sites of interest. The faith would come, I think, in the feeling expressed by Whitehead that "there is no irrelevance" just "neglected modes of relevance"; in the promise, that is, of new meaning in the old and in the assurance that we *make interest, make importance* by raising matters that were apropos of nothing as matters of interest to us. Relevance "saves," writes Whitehead, and "loses nothing that can be saved"; this is its "function"—which brings us back to James's very literary hope that nothing be lost.[32]

2

On the Threshold

Clue, Hint, Poem

In Edgar Allan Poe's "The Raven," a raven, having escaped from its owner, is driven by a storm one dreary midnight to the window of a student whose light is still on. The student, having drifted off while reading "forgotten" books and half dreaming of his dead love, Lenore, is awakened by the sound of flapping wings against the lattice. He opens the shutter to see what is there and inadvertently lets in a raven who alights on a bust just above his chamber door (and sits and nothing more).

In "The Philosophy of Composition," Poe writes that the bust was "absolutely *suggested* by the bird" because of the way the stark contrast between the black raven and the white marble puts the raven into relief. The student was nearly napping, but a strange bird came to him out of the blue and now it has his full attention. From half consciousness to full consciousness, that bird is on the threshold. Overexcited by the effect of a grave raven "seeking admission" in the middle of the night and at such a sorrowful moment when he is mourning Lenore, he finds the bird's appearance very fitting.[1]

But it is an impertinent bird. Having learned by rote the single word *nevermore*, it keeps repeating it reflexively in response to any question, including the demand for its name:

> "Tell me what thy lordly name is on the Night's Plutonian shore!"
> Quoth the Raven "Nevermore."
>
> Much I marvelled this ungainly fowl to hear discourse so plainly,
> Though its answer little meaning—*little relevancy bore*;[2]

Little relevancy bears: after all, "nevermore" is its only "stock and store." And yet the student, who is superstitious and also indulging in his mourning, will not take the bird at its word. He begins to look past the refrain "Nevermore" for evidence of intentions that are not present in it—the bird is evil or maybe a prophet—while the word gives utterance to certain thoughts effected by the melancholy occasion. It seems to answer to the student's fear, for example, that there will be no respite from mourning (*nevermore*) or that there is no heaven and he'll never see Lenore again (*nevermore*). He confuses the meaning of the word *nevermore* with the way it makes him feel, so that the response to the raven is ultimately a response to the reminiscence of Lenore, the accidental by-product of a feeling that seems to reveal a meaning. By the time he commands the bird to leave him and to quit the bust above the door (and the bird replies, "Nevermore"), it is clear that the raven's effect will remain with him, though the raven remains pointless.[3]

There is no getting past the fact that the raven's answers to the student's escalating questions are apropos of nothing. The raven, repeating the single word by rote, is preposterous and even the student keeps smiling at the ludicrous incongruity of a pet bird "croaking 'Nevermore'" in such a ghastly way. The raven is only raving and means nothing by it. Raving is also what the student seems to be doing when he thinks he makes sense of the raven's non sequiturs as if they have final importance. *Raven*, as Jerome McGann points out, would have been acoustically indistinguishable from *raving*, since the *g* terminating an *-ing* ending was mostly an unvoiced letter in rhymed poetry. So the poem "The Raven" might as well be "The Raving," and the bird is absurd. And yet the raven "never flitting, still is sitting, *still* is sitting," and the student, having pulled up a chair to sit in front of it, keeps looking for a meaningful context—epistemological, eschatological, any context—that might justify an impertinent bird.[4] The context he finds that works—a context that finally is determined by his search for relevance—is none other than a poem (let's call it "The Raven"), but more on this in a moment.

There are very few literary works I can find that use any variant of the word *relevance* before "The Raven," and perhaps none that use it outside of a brief mention of proceedings in a court of law. Relevance, as I said, does not have much of a history before the nineteenth century. It was invoked to determine witnesses who might testify in a legal case so that the case could be decided expeditiously and not hampered by too many details. The concept of relevance in the nineteenth century follows from its limited precedent in law, but it does not actually enter into "evidence law" until this time (in ways I describe later), and there are no instances before 1800 of the way that Henry James or William James comes to use it or of the way that Poe uses it here. When the student claims that the raven's answer "little relevancy bore," he means that the bird's answers do not answer to him in any ostensible way. Relevance in the prior, legal sense spoke to a limiting of admissible testimony in order to determine the truth of a case, but truth isn't really at issue here. For all the student knows the raven's name *is* Nevermore, and in any case, the complaint is not that the bird lies but that its answer "little meaning—little relevancy" bears. The problem with the raven is that it does not at first satisfy the student's need to find its appearance meaningful on that stormy and mournful night.

And yet the raven creates a disturbance even if it doesn't mean it. The student was in a sort of stupor—half reading, half dreaming—but then the bird comes to him from out of nowhere and the student *comes to*. The raven is a "mystery," he says, and what is mysterious demands explanation and, in any case, the fact that such a weird bird quoting "Nevermore" enters his chamber where it does not belong excites him. He wheels a seat right up to where it sits in high relief on that white bust. Alfred Schutz, who claims that every search for relevance begins with a problem or disturbance that needs explaining, notes that the Greek root of the word *problem* is equivalent to the Latin root of the word *object*; both originally mean "that which is thrown before" my mind and thoughts.[5] Because the raven is so troubling, it becomes an *object* of attention. It wakes the student up and makes him think. He thinks his way through all the meaningless answers that do not fit the questions until he arrives at questions for which they fit:

> "Is there—*is* there balm in Gilead?—tell me—tell me, I implore!"
> Quoth the Raven "Nevermore."
>
> . . . .
>
> "Tell this soul with sorrow laden if, within the distant Aidenn,
> It shall clasp a sainted maiden whom the angels name Lenore—
> Clasp a rare and radiant maiden whom the angels name Lenore."
> Quoth the Raven "Nevermore."

And the point is that this process of plausible construal, the construction of explanations on the wing (at least of questions that can be answered), is the strange cognitive work that arises from focalizing on nothing but a bird who is doing nothing more, as the student knows, than quoting a single word by rote.[6]

Even so, the cognitive dissonance of *nevermore* echoing in that echo chamber of his begins to resonate. It stretches his mind as far as it can possibly go (to heaven and back). Making such a pointless word worth the vigilance he pays it is what guides his interpretative process, and though he infers so much more than "Nevermore" admits, this does not mean for a minute that what he learns in the process should not be believed. It now dawns on the student, for example, that there is no hope and he will never see Lenore again. Whatever understanding he has gained by the end of the poem, when he finds his soul shattered in the shadow of the raven on the floor, it has satisfied his expectations of relevance. The bird's impertinent words have become pertinent to his sorrow and urgent need for answers and to the dawning, desperate awareness that Lenore is gone.

That the raven takes possession of his mind and thoughts, like the fiend or devil he thinks it is, is only the sign of how compelling he finds it, of how much, at this moment, it appeals to him most intimately. The student says he "marvelled" at it. I am reminded, by the critic Terence Cave, that conscious attention "begins with wonder." Certainly a raven with the mien of a "lord or lady" perching above a chamber door and only answering "Nevermore" is wonderful! The fact that the student turns to it when he had been half sleeping and absentminded seems to suggest what William James suggests in quoting his friend Josiah Royce: "Our own activity of attention will thus determine what we are to know and what we are to believe." The more the student attends to the raven, the more real it feels to him: the atmosphere around it grows "denser," thicker; its eyes, now "fiery," begin to burn into his "bosom's core." All at once, it speaks *to* him. The more he acknowledges the raven's lingering presence, the more salient it becomes. His belief in the raven grows active. James proposes, in *The Principles of Psychology*, that "*our belief and attention* are the same fact," just two names for the same psychological phenomenon. "*Whatever things have intimate and continuous connection with my life are things of whose reality I cannot doubt*"; any relation to our mind at all "*suffices to make an object real.* The barest appeal to our attention is enough for that."[7] We consign our faith to the objects of our attention, as the student devastatingly learns when he "admits" the bird. He really takes it in.

If we grant that the raven bears little relevance and meaning at first but a great deal by the end, the poem makes us wonder what relevance is for and why the speaker keeps pursuing it. Poe, again, is one of the very first writers to think about the value of relevance. He thinks about it in "The

Raven" and "The Philosophy of Composition" (about writing "The Raven") and in other works of criticism, but also in detective stories—a genre he invented—where he suggests that in solving a case, it is "mal-practice of the courts to confine evidence and discussion to the bounds of apparent relevancy." Here the detective, C. Auguste Dupin, continues in "The Mystery of Marie Rogêt":

> Yet experience has shown, and a true philosophy will always show, that a vast, perhaps the larger portion of truth, arises from the seemingly irrelevant. . . . The history of human knowledge has so uninterruptedly shown that to collateral, or incidental, or accidental events we are indebted for the most numerous and most valuable discoveries, that it has at length become necessary, in any prospective view of improvement, to make not only large, but the largest allowances for inventions that shall arise by chance, and quite out of the range of ordinary expectation.[8]

How can the *seemingly irrelevant* be so important?

Or maybe we should first ask, What are the procedures for discovering relevance? Critics sometimes talk about the use of inductive methods in Poe's tales of ratiocination. His detective observes the particulars of a case, discovers new facts, and then infers his theory of the crime in accordance with these facts. The reader of Poe's tales knows that a good detective will take into account what deductive logic alone cannot, namely, new kinds of facts and evidence outside the "bounds of apparent relevancy" to any idea of the crime determined in advance. The detective's knowledge will derive from facts that appear to be accidental, incidental, unexpected, collateral to and diversionary from the main event. He wants us to "concentrate our attention" not on the "interior points of [the] tragedy"—the information that is remarkable to the tragedy—but on its unremarkable "outskirts."[9] To pull a seat right up to something that seems impertinent and turn it over in our minds. In other words, what is "seemingly irrelevant" to the crime may be just what we need to throw light on the problem of solving it.

But the sort of inferring this takes is not exactly inductive, and Poe famously rejected both deduction and induction as "creeping . . . crawling" modes of calculative thought that are incapable of creating new knowledge. Inductive reasoning implies that the facts add up. From circumstantial particulars it draws general rules, and then from the general rules we can deduce and explain further cases. Induction for John Stuart Mill is "the operation of discovering and proving general propositions"—of explaining phenomena by general laws—while deduction verifies these general propositions and determines whether particular cases are consistent with them.[10] In other words, induction recognizes the premises that deduction goes on to apply. We start with the facts and then infer some principle by which they work or fit and by which future, similar cases will work too—while all along the process of induction keeps testing whether the principles adequately explain the facts and particulars we observe.

But for Poe, who mocks Mill's logic, methods of inducing and deducing are not imaginative enough to make the facts meaningful. They are just what the Parisian police do in the detective stories as they systematically work through the evidence of a case and learn nothing. They probe all the pockets of the crime scene, but their practice of investigating only ever follows from their idea of the crime to begin with. In "The Purloined Letter," they look into the nooks and crannies of every hiding place to find the hidden purloined letter without ever questioning what it might mean to hide it *from them*. (The criminal puts it out in the open where he knows they will overlook it.) "They have no variation of principle in their investigations;" says Dupin; "at best, when urged by some unusual emergency—by some extraordinary reward—they extend or exaggerate their old modes of *practice*, without touching their principles."[11]

With deductive arguments, no terms can be discovered that are not already in the premises prima facie. The police either find or do not find what they're looking for. But for Poe, inductive arguments produce no new terms either. Their understanding of the evidence rests on the scrupulous description of the evidence they serve to explain. They believe that the conceptual links among the facts really "exist in the facts themselves," as Mill writes.[12] They assume that data adds right up to theories of data or to "general truths" in consistent ways, just as two plus two equals four.

Poe knows that two plus two does not always equal four. It does not equal four, for example, when two cups of water plus two cups of water spill into a puddle on the table. Two plus two does not equal four when two parts hydrogen combine with two parts oxygen to make water plus some oxygen left over. In areas outside of mathematics and algebra, Dupin says, "it is very usually *un*true that the aggregated parts are equal to the whole." In chemistry the axiom often fails, where the reaction is usually more than the sum of its parts. In human behavior it is not necessarily the case that two separate motives have, as Poe writes, "a value when united, equal to the sum of their value apart."[13] Sometimes motives compete and cancel each other out. Sometimes they don't add up. In Poe's tales, multiple motives usually mean madness.

One cannot simply go around collecting facts, as the philosopher of science Carl Hempel suggests in claiming that there are

> no generally applicable "rules of induction," by which hypotheses or theories can be mechanically derived or inferred from empirical data. The transition from data to theory requires creative imagination. Scientific hypotheses and theories are not *derived* from observed facts, but *invented* in order to account for them. They constitute guesses at the connections that might obtain between the phenomena under study.

David N. Stamos cites Hempel in a book that understands Poe's scientific imagination as importantly attached to this sort of "guessing." Not step-by-step calculus but only an "intuitive leap" can finally grasp the relations between seemingly unconnected facts and observations. These are the "eureka moments" that Poe describes in his "Prose Poem" *Eureka,* a sudden dawning of the way that components come together, the flash of insight that sees all at once a "complexity of relation out of irrelation."[14]

Poe sounds less like Mill in *Eureka* and much more like Mill's rival in the 1840s on the topic of induction, William Whewell, who believed that we need to bring intuition and imagination to inductive inference in order to discover something new. Whewell described the intuitive leap that knowledge requires as a "colligation of facts": a process by which the "discoverer" invents, tries, selects, and rejects "many conjectures, till he finds one which answers the purpose of combining the scattered facts into a single rule." More than observing facts, more than synthesis, "colligation" is the work of inspiration. It connects and unifies facts through "suitable Conceptions" brought speculatively *to* the inductive process rather than abstracted from it. In order to colligate facts, we "believe more than we see." The mind, by "superinducing" on the observed facts some idea that unites them, contributes a new element to them with "the very act of thought by which they are combined." Whewell says that the minds

> that feel a conviction of principles of unity as yet undetected, that believe in the existence of truths wider than they can limit by phrases habitually current, and that assent to the possibility of a connection among laws

> that seem far asunder, while they acknowledge their ignorance what the connection is; these are minds which have the best chance of discovering new principles.

Eventually, after trial and error, the scientist or detective will become conscious of the "*unity or totality of interest*" in how the collected facts are valuable and constitutive of some important idea. The idea might even be as important as God, since Whewell believed this sort of inferring is the only method of arriving at the ultimate truth we cannot see (but much more on God later). The point is that the evidence at hand suddenly clicks—and while the moment may have been prepared for by a long and slow investigation, it arrives as one instantaneous "lightning flash," a revelation in the dark.[15]

I think that for Poe this flash is the dawning of relevance. Everything fits! But before it does, it is hard to trace the "shadowy," half-conscious steps, the onset of understanding in which the incomprehensible pieces get slotted into place. Poe sees this sudden recognition of *fit* as the consummatory moment of what he calls "poetic intellect" in which the promise of meaning comes in the adaptation of all the "irrelative" and component facts into a unifying idea. This is why in *Eureka*, a metaphysical work about the origin and nature of the universe, Poe's cosmological vision of the interconnectedness of all things is likened to the harmony of a poem. The universe "is but the most sublime of poems" and "therefore to be treated *poematically*." Poe claims that he wants *Eureka*, a book speculating about the "Original Unity" of the universe, to be judged not as science or as philosophy of science but "as a Poem only."

In Poe's detective tales, the detective who thinks poetically can see consistency, design, or a single plot in loose facts that are outside the "bounds of apparent relevancy." For the poetic thinker, *seemingly irrelevant* information is not beyond conjecture. But it takes a form of conjecture to "solve the problem as a big picture, in terms of overall consistency" and to recognize the missing piece.[16] It takes poetry to show how seemingly irrelevant things might really count.

What makes a crime scene like a poem? When Dupin in "The Purloined Letter" infers how the clues come together and come to matter, it is because he is thinking like a poet (he admits he has been "guilty of certain doggerel" in his day). That the various clues amount to a crime that only a poetic imagination can solve proves that only a poet could have done it.

(We learn that the cabinet minister who has stolen the letter from the royal apartments of the woman he blackmails is also a "poet" or, as Dupin adds later, a "poet *and* mathematician.") It is not just Dupin's ability to think analogically—to imaginatively identify with the mind of the criminal and to think *like* him. Like him, and unlike the police, Dupin can seize on truths beyond applied principles or at least extend the applicability of these principles so outrageously far as to imagine that something might be hidden in plain sight. But the point is also that Dupin has the ability not to find more facts than the police but to see more of the found facts *as* evidence, to recognize that something the police pass over as irrelevant might be admitted as relevant to the case.

What they miss before their eyes in the minister's hotel room Dupin sees as having been there all along: the soiled, crumpled, purloined letter placed "contemptuously" on display in a card rack. The minister, "D—," has put his large, black seal on it, so that the invitation to notice the letter comes, in Dupin's words, "bearing the D—cipher *very* conspicuously." (Decipher, it announces! Perceive this and solve!) The letter is turned inside out to reveal everything, but only Dupin is capable of the revelation because only he perceives what they ignore. In other words, the letter right out in the open on a card rack suspended in the middle of the mantelpiece dares everyone to notice it, but "the hyperobtrusive situation of this document, full in the view of every visiter," proves that nothing is more invisible to most of us than the ordinary objects surrounding us. The criminal shows his cards. He sets them down squarely. But the police will never be able to recognize something so ever-present as a card in a card rack as worthy of attention, to see it as standing out enough to call it out. Therefore the minister, crumpling and tearing the letter and throwing it unsubtly into so obvious a place for a letter as a card rack, is aiming, in Dupin's words, "to delude the beholder into an idea of the worthlessness of the document."[17] The police never will have the imagination to find something so seemingly unimportant important enough to give it a thought. They will never take note of the kind of things they have never found notable. After all, papers thrown on racks of paper do not usually capture our attention. Only Dupin finds the letter interesting enough to see its value.

For Poe, the detective who thinks like a poet finds apparently worthless details of great worth. They capture his attention. He detects significance in items that seem so negligible, trivial, or commonplace that no one ever cared to notice them before. These include the quality of an overheard voice in "The Murders in the Rue Morgue" (what if it wasn't human?) and a seemingly pointless naval officer buried in the background of the life of the murdered Marie Rogêt. Certain items in the reports pop out for Dupin but not for anyone else in a way that changes the shape of his thinking. He sees them as meaningful, as *clues*. He starts the process of gathering these "small insights," in Carlo Ginzburg's words, within a "conjectural paradigm," of arranging the loose threads in a tight weave. If he can make all the points come together and fit, they will no longer be beside the point, and he will have solved the case. But, again, Dupin's originality consists in the aptitude for finding in the facts that are already found the clues to an "insoluble mystery." What was in the background (say, in Marie's background or in the background of a news report or, in the case of the purloined letter, in the background of a room), Dupin draws out. This is why he can solve the mystery in "The Mystery of Marie Rogêt" from his accustomed armchair "at a distance from the scene of the atrocity" and with no other means of investigation but what the police reports and newspapers provide: he works with the same material as everyone else.

The "mass of information" is readily there, but Dupin has a better sense than everyone else of which items to focus on. "Divert[ing] inquiry" from the crime itself to the "circumstances which surround it," Dupin turns his attention to all the incidental, accidental, and diversionary information that appears to be outside "the bounds of apparent relevancy." He resolves "to *calculate upon the unforeseen*," arising by chance—the aspects of the reports that are apropos of nothing—and then to construct a scheme or explanation that develops the suggestions and bears them out. So while the narrator in the tale, upon reading the newspapers that Dupin brings to his attention, says, "they not only seemed to me irrelevant, but I could perceive no mode in which any one of them could be brought to bear upon the matter in hand," Dupin finds that the very same extracts, if you handle them rightly, do matter "most fitly." He does not collect or uncover evidence so much as put a spotlight on what is already in plain view but imperceptible to the police, the narrator, and the reader, seizing on facts that have been ignored or overlooked and bringing them out like flares. The solution to the crime he dreams up from his armchair works not because he has discovered new facts and induced a theory from them but because, in his feeling for how apparently insignificant and diversionary things might ultimately count, he discovers relevance. The relevance of the "deviations" *is* the eureka moment for the detective who, in Dupin's words, "embrace[s] *all* contingencies."[18] The detective catches these red herrings red-handed.

In Ginzburg's classic work on how looking for "clues" becomes a model for knowledge, he describes how Sherlock Holmes values—actually, overvalues—"apparently negligible details." Fixing his attention on trivialities, accessories, incidentals, marginal information, and inadvertent gestures, Holmes inflates them into clues that point fantastically to a larger truth. The slightest hint will open onto the gravest reality. The smallest moment might prove to be momentous if only we know where to look. Like the symptom for the physician, the clue can be either diagnostic or prognostic. It suggests "an attitude oriented towards the analysis of specific cases" that can be solved only through nearly imperceptible hints that are "usually considered of little importance." It is an epistemological paradigm, Ginzburg writes, "characterized by the ability to construct from apparently insignificant experimental data a complex reality that could not be experienced directly."

These clues, after all, are "thought to be irrelevant" in the eyes of most people. Knowledge of this sort is based on concrete experience but is ultimately conjectural. For Ginzburg, it falls just outside of logical methods (including inductive methods) because the detective infers relationships between the facts that are much too subtle and so much deeper than the little clues could ever verify. "Imponderable elements come into play: instinct, insight, intuition." And while this evidentiary paradigm has very early roots—even as early as the first hunters studying the tracks of their quarry—Ginzburg says that it only begins to assert itself as a paradigm in the arts and sciences of the late nineteenth century: in Arthur Conan Doyle's detective fiction (influenced by Poe) and in other forms of detection that "laid stress on the significance of minor details." For example, the Italian art historian Giovanni Morelli, in his forensic work of attributing unsigned paintings in the 1870s and 1880s, looked for the signature marks of an artist, not in the distinguishing characteristics of a work, which could be imitated (Leonardo's smiles), but in a work's most trivial details: the shape of earlobes, fingernails, or toes. Ginzburg sees a similar method in the early work of Freud, who read Morelli and believed that the art historian's mode of inquiry was "closely related to the technique of psycho-analysis." What puts more faith than psychoanalysis in the meaningfulness of the unapparent and inadvertent details of a life once you isolate them and bring them to consciousness, pull them to the surface as the most valuable clues to individual character? Psychoanalysis reconstructs coherent narratives from traces of memory in the way a hunter sees a broken branch and knows that something *has passed*.[19]

Knowledge on this model comes, Ginzburg says, "from gestures and glances," and I am reminded of Dupin's claim in "The Murders in the Rue Morgue" that "important knowledge" is like looking "at a star by glances." Glancing at a star "in a side-long way" is the only way to comprehend a luster that grows dim and less refined the more we turn our eye to it directly. We infer the heavens through the feeblest hint of them, a slant of light shot in the corner of the eye. Ginzburg claims that detection (including detective fiction) is a late nineteenth-century achievement; so is looking for clues. Franco Moretti confirms that "the final triumph of clues" from the 1890s forward meant that just a decade or two later "clues would be everywhere." But what clues suggest about forms of inquiry and analysis, about the ways in which the slightest things get noticed and brought to attention—how they then gain importance and value precisely because they seem to fit, to answer to the framework into which they are brought—all this suggests new ways of finding importance in the nineteenth century and the kind of creative perception needed to find it.

This is the art of relevance. I shall go so far as to say that there were no "clues" before the discovery of relevance as a value, or rather that the discovery of clues suggests the art of searching for relevance that emerged around this time. It is an art in the hands of Dupin or Sherlock Holmes because it cannot be reduced to a logical operation determined by a set of rules. Inferring from clues is freely creative. It constructs a complex theory that explains the clues at hand but proves nothing decisively and so breaks out of the classic opposition between "rationalism" and "irrationalism," as Ginzburg suggests. The detective in Poe or Doyle is usually "lost in . . . thought."[20]

Critics have long remarked that Dupin may not actually solve the crime in "The Mystery of Marie Rogêt." Some suggestions in the tale are not borne out, and there are noticeable discrepancies in the daily papers that Dupin never bothers to clear up. There is such an overwhelming mass of information that most readers have neither the patience nor wherewithal to know whether it all coheres. The critics who have looked closely suspect that it does not. Sometimes Dupin is contradicted by Poe's own footnotes. Dupin's hypothesis—that Marie was murdered by the naval officer—cannot be corroborated in part because Poe based the tale on the real-life murder of Mary Rogers in New York, which went unsolved. Critics occasionally wonder whether the story is really about the epistemological limits of the detective story or else, given Poe's mischief, an outright hoax. The emphasis, for certain, is less on a verifiable truth than on Dupin's integrative, imaginative act of accounting for "*all* contingencies." His job is to make "a series of scarcely intelligible *coincidences*" meaningful by folding the seemingly irrelevant details into a tale of a crime that depends on them all. In "The Hound of the Baskervilles," Sherlock Holmes also takes an "apparently purposeless series of small mysteries" and "a line of inexplicable incidents" and then "[endeavors] to frame some scheme into which all these strange and apparently disconnected episodes could be fitted."

But first, the detective needs to have a sense for which seemingly purposeless details will serve his purpose. He may go first in one direction and then another, looking in either case for clues. The detective pays attention where there has been a failure of attention. "I wish," Dupin will say, "to call your attention" to this apparently impertinent thing.[21] The detective selects some of these things and lifts them into relief while letting others fall back, and all along his insight, his *discernment*, means that he knows which to call out and which to emphasize as clues. Considerations that are passed over as negligible loom up. For the detective who never leaves his armchair, this heightened interest is the same as discovery. He takes nothing for granted.

In the case of Marie Rogêt, these clues are set down in the newspapers as squarely in full view of the reader as a purloined letter on a mantelpiece. But the papers absorb the public's attention with the most sensational items only. No one but Dupin notices, for example, that the strips of Marie's frock reportedly "torn off" by bushes in her struggle could not possibly have been "torn off" by bushes. Torn, for sure, but not "torn off," as the newspapers say, in perfectly vertical strips by the simple "agency *of a thorn*." So while the public gives no notice to the slight words, Dupin manifests them as clues that are material to the case, bearing on the idea they suggest—and that they finally bear out—that the scene of the torn frock is not the crime scene at all but staged as a decoy after the fact (the strips having been torn off and placed by hand). The point being that the paramount insight of the detective comes in not missing the missing piece because it is buried below the lead. Reading the reports, Dupin finally finds Marie's frock—also her petticoat, scarf, parasol, gloves, and handkerchief—to be so much more material than the mere accessories they are taken to be. Like Watson's description of Sherlock Holmes, he will have spent hours of intense mental concentration in which he "weighed every particle of evidence, constructed alternative theories, balanced one against the other, and made up his mind as to which points were essential and which immaterial."[22]

In *How We Think*, John Dewey suggests that all reflection is like hunting for clues: "To turn the thing over in mind, to reflect, means to hunt for additional evidence, for new data, that will develop the suggestion, and will either, as we say, bear it out or else make obvious its absurdity and irrelevance." Defining thought on the principle of detection means that we only start to think in the face of a mystery, perplexity, or problem that makes us uneasy. (This is also to say that reflective thinking is always more or less troublesome because "it involves willingness to endure a condition of mental unrest and disturbance." Plain sailing never makes us stop and think.) Then whenever there is a mystery, we look into the situation for a sort of "signboard or a map" to solving it. It takes vigilance ("alertness of observation") to discover the "signs, clues, indications" that will support a conjecture or belief. But how can we know what those clues might be? Something in the nature of the total situation strikes us, Dewey says. It captures our attention. It acquires importance and vividness relative to other objects that recede and fade. The mark of the critical thinker for Dewey is fundamentally this ability to seize on what is evidential or significant and let go of the rest. To think, he says,

> is to have a sense of the relative indicative or signifying values of the various features of the perplexing situation; to know what to let go as of no account; what to eliminate as irrelevant; what to retain as conducive to outcome; what to emphasize as a clue to the difficulty. This power in ordinary matters we call *knack, tact, cleverness*; in more important affairs, *insight, discernment*.

If we take situations just as we find them, "they contain much that is irrelevant to the problem in hand, while much that is relevant is obscure, hidden." Thoughtfulness, for Dewey, is just the same as knowing how to focus on what counts.

Our progress in knowledge always consists "*in the discovery of something not understood in what had previously been taken for granted as plain, obvious, matter-of-course*." Reflection, then, is the mental process of selecting for emphasis those aspects of a situation that will matter most—that will help us get a clue. It involves sorting through an abundance of information while concentrating on only some of it. The *insight* of which Dewey speaks is a "certain feeling" for which things might help more than others and for making sure that nothing significant is overlooked.[23] Dupin, of course, has a knack for this. Turning over the object that strikes him, he tests whether it will meet his need and prove consequential for how it speaks to the mystery at hand and to any solution or explanation that coalesces around it. Progress in knowledge consists in not taking for granted what was taken for granted.

So, again, thinking in *How We Think*, involves, first, the sifting out by analysis of what is likely to be irrelevant (since, as Dewey says, there are no tags or labels on any trait announcing "This is important" or "This is trivial"), and second, the accentuation or taking up of what seems relevant as the key to making sense of a difficult situation. By virtue of its relevance, such an object redefines the whole situation it brings into view in a meaningful and comprehensible way. It plays an important role in the scheme of things. It moves us toward a coherent interpretation in which everything fits. This is what Dewey means by describing the process of analysis, then synthesis in thinking:

> As analysis is *emphasis*, so synthesis is *placing*; the one causes the emphasized fact or property to stand out as significant; the other gives what is selected its *context*, or its connection with what is signified. Every judgment is analytic in so far as it involves discernment, discrimination, marking off the trivial from the important, the irrelevant from what points to a conclusion; and it is synthetic in so far as it leaves the mind with an inclusive situation within which the selected facts are placed.

Relevance is always an act of criticism, of discrimination. It reflects the process of *appreciating* objects that have been considered of little value *as* the clues to meaning. We hope that whatever predicament we find ourselves in, the thing we choose to regard, to the best of our knowledge, works. That it will be just what we need to clear up an ambiguity, solve a mystery, or get on with a task—to think it through. Until we find relevance, we won't have a case.

Dewey links critical thinking to the logic of induction, with its observing and processing of data. But he says that it also requires a form of perception that John Stuart Mill would never admit and that calls the attention powerfully into play. *Thinking involves a feeling for what is interesting.* "But in any case," Dewey writes,

> there is a certain feeling along for the way to be followed; a constant tentative picking out of certain qualities to see what emphasis upon them would lead to; a willingness to hold final selection in suspense; and to reject the factors entirely or relegate them to a different position in the evidential scheme if other features yield more solvent suggestions. Alertness, flexibility, curiosity are the essentials; dogmatism, rigidity, prejudice, caprice, arising from routine, passion, and flippancy are fatal.

The feeling to be followed, which Dewey earlier calls an "intuitive" judgment, always follows *on* curiosity and means so much to him that he declares it to be the difference between "the artist and the intellectual bungler."[24] The idea is simple: we will never know what is important or truly matters unless we're curious.

I cannot overstate the importance of *being interested* to Dewey—and also to Poe, Emerson, William James, Henry James, and so many others for whom finding relevance is "an expression of interest" that "depends upon the sensibility which makes us alive in the real world to things that to one not sensitive would not exist." That is, people with "keen interest" are alive to objects that others simply disregard. Their selective attention gives vivacity to these objects much the way the raven becomes increasingly concrete and palpable for the student the longer he stares at it. These objects are not just "matters of fact" but "matters of concern," whose coming into existence depends utterly on the attention of those who are able to appreciate them. The interested mind never stops seeking relevant material for thought—it is perpetually brought into "intimate contact" with strange, unexpected, and uncomprehended objects—while the rigid, dogmatic, or prejudiced mind takes nothing in. Only boring people get bored. We hear again and again that detective work keeps Sherlock Homes interested; "it saved me from ennui," he says.

Dewey, in offering an etymology for the word *interest*, from *inter-esse*, meaning "to be between," says that interest points to a dynamic transaction and "organic union" between an object and the subject who is "actively concerned" with it.[25] The subject *admits* this object in the sense of taking it in and taking it to heart but also in simply admitting it, acknowledging its existence when most people couldn't care less. And for Dewey this subject, more often than not, is the artist or poet who is distinguished by just this perceptive capacity to find unremarkable things of interest. By a feeling for what is interesting. The capacity is something like an impulsion toward experiencing the world as filled with meaning and worth. We saw, in "The Open Boat," that its opposite is a fatal indifference.

Needless to say, Dupin thinks well. He also has knack. He is very good at finding relevance. What makes him look where there has only been oversight? How does he redeem irrelevant things? Nothing falls outside his interest. Unlike the police with their programmatic thinking, he is into everything. Like the narrator in Poe's story, "The Man of the Crowd," who keeps trying to distinguish one face in the crowd, he feels "an inquisitive interest in every thing" ("so precisely the converse of *ennui*," a mood "of the keenest appetency"). The fact that Dupin, as we are told, is always "deeply interested" or "singularly interested" means that more things command his attention. Reading the newspapers, he appreciates and takes into account what the police ignore. There may be a depth of significance in unremarkable details. There may be so much more that matters in heaven and earth than the police could dream of. If you are looking for clues, Moretti writes, "each sentence becomes 'significant,' each character 'interesting'; descriptions lose their inertia; all words become sharper, stranger." When the detective moves from the facts to the flash of insight that brings the facts together as relevant, he experiences this in the way that Poe describes the effect of a good poem (in a phrase he takes from A. W. Schlegel's *Lectures on Dramatic Art and Literature*): as a "*unity or totality of interest*."[26] The attitude of being interested "in everything"—showing itself in an attentiveness to and consciousness of one's surrounding in ways that are aimed at sustaining and rewarding that interest—is the ultimate attitude of the poet or artist in ways I return to at length. For now I will just say that this attitude is like detective work because it depends on a knack for identifying new items and *persons of interest*.

F. C. S. Schiller, that British pragmatist whom Dewey credits with the philosophy and "principle of relevancy," describes "the fatal omission of Relevance by inductive logic." So long as we believed, he says, that the "facts" from which induction argues are objectively "given" to an observer—so long as "no inquiry need be undertaken to discover how a reasoner came by them" (that is, came to take an interest in them)—induction could seem like a "contemptibly easy job, which demanded little intelligence and no vigilance or alertness of mind but only mechanical accuracy." We used to believe, Schiller continues, that all an inductive reasoner had to do is observe the facts and then, having observed them, or as many as "would suffice mechanically to 'validate' his inference, he had merely to recognise the universal principles or laws into which they spontaneously condensed themselves." Since we believed that facts add up to universal principles, there was no need for any kind of "special ingenuity or mental activity, either in observing the 'facts' or in formulating the 'laws.'" The point is that inductive thinking seemed so mechanical that logicians even imagined the day in which machines could make valid inductions, but it never occurred to them "that no forms are universally valid, that valid forms are no guarantee of real value, and that real reasoning does not require valid forms."

What real reasoning requires that no one ever noticed before is "the notion of Relevance" that enters into induction at every step. Because every inquiry is "clogged with masses of irrelevance," thinking requires acts of "choice, preference, and valuation" to sort out irrelevant facts from *facts for the purpose in hand*. It takes selective attention to see which facts might be the "clues to reality" right now—to the real need, for example, to solve a particular case or to cope with a problem and decide what we had *better do*. But all those other facts that are irrelevant to the purpose in hand are still, in fact, phenomena out in the world that might come to matter at another time. "Irrelevant facts are *just as much facts* as relevant—though they do not lend themselves to our purposes in knowing." The "essences" we allege are really only the essential facts that are relative and relevant to our proposes. This is why facts are never always "valid" or "given" but flexibly selected for their relevance to the actual circumstances of a case. And this is why in all thinking—not only inductive thinking—"relevance is a far more valuable notion" than validity and "is incompatible with validity." What is relevant continually evolves as an inquiry proceeds, and "the least change in the circumstances of the situation, in our interests, in our knowledge of the facts, may render relevant what was irrelevant before, and irrelevant what seemed most relevant." I look closely at the logic of relevance later, but Schiller takes particular pleasure in showing that no logic, reason, or intellectual work "can attain to consistency until it has wholly purged itself of every vestige of Relevance."[27]

And what is this "special ingenuity" that lets us sort out the irrelevant facts from the satisfying facts? How do we know what to focus on? One of the key claims that philosophers of relevance make is that any perception involves the selection of what to regard and disregard, what to extract from the background and what to bring out and into relief as the essence of a situation. "'Consciousness,' in other words, is only a very small and shifting portion of experience," and there is always a great deal we can't take in. Successful thinking implies the principle, "Never consider the whole but only the relevant part." But partiality is not an intellectual shortcoming or a sin of omission. It is selection that we justify by "ascribing it to conscious, willed, purposive, and rational *concentration* upon *the point*." So Schiller develops the idea that perceptiveness is the name for being interested in certain evidence out of the preponderance of evidence, for feeling that some of it is interesting enough at this moment to excite attention exactly because it serves our interests in turn. Our interests open up the empirical world in light of its potential meaning for us, and so it is our interests that cast the widest net, catching in its meshes what fits. The interested person regards so much more information as potentially relevant while sensing that incidental or diversionary evidence has the potential to be central (that *that* red herring might be the point of it all). The interested person asserts this romance of details, this unfathomably human purpose, in bare trivial facts. She falls into the habit of looking imaginatively at inert, dumb things so that, like the eyes of the raven, they begin to flame in the dark. Maybe they will serve a vital purpose and answer a need. She is like the detective that G. K. Chesterton describes in "A Defense of Detective Stories" who, "amid a babble of pedantry and preciosity, declines to regard the present as prosaic or the common as commonplace."

And why did it take so long for us to begin to think, in Schiller's words, that the "discovery of any truth is always a process which *moves away from* the *data* it started with, and transforms, corrects, and revalues them?" That the *true* facts of a case may be indistinguishable from the *valuable* facts that appear to work as we "revalue" and appreciate them according to our interests and purpose? Why did it take what Schiller claims to be "2000 years" of logic and philosophy before anyone managed "to recognise the existence and importance of Relevance" in thinking; before anyone considered that real knowing is conditioned by our interests and that the more we find interesting—and the more objects "arrest [our] attention," as they do for Sherlock Holmes—that much more will be meaningful and come to matter?[28]

Schiller would say we hadn't a clue.

...

Once upon a midnight dreary, a student who is reading in his chamber, though half dreaming of his dead love Lenore, cannot make sense of a raven who seems more like a red herring. The appearance from out of the blue, the ludicrous incongruity of the black bird on the white bust, the bird's monotonous repetition of the non sequitur "Nevermore"—it is all extremely diverting. Let's describe the raven's appearance as a change in the student's cognitive environment. He was nearly napping but now is fully awake and conscious of the ingression. He feels the need to come to terms with it. It has ruffled feathers. And while the student begins to query the raven in jest—and while reason assures him, as Poe tells us in "The Philosophy of Composition," that the raven is not actually prophetic nor demonic but "merely repeating a lesson learned by rote"—the student still treats it like a "mystery." The raven excites within him an "intensity of interest"; he wheels that cushioned seat right up to it, and the longer he sits the more intense his interest grows. The bird captures and holds his attention. Poe writes that he is "startled from his original *nonchalance*." The raven takes extraordinary possession of his mind in that close chamber, insulated against the storm, where the student and raven are brought together and where the "close *circumscription of space*" has the indisputable power, Poe says, of "keeping concentrated the attention."

The melancholy character of the word *nevermore*, repeated often by an ominous sort of bird, may be nonsense but it nonetheless produces "novel effects," and the student responds by explaining these effects intuitively. He responds, in other words, by reflecting on this interesting phenomenon and by making its effects salient in thought. Thinking and feeling his way through each "Nevermore," he starts the process of possible construal in which he imagines a solution for which the mystery of "Nevermore" is the clue. All the while, "the effect of the *variation of application*" (again, I am quoting from "The Philosophy of Composition")—the effect of fitting the refrain into the various contexts the student frames for it by his questions—produces in him a "phrenzied pleasure in so modeling his questions as to receive from the *expected* 'Nevermore' the most delicious because the most intolerable of sorrow." If he luxuriates in the sorrow and self-torture, it is also in the pleasure of having ultimately produced an answer, of the real *knowing* that there is no heaven and he will never see Lenore again. It is the relief of building out a theory for which, in Poe's words, "'Nevermore' should be in the last place an answer."[29] He searches for a makeshift concept that allows the raven that takes possession of his thoughts to *be* the answer to his melancholy. That gives this diverting thing salience. That satisfies the expectations of relevance for an utterance that "little relevancy bore." The pleasure is in the satisfaction of the way the diverting words now fit. The search for implications in words that might be made relevant and answer to him in some meaningful way is what drives his questions. Insofar as the speaker is a student trying to make sense of the raven, even as we now *read* "The Raven," the need to satisfy the hope for relevance is also what guides the interpretive process.

The idea of "ad hoc concepts" has been developed by relevance theorists since the 1980s as an analytical tool for processing and understanding an utterance. Further on I give relevance theory due consideration, and my hope is that certain ideas that anticipated or came to bear on it also will become clearer as I go. In the meantime, I introduce it now because "The Raven" might be taken as exemplifying relevance theory's model of how concern for relevance plays a fundamental role not only in all communication but in cognition. Its theorists claim that "human cognition tends to be geared to the maximization of relevance." The relevant meaning of an utterance depends on the speaker's intent, but it also depends on much more, including the full cognitive environment in which the utterance is heard. That is, it depends on all the facts, nonverbal sensory information, and cognitive resources (prior knowledge and experience, cultural habits, beliefs, etc.) that are available to the listener at that time. Utterances create "contextual effects." This means that they change a listener's cognitive environment by making some of these facts and resources manifest or more manifest by calling attention to some things over others in ways that convey a certain import.[30] In our case of "The Raven," the contextual effects of the raven might be said to include a heightened awareness of the storm and the close confinement of the chamber; the emphatic, haunting force of a refrain; the sonorous quality of the word *nevermore,* in which the *o* and the *r* could be protracted for emphasis; the white bust that puts the black bird in highest relief; the mythological association of ravens with omens; and then, too, the student's state of mind; his melancholy memories of Lenore; the shock of being awakened from his *nonchalance*—all these bear on the relevance of the word *nevermore* to him. They all become part of what the lover admits when he admits the raven.

Relevance theory, also known as cognitive pragmatics, was inspired by the philosopher Paul Grice's "inferential model" of conversation and first proposed by the linguists Deirdre Wilson and Dan Sperber in their founding study from 1986. It is essentially a model of cognition that (1) suggests that understanding what words mean is always inferential or interpretive and (2) attempts to show how listeners (or readers) manage to infer relevant meanings from utterances—the sort of processing this "optimally" takes—when words always fall short of stating outright everything you can assume about them at the moment you hear them. To take an example from Sperber and Wilson, if you say to me at a party, "My glass is empty," I might relevantly infer that you are asking me to fill it. Or I might infer, depending on the context and how well I know you, that you are finished drinking for the evening, having made it through the one glass you allotted yourself in order not to drink too much, or that you have already had too much to drink and couldn't help it, having finished that glass, too. The relevance of your words will depend on the context in which you say them and on your tone and expression, how you look at me and put the glass down in front of me, and how much I know about you and your behavior at parties as well as whether you have had a long day or are simply thirsty and what was in that glass to begin with. Intuitively, an input (an utterance, a sound, a look, a gesture, a movement) is relevant to me when it connects with background knowledge I have to yield conclusions that matter to me: here, by letting me know how to proceed and respond and what to believe. Or, to take a nonverbal example from Sperber and Wilson, since they take relevance to be a potential property not only of utterances but of any perceptual stimulus: if there is a distinct smell of gas in the house, I can make the relevant assumption that there is a gas leak. I am less likely to think that "the gas company is not on strike," even though the smell of gas would make this apparent too.[31] That the gas company is not on strike is *not* the most relevant conclusion I could draw when smelling gas in my house (although perhaps one can imagine a situation—say, after negotiating a new union contract—when the sign of gas would mean most of all that the gas company is not on strike). A gas leak is not the only thing I can assume when smelling gas, but the moment I recognize the smell at home, it very well may be the most relevant thing: the information that for me at that moment is most worth having.

Why do we make certain assumptions and not others? Something, a stimulus, a new piece of information, will preempt our attention: the smell of gas, a shout, a flashing light, a siren, a crying baby (if the baby is yours), a waving hand, a sudden movement, the tapping of wings on a window in a storm. Most importantly, for relevance theorists, spoken utterances addressed to us "automatically impinge on the attention"; they are hard to filter out as background noise. A stimulus is relevant if its array of contextual effects, when added to our existing assumptions and knowledge, "produces a worthwhile cognitive effect: say, by answering a question, settling a doubt, correcting a mistake, suggesting a hypothesis or a plan of action." Relevance theory claims that our mental efforts are fully dedicated to picking out these potentially relevant stimuli and to processing them in "the most relevance-enhancing way."[32] We are perceptually drawn to these stimuli, and then we process them in order to discover what to do in the face of them and what they mean to us. We reflect on them until they answer a question or settle a doubt.

Now obviously the raven means nothing by it. Still, the student, who knows better, acts as if it does. "Nevermore," uttered over again in response to every question, raises expectations of relevance, so the student quickly assumes a demonic or prophetic intent. According to relevance theory, we *have* to assume that an utterance communicates some intent when we try to interpret it: the best "ostensive stimuli" would be entirely "irrelevant unless they are treated as ostensive." Why try to make sense of words if there is no reason for them at all? But relevance theorists also suggest that the point of an utterance is not necessarily "to induce a specific belief in the audience, but to make an array of propositions *more manifest* to them. A proposition is manifest to an individual to the extent that it is salient and strongly evidenced, or, in other words, to the extent that the individual is likely to entertain it and accept it as true, or probably true." An utterance can have "strong implicatures" but also "weak implicatures" in a range of contextual effects that go beyond its linguistically encoded purpose; it may reveal a tone, mood, feeling, or sensation—it may reveal an irony or ambiguity, all requiring an act of imagination to explain them—and then each of these may reverberate in a number of unexpected ways for the listener. These manifestations are what relevance theory calls "echoic utterances" and "poetic effects."[33]

I see them as the raven's "butterfly effects" (fig. 1). As "Nevermore" echoes in his chamber, the student tries to imagine some context for the word that explains its resonance. That explains why the raven is "beguiling" and why the student keeps sitting there, having oriented his whole being to the raven whose one, once-insignificant word seems to have the widening power to shape the heavens and earth around it and to move him too. The search for relevance is always a way of justifying what we ultimately choose to listen to. The presumption of relevance always also presumes that it is worth the attention we give it.

Relevance, in relevance theory, begins with an utterance that gets us to

FIGURE 1. Gustave Doré, "Perched upon a bust of Pallas just above my chamber door— / Perched, and sat, and nothing more," engraved by R. G. Tietze. From Edgar Allan Poe, *The Raven*, illustrated by Gustave Doré, with comment by Edmund D. Stedman (New York: Harper, 1884). The Library of Congress, Rare Books, Special Collections Reading Room (Jefferson LJ239).

notice it. We process this stimulus by inferring different assumptions about its meaning, based on all that it calls up for us, until we find a context for understanding it that seems relevant. These contexts are constructed ad hoc. They involve, in Terence Cave's words, an "on-the-spot readjustment" and responsiveness to new information, a "constantly shifting engagement between cognition and environment" as new properties demand attention and others fade into irrelevance. "The rapid construction of ad hoc suppositions may be reinforced or discarded as the utterance proceeds," writes Cave, in a series of provisional theories that allow the listeners to keep listening and constructing theories until one fits. Cave invokes Donald Davidson's idea of "passing theory" as an appropriate term for the way ideas of significance emerge and evolve in the effort to maximize relevance. Cave, who is one of the very few literary critics to think about the implications of relevance theory for literary study, also says that "passing theory" would be "an equally suitable term for the way that readers of a detective novel (or indeed any plotted narrative) construct provisional interpretations of the action that make enough sense for the reading process to proceed, even though they may sooner or later require considerable adjustment."[34]

The student-reader of Poe's poem, like the reader of a detective story or the detective on the case, is doing just this work of "inference to the best explanation." The evidence for it will always be gestural—merely a clue.[35] It will depend on context and the way assumptions and beliefs link up with context, and it will depend on what Poe describes in "The Philosophy of Composition" as "some amount of suggestiveness—some under-current, however indefinite of meaning." An utterance will never "fully encode" a meaning, but it will "provide some evidence about that meaning, just as patting an empty chair may provide some evidence that the communicator intends to invite the addressee to sit down."

I like to think that that raven came "tapping, / As of some one gently rapping" and invited the student to sit down:

> Then, upon the velvet sinking, I betook myself to linking
> Fancy unto fancy, thinking what this ominous bird of yore—
> What this grim, ungainly, ghastly, gaunt, and ominous bird of yore
> Meant in croaking "Nevermore."

As the student sits "engaged in guessing," he thinks of contexts that will bring meaning to the word and then discards them and by degrees recalibrates, drawing an impertinence into new and newer frameworks into which it might pertain. Is "Nevermore" a name? Will the raven leave him tomorrow as others have left him (*nevermore*)? Will Lenore come to him—in a visitation like this visitation (*nevermore*)? And the more he sits "divining," the more he recontextualizes that raven until it meets his need for comprehension, until he articulates, "the order that is proper to the assimilation of this fact," and into which the most inappropriate raven can be "enfolded." As though from a single word, he could infer the heavens and earth. The imaginative scaffolding on which the raven perches and from which he sees his grounded soul is the context that ultimately frames this alien presence as meaningful. This is the student's colligation of facts. But it is a never-ending process of adjustment in which the relevance of the raven keeps unfolding with its effects and the student's attitude toward it, so that by the poem's end, the Raven "never flitting, still is sitting, *still* is sitting." Perched under the spotlight of the "lamp-light o'er him," the raven that "little relevancy bore" may never stop concerning the student.[36] Seated in front of it, he will continue to care. As a continual object of concern, the raven bears not only relevance but enduring relevance.

. . .

Then again, the final context into which the student places the raven is actually the poem that he gives us as its speaker. That the expectation of relevance is ultimately answered by the poem "The Raven" is also the point of Poe's "The Philosophy of Composition," in which he explains how the poem was "put together." Versification, for Poe, is something like the art of successful detection. He began writing the poem with the "consideration of an *effect*," then he went about discovering how the effect might be "wrought." Working backward from the effect to its cause required "induction," which Poe defines as a makeshift process of "construction" in which the explanation for the feeling took shape only after "selections and rejections," "erasures and interpolations." It required, he says, "the tackle for scene-shifting—the stepladders and demon-traps," adjustments and recalibrations until it all came together—a "totality" in which everything fit.

("The thing takes shape, Watson" says Sherlock Holmes. "It becomes coherent. Might I ask you to hand me my violin." Sometimes in the midst of a case, Watson says, Holmes "would talk of nothing but art.")

The effect Poe sought to achieve—one that "intensely excites" and would be "so obvious and so easily attainable a source of interest"—was, as he famously says, a sense of Beauty inflected by Melancholy. But there had to be some stimulus for it, so, having settled on an effect, he looked for a device that might serve him "as a key-note in the construction of the poem—some pivot upon which the whole structure might turn." The device he selected was the one that simply came to him as best serving the need: "Nevermore" was indeed "the very first which presented itself."[37] What was left for him to do was none other than what is left to the student of the poem: to give this arousing refrain a sense of purpose. "The Raven," then, is composed in order to give meaning to a refrain that mysteriously moves its audience, that draws us in as surely as that raven on the bust has the centripetal power to keep the student in his seat. The point of the poem is to make the refrain that excites us relevant within the explanatory context that the poet has "put together." The poem will give this feeling its ideal object.

In the meantime, "The Raven" will keep us in our seat, too, since the poem was written to be read in a "single sitting," the intensity of the intended effect depending on the concentration of attention and the exclusion of everything else for the time being. Poe wants the experience to be coherent to an unusually high degree, to create a "unity of impression." He wants all these effects and feelings to crystallize in the object of the poem, which is why in "The Rationale of Verse," Poe likens a good poem to a "crystal." The pleasure we derive from it comes from the way all the parts are arranged in the formal constitution of something solid or concrete, the way that they each gain contributive value from being a facet of the arrangement to which "all the moods of verse—rhythm, metre, stanza, rhyme, alliteration, the *refrain*, and other analogous effects—are to be referred." He would have agreed with William Hogarth that the sense of the beauty of the whole depends most of all on the "fitness of the parts to the design for which every individual thing is formed" and that any parts that are ill adapted and disproportionate for the uses to which they are put "lose their beauty with their fitness." Poe would have agreed with Emerson that "it is a rule of largest application" that "any real increase of fitness to its end is an increase of beauty." Emerson also says, "Fitness is so inseparable an accompaniment of beauty, that it has been taken for it. The most perfect form to answer an end, is so far beautiful."[38]

Versification, Poe writes, is the "actual arranging" of these elements into meaningful, purposeful relations—the "collating" of words and sounds into a comprehensible form in which they are all "fitting" and "appropriate." "*Verse* originates," he says, "in the human enjoyment of . . . fitness" (of "the fitting" and "the appropriate") and in the poet's effort to gratify this pleasure in *fits*. Monroe Beardsley describes an aesthetic experience as the mental state created by a perceptual field "on which attention is fixed with a feeling that things are working or have worked themselves out fittingly." It is a "sense of actively exercising constructive powers of the mind, of being challenged by a variety of potentially conflicting stimuli to try to make them cohere; a keyed-up state amounting to exhilaration in seeing connections between percepts and between meanings, a sense (which may be illusory) of intelligibility." Like the archaic sense of a poetic "fit" (or "fytte") as a unit of verse—a sense of "fit" that is revived by Byron and others in the nineteenth century—these poetic experiences (or *convulsions*, in that other sense of *fit*) are insulated from others. They hold their own.[39]

We have to distinguish Poe's fits, however, from organic ideas of poetry around this time that also emphasized the inextricability of form from meaning and the interdependence of parts and whole. Poetry for Poe does not have the "purposiveness" that Kant assigns to aesthetic objects and natural things alike: an inner principle of growth and organization, an inner logic of relations. When Coleridge imported ideas of organicism from Kant and A. W. Schlegel into the world of English poetry, he distinguished between organic form (as innate to a work of art and self-evolving) and mechanical form (as imposed from outside). And then when Cleanth Brooks and the New Critics drew on Coleridge's "multeity in unity" to describe the internal coherence of poems, they also treated these poems as a kind of special thing apart: highly organized, autonomous structures that could only be appreciated on their own terms. For these scholars of "organic form," art is remote from the interests of life, and appreciation of it is "disinterested." But Poe, as we said, wants to *hold* our interest above all. He wants to take so obvious a "source of interest" from life as the experience of beauty is to us and to concentrate it in the poem.[40]

A good poem, Poe suggests in "The Philosophy of Composition," will seize on whatever is characteristic or essential in the perception of beauty and, drawing it out with crystalline intensity, make this perception intelligible. Readers should be as keyed up as our surrogate student-reader in "The Raven." Consider, Poe suggests, that a poem is not isolated from nature or life but life extracted into a single, coherent perception. Disentangled from other perceptions, it has the effect of "keeping concentrated the attention" with all "the force of a frame to a picture." Everything that is fitting or appropriate for the expression of this experience will be reworked within the frame of the poem, and any thoughts or feelings that would distract from its intelligibility will be excluded as unfit. We will not have internal coherence so much as a feeling or perception rendered coherent in connection with the poem under construction. The "totality of effect or impression" that Poe tries to achieve will provide his readers with the kind of aesthetic experience that Dewey recognizes in Poe's poetry and describes as forming "a whole in perception." It gives us the "undefined pervasive quality of an experience," Dewey says; it "binds together all the defined elements, the objects of which we are focally aware." All that goes into it is "integrated through its inner relations into a single qualitative whole." Laurence Buermeyer, who worked with Dewey at the Barnes Foundation (I'll say more about their collaboration later), writes in *The Aesthetic Experience*, "in a work of art everything is relevant to the feeling which is to be expressed, and there is no residue of brute fact, destitute of meaning."[41]

Poe calls "The Philosophy of Composition" his "best specimen of analysis." In all of his reviews and criticism, he judges the success of a literary work, including his own, on whether it provides pleasure "in the contemplation of the picture *as a whole*." Does the poem achieve, he asks, a "totality of effect?" In a positive review of Lydia Sigourney's poems in the *Southern Literary Messenger*, he says they often depend on the "nice adaptation of constituent parts" so that the mind of the reader is able "to include in one comprehensible survey the proportions and proper adjustment of the whole." But other literary works simply do not hang together, like the poor poem by Rufus Dawes that Poe elsewhere calls "a mere mass of irrelevancy" in which "the continuous lapse from impertinence to impertinence is seldom justified by any shadow of appositeness or even of the commonest relation."[42] A novel, too, "may be described as a building so dependently constructed, that to change the position of a single brick is to overthrow the entire fabric."

When "properly defined," Poe writes, a plot "is *that in which no part can be displaced without ruin to the whole*." But the novelist Edward Bulwer Lytton stumbles, for example, in his novel *Night and Morning* because any pleasure the reader derives from it "is disjointed, ineffective, and evanescent" and built up with care to its "constituent parts" only. It may have the "peculiarity of being appreciated in its atoms by all, while in its totality of beauty it is comprehended but by the few." Poe clarifies that here he means "that species of unity which is alone worth the attention of the critic—the unity or totality *of effect*." Poe says that, among other things, Bulwer Lytton adds descriptive passages that are adventitious and "might have been omitted with advantage (because without detriment) to the whole." Signs of the writer's "slovenliness" include an "incident utterly without aim, and composed at random." Bulwer Lytton "flounders in the vain attempt to keep all his multitudinous incidents at one and the same moment before the eye" so that "the mind cannot comprehend at one time, and in one survey, the numerous individual items which go to establish the whole." His novel, then, "must inevitably fail of appreciation," since critical appreciation depends on the reader's sense that every seemingly nonessential occurrence—much as every accessory, incidental, and chance-like detail—is meaningfully included and there for a reason.[43] Passages "trifling, perhaps, in themselves" should be "important when considered in relation to the plot."

In a review of Nathaniel Parker Willis's *Tortesa*—a plot that "hangs better together" in Poe's own summary of it than in the flabby, overcrowded play that will "fatigue [our] attention"—Poe says, once again, that "a plot, properly understood, is perfect only inasmuch as we shall find ourselves unable to detach from it *or disarrange* any single incident involved, without *destruction* to the mass. . . . Practically, we may consider a plot as of high excellence, when no one of its component parts shall be susceptible of *removal* without *detriment* to the whole." But in Willis's play is "a vast lowering of the demand," since "with him the great error lies in *inconsequence*. Underplot is piled upon underplot (the very word is a paradox), and all to no purpose—*to no end*," Poe says. It suffers from that "irrelevancy" that "disfigures and very usually damns the work of the unskillful artist." Poe has set out to show, in Willis's boring, miserable play, "how much was irrelevant."[44]

But relevance is the condition to which "The Raven" aspires as a poem, giving every aspect of this "insulated" scene a role in the spellbinding effect—plus every rhyme, alliteration, and metrical line—so that there is no "residue of brute fact, destitute of meaning." Relevance is also, as I keep suggesting, the value the poem brings home to us even as the raven comes home to the student in his chamber. The poem is about this kind of coming home to him—about the course of a realization. At last the bird is no longer absurd but full of meaning and real consequence. There is a sense finally of "seriousness and importance," Poe says, and this "revolution of thought . . . on the lover's part, is intended to induce a similar one on the part of the reader."

And now, when I think about the raven "perched upon the bust of Pallas," "perched above the chamber door," I cannot help also thinking about the way William James likens consciousness itself to the alternate "flights and perchings" of a bird's life. Every "perching," he writes, is a moment of "undergoing" in which preceding experiences are "held before the mind for an indefinite time," in which the consequences and accrued meaning of these doings or flights get "periodically consolidated, and always with a view to what is to be done next." The perchings are the moments when these consequences are, as Dewey describes them, "absorbed and taken home."[45] Perception is the effort to take in experience in this concrete and heartfelt way. So, in "The Raven" we have a perching one midnight in which a raven comes home to a student, and we have a lover in mourning making meaning on a wing. However the raven has managed to come to him, he has taken it in and to heart: "Take thy beak from out my heart," he says.

The discovery of seriousness and importance—the coalescing of this scene into an experience the student undergoes—happens, Poe says, in the two concluding stanzas of the poem, "their suggestiveness being thus made to pervade all the narrative which has preceded them." "The under-current of meaning is rendered first apparent" in the line about the heart I just quoted:

> "Be that word our sign of parting, bird or fiend!" I shrieked, upstarting—
> "Get thee back into the tempest and the Night's Plutonian shore!
> Leave no black plume as a token of that lie thy soul hath spoken!
> Leave my loneliness unbroken!—quit the bust above my door!
> Take thy beak from out my heart, and take thy form from off my door!"
> Quoth the Raven, "Nevermore."

This, Poe writes, is "the first metaphorical expression in the poem": the beak is only in the student's heart figuratively; not the bird but the bird's "form" is on his door. From now on the speaker, like the reader, will see the raven as emblematic—of mourning, of remembrance, anything really that comes to mind through the metaphor. The "intention," that is, "of making him emblematical . . . is permitted distinctly to be seen." As a form or figure, the raven finally has a range of poetic effects. They communicate nothing exactly or nothing specifically, but taken together they create an "impression." A metaphor, with its "under-current of meaning," is a clue to meaning only.[46] It guides the listener to do the constructive work of picking up on its suggestions, of making connections between the seemingly incongruous things that metaphors bring together as instruments of thought. As a metaphor, the raven is adjusted in relation to the new context (say, the context of mourning) in which the raven is conveyed and certain qualities of the bird emerge as fitting to this context and have new value in the light it provides.

How does the lover know what the raven ultimately suggests? He looks for salience. He looks for the "application," as Poe puts it, that best fits all the raven implies at the moment it appears; that makes the experience of the raven "hang together"; that takes into account not only its portentous refrain but its appearance that midnight, the storm, the confines of the room, the marble bust, the state of being suddenly awakened, the feelings a raven saying "Nevermore" would activate in the mind of the bereaved. He will keep stretching his interpretation of the raven until it adequately answers the question of the function it serves in that context in which it so impertinently appeared. He will go on looking until "Nevermore" is not the empty echo of a mocking bird but *speaks to him*, heart and soul. The more "suggestiveness" it has, the more relevant it can be.

In his essay, "The Poetic Principle," Poe rejects what he calls "the heresy of *The Didactic*" in poetry, or the assumption that all poetry should inculcate a moral along the lines of all those early national epics that were often also topical and popular, earning the praise of the press. While the "epic mania" has been "gradually dying out of the public mind, by mere dint of its own absurdity," Poe says that Americans especially remain attached to "verses of society," having taken it into their heads that "to write a poem simply for the poem's sake, and to acknowledge such to have been our design, would be to confess ourselves radically wanting in the true Poetic dignity and force."[47] Of course, Poe shows himself to be radically wanting—flouting the expectation, made known in moral terms—that a poem has worth to the degree that it produces a consciousness of current events.

This does not mean that a poem written for a poem's sake is irrelevant. Poe's basic message in these essays is that the function of literary analysis is to demonstrate how the sort of poem "The Raven" is might meaningfully *be* relevant. His premise seems to be this: criticism shows how some unknown, unregarded aspect of life is made fit for poetic appropriation, made appropriate to the contents of a poem. The poem concentrates our attention on this aspect of life, making apparent and manifest something we never would have admitted otherwise. We stay focused because the poem raises the expectation that there will be something there worthwhile, that the heightened awareness will not be in vain and arouse us for no reason.

The reason is to make some feeling intelligible for ourselves. The beauty, according to Poe, that pervades the world and which all life in some degree reveals, is a poem purged of what is irrelevant or distracting enough for us to experience it in earnest. When I think that Poe sees the work of a poem as raising consciousness like this and at a moment when the idea of *relevance* was only beginning to take focus—when I think, after all, that Poe appears to be one of the very first writers to focus on relevance, though always in relation to a poem for a poem's sake and all that he says it comes to bear—then maybe nothing is more relevant than "The Raven."

3

The Relevance of the Interesting

There is a moment in Emerson's journal that has become for me a way of describing what is at stake in thinking about the value of relevance that is also as close to the heart of Emerson's philosophical project as many of us have come to understand it and as any one passage might be. I am thinking in particular of Emerson's line, "What attracts my attention shall have it," from his essay "Spiritual Laws"—how Stanley Cavell sees this receptiveness (that of Emerson's "being drawn to things") as the most persistent note of a writer who keeps trying to redeem his ordinary world by finding it full of interest. But I am getting ahead of the passage.

Imagine proceeding from the assumption that relevance is what Poe says it certainly is not and that to be relevant as scholars is to set ourselves the task of identifying how the texts we read speak to our current moment most topically. Suppose you start with the assumption, too, that certain texts are more relevant and worthy of attention than others because they are didactic or else seem more applicable to those topics (say, because they are about social or political conditions in their own right or can be read allegorically). Then you come across an entry in Emerson's journal in which he responds to the charge that his reading is "irrelevant" by saying "yes, for you, but not for me," as if relevance is nothing but the fact of caring about a book in a certain way—as if to make a book relevant, all you have to do is keep reading it until it matters:

> *Scholar, Centrality Centrality.* "Your reading is irrelevant." Yes, for you, but not for me. It makes no difference what I read. If it is irrelevant, I read it

> deeper. I read it until it is pertinent to me and mine, to nature and to the hour that now passes. A good scholar will find Aristophanes and Hafiz and Rabelais full of American history.
>
> I believe in Omnipresence and find footsteps in Grammar rules, in oyster shops, in church liturgies, in mathematics, and in solitudes and in galaxies. I am shamed out of my declamations against churches by the wonderful beauty of the English liturgy, an anthology of the piety of ages and nations.

Emerson was forty-three years old when he wrote this entry in the spring of 1847, during months when he also found himself wishing "for a professorship." He says that if he had the "liberty to do so," he should withdraw himself "for a time from all domestic and accustomed relations and command an absolute leisure with books." What the professor would do with all these books and time is find relevance, but he means by it a specific kind of intimate "connexion" with the books that he also writes about in his journal in these same months when he says, "A man must be connected."[1] As a scholar, I might find relevance "to me and mine" just about anywhere. "It makes no difference what I read," Emerson writes. "If it is irrelevant, I read it deeper. I read it until it is pertinent to me and mine, to nature and to the hour that now passes." What attracts his attention shall have it, and it makes absolutely "no difference" whether it is Aristophanes, Hafiz, or Rabelais, the point being that indifference will be converted into interest and that a good scholar does the trick of discovering interest in unexpected places (even, for this heretic, in the church).

Emerson might say that the good scholar is *hospitable* to all these books and to everything else besides. What is the scholar for "but for hospitality?" He finds out that he has relations everywhere and that these very distant, foreign words, encountered in a desultory way, are coming home to him now—"as from exile," Cavell says. The scholar, Emerson writes in "Lecture on the Times," will be the "asylum" for every unfamiliar, untried thought; the world and history are filled with unacknowledged objects of potential significance to him. "A good ballad," Emerson says, "draws my ear and heart whilst I listen, as much as an epic has done before. A dog, drawn by a master, or a litter of pigs, satisfies, and is a reality not less than the frescoes of Angelo. From this succession of excellent objects, we learn at last the immensity of the world" ("Art").

Emerson defines a "genius" as having "an enthusiasm not subject to his control, which takes him off his feet, draws him this way and that." Genius is just the capacity to be drawn to objects, "this feeling of *relationship* to that which is at the same time new and strange; this confusion which at the same time says, It is my own, and, It is not my own"—so that something as remote as Aristophanes or as once unremarkable as an oyster shop will be met attentively and with "entire welcome" ("Genius"). "There is nothing but is related to us, nothing that does not interest us—kingdom, college, tree, horse, or iron shoe, the roots of all things are in man." Emerson calls both for an "intellectual nomadism" that wanders far and wide but also for a "home-keeping wit" that brings certain objects out of the "miscellany of objects" home to us and makes them intelligible in that feeling of being "related to us" and in the confusion, as he calls it, of being pertinent (our own) while recognizing how worthy they are in themselves ("History"). The "motive of all intellectual research," he writes in "Home," is "to find that which is within without there in nature," to feel, as Branka Arsić suggests, a kind of homesickness for the places we have never been and things we have never experienced as if what is beyond us still somehow belongs and relates to us. The mind enjoys each new interest and adventure, Emerson says, "as if coming to its own again."[2]

But out of this "miscellany of objects," how does any one thing ever come home to us? In "The American Scholar," Emerson regrets the "constant accumulation" of facts that "cannot be gathered" or grasped in any productive or meaningful way. The expansion of information and the rapid proliferation of books and other printed media, including the news, at a massive and unprecedented scale midcentury were never far from Emerson's mind, as Cary Wolfe and Maurice Lee suggest. I suppose anyone thinking about a relevance principle is bound to come up against this revolution in news and information. I will turn to it later and also to what it meant to "sort" or "rank" for relevance long before our search engines could and especially in answer to the intellectual and emotional demands for which even now they cannot. But certainly, when Emerson writes in his journal that books are a "usurpation and impertinence" it is because the surfeit of them and of facts, objects, and information in this complex and modernizing world is overwhelming.[3] There is far too much to read and know, so he is trying to get a handle on some of it while being awash in all of it.

But, again, why certain things come to matter over others was the particular problem for Emerson. So much might claim our attention every day, but only some of it will take. The question of how in the disarray—in that "succession of objects," as Emerson also calls it—anything at all gets cast and lifted into an object of experience is the question of "relevance" that he raises in his journal as if to ask how any essay, poem, or work of art "makes interest, makes importance," to remember the words of Henry James. Some aspect of life that is remote, unfamiliar, or obscure—or else, so utterly familiar and that it, too, is invisible to us because we take it for granted—gets taken in at last as if "common daylight was worth something." An artist can show us the secret of things, Emerson writes, "that require no system to make them pertinent," but "make everything else impertinent."[4] But first they have to be admitted as important and meaningful to us. They have to be worth the attention we give them. How do we even begin to notice Aristophanes or an oyster shop—or, let's face it, some obscure passage in Emerson's voluminous journals—enough to study it, to dedicate ourselves to thinking about it and deciding that *this* thinking and *this* studying is relevant to me and mine, to nature and to the hour that now passes?

"Where do we find ourselves?" Emerson asks at the start of "Experience." The hope, to return to that passage from his journal, is to find "footsteps" wherever they may happen to be. He suggests that an attentive mind might discover a foothold anywhere; something, in other words, will be gripping enough in Aristophanes and Hafiz, so who is to say that Emerson's reading is ever irrelevant and that there can be no purchase in studying grammar rules, oyster shops, or church liturgies too? He will find traction in them all. I think that William James offers a similar notion of relevance when he says, along these lines, that he will try not to be a "footless waif"; that his mind can translate even the idea of God—or an idea as abstract as a "universal essence"—into terms of "emotional pertinency" so that he can care for it and feel connected to it. So that he can "be a match for it . . . and not a footless waif."

He says that to believe in whatever commands his attention he only needs "the mere assurance that my powers, such as they are, are not irrelevant to it, but pertinent; that it speaks to them and will in some way recognize their reply." But James also says that we are all different and that "although all men will insist on being spoken to by the universe in some way, few will insist on being spoken to in just the same way." It is why he always insists "that the knower is not simply a mirror floating with no foothold anywhere, and passively reflecting an order that he comes upon and finds simply existing." The "knower is an actor" instead, who chooses footholds for thinking and feeling in his vast surroundings by attaching to certain things over others. Emerson also suggests that we choose what we hold onto for an indefinite time and for periods of comparative reflection.[5]

In studying topics as alienating as grammar rules or as unremarkable as oyster shops, Emerson will make them matter. To "fill the eye" and the hour that now passes, what interests him becomes part of his "reality." He finds that contact with once remote or recalcitrant things has touched him and, as James writes, "whatever things have intimate and continuous connection with my life are things of whose reality I cannot doubt." They feel vital, no less so than the once-vacuous words of the raven for the student who, closely studying it, comes to believe it. That Emerson dismissed Poe's poems as the trivial rhymes of "the jingle-man" only suggests to me that he did not read them deeply or patiently enough to find them pertinent to him, since he usually waited long enough to see how, "like a traveller, surprised by a mountain echo," even the most "trivial word returns to him in romantic thunders."

Later, when Alfred North Whitehead, also along these lines, writes of the "foothold of the mind in nature" in *The Concept of Nature*, he means that to an attentive mind, nature, which is otherwise so elusive and massive and so unnavigable, will offer a succession of things to hold fast. In Isabelle Stengers's words, Whitehead's "'foothold' does not designate the act of taking hold but what the mind, or knowledge, requires from nature, what it needs to be offered by nature if its operations are not to be illusory, if the trust that leads us to speak of a knowledge about nature is to be confirmed." How do we find a foothold? For Whitehead, it is represented by a pair of events: first, an awareness of something (being drawn to it all of a sudden) and then the consciousness of this perception's availability to satisfy or meet a need, like a ledge for a mountain climber. "The primary glimmering of consciousness reveals, something that matters," he says. In other words, the consciousness that follows from an initial awareness gives the awareness its consequence and value. Our "due attention" to something translates the way that it has taken possession of the mind into some purpose that justifies that attention.[6]

(A raven perches above a chamber door; the student who is drawn to it will find it fitting.)

Whitehead is simply trying to understand how we manage to find anything at all to give us a grip, anything as particularly meaningful at a given moment as a foothold to a mountain climber, when the world feels, in Emerson's words, like a series of "slippery sliding surfaces" evading our grasp. The value and appropriateness of our due attention is also what Emerson and James are trying to understand and what Emerson registers in his journal, for a start. If we think of a mountain climber, practically *everything* depends, in Stengers's words "on the relevance of what this choice offers to knowledge" and especially on the irrelevance of everything outside of our attention at that decisive moment.[7] Life always depends, that is, on finding a foothold—on discovering the relevance of whatever it is we feel our way to and with which we make contact.

So to read, for Emerson, is to discover things that pertain to our situation and that can help us along. And it does not matter whether we are reading books or the world around us, because everything in nature, he says in his lecture "The Poet," and

> every word we speak is million faced or convertible to an indefinite number of applications. If it were not so we could read no book. For, each sentence would only fit the single case which the author had in view. Dante who described his circumstance would be unintelligible now. But a thousand readers in a thousand different years and towns shall read his story, and find it a version of their story.

This sounds like reading for relevance as we ordinarily understand it: Dante may have had his own circumstances in mind, but his words can be made to "fit" our circumstances too. Remember that from its etymology, to *relevate* is to raise again or to lift back into attention. So to find a book relevant is to raise it in another context on another occasion. Dante's words can be carried to "a thousand readers in a thousand different years and towns," and if they seem to fit these other times and places and seem appropriate to them, then they are relevant to them, and if they seem inappropriate, then they are irrelevant. But Emerson believes that "every word we speak" has "an indefinite number of applications" and that it takes only the right occasion to see how what was spoken elsewhere can be made to speak to us now. "There is nothing which comes out of the human heart" which is not "thousand faced,—so that if perchance strong light falls on it, it will admit of being shown to be related to all things."

This is why an old, abstruse book can seem relatable and "intelligible" in a new light, part of the domain of our current knowledge from a certain perspective. Maybe we never could have realized it before. Though objects "successively tumble in," only some fall into place—only some are "clamped and locked by inevitable connection as a planet in its orbit." We will have to wait and see which ones draw us in if they are to seem fitting and useful now. "He has it who can use it," and, with patience, "at last the elect morning arrives":

> One author is good for winter, and one for the dog-days. The scholar must look long for the right hour for Plato's Timaeus. At last the elect morning arrives, the early dawn,—a few lights conspicuous in the heaven, as of a world just created and still becoming,—and in its wide leisures we dare open that book. ("Works and Days")

One day it simply might dawn on me to open up Plato's *Timaeus* (to "dare" to open myself to Plato). If the time is right, a scholar can get attached to any obscure, overlooked book and, at the same time, reattach or reconnect that book's words to life—bring them out of obscurity. It simply took until this moment to know what to do with it.

Describing in the same essay how "the day fits itself to the mind," Emerson suggests, not so much the subjectivism of knowledge (the mind coloring the day) as the way we might find something fitting in each day and answering to our moods, if only we pay attention.[8] Each day yields fresh "points of interest" to the person who is not uninterested in what it can offer. This does not suggest the projection of thought onto a moment but the process by which a moment becomes an object for thought, guiding the mind toward an intelligible experience of it. The point is to respond appropriately to the moment or in an advantageous way. I believe the implication is the same when he says in the essay "The Poet" that "thought makes every thing fit for use," the point being that when we care about something enough to reflect on it, we fit it for ourselves and give it purpose within our current frame of reference. It probably also means that if the moment is not right, say, for reading Plato's *Timaeus*, it is because the "elect morning" has not yet arrived and we are not receptive enough to care and find it worthwhile. We better be patient. "We animate what we can, and we see only what we animate. Nature and books belong to the eyes that see them. It depends on the mood of the man, whether he shall see the sunset or the fine poem."

A book may be fit for perpetual use because it can draw fresh interest on every subsequent approach, yielding new emphasis and forms of understanding even for the same reader at different times. "Why covet a knowledge of new facts?" Emerson asks. "Day and night, house and garden, a few books, a few actions, serve us as well as would all trades and all spectacles. We are far from having exhausted the significance of the few symbols we use." Just a few facts or books serve because they are each "inexhaustible." They are endlessly interesting. Just when you thought you knew their meaning, "today you come into a new thought, and lo! all nature converts itself into a symbol of that; and you see it has been chanting that song like a cricket ever since the creation." A thought, writes Emerson in "Natural History of Intellect," once "[hurled] . . . into the world" as a book or any form of expression, "has no limit to its value"—it "is of inestimable value"—because it offers something on which to keep reflecting and remains available for future experiences. As we turn it over in various lights and in connection with changing moods, it sustains and rewards our attention by revealing new aspects of itself that have been there all along.

"It has been chanting that song like a cricket ever since the creation"; "People wonder they never saw it before."[9]

There is always more to see even if there is nothing new to see, and this "more" expresses itself as a striving or movement forward. The best thought or book is the one that we keep turning over, circling all sides, seeing to it that there is *more to it* than we knew, especially when we thought we knew it already. The making a matter "the subject of thought, raises it," Emerson writes ("we behold it as a god upraised"). If it has a way of being resurrected later as fit for thoughts and use—if we keep raising it because it promises further revelation and because it continues to sharpen our vision and illuminate our thoughts and moods as perennially as the light of day "fits itself to the mind"—then it is relevant "to me and mine" for Emerson.

To make a book relevant does not do it violence. It is not the contortion to our purposes it might seem to take Dante's words, addressed to his times, and find they speak to our times, beyond their original context as though they are no longer to their own intent and purposes. Dante's intent matters a great deal, but he never could have known that the words he "[hurled] . . . into the world" would continue to generate awareness—that readers would come back to them and still find them interesting. What Emerson might call their "largeness of suggestion"—how they communicate enigmatically by "hints, omens, inference"—means that they will always invite more interactions. If readers take them not "literally, but genially"—if readers are *hospitable*, that is—then there is no reason they cannot stay worthwhile.

They have an "indefinitely expansive and radiating instrumental efficacy," to use a phrase that John Dewey uses to describe something similar to the "poetic effects" we saw in Poe. A little goes a long way for Emerson because a good book continues to excite attention and because a good reader finds that words written and read a while ago acquire new value in time. "Any piece of knowledge I acquire today, a fact that falls under my eyes, a book I read, a piece of news I hear, has a value at this moment exactly proportioned to my skill to deal with it. Tomorrow, when I know more, I recall that piece of knowledge and use it better."[10]

If there is anything we learn from reading "The Raven," every new question asked of the same rote words can bring forth a revelation. So the point is not that books change over time but that our relationship to them changes because they continue to be satisfying in ways we never could have anticipated. They become more intelligible as we ask more of them. Our "onward thinking" discloses more to us each time, widening the promise of relations. There is also, for Emerson, "the adventitious," or the changing conditions under which you happen to read, that enlarges that book's largeness of suggestion: your mood, the moment, the stimulus of the occasion for reading the book, much as the pleasure of viewing a temple is "only in part owing to the temple" and "exalted by the beauty of sunlight, the play of the clouds, the landscape around it, its grouping with the houses, trees, and towers, in its vicinity." The accidental circumstances in which you see it produce that quality of wonder at discovering something you would have missed otherwise.[11] For Emerson, some quality of Aristophanes, Hafiz, or Rabelais might even seem "full of American history." It is not that the scholar looks for a prehistory of American history in Aristophanes or Hafiz or even that classical Greece or fourteenth-century Persia might be a correlative to American history. It is simply that certain aspects of these texts, in them all along, did not speak to us so purposefully until we found ourselves in the situation where they did. It took until now for their importance to us to dawn on us. (At last the "elect morning" arrives.)

So, again, finding relevance for Emerson is not about twisting the meaning of words to suit our purposes. It is not about homing in, for example, on representations of political conditions in novels, poems, and other works of art to provide a critical vantage point on the politics of the present. At least it is not about reducing the function of a text to this single, "relevant" purpose in a way that would limit its value. Emerson sees all books as "property at interest" that keep accruing "undreamed-of value" as different circumstances make more in them apparent and recognizable than before. "And who shall set a boundary to this mounting value?" If we keep looking for the same kind of connections, we will easily "exhaust" these works' significance, and the point of reading them would be settled. They would lose interest. It would be like approaching them with what Emerson calls "impudent knowingness"—with the significance of a book dogmatically in mind—which is the opposite for him of the adventitious and the stance of wonder in which a book reveals itself and continues to impress us. The fact that a book that feels old or too familiar (much the same as one that feels too remote) still can manage to surprise and compel us suggests that one only wants the mood, the guiding moment, for that book to yield one of "an indefinite lifetime of further revelations," in Cavell's words, "all felt to be in it, there." The feeling, for Cavell, is something like the need to penetrate "some barrier to or resistance in" the book that baffles, bores, alienates, puts off, forecloses any connection until we discover an opening by surprise—a foothold.[12]

The function of reading at the present time is not about finding what isn't there (say, our present situation in an old book) but about recognizing what was there all along as an opening to think further. Emerson likens it to the parting of clouds or to revelations in the dark in flashes of light. It is the discovery that something even more significant has been right there in that book even if people could not see it, maybe because the moment was not yet right for it to be apparent in just this way. But, then, in a flash, "people wonder they never saw it before."

Relevance reveals new worth in the old. That old book may have been "chanting that song like a cricket ever since the creation," but we were never attuned enough to pick it out until the day when it was music to our ears. "By persisting to read or to think," writes Emerson in "Experience,"

> this region gives further sign of itself, as it were in flashes of light, in sudden discoveries of its profound beauty and repose, as if the clouds that covered it parted at intervals, and showed the approaching traveller the inland mountains, with the tranquil eternal meadows spread at their base, whereon flocks graze, and shepherds pipe and dance. But every insight from this realm of thought is felt as initial, and promises a sequel. I do not make it; I arrive there, and behold what was there already. I make! O no! I clap my hands in infantine joy and amazement.

If we keep reading, expanding not the range of what we read but the "range" of our "faculties of observation," something fresh is added to the world, something like a miracle occurs. We do not create it but arrive and behold what was there already. The "invariable mark of wisdom is to see the miraculous in the common." The consciousness of wonders deep in the neighborhood of the old and worn. "'Tis the old secret of the gods that they come in low disguises," writes Emerson, and the debt we owe to genius is that of "lifting the curtain from the common, and showing us that divinities are sitting disguised" there.[13] Again, we are far from having exhausted the significance of what an old book can yield. Commonplaces sparkle. They prosper by fits. The important fact of that old book is that we can learn to like it more.

Dewey writes, "The only objects, insights, perceptions, which remain perennially unwithered and unstaled are those which sharpen our vision for new and unforeseen embodiments of the truth they convey. The 'magic' of poetry . . . is precisely the revelation of meaning in the old effected by its presentation of the new." *The revelation of meaning in the old effected by its presentation of the new* is one of the best descriptions I can find for the relevance that Emerson suggests when he writes in his journal that he reads a work "until it is pertinent to me and mine, to nature and to the hour that now passes." The ability to see old works as mattering still, to readmit them into the orbit of interest so that an old poem is given new life by meeting the new and unusual situation of the present: I think this is what Emerson means in his journal when he says that he believes in a book's "Omnipresence." He is consciously readjusting the value of the old in the new. "'Intuition,'" Dewey says, "is that meeting of the old and new in which the readjustment involved in every form of consciousness is effected suddenly by means of a quick and unexpected harmony which in its bright abruptness is like a flash of revelation." *Intuition* is much the same for Emerson. It is the flash of revelation that there is value beyond our current standing or situation (beyond ourselves), that something already out there—age old, common, perennial, quotidian—can be pressingly important and brought to bear. It can fit or click or lock or fall into place—like a foot in a foothold.

I will not pretend that Emerson always calls this kind of "magic" relevance the way that he does in his journal. In fact he almost never actually calls it "relevance," and it is surprising to me that in 1847 he chose to use the word at all. But the concept that William James, Henry James, Schiller, Dewey, Whitehead, Schutz, and so many others do call "relevance" builds, more or less directly, on this sense of it in Emerson and especially on his relish of the extraordinary vibrancy of existence, by which I mean Emerson's faith that anything out there would feel "alive and significant" if only we could manage to pick it out. Emerson writes, in a line that for me is epitomizing, "The world is enlarged for us, not by new objects, but by finding more affinities and potencies in those we have."

He is at last our greatest philosopher of making the irrelevant count. Nothing is too old, obscure, or boring to have fresh meaning; nothing is too ordinary to feel like a kind of revelation. I will return to the sudden adjustment of the old in the new later, to a moment, for example, when Dewey describes, "that fusion of old meanings and new situations that transfigures both (a transformation that defies imagination)" and that renders any experience, including aesthetic experience, conscious. Value for Dewey always depends on this kind of resurrection in which old or "stored" facts, sensations, and memories, after a long period of incubation, are brought together with novel experiences "like sparks when the poles are adjusted."[14] *This* is the spark to "relevant" thinking in Dewey and also in William James, who goes so far as to call his book of philosophy for a changing and evolving world *Pragmatism: New Names for Some Old Ways of Thinking*. But for now I am only asking how Emerson imagines that transformation takes place in which a book becomes relevant or in which anything in the vast, extant, "unapproachable" world becomes a foothold or else the hook to hang our hat on.

There is always a "succession of objects" in Emerson. In "Art," he describes the "succession of excellent objects" from which "we learn at last the immensity of the world." In "Experience," the "succession of moods or objects" is necessary, but grieved because onward thinking and the "onward trick of nature" means that we are always straying and leaving things behind: "Gladly we would anchor, but the anchorage is quicksand." So, Emerson describes his changing interest in books as new books attract him and he tires of old ones. "Once I took such delight in Montaigne," he says, "that I thought I should not need any other book; before that, in Shakespeare; then in Plutarch; then in Plotinus; at one time in Bacon; afterwards in Goethe; even in Bettine; but now I turn the pages of either of them languidly, whilst I still cherish their genius. So with pictures; each will bear an emphasis of attention once, which it cannot retain, though we fain would continue to be pleased in that manner."

Wherever we find ourselves in Emerson, we get a series of attentions and distractions in alternation, takings and leavings (or relievings). This is why Sharon Cameron, Cavell, then Arsić after them believe that we only come to terms with Emerson if we take seriously his belief that the way of life is "by abandonment" and that knowledge must be, in Arsić's words, "unrelentingly adjusted to the fluctuations and mobility of the external world." In Emerson, nothing can be trusted as a "lasting relation." There will be no "foolish consistency." Whatever "streams with life" will "act or endeavor to reach somewhat beyond." "That rushing stream will not stop to be observed," he writes in "The Method of Nature": "If anything could stand still, it would be crushed and dissipated by the torrent it resisted, and if it were a mind, would be crazed; as insane persons are those who hold fast to one thought, and do not flow with the course of nature."[15]

This is not to say that anchoring is not important. In fact, the moments we feel to be important are precisely the ones that ground us briefly at full speed. Sometimes we have to stop and get a grip in order to carry onward and just keep going. If natural life is really a "torrent," then some grappling hooks can help. We attach and let go in alternation. "An innavigable sea washes with silent waves between us and the things we aim at and converse with" ("Experience"), but there still will be moments of accidental contact—Emerson calls them "hits" or "casualties"—when objects or other beings or human beings manage to strike us. Yes, the "evanescence and lubricity of all objects" means that they, too, will slip through our fingers. Emerson takes this "to be the most unhandsome part of our condition" in a line that Cavell famously sees as a play on the inability to grasp or to keep anything *at hand* as that most *unhandsome* part. But Emerson also writes that "by skill of handling and treatment," a man "can take hold anywhere" so long as he remembers that his "office is with moments," and who cares if the "duration" is "short?"

"Life itself is a mixture of power and form," he says, "and will not bear the least excess of either. To finish the moment, to find the journey's end in every step of the road, to live the greatest number of good hours, is wisdom." Life is in perpetual motion—it has momentum (power)—but there are moments that nonetheless coalesce and come together. There are *formative*, shaping moments of perception along the way when in "a new and excellent region of life" and "by persisting to read or to think, this region gives further sign of itself, as it were in flashes of light, in sudden discoveries of its profound beauty and repose." These are the times when for Emerson the clouds part at intervals, letting the traveler "behold what was there already." There are times when Emerson can "behold" other people, too, by which he means that he can really regard and attend to them and also hold (in the sense of *believe in*) them—when he can "treat them as if they were real: perhaps they are."[16]

So, in the essay "Experience," for all the ways in which Emerson feels the world does not touch him and that he is gliding through it "ghostlike" and unaware, he knows that something will always materialize for him again. It is what he tells himself when, feeling numb with grief after the death of his young son, Waldo, he ultimately has faith in the knowledge, since he has no choice but to keep going, that he will get a grip somehow. One day there will be something else to hold on to, then something else down the line. Other things will come to matter to him. They will surprise him. They will feel substantial, rock solid, and shake off the lethargy and indifference and be important all over again. They will strike him. If he can wait, they will be pertinent at last to him and his, "to nature and to the hour that now passes." He will fill that hour! He will hold on.

But how will anything else ever matter when his son is dead and he no longer cares? He simply knows by the end of the essay that he will feel interested again. That he will be drawn to something enough to treat it as if it mattered. Of all the "objects" that "successively tumble in," one eventually will fall into place. "Up again, old heart!" he says. He will find a new objective and "care enough for results."[17] He will not always be this unmoored.

. . .

I want to think for just a moment about Emerson's sense of being and staying interested. In that "innavigable sea" of life, though he often feels like he is drowning (so much washes over him), he still gets hooked on certain objects. He gets lured. It may be Aristophanes, Rabelais, Hafiz, Montaigne, or Shakespeare. It may be grammar rules and oyster shops. Remember there is "nothing," he says, "that does not interest us,—kingdom, college, tree, horse, or iron shoe, the root of all things are in man." Like Poe, he could be interested *in anything*. He believes the debt we owe to genius is the ability to stay interested and to fight off boredom somehow, to keep expanding the mind's range, like the circles in the essay "Circles," that "[rush] on all sides outwards to new and larger circles, and that without end" from an idea that was at first "imperceptibly small."[18] The mind can keep taking objects in, or else find more to absorb in the same book or object, the difference between the genius and anyone else being a capacity to focus better and longer by bringing more associations, purposes, and interests to his object.

What does it mean to find a book still interesting after all this time?

In *Our Aesthetic Categories*, Sianne Ngai describes how literature became "interesting"—or was suddenly understood to be "interesting"—in the first decades of the nineteenth century. She turns to the German romantic critic Friedrich Schlegel, who first distinguished in his early work *On the Study of Greek Poetry* (1797) the *beautiful poetry* of classical antiquity from the *interesting poetry* of modernity. "At a moment," Ngai writes, "marked by a radically expanded and accelerated circulation of printed media and the emergence of a bourgeois public sphere, by an unprecedented explosion of new literary genres and the nascent professionalization of literary criticism, it was Schlegel who first defined modern, interesting literature in direct opposition to the beautiful art of the Greeks." Schlegel sees modern poetry as "striving"—an aesthetic development keeping pace with a restless, liberalizing age. While Greek poetry is disinterested, rule bound and, in Schlegel's words, "universally valid" (having reached its highest purpose as an expression of divine and absolute truths), modern poetry is individualistic and idiosyncratic. "The general orientation of poetry—indeed, the whole aesthetic development [*Bildung*] of modernity—toward the interesting," writes Schlegel, "can be explained by this lack of universality, this rule of the mannered, characteristic, and individual."

Interesting poetry is always expanding its range of reference and applicability into magnitudes that "can be multiplied into infinity." It can be about anything and express anything. It defines a moment, Schlegel suggests, of unprecedented pluralism in art—an "anarchy" of literary genres and forms and also a new hybridity among these forms—so that, while poetry accounted for more than ever before, more than ever before also counted as poetry. "Content to take nothing less than everything for its province; resolved to possess and to express the entire range of human experience," poetry also demands unlimited "receptiveness" on the part of the reader. It is not simply that there is so much more of it to take in and each in its own particular form. The "real essence" of modern poetry, Schlegel suggests, is that it is forever "in the state of becoming" and never "finished," by which he means that poetry "can be exhausted by no theory" or attempt to understand it. The reader can never settle on the *point* of interesting poetry because "there can be no *endpoint* when it comes to the *interesting*."[19] A poem is always in excess of its interpretation; it can always do *more*. This means that, so long as a reader remains interested, the work of finding meaning never stops.

In his essay "The Relevance of the Beautiful" (*Die Aktualität des Schönen*), the hermeneutic philosopher Hans-Georg Gadamer points to the same moment in the early nineteenth century when romantic critics began to understand the experience of a work of art as being open ended or interminable, as he describes it. It is the moment when G. W. F. Hegel, giving his lectures on aesthetics, declared that art was for us a "thing of the past," by which he, like Schlegel, meant that art's "highest vocation" is over; the work of art no longer manifests the absolute truths that we revere. Once long ago in classical Greece, art was a manifestation of the divine, but it is no longer immanent in this way. The role played by art in the past is now fulfilled by philosophy or systems of belief, including religious belief, that transcend it as a means of expression.

The classical experience of art must have been "incantatory, magical," but then art, writes Arthur Danto in *The Transfiguration of the Commonplace*, underwent a transformation from being simply part of reality, "itself magically structured by virtue of the fact that special things, regarded as possessing special powers," were capable of being present in multiple ways, into "things that *contrasted* with reality, standing outside and against it, so to speak, as reality itself underwent a corresponding transformation in which it lost its magic in men's eyes." For Gadamer, the early nineteenth century comes to register this ontological divide: as soon as art is no longer *present* in reality but only a presentation of reality (in which the artwork brings to mind some state of affairs beyond it), the peculiar question of its value arises. Because art no longer could be what it had been, it became self-conscious. It needed to make a claim for its relationship to the world and for its validity and connectedness. The historical fate of art, writes Gadamer, is that it "inevitably appeared to require justification."[20]

By the early nineteenth century, in other words, the integration of art with life and the understanding of the artist's essential purpose within life were no longer "self-evident." Given art's challenge to the expectation of truth, as Robert Pippin suggests in *After the Beautiful*, it came to understand itself as something novel under new historical conditions that needed to be appreciated in new ways. Hegel's lectures on the "pastness" of art mark a historical shift that ultimately leads to the crisis of modern art of "having to confront, rather than simply assume, its continuing possibility and importance." After the beautiful, after Hegel, art "gives us to understand, first, what 'it feels like' to occupy, at various stages, such an unreconciled status and then what it is to 'live out' some achieved status that is, as Hegel says, more and more 'reconciled with itself.'" The moment art is no longer a manifestation of *the* world, it creates its own world as appropriate to its "pluralistic situation" and as one frame of reference among many. It enters into "openly admitted competition" for legitimacy by asserting "that [its] own particular form of creative expression" is the true one (Gadamer).[21] But there is always the possibility of conflicting interests and consequently of doubt whether the world made present within the frame can be taken for granted beyond question and really believed.

Again, for Schlegel, modern poetry is "interesting" because it will never stop striving. Its crisis is that it will never be "universally valid" again. A faith in the enduring truth of art gives way to a faith in its enduring relevance: to a philosophy of how art might stay interesting, paramount, and most of all meaningful for coming to terms with the predicament we are in. If the logic of art is not now its own proof, then it needs to make claims for its relevance.

This is the moment, for Gadamer in "The Relevance of the Beautiful," when the beautiful becomes relevant. The beautiful becomes interesting. It is not long before Poe proclaims "Beauty" to be "the sole legitimate province of the poem" that will keep his readers in their seats. Again, the work of justifying a poem, of giving it purpose and attaching or reattaching it to truth (including a true relationship to the reader), is interminable or "inexhaustible." Since "there can be no *endpoint* when it comes to the *interesting*," we simply have to keep asking what the point of the poem is. So Gadamer, then Pippin and others looking back to German romantic writers of the nineteenth century, understand this to be a critical moment—a moment, that is, of *criticism*—suggesting the need for conceptual articulation but also a deep and ongoing relationship with a work whose significance is particular to every encounter and whose final intelligibility will take all the time we have.

In the early nineteenth century, Schlegel understood this, too, as Ngai explains: "For Schlegel, 'interessante' also seems to mark a convergence of art with conceptual discourse about art, or an internalization by art—which consequently becomes philosophical or 'reflective'—of the 'relation between theory and praxis.'" Pippin writes that around the time of Hegel's lectures, the treatment of art "began shifting from 'aesthetics' to the 'philosophy of art' (i.e., from the sensible appreciation of beauty to art's interrogation of its own nature and possibility)." Art's crisis of its own possibility meant, in Hegel's words, "What is now aroused in us by works of art is not just immediate enjoyment but our judgment also, since we subject to our intellectual consideration (i) the content of art, and (ii) the work of art's means of presentation, and the appropriateness or inappropriateness of both to one another."[22] There is in the end (or in the end of art as Hegel describes it) the distinct possibility that art's presentation of the absolute truth it no longer manifests is somehow unfitting or *inappropriate*. After the beautiful, after all, art may be apropos of nothing, but it is the abiding work of criticism to find out.

To return to an earlier point, Schlegel suggests that "interesting" poetry is subjective and endlessly particularizing, assuming an "entirely individual stamp and peculiar local color" every time. It appeals to the modern subject's "restless" need for novelty and "longing for a complete satisfaction" that will never be met "by the individual and mutable, the more ardent and restless it [becomes]." A life full of interest marks the gap between itself and the satisfaction of the truly beautiful (the "universally valid, enduring, and necessary"), which always exceeds its grasp. Only "the *objective*—can fill this great gap." But the modern subject keeps longing for this satisfaction nonetheless, and later, in his critical and philosophical fragments, as Ngai and others admit, Schlegel comes to associate Romantic poetry (an idea he derives from "interesting" poetry) with not only the irony of the human condition as defined by this gap but with the subject's "striving toward knowledge of the infinite" and its quest for "the *objective*" and absolute truth.

So while "interesting" or Romantic poetry embraces a relativist aesthetic, it also happens to register this distinctively subjective, individualized striving *in* its shift toward objectivity and detachment, *in* its reflective, critical stance, and *in* its desire to reunite poetry with philosophy. In other words, beauty and truth remain the great *objective* of the romantic *subject*. This is simply more of its irony. We might go so far as to say, right along with Schlegel, that the striving for some truth that is universally valid is, "like everything objective, infinitely interesting."[23]

Emerson was interested in Schlegel, having borrowed from Boston libraries several volumes of his essays and lectures on literature, including a volume of early collected work in which he might have read, with the help of his German dictionary, *On the Study of Greek Poetry*, and also critical fragments that later appeared in the *Athenaeum*. Who knows if he was thinking of Schlegel when he claims that there is "nothing that does not interest us," or when he finds his books to be so interesting himself? Cavell suggests the influence of William Wordsworth instead, who writes, in the preface to *Lyrical Ballads,* that the "principle object" of the poems is to "chuse incidents and situations from common life" and to "make these incidents and situations interesting." Of course, Wordsworth was also interested in Schlegel—at least he shared his interest in the interesting. And so did Samuel Taylor Coleridge, who influenced Emerson just as much and whose literary criticism often points to the "continual rising of interest" or "requisite interest" that we have in the objects of our thought.[24]

In any case, achieving a state of "interestedness" is a goal that Cavell sees as being aligned in Emerson with Romanticism's aim to *make* things *interesting* to a reader so that "what is to happen to that one is that he or she become[s] interested in something." Cavell sees it as the "presiding ambition" of Emerson and also of Henry David Thoreau, who perceive us as being "empty of interest," in the condition of boredom or indifference, evident especially in the cheap entertainments or "stimulants" of modern life that boredom craves and that Wordsworth describes in his preface. So the state of what Thoreau calls "being interested in" is a state of "self-consciousness" and "absolute awareness of self without embarrassment" that is the opposite of lethargy and torpor (although for Emerson always slipping away). It is simply the state of being aware that I am actually experiencing some aspect of the world—that, for example, the strange book that I am now reading, *Walden,* has become an experience that is happening to me and is imposing on me somehow.

This means that Cavell would agree with Pippin that "interesting" literature did the philosophical work of "working out" the "subject object" problem of its day: the problem, that is, of recognizing the unbridgeable gap between the self and the world while denying any "metaphysical dualism." The subject-object problem, Pippin writes, "encompassed everything from how subjects can know objects" as they really are to how the art objects that interest us can be said to bear meaning for us. Our interests let us ask what the world means to us. But because feelings of interest are not free floating or enjoyed for their own sake but for the sake of the object that calls them forth (and in which they are fully absorbed as *abiding interests*), these feelings are very much *about something* and occupied by that thing and not about us. They are not "merely subjective." This is why Schlegel can describe "everything objective" as "infinitely interesting" to romantic *subjects* who keep striving beyond themselves in the most personal and heartfelt ways.

It is also why Emerson says that in art, "nothing interests us which is stark or bounded," but only what endeavors to "reach somewhat beyond" (being all the more interesting if it demands that we reach way beyond, in the direction of the "vast & divine"). Cavell suggests that in both Emerson and Thoreau interestedness "is already a state—perhaps the basic state—of relatedness to something beyond the self, the capacity for concern, for implication. It may be thought of as the self's capacity to mediate, to stand, between itself and the world." In *Walden*, for example, Thoreau uses the word *interest* whenever he wants us to "assess our commitment and orientation" toward his words and the words of others, the presence or distance of these words from us being the measure of how invested we have become in them and how deeply we have taken them in. "It would be a fair summary of the book's motive," Cavell writes, "to say that it invites us to take an interest in our lives, and teaches us how."[25]

How attached are we to the world out there? How interested are we in it? "An interest is objective," writes Albert Barnes and Violette de Mazia, after Dewey, in one of their books on aesthetic experience. "It is a concern, and an abiding concern, with something which is real independently of us. . . . Feelings which do not thus take us outside ourselves into something objective, and keep our attention fixed upon it, are unstable and trivial, they are a welter of emotion which may justly be stigmatized as sentimental." Emotion, they say, is "abiding only when it has an abode, a body; when it is feeling *about something*, to which it is so organically bound that the two are inseparable," whereas "excess of emotion is unabsorbed feeling" and points to a lack of interest; "it spills over into a vacuum and inhibits the process of perception." Cavell writes, "Let the object or the work of your interest teach you how to consider it."

Put differently, our personal interests are objective because they are absorbed in their *object*. They have a kind of teleological focus on or intent toward the object they have in view and to which they tend and are dynamically oriented. It is not so far from saying that our interests are really "disinterested" because they do not consist entirely of personal or private gratification but contain an element of pressing forward and seeking through thought. Emerson writes that "our greatness is always in a tendency or direction." We *attend* to things, meaning, literally, *stretch toward* them. "Only when we are dulled by routine and sunk in apathy," Dewey writes, "does this eagerness forsake us."

Interest leads thought (this time in Dewey's words) "to something beyond itself." In the case of an art object, for example, it is the task of the observer to respond appropriately to the work, to "work with the work," whereas an excess of emotion is never really *about* the work but the opposite of feeling interested in it and attached to it. An excess of emotion "lacks any specific relevance to its object." Dewey writes that a person experiencing a work of art "loses himself in irrelevant reverie unless his images and emotions are also tied to the object, and are tied to it in the sense of being fused with the matter of the *object.*" *That* is the experience "worth having, not merely an indulgence in irrelevant sentimentality."[26]

I doubt anyone would accuse Emerson of being too sentimental. He does not gush, if "Experience" is any indication. He is looking for relevance in objects that had once seemed irrelevant and not indulging in "irrelevant reverie." His moods and emotions draw him fittingly toward the objects that orient him toward the world and let him face it. He treats these objects "as if they were real: perhaps they are."

William James writes, "The mere fact of appearing as an object at all is not enough to constitute reality. That may be metaphysical reality, reality for God; but what we need is practical reality, reality for ourselves; and, to have that, an object must not only appear, but it must appear both *interesting* and *important*. The worlds whose objects are neither interesting nor important we treat simply negatively, we brand them as *un*real." He continues, "reality means simply relation to our emotional and active life. . . . In this sense, whatever excites and stimulates our interest is real."[27] "The unreal is the uninteresting," Barnes writes. Think about how dreams can be so boring in retrospect. Lacking substance, the unreal is incapable of compelling or moving us in any real way. The unreal cannot represent an object or situation "in its concrete fulness," which makes it *uninteresting*, whereas interest needs an object (no less so a love interest).

In other words, interest finds meaning and importance embodied in objective form—something with facticity and force all its own that is capable of exerting a force on us, an active agent. The uniqueness—the ontological strangeness of that object that makes it interesting—means, for Dewey, that it is perceived as an obstacle or problem to the perceiver. "The object is that which objects," he says. When objects *object*, they can be said to impose themselves on us. They strike us in some palpable way. They are, Schutz writes in reference to Dewey, the "ontological structure[s]" of nature with which "I have to come to terms."

Schutz defines *relevance* as a form of "interest" that motivates an individual to be attentive to some objects over others. Certain objects command my attention out of all possible objects in a perceptual field, and it is not a mere act of will or projection on my part, since *they* interest *me*. They draw my attention to themselves. I come to terms with my environment by way of these objects that concern me. They are, as Calvin Shrag writes, my "mode of entry into the world," and I construct my sense of reality—of what it is in the world that actually matters to me—around them. My interests form a certain outlook. Through their auspices, certain "dimensions of the world *as I exist in it* are uncovered and brought to light." Interests imply concern, not with myself, but with the objective things that draw me in *in* recognition of them. "Interest depends," Barnes writes, "upon the sensibility which makes us alive in the real world to things that to one not sensitive would not exist."[28]

When Dewey, in *Interest and Effort in Education*, offers the etymology of *interest*—from the Latin *inter-esse*, "to be between"—he suggests not only that interest is formed in the transaction between a subject and an object but also that "interest marks the annihilation of the distance between" them. It is the sign of their "organic union." It sounds almost cabalistic, but it is not so hard to see: the interested subject simply *experiences* its object (with *experience* always being the key word for Dewey but also for Emerson in "Experience"). In *Art as Experience*, Dewey calls the emotion that results "impersonal" because the feeling is not about the self but about the object in recognition "of which the self has surrendered itself in devotion." It is about an eagerness to be touched and transformed by this object by being faithful to it. Sometimes Emerson even describes being "ravished," because, again, the point of an interest is to be *taken* with an object (even more so a love interest).[29]

Sharon Cameron's essay on the idea of "Emerson's impersonal," first published in 1998, challenged the long-held critical sense of the Emersonian person as egotistical and assertive, projecting his visions onto the landscape and everything else. Cameron finds instead an "erasure of personality" in Emerson's works, the relinquishment of a personal perspective in favor of moments of "interpenetration" with something like a "divine presence" (that Emerson sometimes calls "God"). In "The Over-Soul," he describes this presence as "an influx of the Divine mind into our mind" that is otherwise known "by the term *Revelation*." What then is revelation? It is the distinct apprehension of some *objective* or absolute principle, the wonderful perception of a new truth and, then, the fact of being drawn to it, like the "ebb of the individual rivulet before the flowing surges of the sea of life."

In "Intellect," he says that ordinarily a person is more like "a ship aground," so entirely at the mercy of coming events and so "battered by the waves" that "every man beholds his human condition with a degree of melancholy." Most of the time we are overwhelmed. But there are moments of apprehension by which some fact of life, "disentangled from the web of our unconsciousness, becomes an object impersonal and immortal." This fact announces itself and takes hold. The insight we gain is nothing new. It is the revelation of something that was out there already but is now "disentangled" from the unconscious and raised as a conscious object. "We behold it," Emerson writes, "as a god upraised."

We become aware of the "self-existence" of a fact or truth beyond the self's existence and beyond anything we have yet to experience. We own it "as other," as Cameron puts it, and take it to be "different in both magnitude and category" from everything that we have known before and without comparison—"as if it alone were real." Something that was undistinguished in the immense "sea of circumstance" gets elevated and exaggerated. And whenever this happens—whenever some undistinguished object is separated out in perception from the "succession of objects" and made vital in our minds—we show ourselves to be "intellectual beings." We show ourselves to be capable of thinking about something (capable of *having an object*), since the alternative to the "impersonal" in Emerson's essays is always a kind of stupor.

I think what Cameron calls "the process through which the personal becomes the impersonal"—this coming together of subject and object in the concrete way in which a person comes to be identified with an object (or to have one in mind)—is much like what it means for Emerson to find himself interested in the world, in its objective reality. He wants to feel tied to what is otherwise so alien, to establish a connection with it. In this integrative moment it can be said most fully that a person is a being in the world and realizes consciously a way of inhabiting it. "Thus inevitably does . . . every object fall successively into the subject itself," Emerson writes in "Experience." "As I am, so I see," the point always also being that it does not matter how trivial or insignificant the thing is I see, since my interest in it gives it purpose and life-changing importance.[30]

"A subject and an object,—it takes so much to make the galvanic circuit complete, but magnitude adds nothing. What imports it whether it is

Kepler and the sphere; Columbus and America; a reader and his book; or puss with her tail?" The point is to try to make a connection, to be set in motion to make it. It might be a reader trying to get a handle on a book, or it might be puss chasing her tail: who cares what the object is so long as it moves its subject? Kepler pursuing the heavens may in the end not be very unlike a cat chasing its tail; in any case, what until then had been taken for granted is now brought into question. What had been taken for granted is brought into view. The hope this object gives its eager subject is that the attention will pay off and that something will be grasped.

It actually might be more in keeping with Emerson to call the process that Cameron describes one "through which the impersonal becomes the personal" instead—proceeding the other way around, from objectivity to subjectivity. What was objective now matters to me and has become part of who I am and how I am constituted right now. I have come to value it as the object of my thoughts, concerns, and desires. It has become a fact to know about me. It is *in my interests*. It has been made relevant to me and mine, and so forth. Emerson says, "How respectable the life that clings to its objects!"[31] Always the choice is between going through this world in a kind of stupor or else being engaged enough to try to get a hold on it.

"Most persons do not see the sun," Emerson writes in *Nature*. Most of the time it is, as John Ruskin might put it, "actually unseen, not merely unnoticed, but in the full, clear sense of the word, unseen." But once in a while someone like Emerson manages to see it; it shines explicitly for him and he takes it in ("part of his daily food"). It is the sort of thing that gets classified, in his essays, as a miracle. He feels it never could happen and probably will never happen again, but it occurs all the same, and someone really does see the sun despite the expectations.

The miracle "is a phenomenon called consciousness and its tendency toward individuation." It creates a unique consciousness, like the one that Emerson's readers find in each one of his essays. Every single day the miracle is that some object creates awareness. How anything manages to do this and the value it has when it does is the persistent question of Emerson's essays.

The objective or "impersonal," Dewey writes, "quickens us from the slackness of routine and enables us to forget ourselves by finding ourselves in the delight of experiencing the world about us in its varied qualities and forms." Being "impersonal" is simply a way of forgetting ourselves by finding ourselves in the act of experiencing an object. By "object," both Emerson and Dewey mean something pulled out of the perceptual field in the sort of realizable state in which we can experience it and reflect on it and in which our engagement with it can be purposeful. It is an aspect of life that gets raised out of the sensorium as mattering explicitly. I cannot emphasize enough how often we find Emerson chasing after these decisive encounters with some object that he had taken for granted and with which he never bothered but that he suddenly finds to be interesting. Cameron calls them "heroic" moments of "contact with the real." Emerson himself describes them as the "common gifts" for which "necessity makes pertinences and beauty every day."[32]

It is unsurprising that this interesting object is sometimes animated or personified in Emerson, as the "influx of the Divine mind into our mind," yes, or as something else. "A subject *and* an object," as he puts it (though the italics are mine). These are the moments when we become "alive in the world to things that to one not sensitive would not exist" but that now appear to be perfectly vital themselves. They rise up and take shape and are able to strike us and we resound like bells. "Nature says,—he is my creature, and maugre all his impertinent griefs, he shall be glad with me." A personification. Emerson may feel an "occult relation" with the fields and woods, too, understanding in their presence that he is "not alone and unacknowledged." "They nod to me," Emerson says, "and I to them."

In the presence of nature, Emerson's experience is not unlike that of the correspondent in Crane's "The Open Boat," who feels "perhaps, the desire to confront a personification" just when the waves become "important" and shut out all else from view. These are the moments in which we *make pertinences*, make importances, and in which other thoughts become "impertinent" by comparison (Nature says, "maugre all his impertinent griefs"). Crossing a bare common, in snow puddles, at midnight, "all mean egotism vanishes" in spite of "real sorrows," because something other than these sorrows has come to bear and to act on him. It feels powerful. "The currents of the Universal Being circulate through me," he writes; "I am part or particle of God." He forgets himself in finding himself moved by this impersonal thing. It is the feeling Crane's correspondent gets, too, when, exhausted from rowing and nearly resigned to die at sea, he keeps managing to find a larger sense of meaning in the "impersonal" connections that come to consciousness at that exigent moment. In the waves, but also in the memory of the poem about the dying soldier in Algiers that "moved" him "by a profound and perfectly impersonal connection" and that comes to mind in the midst of the waves. For Emerson and Crane, these are exhilarating, life-giving moments that keep us going because something out there appears to answer to us and address us just when our own thoughts might consume us. Something else feels pertinent and full of worth notwithstanding our griefs. It may be the hardest feeling to sustain, but for the time being these griefs are "impertinent griefs."[33]

Take Emerson's description of a childhood memory, which sounds surprisingly like the correspondent's childhood memory of the poem about the soldier in Algiers. A past action or event gets stored in the deepest recesses of memory and remains there, "immersed in our unconscious life," for an indefinite period of time. It is a part of life, but "we no more feel or know it, than we feel the feet, or the hand, or the brain of our body." But then, "in some contemplative hour, it detaches itself from the life like a ripe fruit, to become a thought of the mind." It gets "disentangled from the web of our unconsciousness," and—to return to the passage in "The American Scholar,"

> Instantly, it is raised, transfigured; the corruptible has put on incorruption. Always now it is an object of beauty, however base its origin and neighborhood. Observe, too, the impossibility of antedating this act. In its grub state, it cannot fly, it cannot shine,—it is a dull grub. But suddenly, without observation, the selfsame thing unfurls beautiful wings, and is an angel of wisdom. So is there no fact, no event, in our private history, which shall not, sooner or later, lose its adhesive inert form, and astonish us by soaring from our body into the empyrean.

That old forgotten event or fact, that storybook rhyme we never knew was there but was with us all along, might come to mind at any time. "Out of darkness, it came insensibly into the marvellous light of to-day," writes Emerson elsewhere of a memory, and then all at once he was aware of it; "always we are fishing up some wonderful article out of that pond." No fact, no event, is too ordinary or despicable to astonish us one day by coming to consciousness like this. Lifted out of our private history, it gets "raised, transfigured" as "an object impersonal and immortal." It becomes an "object of beauty." It is "the advent of truth into the world, a form of thought now, for the first time, bursting into the universe, a child of the old eternal soul" brought into the present moment.

Out from "all that mass of mental and moral phenomena which we do not make objects of voluntary thought," this one neglected fact or event gets raised as a "sensible object" of thought right now. Why now? Because it is relevant. It acquires "an emphasis in your memory out of all proportion to [its] apparent significance" because it answers to this moment and fits our mood and because, for Emerson, "the soul's emphasis is always right."[34] If we think about it, it is exactly what we need and can use. Remember how Emerson writes that Dante might be significant all over again if the time is right? Or how Aristophanes more than two millennia later could have a lot to contribute to American history? Anything may become important, like the verses of the poem learned so long ago the correspondent cannot remembering learning them but that suggest themselves on the open boat as he rows.

Emerson portrays the sudden relevance of a memory as a kind of resurrection. "The making a fact the subject of thought, raises it," so he keeps imagining that fact soaring out of its buried state and coming to light as a "divine" being. That shabby, corruptible, selfsame fact unfurling its wings into "an angel of wisdom": this is the mystical process by which Emerson suggests that memory throws up the strangest things, by which any old perception can get raised again and come to mind a radiant, shining presence. It is also how Emerson believes that new circumstances call on old knowledge and give "new undreamed-valued to the old" and how the old or age old calls out the current moment in turn, revealing something wonderful or significant about it. For Emerson, the relevant fact is like an annunciating angel.

Dante might be true to the current moment. Any memory might be true to the occasion. "So lies the whole series of natural images with which your life has made you acquainted, in your memory, though you know it not, and a thrill of passion flashes light on their dark chamber, and the active power seizes instantly the fit image, as the word of its momentary thought." Of course, what we might recognize as relevant to any given day depends entirely on the day, on our mood, and on the hour that now passes. It depends entirely on the situation in which we find ourselves. The moods that define awareness are contingent on our circumstances, which is why Emerson calls them our *fate*. "Whatever does not concern us is, concealed from us," he writes in "Nominalist and Realist."

> As soon as a person is no longer related to our present well-being, he is concealed, or *dies*, as we say. Really, all things and persons are related to us,

> but according to our nature, they act on us not at once, but in succession, and we are made aware of their presence one at a time. All persons, all things which we have known, are here present, and many more than we see; the world is full.

The objects that attract us change day by day because what fits our moods and answers to our needs and desires keeps changing, and so does the "facility with which Nature lends itself" to our thoughts and "the aptness with which a river, a flower, a bird, fire, day, or night, can express [our] fortunes." On other days, each of these things may be less apt, less apropos.

Emerson writes in his journal, "We are partial & only (select) pick, like birds, a crumb here & there. Tho' the world is full of food, we can take only the crumbs fit for us. The air rings with sounds, but only a few vibrations can reach our tympanum, deaf to all the thunders around us."[35] Or, as he says,

> Teach me never so much and I hear or retain only that which I wish to hear, what comports with my experience and my desire. Many eyes go through the meadow, but few see the flowers. A hunter finds plenty of game on the ground you have sauntered over with idle gun. White huckleberries are so rare that in miles of pasture you shall not find a dozen. But a girl who understands it will find you a pint in a quarter of an hour.

There is much more than we can use, and so we only hear and retain what we wish to hear and pick up on what we can, "as each tree can secrete from the soil the elements that form a peach, a lemon, or a cocoa-nut, according to its kind." We are indifferent toward everything that is less "fit for us," and when we do not attend to these things, we hardly see them, since they come duly only to those to whom they pertain, as game to the hunter or huckleberries in the meadow to the girl who is inclined toward them. The world is full of these objects that advance and recede by turns. As soon as a person "needs a new object, suddenly he beholds it. . . . When he has exhausted for the time the nourishment to be drawn from any one person or thing, that object is withdrawn from his observation, and though still in his immediate neighborhood, he does not suspect its presence," which is not to say that it cannot become intelligible some other time, since "necessity makes pertinences and beauty every day."

I think it is part of Emerson's achievement to help us see that even reading his obscure and recalcitrant essays might now and then answer and pertain to us. "He has it who can use it": one day the time may be right for them to come into focus. They will be what Ross Posnock calls "belated revelations." In the meantime, what the poet, intellectual, or scholar at least can do is bring some aspect of life to attention—raise it as an object of interest that we might raise our sights to it. "Trifles so simple and fugitive that no man remembers the poet seizes and by force of them hurls you instantly into the presence of his joys." Then maybe we, too, will "[seize] instantly the fit image." Maybe it will take. It would be like the soldier in Algiers to the correspondent in the boat or like the nutrients in the soil to make a peach, if only we were peach trees: "the world is full of food."[36] But to pick up on them, requires both an appeal on Emerson's part and an opening up on our part. There has to be the felt promise of meaning or the immanent sense of mattering; and when there is (when interest wins), it will be the triumphant recognition of something we disregard most of the time, like the sun or the flowers in the meadow for Emerson.

A child, for example, will pick up on almost anything. So, for Emerson, will an intellectual, admitting more and more objects into consciousness, like the opening of the shutter where they imprint themselves. "A man is intellectual," he writes, "in proportion as he can make an object of every sensation, perception and intuition." At the heart of Emerson's essays is the effort to understand how we might pick up on more, make more of the world into objects of consideration—and, also, what writing or any sort of art has to do with making interest, making importance, to invoke Henry James once more. Art is a world in which, in James's terms, "everything counts," everything has contributive value by rewarding and sustaining interest and by showing whatever the artist has been conscious of by making us conscious of it in turn. The writer "is pledged thereby to remember that the art of interesting us in things—once these things are the right ones for his case—can *only* be the art of representing them," writes James. So, again, what Emerson is after when he writes that "necessity makes pertinences and beauty every day" is how consciousness will be raised in the first place, so that even the "trifles" we had taken for granted become explicit and important. He is after how anything, let alone more things, might come to matter for us and ours when "most men's minds do not grasp anything." It is also what Emerson's readers—including William James, Henry James, John Dewey, and others—are after in their own reflections on how certain aspects of life rise into importance over others and how we orient ourselves toward these aspects that we might not be indifferent. For all of them, finding relevance requires considerable reflecting on the psychology of "selective attention" and on the process by which something gets picked up as an object of interest (no less so a love object).

Then, for all of them, too, I'll leave off here with Emerson's contemporary, Søren Kierkegaard, whose work "Diary of the Seducer" links our attractions to a similar sense of their fatefulness. That object that so enigmatically excites our attention seems to hold out the promise of rewarding it with emotional pertinence—like a stranger who appears out of nowhere, but in some unique connection with the self. The seducer is a good figure for this object; Poe makes the raven a good figure for it as well. The emotional side of consciousness is what comes to be called *relevance* and, in Kierkegaard's words, "the interesting" is thus "the field on which the battle must be waged."[37]

4

Attention and Selection in a Phenomenal World

Figure and Ground

On the early morning of April 18, 1906, William James was still in bed in his apartment at Stanford University, where he was lecturing in philosophy, when the bed began to tremble and the plaster cracked. Everything that was on anything fell off. The furniture toppled; there was an awful, grinding roar and, all across campus (as the roar reached "*fortissimo*"), the floors split and the walls, rafters, and chimneys came down. It was all over in forty-eight seconds, and the people who had lived through the earthquake came into the streets in their pajamas if they were not pinned in by the rubble.

You would think that an earthquake would be *unwelcome*, but not to James, who says in his account of it that for him "it was pure delight and welcome" and who seems, despite "the material ruin that greeted [him] on every hand," to have been shaken into some kind of firm hold on the value of the experience that *he* greeted with Olympian "glee at the vividness which such an abstract idea or verbal term as 'earthquake' could put on when translated into sensible reality and verified concretely." ("'*Go* it,' I almost cried aloud, 'and go it *stronger*!'") So it seems that in 1906, with the ground cracking and his wife's safety in another room still unknown, James comes to verify that abstract ideas—as hypothetical as *the* great San Francisco earthquake—actually exist and are among the realities of experience. "Here at last was a *real* earthquake," he says, "after so many years of harmless waggle!"

This earth-shattering realization is the adventure that he welcomes in bed that morning when he "felt no trace whatever of fear," as the earthquake becomes for him a "living" thing—or, let's call it, one of the greatest personifications in the history of philosophy:

> First, I personified the earthquake as a permanent individual entity. It was *the* earthquake of my friend B.'s augury, which had been lying low and holding itself back during all the intervening months, in order, on that lustrous April morning, to invade my room, and energize the more intensely and triumphantly. It came, moreover, directly to *me*. It stole in behind my back, and once inside the room, had me all to itself, and could manifest itself convincingly. Animus and intent were never more present in any human action, nor did any human activity ever more definitely point back to a living agent as its source and origin.
>
> All whom I consulted on the point agreed as to this feature in their experience. "It expressed intention," "It was vicious," "It was bent on destruction," "It wanted to show its power," or what not. To me, it wanted simply to manifest the full meaning of its *name*. But what was this "It"? To some, apparently, a vague demonic power; to me an individualized being, B.'s earthquake, namely. . . .
>
> . . . For "science," when the tensions in the earth's crust reach the breaking-point, and strata fall into an altered equilibrium, earthquake is simply the collective *name* of all the cracks and shakings and disturbances that happen. They *are* the earthquake. But for me *the* earthquake was the *cause* of the disturbances, and the perception of it as a living agent was irresistible. It had an overpowering dramatic convincingness.

I will not dwell too long on how much James claims to have welcomed the earthquake despite its awful destruction. (Fires erupted everywhere afterward and the water supply was cut; James tells us how the dynamite detonations to clear all the buildings hanging by a thread made for even more destruction and smoke.) But it was exciting to face the earthquake that had been there all along: "a permanent individual entity," lying low and "holding itself back during all the intervening months" he had been in residence at Stanford until the moment it snuck in behind his back and released that shocking roar. The earthquake is something whose power it is *to appear* with exquisite intelligibility. It came, he says, *directly* to *him*. It aroused him right out of bed and more. "It had me," James says, "all to itself," which is to say that it made itself felt as a consummatory experience. What had been the vague intimation of an earthquake in harmless tremors (or his friend B.'s augury) had now come out definitively. It "expressed intention," with *intention* meaning, literally, that it *stretched toward* him, as if with purpose. It even seems to have waited in its subterranean hole until that surprising moment when it "could manifest itself convincingly" to James as an "individualized being"—an objective reality.[1]

"These vivid accidents," writes Alfred North Whitehead, "accentuate something which is already there." The "power" the earthquake seems bent on showing James is exactly how fully it commands his attention that April morning to become the predominant object of his feelings and thoughts. "As soon as I could think," he writes, "I discerned retrospectively certain peculiar ways in which my consciousness had taken in the phenomenon." In other words, that the earthquake *comes to him* directly and irresistibly is a perfect example of the phenomenon *of* consciousness with which he wants to come to terms. The earthquake "manifests itself" to him; on James's part, it is a triumphant recognition. It materializes for him as an alien "entity" of whose existence he could never have been sure but now welcomes with an openness to the meaning of experience, even disastrous experience, that also drove his interest in radical empiricism, panpsychism, and most of all pragmatism at this time. His book *Pragmatism* was finally completed just after the earthquake and published the next year. Far from "inured to the rough kiss of experience," as Jacques Barzun describes it, James wants us to know how much he's been shaken—like "a terrier shakes a rat," James says.[2]

In that "stream of sentiency" that, for James, bears us along, there are all kinds of evanescent things that pass through the "fringes and halos" of consciousness, "inarticulate perceptions, whereof the objects are as yet unnamed, mere nascencies of cognition, premonitions, awarenesses of direction." But, James writes in "On a Certain Blindness in Human Beings," "wherever a process of life communicates an eagerness to him who lives it, there the life becomes genuinely significant." Wherever this eagerness is found, "there is the zest, the tingle, the excitement, of reality; and there *is* 'importance' in the only real and positive sense in which importance ever anywhere can be." I think it is fair to say that nothing could be more important than the great San Francisco earthquake to the people who felt it that morning, and James depicts the moment at which the earthquake comes to matter. It appears as a dramatic figure against the ground it so powerfully shook. Something that was below the surface suddenly emerged as "sensibly real" to James, who felt its potency and dynamic connection to his life. If

James welcomed it, it is very much in the way that Emerson describes how the attentive mind ("the Soul attentive") greets with "entire welcome" any "feeling of *relationship* to that which is at the same time new and strange."

So much of James's work is about this *focused apparency*, to use a term that that other pragmatist, John Dewey, uses to describe how out of the flux of consciousness, something rises into importance and becomes "momentarily focal." James is fascinated by how anything out of everything makes itself felt or communicates an "eagerness" in this way, the earthquake being the most powerful example of what happens when suddenly we find some aspect of the world completely compelling. This is what James means when he repeats the general impression that the earthquake "expressed intention" and that "animus and intent were never more present in any human action."[3] The earthquake compelled everyone all at once. It refocused attention in those forty-eight seconds but also in the long aftermath of response to it, including the collective efforts to recover from it and James's later reflections on it in his essay.

Intention and attention are two sides of the same coin: etymologically the same, from the French *attendre*, meaning to *stretch toward*, so that the earthquake's intention toward James draws his attention in turn. James wants us to visualize the earthquake tending toward him as he attends to it: a moment of maximum *tension* as that roar hits *fortissimo*. In its surprise, the earthquake seems to reify for James the concept of attention itself and the fundamental state of being compelled by whatever demands his attention like that. So he invokes the musical dynamic *fortissimo*. The earthquake is the bugle call that commands its troops, the reveille that woke everybody up that April morning. It is a wake-up call, a call to action.

The purpose of the earthquake insofar as it expressed intent was not only to make for an experience "too overwhelming for anything but passive surrender to it." Beyond the "almost joyous" confirmation that a *real* earthquake was "here at last" was the phenomenon of concentration, of consciousness of which, for James, the earthquake provides the signal instance. Its call to attention lasted well past the main shock; "above all, there was an irresistible desire to talk about it, and exchange experience." And then there was the immediate mobilization of "an entire population in the streets, busy as ants in an uncovered ant-hill," saving what they could from houses, many on fire, and carrying bundles or dragging trunks to spots of temporary safety. There was "no appearance of general dismay," only coordinated excitement and *seriousness*:

> The inert elements of the population had mostly got away, and those that remained seemed what Mr. H. G. Wells calls "efficients." Sheds were already going up as temporary starting-points of business. Every one looked cheerful, in spite of the awful discontinuity of past and future, with every familiar association with material things dissevered; and the discipline and order were practically perfect.

James finally emphasizes the "rapidity of the improvisation of order out of chaos." Within twenty-four hours, "there seemed to be no possibility which there was not some one there to think of" or that was not somehow provided for by one of the volunteer committees: "rations, clothing, hospital, quarantine, disinfection, washing, police, military, quarters in camp and in houses, printed information, employment," you name it. While anxiety and anguish poured in from back east, James did not hear "a single really pathetic or sentimental word in California expressed by any one." Though absolutely everyone was suffering to some extent, the tendency was "more toward nervous excitement than toward grief." Private misery receded in the face of "the all-absorbing practical problem of general recuperation," confirming for James how "directly practical" human nature can be. "In our drawing-rooms and offices we wonder how people ever *do* go through battles, sieges and shipwrecks," he says. But we do: there is a mental focusing that takes place at the "place of action" that keeps our eye on the object. It keeps us from being sentimental and pathetic. We can only focally attend to one thing at a time, and so from that *fortissimo*, as if at the bugle's call, the people who experienced the earthquake focused with military discipline ("the discipline and order were practically perfect"), this kind of attention being, for James, the organizational force of our conscious life. "Like soldiering," he says, "it lies always latent in human nature."[4]

James's reflection on the San Francisco earthquake is a portrayal of how something can surprise us at any time. What was implicit—"lying low and holding itself back"—becomes explicit and "manifest[s] itself," and James wants to know how our consciousness "[takes] in the phenomenon." He is interested in what happens when that thing that the earthquake so fully figures captures our attention and how this new awareness focuses and organizes our thoughts so that we know what to do in the face of it. Following James, Alfred Schutz writes, "By the term '*wide-awakeness*' we want to denote a plane of consciousness of highest tension originating in an attitude of full attention to life and its requirements." He also is drawing on Henri

Bergson, who was the first to suggest what came to be known as process philosophy and whose idea of *attention à la vie* defines, in Schutz's words, "the realm of our world which is relevant to us" and the "basic regulative principle of our conscious life."[5]

Consciousness brings forth certain thoughts while putting others in abeyance. In a crisis, some thoughts come into relief because they offer relief by suggesting the practical means of moving forward. Right away there is a new sense of *importance*. Thc victims of the earthquake attend to the task at hand ("rations, clothing, hospital, quarantine") while all along their personal grief is put on hold, and this keeps them going as much as those new objects that interest Emerson after the death of his son hold back his grief and keep him going. Something else rises into attentional prominence and lets you refocus. Something else lets you cope. Other things are not nearly so relevant right now.

. . .

Relevance, for James, is about how importance is made at any given moment, and our attention has everything to do with it. In *Principles of Psychology*, he is after both a distinctive phenomenology of attention and its epistemic role: "what-it-is-like to attend" to an object and what that attention can do. He understands attention to be the concentration of consciousness, but he also suggests that it is a way of responding to consciousness purposefully and meaningfully. "Attention is a distinctive way of being conscious," as Wayne Wu puts it, writing of James. Attention to an object distinguishes it and brings it into the foreground. It "phenomenally individuates an object so that one can think demonstratively about it." It suggests not just that we hear the sound or see the flash of light or feel that earthquake but that our consciousness of these things has an "upshot."[6] They "shake" us and make us think. The move us in some way.

The earthquake gets James's attention and makes him respond. It makes everyone respond. (This is what James means by its "intent," its purpose.) The figure of an earthquake pops out of the ground and it gets James thinking about how consciousness works. After all, an earthquake turns out to be a great figure for the ideas of "figure" and "ground" that were already implicit in his work from over a decade earlier describing how attention brings out certain figures from the "dim background" of perception. The earthquake suggests what happens when anything becomes perceptually salient and gets detached, figure-like, from the fringes of our awareness and emerges as a coherent thing for us though we had never been so conscious of it before.

It was the Danish graduate student Edgar John Rubin who later highlighted the concepts of "figure" and "background" for theories of perception in his 1915 dissertation filed at the University of Copenhagen, "Figure and Ground." The so-called Rubin vase, or faces-vase picture, featured in his dissertation came to stand for the figure-ground model of perception in which certain figures rise into prominence against an indistinguishable background. We only see the vase or the faces in alternation but never simultaneously. As we pay attention to the contours of the vase, we cannot perceive the two faces, which do not figure as figures but as a background for the vase. But then if we shift our attention to the edges of the vase on either side and trace its outline, we can see the shape of a brow and the projection of a nose and the double indent of a mouth, and we experience a "Gestalt switch" between seeing the image as a vase and seeing it as two opposing faces. The point is that recognition depends entirely on where we focus our attention. As one figure rises into prominence and becomes a distinguishable "thing," everything else surrounding it is perceived as "nonthinglike." As we concentrate on the vase, what was two faces once again becomes mere background, a negative space or surround that is practically invisible.

Before Rubin, James tried to understand how we distinguish figures from the background in which they are perceptually embedded. He wanted to know how anything at all comes into prominence and takes shape and focus against surroundings of less importance relative to the figure that rises into relief the moment we focus on it. In *Principles of Psychology*, he describes how the kind of attention we bring to the world changes what we find there, so it would not have surprised him that sometimes we see a vase and sometimes we see faces. Shifts in attention have significant experiential and even philosophical consequences.

When Ludwig Wittgenstein refers to the "duck-rabbit" in *Philosophical Investigations*, a figure that can be seen as either a duck or a rabbit, he says that most of us will have the experience of seeing the picture *as* two unique pictures—that both the duck and the rabbit might impress themselves on us in some inexplicable way. Depending on how we focus, we can flip between the duck and the rabbit and discover every time something that was hidden in plain sight. Our attention at any given moment is not an interpretation of the picture or an argument about the picture, and certainly the picture itself never changes. It is very much about having some aspect of the picture suddenly dawn on us and also the surprise and excitement of picking up on these aspects in alternation and having one appear while the other disappears, as, for example, the duck's bill becomes the rabbit's ears. The ambiguous duck-rabbit figure is not an optical illusion but a perceptual phenomenon that points to the role of expectations and world knowledge in what we happen to notice and not to notice (whether, i.e., we are predisposed to see a duck or a rabbit in the first place) and to the nature of our attention and what compels us to direct it toward one aspect over another of the same, unchanging object. (Maybe it is the time of year or whether, for example, we are by a lake and thinking of ducks or whether we are accustomed to seeing rabbits.)

The duck-rabbit that Wittgenstein made iconic for a "change in aspect" was based on the figure originally discussed by the American experimental psychologist Joseph Jastrow in works from 1899 and 1900 (having seen a version of the conceit in *Harper's Weekly* in 1892, itself based on a figure that had appeared earlier that year in the German humor magazine, *Fliegende Blatter* [fig. 2]).[7] Jastrow—who studied with G. Stanley Hall and Charles Sanders Peirce at Johns Hopkins and then taught at the University of Wisconsin—was the first American to receive a doctorate in psychology. His experiments focused on the role that "subliminal" or "subconscious" mental states play in perception, including nonvisual forms of perception. In his book *The Subconscious*, he tracks how consciousness emerges from everything that "lies below the surface" or "below the threshold of our fully waking minds" but also how "to live means to be variously conscious." That is, though we only attend to some impressions, we always have an "inner awareness," in the recesses of consciousness, of so many more:

> By the activity of the one kind I am made aware at the present moment that I still have some of the unpleasant after-effects of a lingering cold in the head, that I have been wearing a new pair of boots all day, that occasionally I still feel a little annoyed because in the after-dinner speech I made last night I omitted some of my best points, that in the interstices of the attention which I am giving to my present task I am groping about to recall the address of one of my correspondents, that I am just dismissing from my attention a rambling reexperiencing of my last night's dream, and that in anticipation of the writing of a note—for which I must in a moment interrupt my present occupation—I am looking about for the most

FIGURE 2. From Joseph Jastrow, "The Mind's Eye," *Popular Science Monthly* 54 (January 1899): 312. Biodiversity Heritage Library.

> presentable reasons for declining an invitation that promises little pleasure. By the other form of awareness I come to realize—and as before to a more or less absorbing extent—that the inkstand needs refilling, that the wind is blowing in the trees, that the clock is sounding a premonitory whirr which I recognize as the herald preceding by a few minutes the stroke of the hour, that the lamp has been smoking, and that my paper is lying partly in the shadow of a row of books to my left.[8]

Jastrow describes the act of mental focusing that reveals each of these things in alternation so that anything might come up at a particular time. It might dawn on him that he plans to decline the invitation that promises little pleasure for reasons that precede this moment or he might think about the omissions in last night's after-dinner speech. Something else might come to mind from his recent experience or background or from the background of the room (the near-empty inkstand, the whirring of the clock, the shadow on his paper) or from the world that comes to bear on this room and makes its presence felt in the sound of the wind and more:

> Naturally these several forms and directions of awareness do not appear with equal distinctness at the same moment. They are fitfully revealed by the sweep of the search-light of attention as it plays upon this and that detail of the composite picture; yet they are all present in the shadowy background and contribute something to the *genre* of the whole. Naturally also do the two kinds and the several manifestations of awareness constantly intermingle and antagonize and cooperate in the ceaseless flow of moods and states, of occupations and attentions,—wave upon wave of complex emotional, intellectual, and volitional content. Thus I may explain that it was because I was too much absorbed in my inward contemplations that I did not sooner notice the soot from the lamp; and because of an indolent disinclination to interrupt my present business that I was not sufficiently disturbed by the shadow on my paper to induce me to stop and remove the pile of books.

There is an "inner awareness" and then an "outward awareness" that, for Jastrow, is "information-bringing" and purposeful and assumes an intellectual or critical attitude toward its object. Not everything takes conscious attention; much of what we do is automatic. So Jastrow is trying to isolate the "function of consciousness" at the "threshold of awareness": how we attend to certain things while subliminally registering others except at the very moment when they need our attention and we turn to them instead. We are able to focus on the content of our writing without reflecting on our fingers moving habitually across the keyboard. We can talk to a friend over dinner while our hands manipulate our utensils without thought. But if we are served fish at dinner and need to look for the bones, we will momentarily attend to the utensils. We walk mindlessly until we reach a stretch of slippery sidewalk that requires deliberate steps and a lot of concentration. Our consciousness has a "functional utility." In the passage above, Jastrow will not attend to the soot and smoke from the lamp unless there is enough of it to alert him to the fact that the flame is burning dangerously high and needs to be adjusted. Consciousness guides our conduct to an appropriate response, which is why Jastrow cares about the "evolution of consciousness" and also about consciousness as an evolutionary function that directs a fit response to our present circumstances and a way of handling them, sometimes even surviving them. He wants to know just how that "search-light of attention as it plays upon this and that" selects something in particular out of all that is available and brings it to light.[9] His experiments record the exact moment when this selected information comes into focus and is distinctly perceived—when that "search-light of attention" fixes on its object and becomes like a spotlight instead. Everything outside of its beam loses clarity and fades in the dim shadows. What the mind disregards is banished from our sight.

Obviously, the ability to see a picture as a duck or as a rabbit is not about the survival of the fit (although one can imagine circumstances when spotting a duck or rabbit matters greatly, and I'll turn to this when I turn to camouflage). But it does demonstrate what Jastrow describes as the "manner and distribution of awareness," the way that a "figure" and "background" might be said to represent what we do and do not attend; the way, too, that we can flip between figure and ground, so that what had not been noticed comes to figure while something that had figured prominently for us dissolves into the background.

The sociologist Eviatar Zerubavel writes that as we focus our attention on some figure, everything else "seems effectively shapeless and, as such, remains practically invisible." The concept of figure and ground helps us to describe what we notice and also the extent to which we "reduce so much of what we can potentially experience both perceptually and conceptually to a mere 'background' that we so casually ignore." He sees these extracted figures as being "raised (practically as well as symbolically) above their background-like surroundings," like the sculpted figures in an ancient Greek relief. And while Zerubavel does not make the etymological connection between figures in *relief* and relevance, he does see "figure (and for that matter foreground) and background" as constituting "metaphors for relevance and irrelevance" in which what is remarkable in our phenomenological world is always up against what is unmarked or irrelevant to us at the time.[10] In the psychology of attention, we tend to filter irrelevances out. It is not just that we are inattentive to those sensations, impressions, and other things, even, ultimately, those other beings and persons that we do not right now care about. We are simply unaware of them, incapable of recognizing or conceiving of them, in the way that a rabbit seems impossible when we have only a duck in mind. This is why for Zerubavel, and other sociologists, the questions of figure and ground have such high sociological stakes.

In his 1905 book, Jastrow depicts the process of recognition like this:

"relevant and irrelevant claimants," he says, "must frequently meet and jostle one another at the portals of the mind; and this busy and diverse traffic brings it about that a given attitude is favorable to one claimant and not to another." Entry into this psychic forum "implies some act of reception, some incorporating procedure." The manner of incorporation, he writes, "depends upon the interest or cordiality of the welcome that goes out to the new claimant." We can think of James's sense of "pure delight and welcome" the moment the earthquake made itself felt or the way that Emerson suggests that the "Soul attentive" will greet with "entire welcome" something new and incalculable. For Jastrow, these all would be relevant claimants.

Jastrow wants to know how the mind behaves at the threshold of a particular awareness, the "hidden springs, that operate this psychic mechanism" when the gates open and subconsciousness flips into consciousness and the mind admits something new. What are the "complex conditions of ingress . . . enforced at the gateways of consciousness?" What makes us attentive and aware when we are ordinarily so unaware? Sometimes those doors seem "generously ample" and sometimes they seem "narrowly exclusive," but there is never an "open door" policy. Admission depends on the character of the applicant and, equally, on how the senses "are sufficiently trained in subconscious service to readily catch" these impressions in a glance. Something in our background readies us, in those subliminal intervals, to be interested in this object and not in that. Maybe this object has "special pertinence to [our] dominant interests."

Then admission also depends on how the recognition of it gives rise to a sense of "deliberate purpose." "The interpretation of the entrance of an appeal," Jastrow says, "is inevitably bound up with the further spread of significance of that appeal, as it . . . becomes effective in thought or revery." The soot on the lamp might catch Jastrow's attention in part because past experiences make him capable of noticing the soot. It might come to be more relevant to his interests right then than last night's after-dinner speech or whatever he is committing to paper. If so, it will prove "effective in thought." Jastrow will turn down that lamp and avert a disaster. In all the "selective preferences" that happen at every moment, that lamp finally comes up. Insofar as it brings consciousness out of subconsciousness, it is also how Jastrow *comes to*.[11]

Jastrow engaged with William James throughout his career, and James cited Jastrow's early work on perception several times in *The Principles of Psychol-*

ogy. They shared, along with their interest in conscious experience and acts of mental focusing, an interest in the psychology of belief and of spiritualism and other claims to paranormal phenomena. They both were influenced by Wilhelm Wundt, founder of experimental psychology at the University of Leipzig, whose studies of conscious experience, or what he called "apperception," earlier inspired G. Stanley Hall's pioneering efforts in psychology at Johns Hopkins. In 1883 Hall established the first American laboratory and doctorate in psychology, of which Jastrow was, again, the first recipient.

At Cornell, the English scholar Edward B. Titchener established his own lab in experimental psychology after earning his doctorate at Leipzig under Wundt. In his textbooks on psychology, Titchener addresses problems of attention at length, drawing on German work in applied psychology, including that of Wundt and also Oswald Külpe on attention and Hermann Ebbinghaus on conscious experience in relation to memory. Titchener describes how the "attentive consciousness" is arranged as "clear or obscure" and how an object's "clearness" depends on the attention one pays it. A "weak" sound, for example, gets intensified with attention: "you can hear, with attention, a faint sound that you cannot hear if you do not attend." Attention "[sharpens] to the sound," so that, once you become aware of the bell in the clock tower, you hear it more sharply; it sounds for you, but not for everyone, above all the other sounds of the city as it finishes its midday chimes. That bell resounds according to the "law of prior entry," meaning, for Titchener, that the stimulus for which you are now predisposed comes to consciousness more quickly. An "accommodation of attention" takes place. Because it is a sound that already has your interest, you can follow the upward course of the last chimes to the top of the hour. They come right to you over the din of the streets.[12]

Titchener also suggests that there are always "two levels of consciousness" and that "increased clearness of any one part-contents of consciousness implies the decreased clearness of all the rest." There is a sort of conservation of the "energy of attention" in which conscious attention to one thing inhibits the perception of something else. Suppose, he writes,

> that I am working or reading quietly, and that a telephone message or the entrance of a visitor suddenly demands my attention. The first thing that happens is that there is a redistribution of the entire contents of consciousness. The incoming ideas—my friend's business or the subject of the message—drive to the centre, and everything else, my previous occupation

> as well as my sensory surroundings, are banished to the outskirts. Consciousness, in attention, is patterned or arranged into focus and margin, foreground and background, centre and periphery. And the difference between the processes at the focus and the processes at the margin is, essentially, a difference of clearness: the central area of consciousness lies clear, the more remote regions are obscure.[13]

The self is constantly interacting with its milieu, but the selective nature of attention means that only certain aspects of this immense terrain come into focus while others get relegated to the "obscure background of consciousness." Külpe describes this focusing as a process of "abstraction" in which what is "logically or psychologically effective" at a particular moment is abstracted out of what is "ineffective" and banished in turn to the background and not held in any reflective awareness.

For Titchener, "the whole situation in attention seems, at first sight, to imply a selective and spontaneous mental activity." Leaning back in his chair to think through problems in attention, "I am subject," he says,

> to all sorts of sensory stimuli; the temperature of the room, the pressure of my clothes, the sight of various pieces of furniture, sounds from house and street, scents coming from the room itself or borne in through the open window, organic excitations of different kinds. I could easily lapse into a reminiscent mood, letting these impressions suggest to me scenes from my past life. I could easily give the rein to my imagination, thinking of the further business of the day. . . . But I am, in fact, perfectly well able to ignore all distractions, and to devote myself entirely to a single self-chosen idea,—the idea of the problem that awaits solution.

The "clearness of the idea," he continues, "is rather a matter of the mind's own concentration than of any character of the idea itself," and, anyway, he can turn his mind to something different if he likes.[14] What he sees entirely depends on how he minds it.

Sometimes attention seems more passive and involuntary. There is an attention that we are compelled to give and powerless to prevent, and there are impressions that "take consciousness by storm." We cannot help attending to loud sounds, bright lights, extreme temperatures, intense pain—they are all clear to us by virtue of their intensity and "attract our attention, as the phrase goes, in spite of ourselves." Sudden stimuli produce a powerful effect on the nervous system (although Titchener also says that there are considerable differences between our mental and physiological states, and that some of us will respond to certain stimuli more than others). But whether the attraction is strong enough to hold our attention will always be a matter of choice, made more or less reflexively. There will be a "seesaw of light and sound at the focus of consciousness, a quick succession of primary attentions" that creates a *tension* between habitual objects and "the forcible hold over us that the thunder-clap has from the moment of its appearance in consciousness." There will be a competition between new and old objects, but the question for Titchener and for so many other psychologists at the end of the nineteenth century was how that new object ever comes to structure one's whole conscious field around it.

There are two questions, actually: whether we hear that noise to begin with—and powerfully enough to turn to it (not all of us do)—and whether we stay oriented toward it and respond to it. Attentional capture, says Titchener, is tied to an orienting response. Thoughts, memories, and images will pop into our head just as a noise or a bright light flashes into our sensory field, and these flashes lead to an alteration in our mental state. But when that flash induces us to ponder it further—when that item that captures our attention not only alters our mental state but does so in a such a way that engages a response and moves us in some way—this is "attentive consciousness." Wu calls it "conscious attention." When one "exhibits intentionality" toward an object, "one attends" to it."[15] It is not, then, just a shift in consciousness but what happens when this new object of attention becomes available for thought or meaningful in some way.

We pick up on it, Titchener suggests, because our attention presents it as "relevant," and we discard or neglect other things because, to our present determination and relative to something else at this time, they are "irrelevant." That object simply appears more intensely and clearly because our attention has made it salient in thought. The facts we ignore are not less bright, less loud, or less striking. They are, in other words, no less matter of fact, but, from the standpoint of psychology, "they are irrelevant facts" and not part of our current orientation. I will smell gas in my kitchen more clearly than gas at a gas station because I need to see what is causing it. Novelty arrests the attention, and so do impressions that "are in a sense the reverse of novel," paradoxical as it sounds, if they "fit in with, are associated to, the present trend of consciousness." I hear my child crying over the noise of a room because this matters to me. James says that nurses of patients or mothers of infants "will sleep through much noise of an irrelevant sort, but waken at the slightest stirring of the patient or the babe."

How, Titchener asks, do such useful things come to us just when we need them? How in the world—to vary the question, and thinking back to Stephen Crane—could that poem about the soldier in Algiers pop into the correspondent's head over every other latent memory just when that would keep him going? "Relevant facts and ideas crowd in upon consciousness," Titchener writes; "the mind stands wide open to them, while it is fast locked against the irrelevant; and you surpass yourself."[16]

Does this seem obvious? That I can hear my child over a room full of children or be predisposed to discover a single face in a crowd? Or, that at moments of pressure or crisis, we might discover that we have what we needed all along if only we had realized it, like the correspondent with the poem in the boat or like Dorothy with her ruby slippers (*The Wonderful Wizard of Oz* appeared in 1900). It was not at all obvious to scholars then, and it still is not obvious to the many cognitive psychologists working on attention today.

In other words, it was not at all obvious why some things should be obvious to us while others remain unavailable, mere noise. How we process information so as to pick up on or seize on certain things—this crying, this poem, these musical notes, these flowers in the meadow (to return to Emerson)—was the particular problem of relevance. It was closely tied to the ways in which people started to see attention as the gatekeeper of consciousness and as the means of "[selecting] for action."[17] It had consequences for psychology, for phenomenology, for sociology—and it had consequences for art especially, as I will continue to suggest—that were not obvious at all.

Certain things will always come up, and whatever dominates our consciousness is most relevant to us right now. But Titchener never explains how different things might come to be relevant or how we could ever become aware of anything so relegated to the background as to be invisible enough to draw it out and into our sense of reality. What if we cannot perceive the duck but only the rabbit? The question is not simply one of flipping between the two, between foreground and background, but of having the sort of background in the first place that makes the duck possible whenever it makes sense to conjure it. How do we ever develop the resources and deep store of facts, knowledge, and possibilities to become the person who hears the chimes over the noise of the street and does not ignore them, or to stop and smell the roses and not only the gas in the kitchen?

Momentarily Focal

"Everyone knows what attention is," James writes. "It is the taking possession by the mind, in clear and vivid form, of one out of what seem several simultaneously possible objects or trains of thought. Focalization, concentration, of consciousness are of its essence. It implies withdrawal from some things in order to deal effectively with others, and is a condition which has a real opposite in the confused, dazed, scatter-brained state which in French is called *distraction*, and *Zerstreutheit* in German." Attention always suggests an economy of attention. Out of all possible objects or trains of thought, the mind selects one and lets go of the rest. It simply cannot focus on more right now. This object is brought into the "foreground of consciousness." It gains contours that distinguish and separate it from the wider perceptual field, which is what allows us to perceive or conceive of it in the first place: attention gives accent or brings to light "every creature" that otherwise "would be a gray chaotic indiscriminateness, impossible for us even to conceive." Out of the "gray chaotic indiscriminateness," that creature becomes an intelligible entity that is now available for thought.[18]

There is in James what we might think of as "attentional capture," the mere registering of a change in one's mental state in regard to an object: "a loud sound (or a sudden shift in the pitch of a current sound), a swooping bird, a fragrant smell, a pleasurable memory, a twinge in one's calf, or a disturbing thought." A routine is arrested by an object that was not perceived before, and this is tied to an "orienting response" toward or away from that object. Just as an object pops into my sensory field, so can thoughts and images pop into my head. A "flash of thought is no different than the flash of a change in perception. Both yield alterations in what is given in one's mental states that do not entail or necessitate attention." These flashes are the first conscious apprehensions of what may be a signal to act or respond further. Attention enters the scene when the flash of thought that does the capturing does so in a way that engages further thought and action. Attention, writes Wu, "exhibits intentionality. One attends *to* an X."[19]

James describes an extreme state of distraction in which

> the foreground of consciousness is filled, if by anything, by a sort of solemn sense of surrender to the empty passing of time. In the dim background of our mind we know meanwhile what we ought to be doing: getting up, dressing ourselves, answering the person who has spoken to us, trying to make the next step in our reasoning. But somehow we cannot *start*. . .

> Every moment we expect the spell to break, for we know no reason why it should continue. But it does continue, pulse after pulse, and we float with it, until—also without reason that we can discover—an energy is given, something—we know not what—enables us to gather ourselves together, we wink our eyes, we shake our heads, the background-ideas become effective, and the wheels of life go round again.

There is routine, fatigue, indifference, and monotonous occupations. There is a state in which we are thinking of something as usual or of "nothing in particular." And then there is "what we call the awakening of the attention" in which one principle object comes "into the focus of consciousness" while "others are temporarily suppressed." The change the awakening brings "amounts to a concentration upon one single object with exclusion of aught besides, or to a condition anywhere between this and the completely dispersed state." It is always the case that attention to one thing "interferes a good deal with the perception of the other."[20]

The particular way of being conscious that James calls *attention* also yields a "distinctive phenomenology of attention." In other words, *what it is like* to experience an object while attending to it is for James different from what it is like to experience that object when not attending to it. This is why ideas of conscious attention, as Wu suggests, speak to philosophical work in epistemology. First, attention to an object changes that object in our minds. The sensation of it becomes stronger and more intense. James says if we start "listening for certain notes in a chord, or overtones in a musical sound, the one we attend to sounds probably a little more loud as well as more emphatic than it did before." Although hue itself will never change, colors may seem more saturated or warmer or cooler as we focus on reds or blues. James agrees with the German psychologist Gustav Fechner, who insists that a gray paper can never look white no matter how much "we increase the strain of our attention." The stroke of a pendulum will never sound like the blow of a hammer, and we are never actually deceived into believing that the objects we attend to are not the selfsame objects they have been. But unlike Fechner, James suggests that attention intensifies the perception of any properties that can be understood in terms of magnitude, allowing for *more* or *less*. "Every artist knows how he can make a scene before his eyes appear warmer or colder in color, according to the way he sets his attention," says James. So, again, hue will not change (the red fire engine will remain red), but the sense of saturation might change so that the fire engine appears redder and the sky appears bluer. The sense of volume, speed, size, and contrast might change too. When we pay attention, "a certain intensity or quality of impression will often make us sensibly see or hear it in an object which really falls far short of it." When we turn to a face in a crowd or a flower in a field, we give it emphasis. (Emerson says that we should let these things we regard "have their weight.") My child's cry, as I listen to it, rises sharply above the din of the room. It is the same faintly perceptible cry it always is, but it has grown more impressive. I experience it more intensely than others ever would. The more one attends to an object, the stronger its sensational force, so when attention is concentrated long enough, some objects even retain the "brilliancy of reality" as aftereffects or afterimages well after they pass away.[21]

Second, James believes, like Titchener, that attention renders the attended object more clearly. When we pay attention, weak impressions seem stronger, yes, but also more clear, and what James means by *clearness*, insofar as attention produces it, is "distinction from other things." The attended object comes into focus, while unattended objects lose focus in the fringes of consciousness and become indistinct—even so indistinct as to be imperceptible. If I see a duck, I do not see a rabbit. If I focus on one flower in a meadow, the surrounding flowers blur and the rest of the meadow fades away. The increase in clearness suggests to James that the attended objects "are essentially products of intellectual *discrimination*, involving comparison, memory, and perception of various relations." To perceive something so that it becomes intelligible is to distinguish it from other objects and from the background too. Attention highlights or phenomenally prioritizes a specific object in a field of objects while deprioritizing other objects. It renders *this* object phenomenologically salient in thought relative to all other objects at this time or even to this same object at another time. "Accentuation, foreground, and background are created solely by the interested attention of the looker-on."[22]

At the moment, this object feels important relative to other objects. It has special status. It is phenomenologically salient because I have turned to it and am thinking about it and because attention has changed my perceptual field so as to structure everything around it. It is not simply that attention shapes my consciousness into a center and a periphery; attention flips the center and periphery. It brings objects that are "dimly perceived" in the "fringes of relations" into central focus. They become the object "about which all the members of the thought revolve."

"Millions of items of the outward order are present to my senses which never properly enter into my experience," says James. I register most things as bare impressions of little relation to me and am "only aware in the penumbral nascent way of a 'fringe' of unarticulated affinities" about them. I have a mere "acquaintance" with these images and impressions and not "knowledges-*about*" them; only a "dim awareness" as they pass before me that they are disconnected from me and cannot fill the "gap" at the center of my thoughts. Each sound, image, and impression "swims in a felt fringe of relations" to "this aching gap," as James puts it, but "the gap negates" so many of these impressions "as quite irrelevant." Again, mothers of infants "will sleep through much noise of an irrelevant sort." Mothers will be dimly conscious of all the noises in the background, and if they concentrated on them, they would realize that they were audible all along, but they could not be said to have heard them. These noises will have "relative unimportance" and mean nothing to them.

But then they prick up their ears. One cry arrests the "train" or "stream" of impressions and stands out from all the rest "by reason of the peculiar interest attaching to it." They feel an "affinity" with it. They may feel that their body "adjusts itself to the perception," writes the German American psychologist Hugo Münsterberg, who taught at Harvard with James. Their "head enters into the movement of listening for the sound." Their "eyes are fixating the point in the outer world" as they hold all their muscles in tension "in order to receive the fullest possible impression" of that one sound that matters. The impressions they notice are "funded" and reinforced by the preexisting contents of their minds. The name for this is "apperceptive attention," and it is why, James says, "the lover's tap" will always be heard:

> it finds a nerve-center half ready in advance to explode. We see how we can attend to a companion's voice in the midst of noises which pass unnoticed though objectively much louder than the words we hear. Each word is *doubly* awakened; once from without by the lips of the talker, but already before that from within by the premonitory processes irradiating from the previous words, and by the dim arousal of all processes that are connected with the 'topic' of the talk. The irrelevant noises, on the other hand, are awakened only once."[23]

One sound (or word, image, or sensation), James says, may influence us in "an intensely active and determinate psychic way," whether "rising to answer a problem or fill a pre-existing gap that worried us, or whether accidentally stumbled on in revery." Our interest in it "makes a sort of crisis of it when it comes, induces attention upon it and makes us treat it in a substantive way." Our mental driftings gather round this "central interest" that we distinguish as *relevant* against the background noises that are *irrelevant* and barely perceptible by comparison. We become more than merely "acquainted" with it because we feel it relates to us and are compelled to act in relation to it. "Knowledge *about* a thing," James writes, "is knowledge of its relations." Provided we feel that sound "to have a place in the scheme of relations" in which our interests also lie, it "is quite sufficient to make of it a relevant and appropriate portion of our train of ideas."

In other words, what was dimply perceived in the fringe of relations comes into a felt relation with ourselves. It fills that "gap" at the center of our thoughts (it "completely occupies the mind"). And this is what it means to pay attention. What I attend to is what I am most conscious of, but only certain things ever "properly enter into my experience." Our minds seem to be optimized to select from the "millions of items" present to our senses the ones that present themselves for a particular purpose and to shut out the rest. The attended figure-like object is mentally isolated from its background with an intensity that, excluding all irrelevant distractions, narrowly concentrates the attention on what is relevant at the time. This is why James describes the experience as "a more or less massive organic feeling that attention is going on." There is the overwhelming sense of a "total object, all the parts converge harmoniously to the one resultant concept." "We endeavor to lift into consciousness meaningful units, such as the whole picture, the whole building, the living animal, the stone, the mountain, the tree," writes Whitehead. That unit that seems to be punched out from the background with clear contours is all of one piece. It becomes perceptually coherent. James describes its rising into importance as everything else falls away—also, the way that object comes to us to occupy that gap at the center of thought—as nothing less than a feeling of "consummation."[24]

Within the stream of impressions there are these consummatory moments of attention that figuratively freeze the stream. They are moments of arrest or, to use James's other figurative terms, "perchings" in the midst of "flights." The attended objects never appear in a vacuum but out from a vague background or an immense field that nonetheless remains present in every conscious experience. The bright focus of consciousness corresponds to the point of urgency and immediate importance, but the "fringes" of consciousness never go away even as they are taken for granted or recede far from the center of our concern.

Here is James, for example, writing from the Adirondacks during his honeymoon: "The sound of the brook near which I write, the odor of the cedars, the feeling of satisfaction with which my breakfast has filled me, and my interest in writing this article, all simultaneously co-exist in my consciousness without falling into any sort of spatial order." But even when the writing of this article occupies him in a way that his breakfast does not—or, I guess, his honeymoon does not—even when the writing is central, that feeling of satisfaction remains in the background of the task at hand. It affects his ability to keep writing insofar as he feels satisfied with a full stomach and the sound of the brook on his honeymoon. He may, in fact, have forgotten his breakfast altogether by then, but that noncognitive element of consciousness continues to "fund" his cognitive act, as Dewey would put it.[25]

A great deal is to be included in what James calls the "background" against which a relevant concern stands out. Dewey, following James, calls it the "horizon" against which the focus of our thought appears, insisting that these two elements of experience (the "horizon" and the "focused apparency") are interrelated, each owing its existence to the other. He says that the "scope and content of the focused apparency have immediate dynamic connections with portions of experience not at the time obvious." Dewey continues, sounding a lot like James and also Titchener:

> The word which I have just written is momentarily focal; around it there shade off into vagueness my typewriter, the desk, the room, the building, the campus, the town, and so on. *In* the experience, and in it in such a way as to *qualify* even what is shiningly apparent, are all the physical features of the environment extending out into space no one can say how far, and all the habits and interests extending backward and forward in time, of the organism which uses the typewriter and which notes the written form of the word only as temporary focus in a vast and changing scene.

It makes sense that whatever we focus on is not an "isolated singular object or event; *an* object or event is always a special part, phase, or aspect, of an environing experienced world—a situation" that we choose to isolate momentarily. If the singular object stands out relevantly, it is always in relief from the total background of consciousness that is "taken for granted" and that includes the complex environing world and also our own deep background of experiences: the memories, habits, beliefs, and prejudices that form our interests and that lead us to choose what we do. These precognitive elements "fund" conscious action. This means that in the phenomenology and psychology of attention, the background is always active too. It constitutes what Schutz later describes as all the "possible realities" from which the "paramount reality"—being the most "relevant" and real thing to me right now—emerges.[26]

For James, our ability to concentrate on the most relevant thing actually depends on the ability to keep everything else down or in the background (to prevent these from coming up too). So he tells this anecdote about Sir Walter Scott:

When Scott was in school, he wanted to be the "head-boy" of the class, but there was another boy who excelled even more. During lessons and recitations, this student was in the habit of twirling a button on his jacket. So what did Scott do? He cut that button off the boy's jacket and then, sure enough, rose to the top of his class. Why? With the "button gone, its owner's power of reciting also departed." Fiddling with the button may have helped the boy drain away an excess of anxiety or "overflow" of excitement. But it may also have been "a means of drafting off all the irrelevant sensations of the moment, and so keeping the attention more exclusively concentrated upon its inner task." James says that each of us has some usual means or habit of concentrating thought by discharging "incidental stimuli" through a "downward nerve-path"—of pushing down irrelevant thoughts and feelings in order to "protect the thought-centres from interference from without" ("such as pacing the room, drumming with the fingers, playing with keys or watch-chain, scratching head, pulling mustache, vibrating foot, or what not").[27] That poor boy without his jacket button was overwhelmed by irrelevant feelings, while Scott, concentrating his attention on being on top, managed to make his rival irrelevant.

"What is the attentive process, psychologically considered?" James asks.

> Attention to an object is what takes place whenever that object most completely occupies the mind. For simplicity's sake suppose the object to be an object of sensation—a figure approaching us at a distance on the road. It is far off, barely perceptible, and hardly moving; we do not know with certainty whether it is a man or not. Such an object as this, if carelessly looked at, may hardly catch our attention at all; the optical impression may affect solely the marginal consciousness, whilst the mental focus keeps

> engaged with rival things. We may indeed not "see" it till someone points it out. But if so, how does he point it out? By his finger, and by describing its appearance—by creating a premonitory image of *where* to look and of *what* to expect to see. This premonitory image is already an excitement of the same nerve-centers that are to be concerned with the impression. The impression comes, and excites them still farther; and now the object enters the focus of the field, consciousness being sustained both by impression and by preliminary idea. But the maximum of attention to it is not yet reached. Although we see it, we may not care for it; it may suggest nothing important to us; and a rival stream of objects or of thoughts may quickly take our mind away. If, however, our companion defines it in a significant way, arouses in the mind a set of experiences to be apprehended from it—names it an enemy or as a messenger of important tidings—the residual and marginal ideas now aroused, so far from being its rivals, become its associates and allies; they shoot together into one system with it; they converge upon it; they keep it steadily in focus; the mind attends to it with maximum power.[28]

Another figure in James emerges from the (back)ground. It is difficult to make out at first, and our mind is engaged with other things, though we register the impression in the margins of consciousness. We hardly see it. Even when we do, it "may suggest nothing important to us" and "we may not care for it," and we are easily distracted by rival thoughts. The process by which this figure eventually emerges from the horizon to come to our attention—by which the consciousness of it gets sustained so that all the "residual and marginal ideas" aroused by it converge in a single radiant focus—is also the process that determines what is relevant or not to the situation at hand. This figure, in other words, becomes relevant. It becomes important and we start to care. Some aspect of the environing scene is met by prior knowledge; in this example, the prior knowledge is provided by a friend, creating the "premonitory" image of what to see. Then, imagining that figure might be a problem for us or else "important" in some way, it *comes to us* more and more clearly, down the road.

It is the prior information that makes this figure interesting and gives it emotional pertinence. The figure is a discovery made possible by a readiness to see it. Appearing from out of the blue, it wins emphasis because it appeals to personal interest and stirs up hope or fear. What attracts us from far beyond us receives its meaning and motive force from the inner resources we bring to it. We attend to the sorts of new stimuli that, given our background and stock of knowledge and experiences, offer themselves to us for some present purpose and effect. For James, the attentive process occurs precisely in this contact between the new and old. "In this process the incoming impression is the newer element; the ideas which reinforce and sustain it are amongst the older possessions of the mind. And the maximum of attention may then be said to be found whenever we have a systematic harmony or unification between the novel and old."

It is not clear from James's example what we should do in the face of that new figure in the background, but it is clear that our perception is an effort to incorporate it in a concrete and emotional way—to understand that figure *as* relevant to the knowledge we already have at hand. Meanwhile, whatever else is on the horizon remains part of the "Unclassified Residuum" that is, as James describes it, the "great field for new discoveries." Relevance suggests what happens when "background-ideas become effective." A shift in attention reveals what had not been noticed before, and every shift along these lines—every appearance of a figure from out of that "great field" (everything that somehow *comes to figure*)—suggests an adjustment to the environment on our part and a process of both selection and inhibition in which new aspects of the environment come to matter.

Bergson wrote to James, in response to a fan letter from him, "The more I think about the question, the more I am convinced that life is from one end to the other a phenomenon of attention." Life from beginning to end is a contest among the millions of things that might attract our attention and the rising and falling of an emphasis and the justification of that emphasis for the time being. "For concentrated attention means disregard of irrelevancies;" in Whitehead's words, "and such disregard can only be sustained by some sense of importance."[29] What, then, is importance? Just the quality of anything we find worth the attention we give it right now.

. . .

"Whoever treats of interest," James writes, "inevitably treats of attention; for to say that an object is interesting is only another way of saying that it excites attention." In *Talks to Teachers on Psychology*, James offers advice on how to make a classroom "interesting enough to be attended to" by students whose "minds will soon be wandering again." It is here that he asks what the attentive process is "psychologically considered," and it is here that he describes how an obscure figure that "may suggest nothing to us" and that we "may not care for" might enter our consciousness down the road. The idea that a subject we never would have thought or cared about might turn out to be significant is, for James, as much an educational theory as a psychological one.

He tells teachers they can sustain their students' attention by appealing to their interests. They can present new material in relation to something the students already care about and know. Again, attention is maximized whenever we have "a systematic harmony or unification between the novel and the old." "It is an odd circumstance," he says, "that neither the old nor the new, by itself, is interesting: the absolutely old is insipid; the absolutely new makes no appeal at all. The old *in* the new is what claims the attention—the old with a slightly new turn. No one wants to hear a lecture on a subject completely disconnected with his previous knowledge, but we all like lectures on subjects of which we know a little already." The interesting teacher will "awaken whatever sources of interest in the subject he can by stirring up connections between it and the pupil's nature." If the topic is abstract, make it concrete; if it is unfamiliar, "trace some point of analogy in it with the known"; if it is inhuman, "make it figure as part of a story"; if it is difficult, "couple its acquisition with some prospect of personal gain." Begin with the student's "native interests, and offer him objects that have some immediate connection with these." Only then will the "laws of mind" bring enough "pulses of effort into play to keep the pupil exercised in the direction of the subject." Only then will the new subject in association with the old bring, in Emerson's words, "new undreamed-of value to the old." The student will feel the "sparks" that Dewey describes when the old and new are brought together, like two electrical currents. The teacher will have made the lesson "relevant."

Of course, attention will take great effort on the part of the student. It cannot be forced by the teacher. "There is, in fact, no greater school of effort than the steady struggle to attend to immediately repulsive or difficult objects of thought," James says—not merely to grow interested in these objects but to remain interested. You will not stay focused on anything for long, he says, unless "you ask yourself successive questions" about it, but if you keep asking new questions, you can stay focused on practically anything. Take the extreme example of a *dot* on the wall:

> From an unchanging subject the attention inevitably wanders away. You can test this by the simplest possible case of sensorial attention. Try to

> attend steadfastly to a dot on the paper or on the wall. You presently find that one or the other of two things has happened: either your field of vision has become blurred, so that you now see nothing distinct at all; or else you have involuntarily ceased to look at the dot in question, and are looking at something else. But, if you ask yourself successive questions about the dot—how big it is, how far, of what shape, what shade of color, etc.; in other words, if you turn it over, if you think of it in various ways, and along with various kinds of associates—you can keep your mind on it for a comparatively long time. This is what the genius does, in whose hands a given topic coruscates and grows. And this is what the teacher must do for every topic.

A "subject must be made to show new aspects of itself; to prompt new questions," so that a student's associations with it stay in motion and never become rote or automatic. Otherwise "attention inevitably wanders." That dot must stay relevant for the student if it will continue to mean anything at all.

James addresses teachers to acknowledge the psychological work it takes to keep the classroom interesting, which is just the same to him as making learning possible. Psychologically considered, learning is nothing less than "the steady struggle to attend" to those repulsive or difficult objects of thought "which have grown to interest us through their association." It happens every day in the classroom, but for James (as for Emerson) it can feel like a miracle every time: absolutely anything can *become* interesting, can be made relevant. Just take the example of a dot! Or take the example of a railroad timetable, James says. What could possibly be a "more deadly uninteresting object?"—unless, of course, you are going on a journey, in which case, "where will you find a more interesting object?" Lend a child some books. Then "give them to him, make them his own, and notice the new light with which they instantly shine in his eyes. He takes a new kind of care of them altogether."

These difficult, boring, remote, recalcitrant, repulsive objects we never cared for and that never mattered to us or attracted us come to figure just as much as that figure we never would have seen coming down the road. It is not just that they grow to interest us through their association with us. Since "all consciousness tends to action," James says, these objects become our *objectives.*[30] They move us in some utterly personal and emotional way. They interest us in their relation to us "as means" to a meaning or end.

Students take in the things that interest them. Their minds fill little by little like this with a stock of facts, ideas, and experiences. Each of them may one day come to figure and be relevant if they spark new connections down the road.

The Age of Selection

Why do "millions of items" that are "present to my senses . . . never properly enter into my experience?" "Because," James says, "they have no *interest* for me. *My experience is what I agree to attend to.* Only those items which I *notice* shape my mind—without selective interest, experience is an utter chaos. Interest alone gives accent and emphasis, light and shade, background and foreground—intelligible perspective, in a word."

Schutz tells us that "since the publication of William James's *Principles of Psychology* and Bergson's early writings, it has become commonplace to talk of the mind's selectivity." The function of consciousness is not to record or mechanically react to outside stimuli. Its function is to enable us "always to choose out of the manifold experiences present to it at a given time some one for particular accentuation, and to ignore the rest." We select for attention according to our interests and needs, which is why James writes that interest itself "*makes* experience more than it is made by it." James is arguing against psychologists from the English empiricist school (Locke, Hume, and Hartley), who are "bent on showing how the higher faculties of the mind are pure products of 'experience'" (where "experience is supposed to be of something simply *given*"). "Selective attention," James says, receives "hardly any notice" from them. He is also arguing against Herbert Spencer and other determinists and strict materialists who try to translate the objects of our thoughts "into terms of no emotional pertinency, [leaving] the mind with little to care or act for." We are neither purely receptive nor purely reactive to an antecedent world but shape the world through our preferences and "practical interests." Our consciousness—what we register of the world—"is not indifferent or colorless, but it is regarded as having importance, having value, having *interest*," writes Dewey along these lines. "Selective emphasis," he says, "with accompanying omission and rejection, is the heart-beat of mental life."[31] Our environment presents according to what feels interesting and important as events unfold. *Our experience of it is what we agree to attend to.*

Attention is, at its core, a struggle for recognition. If something in the environment has no interest for us, we simply will not notice it. It will not be a part of our reality. "We actually *ignore* most of the things before us,"

James says. "Out of the infinite chaos" of sensations "of which the outer world consists," the mind "picks out certain ones as worthy of its notice" and "ignores the rest as completely as if they did not exist." It is as if these other things were not real, since, in Dewey's words, people "take that which is of chief value to them at the time as *the* real." Or, to repeat James's words "*whatever excites and stimulates our interest is real*; whenever an object so appeals to us that we turn to it, accept it, fill our mind with it, or practically take account of it, so far is it real for us."

Again, consciousness structures our surroundings into "light and shade, a background and foreground," changing how the world appears to us by making only some things intelligible for the time being. "Out of what is in itself an undistinguishable, swarming *continuum*, devoid of distinction or emphasis," by attending to this or ignoring that, "our senses make for us . . . a world full of contrasts, of sharp accents, of abrupt changes, in a word, of picturesque light and shade."[32] And so, through selective attention, a world takes form like Genesis from the void, and all at once there are lines, distinctions, and lightness and darkness as that unformed continuum gathers in one place and the heavens and earth *appear*.

James writes, "The practical and theoretical life of whole species, as well as of individual beings, results from the selection which the habitual direction of their attention involves." Scholars have pointed out the extent to which James and other pragmatists work from Darwin's theories. Certainly James is drawing on Darwin when he suggests that the life of the individual, like the life of whole species, results from selective attention or when he suggests, in Robert Brandom's words, "that *evolution*, at the level of species, and *learning*, at the level of individuals, share a common *selectional* structure. Both can be understood as processes of *adaptation*, in which interaction with the environment selects (preserves and reproduces) some elements, while eliminating others." It was Darwin who effectively challenged and replaced the concept of *necessity* that earlier philosophies of science took from Newtonian physics, with its insistence on immutable, exceptionless, and universal laws in nature. Darwin brought in contingency instead by showing the conditions under which individual selections over time lead to a collective order that "in turn provides the dynamic habitat to which all must collectively adapt." For Darwin, and also for James, the world and our knowledge of it are construed as contingent products of "selectional-adaptational processes that allow order to pop to the surface and float in a sea of random variability."[33]

Before Darwin, Newton's methodology for science may have been "an overwhelming success," writes Whitehead, but "the forces which he introduced left nature still without meaning or value." In the case of gravity, for example, Newton discovered the "notion of stresses, as essential connections between bodies. . . . But he left no hint, why in the nature of things there should be any stresses at all." He offered a field of moving bodies devoid of "any reason for the concurrence of its factors"—an arbitrary, barren nature that "aims at nothing." Activity, yes, but "activity for what, producing what, activity involving what?" Nature is not a static fact. It has boundless transformative potential in each occasion for the experience it provides and in all the ways in which it presents with different stresses, emphases, and urgencies at different moments. The objective world of facts gives subjective value to the bodies it acts on and that act on it. "Each actual entity is a throb of experience," Whitehead says, and each experience is the result of finding some object from the continuum *to* experience—a selective emphasis that "claims attention, enjoyment, action, and purpose, all relative to itself." After Darwin, Newton's world would never be the same because at last all entities and natural facts have the potential for implication. Everything out there in the shapeless void has the potential to be an object of experience. Now we see that "all entities or factors in the universe are essentially relevant to each other's existence" even where we do not yet see how they might come to bear. Nothing is indifferent; "there is no irrelevance," says Whitehead, only "neglected modes of relevance."

The world made by natural selection aims to satisfy. It is for every entity's "self-enjoyment," as Whitehead describes it. It arises from some way of being *interested* in the environment even when those interests are so habituated, deep seated, or inborn that we are unaware of them. Even then, the environment is "made over in consonance" with the interests that every creature shows in attending to some aspect of its surroundings and, equally, in the efforts to adjust to them. It pertains to us because we reap value from it.

The way that selective interest makes over—or, to use Dewey's word, *reconstructs*—the immediate world is a constantly evolving and transactional process. These selections are what it means to keep experiencing the world and to be a part of it, "sharing its vicissitudes and fortunes" and shaping it even as it shapes us, too. Selective attention to the world is how the living creature is connected to its environment, and there is no such thing as consciousness apart from this, but if there were, Dewey says, it "would be so completely irrelevant to the world of which it is outside and beyond." The living creature "would not be pertinent to its environment nor its environment relevant to it."[34]

Pragmatism's method begins with what Joan Richardson calls "*intellectual sampling*—or, perhaps better, *perceptual sampling*." James writes that "each of us literally *chooses*, by his ways of attending to things, what sort of a universe he shall appear to himself to inhabit." Our attention has the centrifugal power to pattern the world around it; *this* then is the reality we inhabit and to which we are practically attuned. It means that if we want the world to *appear* differently, we need only to *choose* to attend differently, and then a new order will gather itself around that bright new focus.

Robert Richardson compares the selectional process of attention in James to George Eliot's description of the pier glass in *Middlemarch*: from so much rubbing and polishing, the glass "will be minutely and multitudinously scratched in all directions; but place now against it a lighted candle as a centre of illumination, and lo! The scratches will seem to arrange themselves in a fine series of concentric circles round that little sun." The narrator says, "It is only your candle which produces the flattering illusion of a concentric arrangement, its light falling with an exclusive optical selection," since the scratches are random and go "everywhere impartially." So the narrator selects one spot to illuminate and then every impartial and indifferent impression arranges itself in relation to that: "All the light I can command must be concentrated on this particular web, and not dispersed over that tempting range of relevancies called the universe." This suggests, of course, that the potential range of relevancies is always as wide as the universe, but this narrator has chosen the town of Middlemarch. "To poor Dorothea," all things alien or indifferent to the experience of Middlemarch are at first "painfully inexplicable," since "she had never been taught how she could bring them into any sort of relevance with her life." But in time, from this one spot, she expands her circles.

For James, our "selective interest" is the organizational activity of our conscious life—the illumination ("that little sun") that makes a world go round. James uses another analogy in writing about how consciousness consists in the "selection of some, and the suppression of the rest by the reinforcing and inhibiting agency of attention":

> The mind, in short, works on the data it receives very much as a sculptor works on his block of stone. In a sense the statue stood there from eternity. But there were a thousand different ones beside it, and the sculptor alone

> is to thank for having extricated this one from the rest. Just so the world of each of us, howsoever different our several views of it may be, all lay embedded in the primordial chaos of sensations, which gave the mere *matter* to the thought of all of us indifferently. We may, if we like, by our reasonings unwind things back to that black and jointless continuity of space and moving clouds of swarming atoms which science calls the only real world. But all the while the world *we* feel and live in will be that which our ancestors and we, by slowly cumulative strokes of choice, have extricated out of this, like sculptors, by simply rejecting certain portions of the given stuff. Other sculptors, other statues from the same stone! Other minds, other worlds from the same monotonous and inexpressive chaos!

Here we are in the "monotonous and inexpressive" chaos of sensations in which nothing stands out or makes itself felt. But then the mind chips away at the raw material like a sculptor at a block of stone until something takes shape and expresses itself. It literally ex-*presses*, or presses out of, that vague, inexpressive block. The mind does not create it, exactly: "in a sense the statue stood there from eternity," but, with "a thousand different ones beside it," no one could ever distinguish it from within that black, jointless block until the mind, like a sculptor, drew out this one significant figure from the rest. This is what it means to make something matter, to select some object to be part of "the world *we* feel and live in." We carve out very few things "to stand for the objective reality *par excellence*," as James says elsewhere. But it always depends on what we select and deselect from the same "given stuff," a subtraction from the block of stone, and there will be "other sculptors, others statues from the same stone!"

James really insists on the analogy: "We carve out order by leaving the disorderly parts out; and the world is conceived thus after the analogy of a forest or a block of marble from which parks or statues may be produced by eliminating irrelevant trees or chips of stone."[35] The object comes to matter—it materializes and enters our experience—by eliminating all other matters as "irrelevant." There it stands in relief against a meaningless background and, as Emerson would say, "I . . . behold what was there already! I make!" Michelangelo famously saw the angel in the block of marble and carved until he set it free. That angel was like the divinity Emerson claims is always there "in the neighborhood, hidden among vagabonds."

James does not imagine that these extricated things will always matter this much. They, too, will fall away as new things arise from the very same world stuff. There will always be "other minds, other worlds" from this same, inexpressive chaos—other forms of expression will emerge.[36] But pulled out of a chaotic, disorderly world, they feel no less adamant right now.

The nineteenth century is the great age of selection. At least by the end of the century James could suggest that its philosophies, psychologies, and natural histories had all taken shape around the idea of selective attention so central to him, like the world gathering around the candle on the pier glass. "Darwin," James writes, "opened our minds to the power of chance-happenings to bring forth 'fit' results if only they have time to add themselves together," and so all individuals, consciously or unconsciously, choose from the phenomenal field what satisfies our needs, and that is all it takes to bring forth a meaningful world. Darwin and James both believe in the "utility" of consciousness to select what we need and in "emotional interests" as "the great guides to selective attention." So for the individual, so for the species: in our day-to-day lives and in the world at large, these choices keep the environment relevant to us and we to it.

For James, selection is "omnipotent" in every form of consciousness: he defines reasoning, for example, as nothing but selecting, or "the ability of the mind to break up the totality of the phenomenon reasoned about, into parts, and to pick out from among these the particular one which, in our given emergency, may lead to the proper conclusion. The man of genius is he who will always stick in his bill at the right point, and bring it out with the right element—'reason' if the emergency be theoretical, 'means' if it be practical—transfixed upon it." Thus all logical thinking, even more so as it approaches genius, "is but another form of the selective activity of the mind."[37]

Aesthetics also works on the principle of selection for James so long as "the artist has wit enough to pounce upon some one feature of it as characteristic, and suppress all merely accidental items which do not harmonize with this." The artist, like the genius, makes a *point*, by eliminating everything irrelevant to the "main purpose" of an artwork. ("That art is selective is a fact universally recognized," Dewey says.) And in ethics, too, "choice reigns notoriously supreme": "an act has no ethical quality whatever unless it be chosen out of several all equally possible." The whole character of a person and what "he shall now resolve to become" rests on these choices.

By selective attention, we choose how the world appears to us. But while we learn from Darwin that the whole human race "largely agrees as to what it shall notice" and not notice—and "among the noticed parts we select in much the same way for accentuation and preference"—there is still, for James, "one great splitting of the whole universe into two halves" in which each of us draws the line between the halves in completely different places and no two lines are alike. The names for these two halves are "*me*" and "*not-me*," and they divide according to our interests and the psychological fact of what we call *me* and *mine*. What excites and captures my interest is real to me; so to call something "real" is to say that it stands in some relation of interest to myself. The whole "selective function of interest," according to Schutz, organizes and structures the world into "multiple realities"—"strata of major and minor relevance" for different individuals and for the same individual at different times. "Environment," Schutz says, is not "a sector of the world simply imposed upon us from the outside, something which we must take as not of our own making and with which we may come to terms only if we 'adjust' or 'adapt' ourselves to it." The environment is also "the outcome and product of our selection of that sector of the world which we consider and acknowledge as relevant for the functioning of our activities—organic as well as mental—as a whole."

Collectively and alone, we chip away at an undifferentiated, undistinguished world until we discover what matters to "me and mine," like Emerson. It had been there all along even if we had not yet picked it out. "Relevance is selection of the relevant part," writes F. C. S. Schiller, for whom relevance and pragmatic thinking amount to the same thing, the point being for him that the great century of selection is the great century of relevance, too.[38]

Taking Note

The idea that we shape a world through our selective attention to it takes a lot from Darwin, but not only from Darwin. It shares with Emerson a certain debt to an idealist tradition—including Kant—suggesting a practical attunement to new situations, a means of construing them according to one's prior commitments, and a certain responsibility for how they get construed. Robert Brandom suggests that Kant might be thought of as a "pragmatist *avant la lettre* because of the way his normative theory of conceptual *activity* (theoretical and practical) shapes his account of conceptual *content* (both theoretical and practical)." Brandom understands Kant as looking forward to how the pragmatists see us as pulling a distinctive kind of experience out from the world—a "synthetic" experience organized around a particular awareness. Kant does not sound unlike the pragmatists later when he describes, for example, how "objects of sense" are "mere appearances"; how these phenomena can only be known "in the way in which our senses are affected" by them and through categories of the understanding; how, therefore, any sense of "actuality" is "conceded to the creations of thought."

Dewey writes that we "start from the assumption of a sensory-continuum, the 'big, buzzing, blooming confusion,' out of which particular sensory quales are differentiated. Discrimination, not integration, is the real problem. In a general way we all admit that it is through attention that the distinctions arise, through selective emphasis." In Kant, too, this readiness of the mind to concretize aspects of the sensory world involves a choice of how to perceive any given content. It involves a judgment or discrimination about what is appropriate and what works; also, a willingness to readjust prior understandings in light of new ones. Our minds structure sensory content through our discriminations as part of an evolving process.

But Brandom also emphasizes how much of this cognitive processing in Kant should be understood in terms of what he calls *force*: how the judging, discriminating, believing—all of what is *done* to the phenomenal world—should be understood in terms of what one feels one *must do*, "what activity one must engage in, to be judging, believing, or doing it."[39] It is actually Brandom's sense of the needfulness of this choosing for coming to terms with the phenomenal world that he sees as most compatible with pragmatic thought.

Emerson likes the word *force* and uses it often, as when he describes how genius has "force" (or "native force") or how the "force of character is cumulative." "All great force is real and elemental," he says; "every man . . . should find or make a frank and hearty expression of what force and meaning is in him." "Within the form of every creature is a force impelling it to ascend into a higher form." Sometimes Emerson uses *force* interchangeably with *character* and sometimes with *tendency* or *fate*. It is almost always what drives the expressions (the words, writing, art, conduct, manners) that shapes each moment for each of us and gives it form, as if to say that every expression is also fateful and necessary to our tendencies—or, as Cavell might put it, *conditioned* somehow. Our force, for Emerson, is like our interests. It determines what draws us toward aspects of the world and how we process and conceive of them. "Experience" is something like the application of this force.

Again, Brandom suggests how idealism's practice of applying concepts involves the critical awareness of the necessity of applying them in every instance—what it means to have these concepts available to us to make a wholly contingent world intelligible and the work it takes to apply them and keep applying and adjusting them to further contingencies. The idea is that knowing something is the same as the feeling for how to sort it out.

We can see that Emerson does something like what Brandom suggests Hegel started, following Kant: that is, take the German idealist tradition and *naturalize* it by seeing this relationship between the *recognizing* individual subjects and the subjects they *recognize* as being a product of some larger force that informs their consciousness but exceeds it, too. Hegel finds a historical spirit behind a great struggle for recognition in which we develop and institute the norms by which more and more aspects of the world come to light. For Emerson, some elemental "force" supplied by a deep personal history or human history or else something "elemental" or "eternal" (that has been there all along) impels what aspects of the world come to speak to us and how we finally manage to express them (in language, in art, in love and friendship, in the way we live, in any one of his essays). And while I won't elaborate on any of this, I will say that Brandom takes the "selectional-adaptational processes" that he attributes to American pragmatists to be further developing this idealist tradition "by completing the process of *naturalizing* it, which had begun already with Hegel."[40]

Brandom sees the pragmatists as offering a scientific account, informed largely by Darwin, of the emergence of relatively stable forms of order and habit arising and sustaining themselves through interactions with an environment. The pragmatists believe that learning, at the level of the individual, like evolution, at the level of the species, are both, as I cited earlier, "processes of *adaptation*, in which interaction with the environment selects (preserves and reproduces) some elements, while eliminating others." And they see this natural process as being not, as many think, a radical break from but rather a continuation of Kant's rational process of becoming conscious of objects in space through the forms and categories, including the aesthetic categories, we have for sorting them. "The pragmatists' conception of *experience*," Brandom writes, "is recognizably a naturalized version of the rational process of critically winnowing and actively extrapolating commitments . . . which Kant describes as producing and exhibiting the distinctive synthetic unity of apperception. For that developmental process, too, is selectional. . . . Some commitments (theoretical and practical) thrive and persist, in concert with their fellows, while others are modified or rejected as unable to flourish in that environment."

This is only to say that both idealism and pragmatism are working through how an object in the wide world manages to come into consciousness—how, in Emerson's words, "it detaches itself from the life like a ripe fruit, to become a thought of the mind." It requires, in both cases, an act of selective attention for us to conceive of it in the first place and to call it out in some real and intelligible way. We recognize that object by incorporating it or bringing it within our current frame of reference. The idealist, Emerson says, measures according to "the *rank* which things themselves take in his consciousness."

But in both idealism and pragmatism there are also forces behind this selectional act that make it feel necessary or important (categorical), that suggest the ways in which this object works well and *fits* the category or practical application we have ready for it at the moment we perceive it. In other words, our consciousness of an object suggests "a practical attunement to an environment" that offers up what we need in turn. We could say that thinking extracts what pertains to us or that which "rightly belongs to us . . . and which we dare to make ours," to use Emerson's words. "Thought makes everything fit for use," he says.[41]

The following passage appears in Emerson's essay "Spiritual Laws":

> A man's genius . . . the selection of what is fit for him, the rejection of what is unfit, determines for him the character of the universe. A man is a method, a progressive arrangement; a selecting principle, gathering his like to him, wherever he goes. He takes only his own, out of the multiplicity that sweeps and circles round him.

James marked this passage in his collection of Emerson's essays and also copied it, in an index he kept, under the heading *man a selective principle*. The early note he took from Emerson on the "selecting principle" provided much later for his "principles of psychology." "What attracts my attention shall have it," Emerson continues in the essay, "as I will go to the man who knocks at my door, whilst a thousand persons, as worthy, go by it, to whom I give no regard. It is enough that these particulars speak to me."

What we notice in any given situation is only the smallest measure of what might be noticed. What James noticed in Emerson's essays are these passages about the selective function of interest and how it singles out particular people and things "whilst a thousand" others go by. After all not everything around us is interesting to us. Our interest selects certain things as notable, and only *they* present to us, even as the man who knocks at Emerson's door. "Nothing exists unless I maintain it (by my interest, or my *potential* interest)," writes Susan Sontag, who registers this fact in her notebooks as an anxiety as well as the charge to remain always "interested in *everything*" and to signify that interest by at least "noting down" the names of everything ("Beethoven's music, movies, business firms"). By taking note, she says, "I *perceive* value, I *confer* value, I *create* value, I even create—or guarantee—*existence*." So James marks passages too. In his marginalia and index, they are the selective exercise of his attention to passages on selective attention, as if to say, with Emerson, "it is enough that these particulars speak to me" to rivet my attention on them as many more pages of Emerson go by. James was motivated to pull out these passages, fully expecting that what was then ready at hand would soon go out of reach, receding in memory, and that he would need some little index, or mark or contrivance, to reach it again, like breaking a branch to find your way back through the woods.

Later, when James writes that "whoever studies consciousness, from any point of view whatever, is ultimately brought up against the mystery of *interest* and *selective attention*," I like to imagine those passages from Emerson rising to his mind "out of the recesses of consciousness." They would have been an aspect of what Ross Posnock describes (following James and also Heidegger) as "the 'unthought' background of thought . . . under the radar of cognition—blind, intuitive, tacit," then notable once more right when James's thoughts on the psychology of selective attention made them "fit for use." They would have been "selected by thought from the totality of lived experience and regarded as relevant," as Schutz puts it.[42]

Selective attention for James is important from a practical point of view because it helps us transcend the world within our actual reach by relating elements within it to elements outside of it. It is about the "conscious process of experiencing itself" and how far interests can take us beyond our current frame of reference. It is about just how deep and often our involvement in the wider world might be. Our selective attention provides us with the bearings that serve our interests; as our interests evolve, it works to make ever more bear on us in concrete and tangible ways. Selective attention is how we can be sure not to lose contact permanently with so many aspects of life that are lost to us most of the time.

James also marked a passage from Emerson's essay "Nominalist and Realist" I mentioned earlier:

> It is the secret of the world that all things subsist, and do not die, but only retire a little from sight, and afterwards return again. Whatever does not concern us, is concealed from us. As soon as a person is no longer related to our present well-being, he is concealed, or *dies*, as we say. Really, all things and persons are related to us, but according to our nature, they act on us not at once, but in succession, and we are made aware of their presence one at a time. All persons, all things which we have known, are here present, and many more than we see; the world is full.[43]

James annotated these lines of Emerson with the name Bergson, which suggests that he read or reread the passage late, since James was first struck by Bergson while rereading *him* around 1902. He writes in his notes that Bergson is a "magician" who "tells of reality itself." Bergson's idea of *attention à la vie* suggests that persons and things only become real to us if they are relevant to us; that our concern with these phenomena prevents them from being submerged in what he otherwise describes as pure duration, withdrawn from notice. James obviously saw the connection between Bergson's *attention à la vie* and Emerson's sense that "whatever does not concern us is concealed from us." We never see "all the things that really surround us," but it is nonetheless "Emerson's creed," says James, "that everything that ever was or will be is here in the enveloping now."

In "Nominalist and Realist," Emerson brings the idea of inattention *to* attention, like James and Bergson, so that what is taken for granted, though present all along, can be noticed and sharply distinguished. As soon we need it, suddenly we "behold" it. Look at how different the world appears by agreeing to attend to something or someone—how a person might *appear* like magic or like a rabbit or duck that was concealed! The world is full of potential. We can even guarantee the existence of someone just by noticing him; then, at least, he will not be dead *to us*.

A shift in consciousness allows the mind to recognize and reflect on more of reality, and so any philosophy that makes us conscious of the process of becoming conscious is also about increasing our contact with the world's everyday phenomena. To do the work of philosophy, for James, is to understand what we can bring to our daily lives from beyond ourselves. Philosophy, he says, will contain an "assurance that my powers, such as they are, are not irrelevant to [the universal essence], but pertinent, that it speaks to them and will in some way recognize their reply, that I can be a match for it if I will, and not a footless waif." Far from denying our powers "all relevancy in universal affairs," the work of philosophy is how any of us manages to find a foothold and, at least temporarily, hold on.[44]

Relevance in the Rockies

Alfred Schutz's book-length manuscript, "Preliminary Notes on the Problem of Relevance," written between 1947 and 1951 and posthumously published in 1970, was conceived as the first part of a five-part study to be titled *The World as Taken-for-Granted: Toward a Phenomenology of the Natural Attitude*. Schutz was an Austrian philosopher and social scientist who fled to Paris in 1938 just before Hitler's occupation and then moved to New York the following year, where he joined the faculty of the New School for Social Research. He continued to write in German, including his major study, *The Structures of the Life-World* (*Die Strukturen der Lebenswelt*), which he also never finished, but he chose to write "Preliminary Notes on the Problem of Relevance" in English, translating his thoughts into English as he wrote and then thematizing this "choice to use the English language (with all its syntactical rules and terminological implications for the purposes of articulating my thought)." When he devoted a section of *The Structures of the Life-World* to problems of relevance as he worked on his book-length manuscript on relevance, he used the loanword from English, *Relevanz*, suggesting that the "terminological implications" of the word in English have no true equivalent in German, as I also mentioned early on.[45]

I think Schutz saw his relevance manuscript as his most American work, written largely during vacations in Colorado. He took long walks most mornings to the picnic tables outside of a church and wrote there, surrounded by mountains and meadows, and "there it was where the *Reflections on Relevance* came into being." He describes his setting and also the "social background" that guided his choice to use English instead of German all as part of the "background" of the "thematic field" against which his writing on relevance occurs. The manuscript is indebted to Bergson, especially the concept of *attention à la vie*, and to the phenomenologist Edmund Husserl, who was Schutz's close friend and lifelong correspondent. But the manuscript is also the result of Schutz's encounter with American pragmatism, especially the work of James, Dewey, and George Herbert Mead (plus Whitehead, and C. I. Lewis and value theory, to which I will turn later on).[46]

As a philosopher, Schutz draws out a theory of relevance from studies of phenomenology and psychology based in the idea of the selectivity of consciousness and how it organizes experience into objects of more and less importance. By "relevance," Schutz means what James means: the fundamental process by which some object out of all possible objects comes to our attention. But as a social scientist Schutz also wanted to understand the role that a phenomenology of relevance might play in sorting everyday life into various "domains of relevance"—a plurality of shared values and interests around which sociocultural groups and social systems get organized. After all, if what is relevant is what we are "conscious of," then how persons become aware of each other and how persons *appear* to each other is both a phenomenological question and a sociological one. How do others come to matter to us and to our world? How do those persons *fit in*? (Schutz writes at length, for example, about the situation of the "stranger," having been an immigrant himself. The problems of orientation and adaptation for persons who move from one cultural community to another is, for him, a problem of translation between different systems of relevance.) He believed that a theory of relevance would be a theory of social reality that linked phenomenology to sociology. He conceived of it variously as a "piece of phenomenological psychology," a "phenomenology of the social world," and a "philosophy investigating the presuppositions" of daily life.[47]

Schutz begins his manuscript sounding much like Jastrow on his act of writing the day after his after-dinner speech—with a head cold, in that room with the whirring clock, smoking lamp, and inkstand that needs refilling—or else like James writing in the Adirondacks on his honeymoon or like Dewey at his typewriter:

> Before me is the table with its green surface on which several objects are placed—my pencil, two books, and other things. Further on are the tree and lawn of my garden, the lake with boats, the mountain, and the clouds in the background. I need only turn my head to see the house with its porch, the windows of my room, etc. I hear the buzzing of a motorboat, the voices of the children in the neighbor's yard, the calling of the bird. I experience the kinesthetic movements of my writing hand, I have sensations of warmth, I feel the table supporting my writing arm. All of this is

> within my perceptual field, a field well organized into spheres of objects: those within my reach, those which once have been within my reach and can be brought within it again, and those which thus far have never been within my reach but which I may bring within it by means of appropriate kinesthetic movements or movements of particular kinds. But none of these perceived things is at the moment thematic for me. My attention is concentrated on a quite specific task (the analysis of the problem of relevance).

Writing about relevance is the relevant part and holds his attention, while the movement of his hand, the feeling of warmth, and the noises of the motorboat, children, and bird all remain in the background, along with his two books, his house, the tree and lawn, and then the lake, mountains, and clouds further on. They are all within his "perceptual field," some within reach, others out of reach but that can be brought within or back within reach, but none of which interests him right now. Nothing within the horizon "is at the moment thematic" for him as his writing about relevance is. "Writing-in-English-in-longhand-a-paper-on-the-problem-of-relevance": that is his "paramount reality." But even as he attends to his task, he lives "*simultaneously* in various realms of reality, in various tensions of consciousness and modes of *attention à la vie*" that remain, as it were, *behind* that task, or "horizonal, ancillary, subordinate in relation" to it. An accomplished pianist, Schutz compares these "multiple realities" to musical counterpoint in polyphonic music in which two independent themes happen in the same phrase or flow of music; "the listener's mind may pursue one or the other, take one as the main theme and the other as the subordinate one, or vice versa: one determines the other, and nevertheless it remains predominant in the intricate web of the whole structure."[48]

Thus, thinking through the problem of relevance is the theme of his activity, but this activity "is spread over several realms or levels" of his conscious life, "each with its own particular tension, its particular dimension of time, its particular articulations into thematic kernel and horizonal surrounding." Though he spends an hour writing at his desk, he also hears the motorboat and occasionally will be conscious of it. He dimly feels the kinesthetic movements of his writing hand and pen, and at some point he may need to "turn-away" from his writing and "turn-toward" the pen if he needs to refill the ink. At some point the physical state of his body will intrude on his consciousness, and he will have to stop to eat or rest. Someone may interrupt his writing by bursting into the room and demanding that he "turn-toward" them. Plus, the hour he spends at his desk is a "measurable period of outer time" within an ongoing span of "inner life which condenses experiences, skills, and knowledge acquired in the greater part of [his] lifetime into the writing down of a single page."[49] There is, in other words, a long personal history and a lot more behind this moment of writing about relevance in Colorado. It occurs against the background of all of Schutz's knowledge and experiences that fund the theme of the hour. So many aspects of his lifetime have degrees of relevance to the activity of writing that is his present concern right now.

So he proceeds by concentrating on the paramount activity at hand. But if a loud sound from near the lake interrupts the course of his activity, then he might go to the window instead. Anything that momentarily disrupts the world *as given* and taken for granted—anything that is "atypical" or unexpected, "*if it is interesting enough*" to be further explored—may become a new *theme*, as he calls it. Then whatever prevails in daily life is suspended (though it persists in a kind of neutralized form, ready to be reactivated) while he attends to this new consciousness.[50] He reorients himself toward it. It could be a loud noise, a bright flash, an intrusion in the room, even so small a thing as a pen that runs out of ink, making him pause—if it is worth his shift in attention, it is suddenly relevant where it wasn't before.

Schutz asks readers to imagine walking into a familiar room and noticing something out of place. He is elaborating on an example used by the Greek skeptic Carneades in which a man, entering a poorly lit room, thinks that he sees a coil of rope in the corner. Why is it there? But wait, he wonders, what if what appears to be a coil of rope is actually a *snake* instead? And now, uneasy, the man "oscillates" between the alternatives (Husserl would call the snake the "problematic alternative"), moving around his object, trying to determine whether it is dangerous and how to act in the face of it. And first of all Schutz asks why *this* object in the man's "unstructuralized field of visual perception" commands his attention "to such an extent that he makes it the theme of his interpreting activity." There may be other objects in the room, even in the same corner of the room in the same field of vision, that leave him perfectly indifferent. And the answer obviously is that the man would not pay attention to these objects because they do not appear to be problematic in the way that a rope that may be a snake is. Among all the more or less familiar objects, this one object "stands out over against" all the others in the room. "It is," Schutz says, "from the outset—to introduce this term by anticipating later results—*relevant* to him."

That object becomes relevant because it seems so glaringly irrelevant—completely *in*apropos—to a familiar room that may even be his own room and that he expects to find as he left it. In a glance he discovers within a previously "unproblematic" field an unlikely element that "does not correspond to what he had expected." An object like that in the corner does not at all *fit* in this room. It does not "belong to the type of things" the man assumed he would find there. What could it be? Whatever he had been thinking as he entered the room, this atypical object "*imposes* upon him a change of his thematic field. Something which was supposed to be familiar and therefore unproblematic proves to be unfamiliar." "It evokes his curiosity, invites him to pay attention to it." It has imposed on his routine activities and cannot be "left in the indifference" of the background. "It is," Schutz says, "sufficiently relevant to be imposed as a new problem, as a new theme, and even to supersede the previous theme of his thinking which, then according to circumstances, our man will either 'let out of his grip' entirely or at least set aside temporarily."[51]

This is what Schutz defines as "the *first form* of relevance: namely, that by virtue of which something is constituted as problematic in the midst of the unstructuralized field of unproblematic familiarity—and therewith the field into theme and horizon." This form of relevance (that he also calls *topical relevance*) concerns "the way in which an unfamiliar experience imposes itself upon us by its very unfamiliarity." It is "unfamiliar" because it cannot be neatly subsumed under any ready types or categories based on the man's stock of experiences and knowledge. If he has no experience of a coiled object like that in that room, then that object will become problematic and "therefore thematic." A setting he normally takes as a given has become questionable and "cannot be taken for granted any longer." It becomes the central focus of his attention instead. This again, for Schutz, is the first definition of relevance: the articulation of consciousness into attention and inattention, "theme and horizon."

Something turns out to be "otherwise than expected." "Something formerly irrelevant (because just implied in the unexplored horizon of the familiar main topic [in this case, whatever else he would be thinking when walking into a familiar room]) has now become interesting and has been constituted as a new topic." How strange. Arousing the man's interest (with a sense that this bit of the setting may turn out to matter somehow), it leads him to investigate. "*The thing as it appears to him* in its surroundings, the thing as *phenomenon* . . . is now thematically given to him for interpretation." He needs to familiarize himself with it. It means that the task now at hand is that of "translating the unfamiliar into familiar terms," to fit the thing in the corner of the room into some frame of reference and meaning—to make sense of it by referring it to prior experiences and knowledge.

But, of course, not everything in the man's total stock of knowledge can be used to make sense of that coil. "Within the context of his previous experiences (of any kind) as preserved by memory and arranged by previous interpretations into his stock of knowledge actually at hand, there are many which have nothing to do with the interpretation of the object before him, which are entirely *irrelevant* for interpreting this new object." The fact, for example, that the sun rises in the east is completely irrelevant for making sense of this strange object. On the other hand, there will be some previous experiences to which the present experience might be compared, experiences with ropes or knowledge of snakes, knowledge that a snake would eventually move in distinction from a rope, and maybe there are other contexts relevant to interpreting the object: whether the room was by a dock or else by a desert or who had been in there before. Maybe the man is a fisherman or sailor. In any case, these are what Schutz calls *interpretative relevances*, having "*something to do*" with the thematic object that makes it recognizable and meaningful. They refer this unfamiliar object to the resources and store of knowledge one has at hand.[52]

And then, for Schutz (who provides a full taxonomy of relevances that I will not exhaust here), there are *motivational relevances*, which suggest that the man's interest in attending to that coiled object—in determining whether it is a rope or a snake—is "of vital importance" for planning his future actions and behavior. The interpretation of the nature of this object is important *to him*. The "selective function" of "interest" organizes this room for him, and that coiled object is selected as primarily important. However he comes to term with it, however he decides to interpret it, will determine the appropriateness of his response. Does he try to remove it? With his hands? Does he hit it with a stick? In this sense, relevance for Schutz is motivational because it links the *interesting* (what compels my attention) to the *important* (what I plan to do with the thing that interests me or how I respond in light of it). And what exactly does *interest* mean in such cases as the interesting case of the rope or snake? "Obviously," Schutz says, "it refers to the system of motivational relevances which induced me to make a certain aspect of the object in question the topic of my investigation or concern. *Interest in this sense is the set of motivational relevances which guide the selective activity of my mind.*"[53] Interest determines the selective attention I give to the objects and experiences that are motivationally relevant—that may turn out, in other words, to be important to me.

There are imposed forms of relevance—that unfamiliar object that makes me turn to it and make sense of it (the rope that could be a snake, the loud noise, the flash of light, the sudden interruption). And then there are forms of voluntary relevance (under the heading of what psychologists call "voluntary attention"), Schutz says. We may voluntarily shift attention from one topic to another so that, again, what was "horizonal has become thematic." We may voluntarily stop writing about relevance and walk to the lake because that is what we need right now. Our interests voluntarily select objects and experiences that are meaningful to us given who we are. They draw us to things that are *hypothetically relevant* by connecting new and future experiences with past ones.

Schutz sees the whole "life-world" as being organized by "systems of relevance"—frames of reference and provinces of meaning built out of our experiences and stores of knowledge that determine what we find to be interesting and important; that see new objects and experiences as mattering; and that bestow a context of meaning on other realms of experience beyond the everyday world to which we are habituated. Systems of relevance make *something else* stand out as thematic and worth our attention. They determine why we shift attention from one topic to another and how the "counterpointal structure of the stream of consciousness may change its character because other strains of it receive a particular accent through such shifting of attention and thereby obtain predominance."[54] Systems of relevance are the means by which individuals orient themselves in new situations and define these situations as significant in accordance with whatever is interesting and important to them.

In *The Principles of Psychology*, James describes the "many worlds" or "sub-universes" of human experience—the "various orders of reality" within which a person lives. There is the predominant world of physical actions and things but also whole worlds of individual opinions and impressions, of beliefs, of vagaries and fantasies, of sheer madness. "Each world," James says, "*whilst it is attended to* is real after its own fashion; only the reality lapses with the attention." Schutz takes up James's idea of "sub-universes" but calls them instead the *finite provinces of meaning* on which we bestow an "accent of reality." They include not only the paramount world of objects and events "into which we can gear by our actions" but also the world of dreams, of religious experience, of scientific and theoretical contemplation, of phantasms. They include the play world of the child, and they especially include "the world of art." These all become real worlds to us while we attend to them. Each feels "coherent" within its borders and each is characterized "by a specific tension of consciousness" and its own "cognitive style." "Provinces of meaning" are always "consistent in themselves," by which Schutz means that certain things are "relevant" to these worlds and other things are not. He wants to understand just how these provinces of meaning (or what Edmund Husserl had called "unities" of "sense" or "meaning") are constituted, how they arise within the lifeworld with their own constitutive coherence and style, and how the mind chooses to give the "accent of reality" to one or another of them at a particular time.[55]

The everyday world in which we live and work is the "paramount reality" among all possible realities that we simply "take for granted." We do not question it or feel the need to verify it. We are "wide awake" to it, while all other possible awarenesses are relegated to the background of consciousness. The everyday world makes "the other realms appear 'irreal'" by comparison. But perception, as Schutz reminds us, always involves the possibility of choice, and there is always an "alternative." So how do we pass from one "finite province of meaning" to an alternative province of meaning? How in a world in which we take everything for granted or without question do we become aware of an alternative? How do we shift our sense of what figures for us so that something unnoticed or unregarded in the horizon or fringes of consciousness becomes relevant all of a sudden and takes on the "accent of reality" instead? How do we change our *attitude*? Schutz writes that the "paramount reality" of everyday life "seems to us to be the natural one, and we are not ready to abandon our attitude toward it without having experienced a specific *shock* which compels us to break through the limits of this 'finite' province of meaning and to shift the accent of reality to another one."

The shift from subconsciousness to consciousness that we see in Jastrow and James is what Schutz describes as the *leap* between these "various orders of reality." It always comes with an experience of *shock*. There are as many different kinds of shock experiences as there are "different provinces of meaning upon which I may bestow my accent of reality," says Schutz. He describes the *shock* of falling asleep as the *leap* into a world of dreams.

He describes the sudden "inner transformation" at the moment the curtain in the theater rises and we transition into the world of the play. He even describes the "radical change" in attitude we experience in front of a painting that pulls our attention into the world of its frame. This, too, is a *shock* that compels a *leap* between provinces of meaning much as Kierkegaard describes the "instant" of a religious experience as a *leap* into another world of meaning. The theoretical contemplations of scholars also can remove them from the affairs of "this world" in an instant.[56]

Suppose, Schutz asks us to imagine, that he is reading *Don Quixote* but is interrupted so that he cannot finish it in one sitting or even one week, but is sure that whenever he resumes his reading, he can pick up where he left off. Meanwhile, he turns to other topics and themes. These will be in the foreground of his concern, and "other relevances will emerge" from them during the break from his reading. Let's say that *Don Quixote* is not topically relevant to his work as a social theorist or phenomenologist but only figures within plans for his leisure time. Let's say, in his words, the book "does not fit into my plan for work; and while working, it is neutralized, put in brackets, inactive, dormant but nevertheless still in my grip. It is, in short, a topic belonging to another system of plans, to another province of my life; the predominant topic of my leisure time is suspended but persists in neutralized form, ready to be reactivated." Then, of course, at his leisure when he is fully occupied with *Don Quixote*, the topics belonging to his plan for work are themselves "left in abeyance," only to be reinstated when he next turns back to them.

We oscillate between these realms or contexts of meaning, taking each for granted as a matter of course when we are in it. We wake from a dream or leave a novel behind and return to the paramount reality of daily life. But experiences at "another level of reality" do have a way of coming back to us—or, as Schutz describes it, coming "home" to us, our "home base." We remember dreams and novels and reflect on their meaning in the context of our daily world and within the scheme of "interpretive relevances" that prevail within it. The fictional world of the novel gets "translated" into the system of meaning that prevails in our everyday world or, rather, reinterpreted "by means of systems of relevances belonging" to it.[57]

I will return to the idea of translation (that I also mentioned at the beginning of this book in relation to Derrida's famous essay "What Is a 'Relevant' Translation"). But I shall say for now that it is the term Schutz also chooses to describe how the meaning we experience in one realm becomes intelligible or relevant in another. To speak of relevance as "translation" is to ask how anything we experience while reading a book, watching a play, or looking at a work of art—or in any aspect of intellectual or contemplative life apart from our everyday living—might bear on our everyday living with any measure of importance. "Why are we deeply moved by participating in the destiny of the fictitious persons of a tragedy? Why do we gain a new kind of knowledge after having dwelt in the fictitious reality of a great work of art? How is it possible that religious experience reveals as a kind of knowledge, the truth of which cannot be grasped by the scheme of interpretational relevances prevailing in the world of daily life?" What we learn in these other realms of meaning, including the realms of religion and art, enters our memories and our stock of knowledge. They very well may come to mind again in the midst of daily life—not, however, as they were (as an integral and necessary part of the world left behind) but transformed into a "symbol" of what they were, having originated in one context but arrived in another (a substitute belonging to both worlds). And now they can be interpreted in light of this other context as somehow fitting. It is this "symbolic transformation" of some reality in the context of a new reality that makes a fictional character—or a dream or phrase of music or religious feeling—relevant somehow.

"'What is Hecuba to the actor?' asks Hamlet. What is Hamlet to us?" We will have to "watch" to see if a *hypothetically relevant* figure like Hamlet can become *topically relevant*, if something from one realm of meaning (a play) can come to mean something else in another (daily life). These provinces, for Schutz, have "open horizons." What we experience in one of them remains in the "margins" of consciousness and potentially within our reach while we focus on something else. If we find that we can use *Hamlet* at some future moment in our everyday life, at that point it "stands out from a horizon" of other things that are known and stored away. It will be remembered but in "typified" fashion—that is, according to the systems of relevance and categories of meaning that structure our daily life.[58]

But we traffic *between* worlds, so we will also find that when we return to reading *Hamlet* after an interruption, some aspect of our life in the meantime may come to bear on it. An interrupted activity is never actually the same when we return to it, because during the pause other things will have imposed themselves on us and entered our stock of knowledge and resources; meanwhile our own attitude might have shifted a little and might now shift our understanding of the reading that we resume. In other words, our framework for recognizing and making sense of what we read and experience is itself always evolving. Our systems of relevance and meaning are always evolving, which means that we may notice something now or in the future that we missed before. This is why Schutz does not believe in anything like strict "recurrence." A resumed activity "may be substantially the 'same' as it was before the interruption, but it will always have the meaning of '*the same activity but continued after interruption.*'"

Schutz suggests that our lives may take a new turn because we read the same old book at a particular moment. Or maybe we were exposed to that book too soon, "at a time when we were not prepared to deal adequately with it," and so found nothing in it and dropped it for the time being. Most of us will say at some point, "I was too young and inexperienced at this time to grasp the full importance of the event." Or else say regretfully, "If I only had known in my youth what I know today!" Or maybe, I did not back then have the resources to know how that book might be relevant. I could never have known what Hamlet might be *to me*. "We form no guess at the time of receiving a thought, of its comparative value," writes Emerson in "Spiritual Laws."[59]

Again, for Schutz, the lifeworld is composed of so many different "zones" or "regions" or "provinces" of meaning—internal systems of value that determine what counts. We take for granted what is relevant to each situation in which we find ourselves (as Emerson might put it, though Schutz invokes Heidegger's sense of being "in-situation" instead). Schutz writes that the interests he has "in the same situation as a father, a citizen, a member of my church or of my profession, may not only be different but even incompatible with one another. I have, then, to decide which of these disparate interests I must choose in order to define the situation from which to start further inquiry." But mostly Schutz wants us to understand that systems of relevance are "open" and that to speak of them does not mean that they are "each separated from the other by clean-cut border lines." In fact, he says, the opposite is true. "These various realms of relevances and precision are intermingled, showing the most manifold interpenetrations and enclaves, sending their fringes into neighbor provinces and thus creating twilight zones of sliding transitions." Relevance is about everything that is fitting and appropriate to a particular context of meaning and value. But relevance is also about relations and communications between these contexts and how each one of them evolves by assimilating new facts into a set or "sedimented" system and by recognizing what these other facts might be *to it.* Schutz's situation as a father, for example, may come to inform his professional life. So when he describes relevant facts as "disturbances of the process of sedimentation," he is pointing to the way that these discrete systems continually get shaken by the shock or sudden recognition of other, new things in relation to them.[60]

The experience of relevance, for Schutz, is the "experience of transcendence." It is the "irruption" of a world beyond everyday life "into the world of everyday life," and when Schutz describes it, he sounds a lot like Emerson in "Circles" (drawing circles beyond the horizon of every circle "without end")—hemming in a life but then always "[bursting] over that boundary on all sides." Schutz writes, "the world within my actual reach carries along the open infinite horizons of my world in potential reach, but to my experiences of these horizons belongs the conviction that each world within potential reach, once transformed into actual reach, will again be surrounded by new horizons, and so on." Whenever "something formerly irrelevant" becomes relevant, "our daily life is coupled with an idea which transcends our experience of our everyday life," reaching beyond and lying outside our present context. "My actual social environment refers always to a horizon of potential social environments," Schutz says. New environments are brought within the reach of old environments and contexts that then adjust with new relevances. Each one of these "transcendent experiences" transforms everyday life by providing it with elements of "significance . . . which it did not have before."[61]

What is Hamlet to us? It is not simply that, if the moment is right, we might find a place for Hamlet within our everyday lives. Once Hamlet becomes intelligible to us, then that makes other forms of relevance possible too. We restructure our sense of the interesting and important by our conscious attention and by our reception. ("My reception has been so large," writes Emerson, "that I am not annoyed by receiving this or that superabundantly.") "We have to consider," Schutz says, "that . . . not only the range but also the structurization of our stock of knowledge at hand changes continually" and that the emergence of any new experience "results by necessity in a change, be it ever so small, of our prevailing interests and therewith of our system of relevances." Our horizons, too, keep shifting as we incorporate new, previously ignored objects into our "circle of concern."

But as the sociologist Zerubavel suggests, "we notice and ignore things not only as human beings but also as social beings" and as collectives. Across social groups, there are shared ideas of relevance and concern, and shared ideas of irrelevance too. This is why Zerubavel calls for a "sociology of attention" and why Schutz believes that understanding the phenomenon of "selective attention" (which is practically the same for him as the phenomenon of relevance) is of particular importance for "the theory of social action." When Schutz turns to sociology, he considers the hierarchy of values by which any social or cultural group establishes its own "domains of relevances"; how much these values are socially derived from our backgrounds; and how social traditions, biases, conventions, habits, heritages, and backgrounds ultimately underlie any collective sense of mattering. Members of a social group live within a "common situation," Schutz says: they share frames of reference and a "system of relevances" within which individual members feel "at home." Individuals "find their bearings without difficulty in the common surroundings, guided by a set of recipes of more or less institutionalized habits, mores, folkways, etc., that help them come to terms with beings and fellow men belonging to the same situation." There are, in Zerubavel's words, "attentional communities" that set norms for determining what and who belongs and what and who "we come to regard as relevant and to which we therefore attend."[62] These norms function as both a scheme of interpretation and as a scheme of orientation toward other cultures and worlds. Schutz suggests in fact that all social interaction and all communication between persons and groups happen in those "twilight zones of sliding transitions" between different zones or systems of relevance.

In other words, we all have a "preconstituted" or "typified" sense of relevance that determines what we habitually notice and just as habitually disregard. We are thus "'perceptually readied' . . . to seek out and register those details that reflect our collective expectations, while overlooking other details that are equally perceptible." It is easy to see how these shared systems that define what is relevant and important—systems that are passed down educationally and institutionally *as given* and that form our deep backgrounds—define "the social roles, positions, and statuses" of members of a group and also who belongs to the group and who is alien to it. It is easy to see how the system of relevances that Schutz calls "home base" and that guides our selective attention also excludes alien or unfamiliar persons and things—how, within this system, they all are invisible or outside our consciousness even as we take our system of values for granted every day and hardly notice it either.

But this is not to say that we are not capable of learning or taking new things in. "Philosophers as different as James, Bergson, Dewey, Husserl, and Whitehead," writes Schutz, "agree that the common-sense knowledge of everyday life is the unquestioned but always questionable background within which inquiry starts and within which alone it can be carried out." From philosophies of attention we learn that we can be *shocked* into paying attention to something hidden in plain sight; we can find unregarded objects, words, and ideas interesting; we can come to understand disregarded persons as mattering to us. Whenever we *leap* for the time being into different contexts, social systems, cultures, and provinces of meaning, we bring some new consciousness "home" to us. The memory of it will change the "structurization" of "our stock of knowledge," however slightly. A system of relevance is an evolving, "open system" in which "newly emergent and unanticipated relevances . . . supersede and cover the former set." What was taken for granted and unquestioned may be called into question; what was irrelevant may be relevant once we take cognizance of it. Awareness changes our prevailing interests enough to leave us open to further awareness. The more we find relevant, the more we find relevant, and so on. There will be, says Schutz, "an element of surprise" every time.[63]

The phenomenology and sociology of relevance suggests how we choose to ignore, but especially how we choose to recognize what we normally ignore. It makes a theory of the perception of a sudden fit between what is unfamiliar and the familiar world that defines our interests and plans—also, how our world changes just a little in light of every new connection and accommodation. Ultimately for Schutz, the refugee and immigrant, writing about relevance in English at a church in the Rockies, the theory of relevance is a very social theory of *fitting in*—of the feeling of belonging, at least "until further notice," as he puts it.[64]

And as we learned James liked to say toward any feeling of relationship that is at once new and strange: *welcome*.

5

Salience, or Finding the Point

Remember that Dewey had said that "events that have no attributed meanings are accidents and if they are big enough are catastrophes" and that Stephen Crane was trying to avert a catastrophe by insisting that time spent on an open boat in the wake of a shipwreck could be the "best experience" of a life? I would like to turn to another expression of a shipwreck that seems to know itself to be an experience.[1]

Winslow Homer's painting *The Life Line* is one of several paintings from the 1880s and 1890s that is interested in what it means for a work of art to attract attention (fig. 3). It was the most money Homer had ever made for a painting; it transformed his career when it was shown at the National Academy ("the most popular picture in the show"), closely followed by a print that Homer had engraved of it even before the exhibition, displaying "remarkable marketing savvy on his part." But this is not what I mean. I would like to say, without sounding too metaphysical about it, that the painting makes actual *what it is like* to pay attention to something; that Homer in these decades and across his late works, demonstrates that distinctive way of being conscious that so fascinated William James in studying attention and in describing how the "focalization, concentration, of consciousness are of its essence."[2] I think that Homer shows how wonderful a painting can be at seizing something from out of the drift. The painting enacts the phenomenological process that itself was coming to attention at the time in which a particular moment gets so arranged that something we otherwise would not pick up on becomes paramount. Homer floats it as an object of interest.

FIGURE 3. Winslow Homer, *The Life Line* (1884). Oil on canvas. Philadelphia Museum of Art, the George W. Elkins Collection, 1924 (E1924-4-15).

Sometimes in the pictures from this period, Homer literally lifts an object out from a current or stream (fig. 4). It is almost too easy to suggest of an image like *Leaping Trout* that the trout is phenomenologically discriminated from "a gray chaotic indiscriminateness," to recall the way that James describes how "interest" alone provides a foreground and background, accent and emphasis, light and shade.

What can this picture be about but the fact that Homer took interest in a fish and is now showing his viewers how such acts of attention can transfigure even it? Against the current, the monumental trout looms in "heroic isolation." It is pulled out of the wash and a little out of the picture plane, too, which lies against the surface of the water. Its foreshortened head tends toward us a little as we tend to it; it appears to be angling out of the frame even as we stand alongside the presumed angler of this fishing expedition beyond the frame. "What is life but the angle of vision?" writes Emerson, whom Homer read and whose book *Society and Solitude* he kept in his small library in Maine.[3]

FIGURE 4. Winslow Homer, *Leaping Trout* (1889). Watercolor on paper. Portland Museum of Art, Maine, bequest of Charles Shipman Payson (1988.55.7). Courtesy of Meyersphoto.com. © Trustees of the Portland Museum of Art, Maine.

The idea of *Leaping Trout* and other pictures like it seems to be that we might realize these nonapparent objects by seeing them from a new angle. They have that focus on *apparency*, to use again the term that Dewey uses to describe how something gets foregrounded in the stream of consciousness and becomes "momentarily focal." *Leaping Trout* suggests a kind of sudden visualization from out of the stream. A fish rises into relevance and takes on substance like never before. It comes to bear on us by its emphasis. It grows impressive and distinct. For as long as we look at the picture, Homer puts it at the center of our consciousness. It is like the "close-up" that Hugo Münsterberg describes on a film screen that "[objectifies] in our world of perception our mental act of attention." Every work of art, Emerson writes, "is the tyrant of the hour, and concentrates attention on itself." We will pass to some other object soon enough, but for the time being it is the power of the artist "to detach, and to magnify by detaching" and to suggest to us how much "it is the right and property of all natural objects . . . to be for their moment the top of the world. A squirrel leaping from bough to bough . . . fills the eye not less than a lion."[4] Not less than a leaping trout too.

Once more, the word *relevant* suggests the act of lifting or raising into relief. In *Leaping Trout* it is the trout that does the leaping. Insofar as the active agent of this picture is merely a trout, we cast toward something that we almost certainly would have ignored or missed save for the fact that it now acts as a kind of lure. I actually want to say that the trout *is* the orangish-reddish lure to which it is likened in the painting: we can see how the fly to the right mimics the shape of the flying, open-mouthed trout that is the paramount reality of the picture to the exclusion of everything else. In other words, the trout is the bait: how will we take it? Are we hooked? "A 'lure,'" Roland Barthes writes, "endlessly affirmed, against everything, becomes a truth."[5]

"I was absolutely interested," writes John Ruskin, "in marmots and chamois, in tomtits and trout. If only they would stay still and let me look at them." In *Praeterita,* he says that at the root of all he has "usefully become" is this absolute *interest* he has come to take in "the living inhabitation of the world—the grazing and nesting in it,—the spiritual power of the air, the rocks, the waters, to be in the midst of it, and rejoice and wonder at it, and help it if I could,—happier if it needed no help of mine." The *help* that he might give is that interest that makes the air, rocks, and waters alive to him and his readers, which is why they sometimes need his attention or, like the tomtits and trout, let him look at them. In *Modern Painters,* Ruskin writes that the artist's work "is essentially this: it is the gathering and arranging of material by imagination, so as to have in it at last the harmony or helpfulness of life, and the passion or emotion of life." It is not hard to see why Ruskin appreciated the Pre-Raphaelites especially for the special help they gave to the natural world, under whose microscopic lens viewers could see things they had never seen before in art: the vein of a leaf, a blade of grass, a garden stamen by stamen and even, yes, "the spots of the trout."[6] Now a trout could been seen for its texture, proportion, and line. Its flecks of orange and reddishness were important. The new objectivity meant that all these things could be taken on their own terms and *as* vital and to the exact degree that the nature of them admits.

But the key for Ruskin remains that they are *taken,* increasingly admitted into the picture as "vehicles of expression and emotion" and "absolutely and in themselves as valuable as they can be." He writes of the "human, pre-eminently human, feeling it is that loves a stone for a stone's sake, and a cloud for a cloud's" and that makes that stone and cloud matters of interest and care: "a little flower," for example, "apprehended in the very plain and leafy fact of it," but with all "the associations and passions" that "crowd around it." When describing the difference between the "mere botanist's knowledge of plants, and the great poet's or painter's knowledge of them," Ruskin writes in the preface to the second edition of *Modern Painters*, that while the botanist counts the stamens and affixes names, the poet or painter observes every aspect of the plant's color, seizing on the serenity or tremulousness of its hues that he may render all these characteristics as vehicles of expression. "Thenceforward," Ruskin exclaims, "the flower is to him a living creature." It has "passions breathing in its motion." "It is," he says, "a voice rising from the earth."[7]

Whenever, that is, the poet or painter, selects an object for attention, it becomes powerful and no longer inert. It carries the subject who apprehends it "off his feet." It *moves* him, Ruskin says, and "*ought* to throw him off his balance." It makes him want to leave off his accustomed course and "do something he did not want to do before." He feels "shaken" by the object, just like that irresistible earthquake of 1906 (another "voice rising from the earth") shook William James to the core. The object, to return to Ruskin's phrase, is given *help*—the "helpfulness of life"—which is why, if you remember, James says that it is *welcome*.[8]

For Ruskin, a picture is always the greatest expression of the help that interest gives, where "if it *be* drawn for love of it, it will never be wrong." He writes of the "principles of selection" that make a picture "highly interesting" by calling out *that* stone or *that* cloud from the "cold" mix of sensations that "pass perpetually before the eyes without conveying any impression to the brain at all." The chosen object of any picture will seem vital, while other objects "pass actually unseen, not merely unnoticed, but in the full clear sense of the word unseen." So, Ruskin associates selection "with love" much in the way Emerson defines a love object as "a representative of all select things." That fish, stone, or cloud becomes *lovely* when of all things we pay attention to it. In his essay "Love," Emerson says that for the youth love "makes all things alive and significant. Nature grows conscious. Every bird on the boughs of the tree sings now to his heart and soul. The notes are almost articulate. The clouds have faces, as he looks on them."[9]

James writes in "A World of Pure Experience" that "we live, as it were, upon the front edge of an advancing wave-crest, and our sense of a determinate direction in falling forward is all we cover of the future of our path." In Homer's painting, *The Fog Warning; or, Halibut Fishing,* a fisherman's dory is falling forward on the crest of a wave (fig. 5). The future of his path is a fog. He has caught some nice halibut, and as he looks toward the horizon, he sees his ship. But he also sees an ominous fog bank stealing in around the ship that guides his course, and his little dory rocks high on the waves. In the rapid stream of events that, for James, bears us along, there are all sorts of things that pass through the mind in the "fringes" of consciousness—"mere nascencies of cognition, premonitions, awarenesses of direction"—but wherever life communicates an "eagerness" or a problem to the person who lives it, "there the life becomes genuinely significant"; wherever this eagerness is found, there is "the excitement, of reality; and there *is* 'importance' in the only real and positive sense in which importance ever anywhere can be."[10]

In *The Fog Warning,* Homer paints the moment at which the fog becomes important—at which the fog *comes to matter*—showing itself against the background of the horizon with astounding density of form for a fog. Something in the background of the scene emerges as "sensibly real" to the fisherman, to remember how the great earthquake felt to James. In fact the fog is as real to the halibut fisherman as a hook to its prey, which may be why Homer painted the fog to look so much like a traditional halibut hook (specifically designed for the mouth and feeding habits of a halibut and widely distinguishable in the late nineteenth century [fig. 6]). I find that the fisherman is *hooked* in the way that the fog demands his attention. He comes to see its potency and dynamic connection to his life in the dory. The fog in the painting *is* the hook that throughout his writings Whitehead calls the "objective lure" for these feelings of connection.[11]

Something as insubstantial as a fog seems to have solidified and is on the verge of coming to life. We see it, too, as the fisherman presumably does, in the way the right edge of the right streamer of the fog resembles his profile. (Can you see the fisherman's silhouette in the fog? The contour of his nose touches the clouds!). "The clouds have faces," says Emerson, when we attend to them. "Nature grows conscious." We could say that for the fisherman, the fog is as much of a "personification" as the 1906 earthquake was to James. Or we could say that the picture represents what Ruskin calls a "pathetic fallacy," with the fisherman projecting himself and his emotional state onto the natural world so that "nature grows conscious" insofar as it appears to reflect his conscious state of mind.

FIGURE 5. Winslow Homer. *The Fog Warning* (1885). Oil on canvas. Museum of Fine Arts, Boston. Anonymous gift with credit to the Otis Norcross Fund (94.72). © 2022 Museum of Fine Arts, Boston.

But Homer does not give us projection in any false or distorting sense. This is not a case of being so overwhelmed with emotion that the fisherman perceives wrongly, like the poet that Ruskin describes "who perceives wrongly, because he feels, and to whom the primrose is anything else than a primrose." The poet who is consumed by his own feelings and fixes his thoughts on them alone is finally uninterested in the primrose but suffers instead from a kind of sensualism or "disease." He sees the primrose as anything other than a primrose—"a star, or a sun, or a fairy's shield, or a forsaken maiden," as an image or emblem of his emotions. (But Ruskin wants him to stand instead "in his due relation to other creatures, and to inanimate things—know them all and love them.")

Nor is *The Fog Warning* a case of the naive objectivism of the poet or painter who, Ruskin says, "perceives rightly, because he does not feel, and to whom the primrose is very accurately the primrose, because he does not love it." Knowledge for its own sake is what Ruskin calls "asceticism."

FIGURE 6. Halibut hook (nineteenth century). © McCord Museum, Montreal (M13176).

It is the opposite of sensualism, but no better. It is the symptom of someone whose mind is unimpressionable and made up and who will never be "moved" by the things that he perceives. E. D. Hirsch calls knowledge for its own sake a "pathetic fallacy," too, because it makes an autonomous or "independent" entity of something as abstract or disembodied as knowledge, and while that knowledge may be valid, it also may have no value that we can see. Value is always value *to* someone. One should feel that that knowledge is worth having.

In *The Fog Warning*, Homer shows us neither an object without emotion nor emotion without an object. He shows us an object of emotion and concern. His painting has to do with just how the mind comes *to attend* to its object—meaning, again, literally how it gets *stretched out* toward that object as when Dewey writes "attention is most alert and stretched, when, because of unusual situations, there is great concern about the issue."[12] Here the fisherman's mind appears to be stretched out all the way from the dory to that fog on the horizon where we see it take shape.

Homer shows the very moment at which the fisherman notices the fog and makes a connection between the fog and himself. Right now, it comes to matter to him. He realizes it all at once. *The Fog Warning* is the painting of a fog that is culminating in consciousness.

Homer and James were exact contemporaries, born a few years apart and dying in the same year in 1910. What are contemporaries? Whitehead says that they imply the "co-presence" of persons and practices of thought and feeling that are distinct from each other but also capable of being understood with regard to each other. To have contemporaries, in other words, is to suggest what might be out there and available for this kind of understanding, what might be, to use the word that Whitehead uses, *relevant* to each. It is to wonder what difference one person or idea could introduce with respect to another and to imagine how that "objectified entity . . . is a datum in the experience of the subject."

When critics define what it means to be contemporaries, they tend to look to Nietzsche's use of the term *contemporary* in *Untimely Observations*, which translates roughly from German as "those who accompany us in time." It is always with the sense, as Paul Rabinow writes, that "to accompany others in time depends, because 'to accompany' is a transitive verb, on where you are, where you are seeking to go, and with whom you want to be accompanied."[13]

I would like to think of James as contemporary with Homer and as a kind of accompaniment to him and his paintings. To put it differently, I think that James offers occasions that are relevant and available to our understanding of Homer's paintings in which we can assume an attitude of "adjacency in regard to them." And not only James, but maybe Emerson, too, since, in Schutz's words, we can be connected with contemporaries we have "never met"; we even can make a contemporary of a "predecessor."[14] Homer certainly seems to have had contemporaries in James and Emerson in the way that he works, like them, toward a thematization of attention as if of consciousness itself.

I guess I simply hope that it was worth the trouble to discuss James and Emerson before looking at Homer's paintings. The paintings invite understanding of how "importance is made" in terms analogous to theirs. The paintings also exemplify how much the mental activity of attention that James and Emerson helped to define can be just like the experience of looking at a painting: lifting into relief the now-material thing so that it might be resurrected or saved, bringing it into view in an undivided moment. It feels worth it! That moment, to remember James on how deeply red the color red will appear when we really focus on it, seems saturated.

In *The Life Line*, a woman, who appears to be unconscious, is suspended on a breeches buoy between her foundering ship and the shore. She is sitting on the front edge of a lifesaver that encircles a man whose arms and clasped hands encircle her waist. The man's face is completely obscured by a fluttering red scarf that is tied to the rope to signal the location of the buoy—it is a red, red flag.

In the 1880s the use of breeches buoys reduced the loss of life from shipwrecks by up to 75 or 87 percent, depending on the account. For the United States Life-Saving Service, it was much faster and safer than a lifeboat. A cork buoy, with a pair of canvas breeches sewn in, would hang on a single "traveler" or pulley; it created a basketlike seat for a passenger or for a coast guardsman to carry a passenger who was unable to cross alone. Homer began painting shipwrecks and storms at sea while living for a year and a half in Cullercoats, a small fishing village near Tynemouth, England, known for its volunteer lifesaving crews and also for its own breeches-buoy rescue that took place at night by the light of rockets and that Homer narrowly missed seeing when he was there in 1881. Several of his pictures from Cullercoats show figures watching a shipwreck and rescue from the new watchtower. In *Perils of the Sea*, men in oilskins point down the coast while two women grouped above the rail clutch their wraps against the storm (fig. 7). We are meant to understand their sense of being cleaved; their gray isolation and fear of loss.

When Homer returned first to New York and then to the coast of Maine, where he finally lived year-round, he continued to paint shipwrecks with spectators. Even in *The Life Line*, where they are hard to see at the far right, we have figures like the women of Cullercoats watching from the towering cliff on the other side of the ropes. This time, though, the shipwreck feels different, more immediate, since, as viewers, we are given the vantage of watching the action from some intermediate point on the water, as if we, too, were at sea. We get the feeling of being pulled in, the threat of immersion, as those two figures get pulled up in the vapor and mist, bobbing, rocking—and then somehow we are buoyed too. I take it that the reality of life outside the picture is the viewer's own lifeline. We can philosophize about this mechanism of salvation while riding the waves at little risk.

The woman is soaked through, and her dress clings tightly to the round-

FIGURE 7. Winslow Homer, *Perils of the Sea* (1881).
Courtesy of Clark Art Institute (clarkart.edu).

ness of her thighs and her breast, which swells heavily over his hand. Her voluptuous form is pulled down between the man's legs. Her flesh peeks out over stockings where the skirt has ripped and clings higher. The erotic elements are hard to miss. The two figures are separated only by the girdle of the life saver, like a kind of chastity belt, as Jules Prown describes it. The man embraces her tensely just as his thumb seems to be thrusting into the inverted V of her armpit above his clasp. Behind them the tip of the rock juts suggestively toward the crotch of ropes as they meet at the pulley.

The sensuality of the picture was not lost on reviewers, who commented on how the wet clothing reveals the woman's whole form, making the dress cling to her thighs and bust (she is a "buxom lassie," one writes), even as the picture finally would not "shock the most decorous."[15] The two figures rock to and fro on the breeches buoy; the woman has been knocked out but appears in the kind of swooning posture that elsewhere in art suggests ecstasy. In back of them, there is an explosive column of spume.

Why is that red scarf there? Critics have never really figured it out or accounted for the weird effect of having that shock of red at the center of the slate and dirty greenish water and just beneath the fulcrum of the pulley. We know from X-rays that Homer added it late, over the man's delineated face, like a blind. (Prown wonders if we were to unveil the face whether we might find Homer himself; the "blind Homer" with his epic visions; or maybe the image of a very isolated bachelor artist living alone in Maine while sublimating his desires in his paintings. I don't know.)

I do know that the red scarf adds to the sensuality of the picture, ripples of red that seem to emanate from the woman's breast and that alert us to the patches of red elsewhere, on that flashy thigh, for example. Just beneath the pulley, the brilliant scarf at the center of a painting dominated by the dullest greenish tones pulls us in.

The painting is clearly about tension, realized in sexual tension and also in the tautness of the thick hawser and thinner pull line as they meet at the pulley as well as in the heavy bodies tugging downward at the same ropes that keep them suspended. The buoy is traveling right from ship to shore (we infer this, Prown says, because the hawser to the left has been rung dry by the pulley's passage, while drops of water still cling to the right). The buoy is moving forward, but Homer seizes on a moment of suspension in which all the lateral and downward forces and intersecting lines tug and pull. They leave us hanging. Of course, there is the utter suspense and danger of the rescue. The cresting waves that converge in the eruption of white spume just where the pulley is make it that much more charged. So these figures beat on against the current. Can the man hold on?

All the elements of the picture are sustaining and interacting with each other in the way the two figures at the center are. We see, to use Dewey's words, the harnessing of "resistance and tension" in a composition that is vertically bisected by the buoy (with its breeches or harness), the waves cresting on the left and right, the ropes passing in front of both figures and then on each side of the pulley pulled taut (themselves tied to two unseen polarities, left and right). It is a moment of equilibrium that Dewey might call "*an* experience" of some intensity when all the elements of a situation are gathered up into a whole, interrelated picture, and there is no slack. Consciousness arises, he says, when "a situation becomes tensional."[16]

Homer has concentrated our attention at the point of stress. Whatever immanent sense of consummation there may be—in the physical effort and weight of the bodies, in the column of spume, in the experience of looking at a painting dramatizing the interplay between forces and resistances (the water gathering into breakers; the undertow sucking it back)—it all comes to a head just where a head is meant to be but where we see a red scarf instead. At the center of the picture, where everything is just managing to hang together, that scarf makes itself felt as a challenge. What exactly does all this tension bring to consciousness? A red scarf, first of all. It must be more than a mere accessory.

Art theorists of the nineteenth century thought a lot about the role of accessories, as when Ruskin writes to Frederick Leighton about the "theory of accessories" in his paintings or else the "exquisite perspective" that "bandeaux, braids, garlands, jewels, flowers, or anything else" lend to their subjects in the best Venetian paintings. In *Modern Painters*, Ruskin describes how the most "earnest, and pervading thought" of great art is "aided by every accessary of detail, colour." He describes how an artist's power in rendering a subject "will be perpetually showing itself in accessaries and minor points."[17]

The most important book for Homer on the practice of painting was Michel-Eugène Chevreul's *The Laws of Contrast of Colour*, first published in France in 1839, which describes how "accessory" hues and tones, modify a viewer's sense of the dominant colors in a picture. In Chevreul, such "accessories" direct attention toward a picture's main subject by complementing it in a field of relative colors. Homer's brother gave him a condensed English translation of Chevreul's book of color theory in 1860 that Homer cherished the rest of his life. Homer called it "my Bible." Inside his worn copy, he tipped a photograph of a fishing boat in Cullercoats.

Chevreul's treatise teaches that colors have values. They work as an expressive medium in an interactive field of relations and contrasts, so that across a picture every tint has a tonal value within the complex whole. What happens when we think of a color as part of the big picture rather than as a discrete phenomenon? Chevreul's idea, so important to Homer, is that colors get modified in relation to other visual stimuli because the human eye takes into account the manner in which objects reflect and absorb light and also the effect of their reflected light on other objects. Colors can modulate across a canvas, like microclimates. Principal color elements may be true to nature, but accessory hues, tones, and qualities will vary and determine what is visually brought to bear on an object and what it highlights in turn. In other words, color is dynamic and perceived relationally: even a seemingly monochromatic scene is actually resonating with consonances and dissonances of accessory hues, with spots of red in green or spots of green in red. These other colors may be nearly imperceptible but create, in relation to the main color, what Chevreul describes as intervals on the chromatic scale that make us alive to the main color and the feeling it gives. We could not have the experience of red or green without them.

A good artist knows that color needs some other color to make itself felt. So however a color makes itself felt, its depth and force result from the touches of accessory pigments harmonizing or clashing with it. These accessories work by inviting or "fixing" the spectator's attention in certain ways. Primary colors look most saturated, for example, when offset with their complementaries (for red, green; for orange, blue). Colors appear to us as they do because of the way they interact with "accessories," because of what Chevreul describes as the vibration between complementary or adjacent tones. Colors that are near to each other on the chromatic scale (say, yellow and orange) vibrate quickly and create dissonance, while complementary colors (at much large intervals on the chromatic scale—say, red and green) vibrate slowly and create harmony. The different vibrational speeds between hues are what give each scene its energy, vibrancy, and, in a picture, accessories may be adjusted to create a harmonious whole. The psychological capacity of a color to arouse emotion finally results from the chromatic effects of other, surrounding colors acting on it. If that blue makes me feel that I have never seen a better, truer blue, then I better believe it is shot through with orange.[18]

In *The Life Line*, the accessory at the center of the picture is the accessory color in Chevreul's theory, the red-orange to Homer's green-blue sea. The red scarf is an instance both of what Chevreul calls the "draperies, ornaments, in a word, all the accessories" that complement the main figure of a picture and of the patch of color that becomes "accessory to" its theme. Homer's paintings often stage this dramatic encounter Chevreul describes between subjects and accessories; the contrasts and harmonies focus attention on the relations of elements within a reciprocal system and the way that accessories bring their subjects to light.

Chevreul's particular interest in the color of "draperies" as accessories derived from his job as director of dye works at the Gobelins tapestry factory in Paris. His treatise even includes a section on how draped fabrics of different colors complement skin tones in art. The red scarf in *The Life Line* works very much on the principle of the patches of red drapery in the tapestries Chevreul knew well: the red billows of fabric in François Boucher's famous tapestry of Neptune, for example, reproduced in the nineteenth century at Gobelins where Boucher was the director a century before. Neptune, in the flaps of his red mantle, is saving Amymone from rape by a satyr; like *The Life Line*, it is a picture of a sea rescue.

"The greater the number of different colors and accessories in a composition," Chevreul writes, the more difficulty the artist has in "[fixing] the attention of the spectator upon the physiognomy of the figures which he would reproduce." So *The Life Line*, as if in response to Chevreul, has just one accessory that we can see. It offsets the face of the woman and also the monotonous sea that might overwhelm us at any moment except for the way that that red scarf keeps us focused. Speculating at the time about why in the world the red scarf is there, the *Evening Telegraph* writes, "Winslow Homer originally painted the face of the coast guardsman in his masterwork 'The Life Line,' but finding that it scattered the interest, boldly threw over it the shawl of the fainting woman who lies in his arms." The *New York Times* writes that "the hiding of his features concentrates the attention very cleverly on his comrade." Other reviewers comment on the device as "an expedient which succeeds in centring all the interest on the female figure" or else in hiding the man's face, which otherwise would "distract attention from the principle figure to create two centres of interest." In *Principles of Art* (1887), John C. Van Dyke remarks on Homer's effort to "intensify and increase" interest in the woman through the use of the red scarf that is "wrought out for the express purpose of preserving the value of the girl as a principal, at the expense of the man as an accessory." Homer painted the woman from life—from a mixed-race Black woman he hired as a model in New York. He would have learned from Chevreul's book that red fabric is well suited for bringing darker complexions into relief.[19]

Everything in the picture conspires to draw attention to the woman who is being raised on the buoy. Yet Homer especially draws attention to attention's appurtenances: the blotting out of what remains beside the central focus; the way this focus must be accompanied by oversight of the rest. It reminds me of Emerson or James describing how attention involves a choice, a selecting principle. Something will always be accessory to the central focus, whose intelligibility and distinctness depends on disregarding what surrounds it. Here it depends on literally effacing what surrounds it. Another figure is banished from our sight. What gives a work of art its "harmony," its "superiority," James says, "over works of nature, is wholly due to *elimination*."

If the accessory is the first thing we see in *The Life Line,* it may be that Homer wishes to state just how a painting consists in controlling this process. That accessory is his statement piece! He shows that he will devise every element to facilitate a focus. Every last element will be contributory, and the result will be a picture that hangs together just as tightly as the figures on the pulley. The painting will gather together all these elements as relating to each other, interacting and sustaining or resisting each other in this one tensive, dynamic moment. An artist, Dewey says, "cultivates [resistance and tension], not for their own sake but because of their potentialities, bringing to living consciousness an experience that is unified and total."[20]

Dewey calls an aesthetic experience a "consummation." I think that we are meant to see Homer's figures as the sensual embodiment of that experience, pressing intently into each other, rocking at the point of stress between the upward lift and downward pull, the momentum and the undertow. We perceive a work, Dewey says, as "the organized and organizing medium of the rhythmic ebb and flow of expectant impulse, forward and retracted movement, resistance and suspense, with fulfillment and consummation." A picture should feel integrated to the highest degree. It should be held in tension. All the material in it should be "fraught with suspense and moving toward its own consummation." Our sense of its beauty is "the response to that which to reflection is the consummated movement of matter integrated through its inner relations into a single qualitative whole." It is the response to the kind of experimental togetherness we see here, with everything bearing on everything else and all the elements mixing together and gathering force like a column of sea spray about to explode.

"Consider a good picture," Whitehead writes. "No extra patch of scarlet can be placed in it without wrecking its unity." A good picture, he says, "expresses a unity of mutual relevance. It resents the suggestion of addition." Or, as he says elsewhere about the visual perception of a picture, "an extra patch of red does not constitute a mere addition; it alters the whole balance." What appears to be an extra patch of red in *The Life Line,* a mere accessory, is very much to the point. It contributes meaningfully to the "satisfaction" of a picture like this. The painting makes it relevant. We simply would be unable to focus without it.

Beside the red scarf, we shift our attention to the woman on the lifesaver. We perceive this central figure as being saturated, soaked through with the surrounding elements like a woman drenched from the waves, a figure bursting through the fabric and now appearing for everyone to see, a figure whose sensual contours are made visible and "momentarily focal." I think it is the idea of the "consummatory phase of experience" that Homer is trying to float for us here—as if on a buoy.[21]

The lifeline is finally a very elaborate device. Its obvious purpose is to pull someone in.

. . .

How do we create a meaningful object? We need to hold it out from the rest. A painting, Homer suggests, is the result of a changed attention, and it tries to change our attention in turn. It has the quality of bringing out some aspect of the world as prominent so that we become aware of it. It selects in everything we have the potential to perceive the features that are important for some purpose while showing us how to appreciate those features and concentrate on them. Homer wants us to discover the salient point of what we see.

"Saliency," Emerson writes in his journal in 1857, is "the principle of levity, the *sal volatile*, which is the balance, or offset, to the mountains & masses." Any sort of thing can have salience, but for Emerson the essence of it will always be on this "principle of levity": "it is the next finer ascent or metamorphosis of gravity, chemistry, vegetation, animal life, the same thing, on the next higher plane." *Salient* derives from the present participle of the Latin verb *salire*, which means "to leap." So, to have *saliency* is to have this quality of "leaping" or of jumping out. Let's picture it like Homer's *Leaping Trout*. It is, Emerson writes elsewhere, "the antagonist of matter and gravitation." To be salient is to be perceived as leaping out, springing up, or, more figuratively, as becoming prominent or "interesting" in the way that "Rabelais, Homer, and Shakespeare, and Cervantes" are for Emerson the salient figures of their time and place. Their "native force . . . escapes in fine jets, illuminating the time and place where they are" and everything else from their perspective. To be salient is to rise above what is "more or less torpid" and dull, which is why Emerson makes a play on saliency as the *sal volatile*, the smelling salts, that will arouse consciousness and command awareness.[22]

When we speak of the "salient point" of a work, idea, or experience, we are speaking of the aspect of it that best captures our interest and guides our general view. Defining salience as a perceptual process within social psychology, Gianluigi Guido invokes the figure-ground principle: something standing out in a perceptual field triggers those thoughts and memories that bear on that figure and make it feel important. A very old medical term, *salient point* refers to the pulse or beat of the heart as it first appears in an embryo; it is the point from which all else springs—the heart of the matter. The Renaissance physician William Harvey believed that the salient point (*punctum saliens*) derived from the soul of the ovum (hence the heart). (I am visualizing the beats on an electrocardiogram as the salient points.) Emerson describes how Linnaeus, "like a naturalist, esteeming the globe a big egg, called London the *punctum saliens* in the yolk of the world." The salient point comes to mean (of material things) that which stands above or beyond the general surface, jutting out, a projection, and (of immaterial things) that which emerges as most prominent in a person's awareness. In remembering past experiences, the salient points spring to mind. "Ah," writes Emerson at age sixty-two, "the decays of memory, of fancy, of the saliency of thought!"[23]

"This creative saliency, this saliency of thought, this *habit of saliency*" is what, for Emerson, allows us to concentrate on a moment, to recognize in our experience some particular high point that feels meaningful when we reflect on it. Finding salience is how we take only our own "out of the multiplicity that sweeps and circles" around us. It is the "terminus of a past thought" that also leads "to new sallies of the imagination and new progress of wisdom." (Emerson here understands that *salience* and *sally* [forth] borrow from the same Latin root.) This is how thinking progresses, which is why Emerson defines the opposite of salience as "the path of indolence, of cows, of sluggish animal life; as near gravitation as it can go." If only we can see something as important—as giving importance and essential in some way—it will be a kind of uplift, a way of rising out of our sluggishness, thoughtlessness, or routine. We can be like a fish leaping out of its element. And so Emerson associates salience with the moment of "transition" between the past and the future—between where we were and might go—and with "not pausing but proceeding."[24] He associates it with the ability to sally forth. To return to its original medical meaning, if we have salience, we have a pulse.

Again, for Emerson this creative salience is "the moment of transition, as if the form were just ready to flow into other forms." It is the moment in which the flow of existence is gathered together and stalled in some perceivable form before being released again "to flow into other forms." "The experience of poetic creativeness" is "not found in staying at home nor yet in travelling, but in transitions from one to the other, which must therefore be adroitly managed to present as much transitional surface as possible": it is "the seashore, sea seen from shore, shore seen from sea, the taste of two metals in contact, and our enlarged powers at the approach and at the departure of a friend." In his journals, Emerson writes, "Every thing good in nature & the world is in that moment of transition, the foam hangs but a moment on the wave."[25] In mathematics, a salient point is the point at which two branches of a curve with different tangents meet, but do not cross; as the curve passes through this point it "jumps back up." It marks the moment when the curve's function (dy/dx) becomes discontinuous "by changing suddenly of value." Salience, in other words, is the sudden perception of a new value. It marks an immediate surge in the register of value. Every salient fact, Emerson writes, is some "fulcrum of the spirit" on which we pivot, then sally forth.[26]

In Homer's *The Life Line*, the high jet of spume suggests a moment of salience right at the "fulcrum" of the pulley. From its earliest uses, salience finally is a term to describe water (*salience* is "of water") jetting forth, springing, spouting, leaping upwards. A whale's salient spout. A salient spring. Something that "escapes in fine jets," as Emerson puts it. The salience we see in *The Life Line* appears everywhere in Homer: in *West Point, Prout's Neck*, for example, where a single wave, crashing high against the breakers, is the salient event (fig. 8). From the boundless flow, we have this one moment of condensation—a form springs up before our eyes. The shaft of water, so abstracted out, literalizes for me Patricia Junker's observation of Homer's "ability to reduce his subject to its salient forms."[27] The foam hangs but a moment on the wave.

Homer considered *West Point, Prout's Neck* to be the best work he had done—"no ordinary affair," he said—and there really is nothing ordinary about it or about any of these paintings that assert what it is like to see salience or to raise matters we may never have considered as salient for us. In an "ordinary sense, the ocean has long been thought of as a medium invisible to its users," John Durham Peters writes. But Homer takes what is ordinarily invisible and gives it salience, condensing it into animate form, as if to assert, with Whitehead, that "there is nothing in the real world which is merely an inert fact." His pictures are about the *expression* of salience—literally, the *pressing out* or *pressing forth* of these subjects that must have been mere background but now are made to leap out, the way his leaping trout appears to transgress the barrier of the picture and turn its head toward us. The background comes to the surface and brings its contents before the viewer.

FIGURE 8. Winslow Homer, *West Point, Prout's Neck* (1900). Courtesy of Clark Art Institute (clarkart.edu).

These subjects *express*, or press forth, as if from some internal pressure. Look at *Cannon Rock* (fig. 9): we cannot keep *this* "advancing wave crest" at bay, rising up, falling forward, spilling over the frame. It is trying to emerge! It just might become part of our reality. What ordinarily would have been mere background, invisible to us, is raised as the focus of consciousness. We are made aware of its presence. Homer is picturing what it means for it to *come to us* since it is rolling forward, expressively, emptying its contents. It is hard to imagine it won't bear on us right away.

In his lecture, "Human Immortality," James cites the psychophysiologist Gustav Fechner's notion of consciousness as crests of "waves" that rise above a "threshold." He includes in his notes to the lecture Fechner's diagram of a waveform rising above a "horizontal basal line or surface" in which the line represents the threshold of consciousness and in which "whatever lies below the threshold, being unconscious, separates the conscious crests." The threshold of consciousness itself changes under different circumstances. When the threshold falls, the amplitude of the waves that cross above it

FIGURE 9. Winslow Homer, *Cannon Rock* (1895). Oil on canvas. Gift of George A. Hearn, 1906. The Metropolitan Museum of Art, New York.

increases, suggesting how "we grow conscious of things of which we should be unconscious at other times." So, for Fechner and James, those crests represent our "general wakefulness and the general direction of our attention as a wave." Each wave represents a special mental state of awareness of the infinite things of which we are normally unaware but that "float into our finite world" at these heightened moments only as "glows of feeling, glimpses of insight." At these moments they flow into "our special stream of consciousness" from the vast "mother-sea" of consciousness. Maybe they are intimations of "immortality," to use James's word from the lecture, but, in a plainer sense, those high rising waves mark the intense mental state when whatever it is that may be beyond consciousness gets "transmitted" into consciousness. The opposite of this state is "drowsiness."[28]

The feeling of an "aweful power in this creative saliency, this saliency of thought, this *habit of saliency*, of not pausing but going on" is, Emerson writes, "a sort of importation & domestication of the Divine Effort, in a man." I think he means by this hyperbolic claim what he elsewhere describes as the power of thinking and also of art to bring something otherwise vast and unfathomable to mind. It is the ability to bring to us (to "import") in salient form what we had never thought of taking in—or could never otherwise think of at all. It is the power to harness momentarily that otherwise lost to us thing as if in a breeches buoy. Or, it is what Emerson describes elsewhere as "a fixation or momentary eddy in which certain services and powers are taken up" before they are "released again to flow in the currents of the world"; in which they are taken up *as* salient and of the essence right now. A work of art can, for a moment at least, actualize what it means to feel something as important. As to the "*Miracle*" that is poetry and art, Emerson writes in his journal, it can be said, "There is truly but one miracle, the perpetual fact of Being & Becoming, the ceaseless Saliency, the transit from the Vast to the particular, which (one) miracle, one & the same, has for its most universal name, the word *God*."[29]

The Life Line harnesses and lifts up its central figure. It draws our attention to her as if she were as salient as the jet of water that surges in back. The point of all of this is obvious: to preserve what it can on a life preserver. To save a figure from oblivion.

And now when I read Emerson and then look at *The Life Line* and the way the woman on the buoy is held out for our notice, I see that red scarf differently. It looks to me, next to the figure it illuminates, like the annunciating angel in paintings by Botticelli, Raphael, and Rubens, or in so many paintings by Pre-Raphaelites that pick up on these in the nineteenth century (fig. 10). Gabriel always appears with red wings or else draped in the thick folds of red fabric that come to signal the Annunciation. The Virgin is always set off in these pictures by the angel's red wings or billows of red fabric—or sometimes red drapery or bedding on a bed or hung like a tapestry—that serve as surrogates for the angel and the announcement he makes. What is Homer's picture after all but a scene of Annunciation? An act of making known and intimate to the senses, of manifesting to the mind (without words). Like an angel, or "messenger," it *comes to us* bearing messages. It reveals at once an incarnation, a sensible embodiment of shared meaning, a gathering of something unfathomable in a tangible form we can recognize

FIGURE 10. Edward Burne-Jones, *The Annunciation* (*"The Flower of God"*) (1863). Watercolor on paper. Private collection. © Christie's Images / Bridgeman Images.

and experience. This is the miracle of a "transit from the Vast to the particular" that Emerson calls by the name of *God* and sees as the miracle of art. It is a *pregnant* moment, a salient moment. It means that things will be saved and not lost.

. . .

I have been suggesting that the point of Homer's pictures is to express a salient point and that he tends to do this in very tangible ways—by making us aware of how he is holding everything in suspense, taking in the slack,

FIGURE 11. Winslow Homer, *The Herring Net* (1885). Mr. and Mrs. Martin A. Ryerson Collection. Art Institute of Chicago.

arranging the moment to call attention to particular values. His pictures comment on the optical conditions for lifting into consciousness some figure raised out of the drift. From the great flow of things that rush by unnoticed, something will get drawn out or raised. Whitehead would say, "Here is something that matters!"[30] Homer is extracting whatever it is from the undertow and catching it with a net. He is catching, filtering, and bringing it up glistening, as a kind of resurrection.

The cross of the wooden oars in *The Herring Net* is just the most iconic way of saying that these pictures are articles of faith (fig. 11). The fisherman who hoists up the net bows forward in a devotional stance; his oblique lines parallel the cross behind him. The triangular composition of the oars recalls the triangular geometry of the breeches buoy in *The Life Line*. Both pictures preserve the pyramidal shape of religious paintings by Raphael and others since Homer also is giving form to a notion of salvation. I wonder whether maybe their triangulating shapes remind us, too, of the three-point perspective that puts the viewer in relation to the buoy or boat. The viewpoint of the onlooker always comes into play, because these pictures keep projecting outward and spilling into our space. In *The Herring Net*, the foreshortening of the boat has the effect of tilting it toward us like the head of the leaping trout. The waves are too immediate and rolling forward. The viewer stands just beyond the frame somewhere along the lines of where the fishing net submerses to the right, and so we get the sense of being there just underneath with the herrings. Those figures in the boat are also the fishers of men. Maybe they are baiting us to reflect on our own relation to whatever else Homer is putting together for the purposes of this picture—all in the same boat.

In *The Herring Net*, once again a buoy shines front and center, making a theme of the function of raising up, lifting, or floating for our consideration. Like the "life-buoy" of a coffin that pops up at the end of *Moby-Dick*, it is something to hold onto. The buoy in the picture is reddish-orange and, once again, the attentional pull of the accessory colors in Homer, including the red flecks of the herrings' gills, create ocular vibrations within the darker tones of the water. "What attracts my attention shall have it," says Emerson. I think the particular effects of the paintings are premised on their attracting our eye and being seen as having attracted Homer's first. They are visual performances of the way Homer's own vision is "a selecting principle, gathering his like to him," then holding it up for us to see. A person's genius, Emerson continues, "takes only his own, out of the multiplicity that sweeps and circles round him"; it is "like one of those booms which are set out from the shore on rivers to catch drift-wood."[31]

The last picture Homer ever completed was called *Driftwood* (fig. 12). Theodore Stebbins says that Homer "conceived it as a valedictory effort"; his nephew had told an earlier critic that Homer "knew he would never paint again." *Driftwood* shows a massive log wedged between rocks on the shoreline and the bent figure of a man in oilskins with a rope. The waves are rolling forward, and as the water crashes against the rocks, it whips up and sprays. Homer could not decide what to call the picture, having written *Spoon Drift* on the back of the stretcher but calling it *Drift Wood* in a letter to his dealer in New York, and then only deciding on *Driftwood* when the dealer asked which one the title would be. *Spoondrift* refers to the fine mist that blows from the spume on the crashing waves. As the title, it would have drawn attention to the sea itself, but Homer finally draws attention to the foreground instead and to the act of catching driftwood marked by the bent man with the rope and his back to the shore. That figure, in Stebbins's words, "comes as close to being a self-portrait as anything Homer painted."[32]

FIGURE 12. Winslow Homer. *Driftwood* (1909). Oil on canvas.
Henry H. and Zoe Oliver Sherman Fund and other funds (1993.564).
© 2022 Museum of Fine Arts, Boston.

Critics have assumed that the enormous brown log *is* the driftwood to be caught, and I suppose it is possible; it certainly would be a worthwhile catch for the fisherman with his rope. But the smallness of the rope and the man in the face of that enormous task makes me wonder whether Homer intended the log to be not driftwood so much as "one of those booms that are set out from the shore . . . to catch driftwood," just as Emerson describes. Then it would reinforce the work of that Homer figure, who patiently waits for what the water will give up. The culminating task of the artist is this act of catching if he can. He will find in the sea that "sweeps and circles around him" something brought out of the drift. To him, it will appear as salient as spoondrift.

I think it really doesn't matter whether the painting is called *Driftwood* or *Spoon Drift*—either way. The catching and taking up as "our own" that driftwood suggests depends on the springing into visibility that spoondrift implies. Homer seems to say that the subject of the painting is constituted by the fact that he turned to it, "gathering his like to him," and then called it up again in salient form. The hope is that now we will turn to it, like the figure before us with his back to us. That we will find it expressive (pressing) even as Homer invites us one last time (since he wouldn't paint again) to call it out—one last remarkable, salient moment—as if with Walt Whitman, "You sea!"—before sallying on.

. . .

Whatever might be the point of Homer's paintings from the 1880s and 1890s, he seems to make the process of finding the point thematic. I mean "thematic" the way that Schutz uses the term in describing the process by which something dawns on a person as relevant: "*the thing as it appears to him* in its surroundings, the thing as *phenomenon* . . . is now thematically given to him for interpretation."[33] So it seems that Homer is asking us to find the point—the thing we will not have seen at first that then *appears* to be given to us for interpretation—and sometimes we have to go about finding the point in the most literal ways. It is almost comical actually how the secret of Homer's paintings is that *this point* was there all along and then all at once we are made aware of it—that *this* is the point.

Can you see that thing here in Homer's painting *Moonlight, Wood Island Light* (figs. 13 and 14)? There is more in the picture than we realized. That tiny point of red pigment on the horizon to the right is the light of the Wood Island lighthouse. The red flare of the lighthouse on Wood Island, on the southeast tip of Prout's Neck, shines against a nocturnal sea. The moon, hidden behind a cloud on the horizon to the left, throws a silvery beam on the waves that break saliently over masses of rocks. But it is that other beacon, that red dot, that is most salient here. The painting is named for it. It could not be more significant, nor could this ability to spot the steady beam of a lighthouse in the dark night where only the phosphorescence of the moon otherwise lights on a treacherous coast. If we look long enough at Homer's picture, that minute thing in the background comes to the surface at the limits of perception and gets meaningfully activated. And *that* is the point. We should always look for the point of a picture.

In *Eastern Point Light* (fig. 15), we find it again in the tiny dot of red in the gray-light zone of the horizon. Do you see the point? Between two sailboats backlit by the moon, Homer is making a point of the beam from the Eastern Point lighthouse. "The usual practice among painters was to let the horizon fade into visual and conceptual insignificance," writes Charles Colbert. "Homer's inclusion of a significant detail in the distance has few parallels among the work of his confreres."[34]

What does it mean to make a nearly indistinguishable red dot in the remote distance the point of the picture? For those boats, at least, it is the saving grace (the one good point) of navigating at night. At moments like these, on a boat on the open waters at night by a rocky coast, there is nothing more valuable. While most of the time what constitutes the horizon of our perception is left tacit, here it is "consciously apprehended or realized." Homer is making a point of the horizon so that the perceptual experience of the painting is the process of revealing that object deep in the background. It comes to the surface. It emerges into consciousness. Its tininess or remoteness does not diminish its importance but engages the mind all the more actively for discovering that it has been there all along. Here, in other words, is the perceptual process of finding the object that matters.

I will have more to say later about how, by the late nineteenth century, the idea of finding the point or "getting to the point" became a question for the work of understanding and finding meaning and for philosophical inquiry. F. C. S. Schiller, in his writings on "relevance," describes how, in a successful inquiry, "we progressively narrow down the sphere of the relevant and contract it to 'the point,'" his point being that "for any human purpose we consider only part of the total truth . . . nay, even of what is before the mind." Finding meaning, then, is a process of finding the point and not so much a process of discovering truth but only that small part of the whole truth that serves our present purpose. When we ask what the point of a painting is, it is not to suggest that there are not all sorts of true things that might be said of that painting that are not "to the point." It is not that those things are not also true but that they are "irrelevant" to "conscious, willed, purposive . . . *concentration* upon *the point*."

"Have we the right to make such selections?" Schiller asks. "Assuredly, if we have . . . the right to select the *humanly valuable* part, the right to desist from vain attempts to include everything in a whole which could only

FIGURE 13. Winslow Homer, *Moonlight, Wood Island Light* (1894). Oil on canvas. Gift of George A. Hearn, in memory of Arthur Hoppock Hearn, 1911. The Metropolitan Museum of Art, New York.

be a chaos." Such selection, in other words, is not sheer favoritism; "It is the condition of all effective thinking—indispensable, characteristic, and 'essential.'" It is the way that perception orients itself toward what is most valuable for us right now, like the epiphanic revelation of light from a lighthouse at night. Finding the point is what guides us.

I am trying to suggest that Homer's paintings seem to be very much about activating the horizon. What had been, in James's words, in the "immense horizon" or "fringes" of consciousness comes into the "field of view."[35] It is no longer passive in our perception but "momentarily focal." Homer's horizons do not recede like most horizons but focus attention on some point deep within them brought into our line of sight. It is as if the paintings create

FIGURE 14. Winslow Homer, *Moonlight, Wood Island Light* (1894) (detail).

the experience of consciously realizing the point of his paintings and feeling it emerge. In *Eastern Point Light*, the viewer is unnaturally positioned over the waves—there is no terra firma and an expanse that stretches out indefinitely but there finally is a point to all of it that gives the whole its bearing, its significance, "for there is much more in it than is ever immediately or initially apprehended." That point *is* "the point" of the picture; it is nothing less than the Eastern Point lighthouse of *Eastern Point Light*. Seeing it makes the painting what it is much in the way that Dewey suggests that the "creativeness of consciousness . . . makes objects what they are."

What is deep and buried in the background emerges as the meaningful part. Schiller calls it the "relevant" or "essential" part. The picture's whole point seems to be just how it manages to yield this up from the background in some kind of "dynamic connection" with the self. To see the point is to shift our standpoint as a viewer and to orient the contents of our experience of a picture toward that object at last.

In *Searchlight on Harbor Entrance, Santiago de Cuba* (fig. 16), the steady

FIGURE 15. Winslow Homer, *Eastern Point Light* (1880). Watercolor over graphite on cream wove paper. Gift of Alastair B. Martin, Class of 1938 (x1957–116). Princeton University Art Museum / Art Resource, New York. Photography: Bruce M. White.

beam of the searchlight from the American blockade of Santiago's harbor during the Cuban War also makes the viewer its focus. We are meant to become aware of it far away on the horizon. It represents the most distinctive aspect of the blockade in the use of the ship's searchlight to illuminate the harbor at night and to prevent the Spanish from escaping in the dark. The Americans are in fact winning this war with modern machinery like this searchlight that aims its "steady glare" on the obsolete canon on an old fort in the mouth of Cuba's harbor. The searchlight's focus is "on apparency" and also on us, since Homer is employing that same "expressive stratagem" of his other late paintings in "positioning the viewer not as a passive or detached observer but as the focus of the searchlight's beams." Like Joseph Jastrow's "search-light of attention" I earlier described, the light on the horizon focuses on us because the recognition of everything else it illuminates

FIGURE 16. Winslow Homer, *Searchlight on Harbor Entrance, Santiago de Cuba* (1901). Oil on canvas. Gift of George A. Hearn, 1906. The Metropolitan Museum of Art, New York.

depends on us. We see these things at last when we never would have except that now they are brought into bright focus: the technological revelation of objects that are lost—an obsolete canon, a seventeenth-century fort, a country obliviated by modern warfare.

In Homer's penultimate picture, *Right and Left*, two ducks caught in midair are set against a curtain of sky and spray (fig. 17). Like Homer's leaping trout, these humble subjects are lifted into relief, still as sculpture and gargantuan in the foreground. Homer gives them weight. They are fixed at the point of tension, not rest, "as if in some magnetic field of force" that is pulling and repelling across the austere canvas, right and left, up and down. A tiny daub of red in the center marks the parallel line of the horizon right where the gray sea meets the gray sky. Maybe it is meant to be a glint of sunlight, but at least we know that any Chevreul-inspired red stroke in a monochromatic field by Homer is always to the point. It focuses attention in intentional ways. Maybe this time it prepares us for "the visual force that emerges to surprise us" by redirecting interest—by creating expectancy—in the form of another vermillion flash to the left in the middle distance.

FIGURE 17. Winslow Homer, *Right and Left* (1909). Oil on canvas. Gift of the Avalon Foundation. Courtesy of the National Gallery of Art, Washington.

Do you see it? It turns out to be the flash from a hunter's rifle. (The painting's title came from an early viewer's sense of a double-barreled shotgun bringing down birds with succeeding shots, right and left). The hunter balances on a boat and takes aim at a duck, and this feels like an especially charged confrontation because we, too, are in the line of fire with the rifle pointing at us. And now our point of view has shifted, and the new focus on that point in the surrounding horizon "corresponds to the point of imminent need, of urgency," in Dewey's words. "No one can *make* you see this point; but unless you do see it, you won't change your conduct; if you do get the point you will act differently" in response to the sense that it matters.[36]

That second red spot in the gray-light zone of the horizon is now meaningfully and purposefully activated while everything hangs in the balance. Seeing it begins to feel very important, like a matter of life or death, if we are in fact "game." That point of red pigment is the cognitive challenge of the painting, but we are conscious of it now. It is targeting us. This picture, with its gun, knows how to draw.

It is hard not to be aware of the expressiveness of Homer's picture—how it discharges its contents, draws them out. In this split-second moment, caught like a duck in midflight or shot like a photograph, the hapless birds are given so much weight and emphasis. They have been extracted according to Homer's own selective bent and shot forward even as the left duck's foreshortened head tends past the picture plane toward us. What do we see when we see the point? We see that what turns out to be significant—to be *humanly valuable* to see—would have been far from obvious at the start. This is a picture that concerns ducks, and it concerns human beings too. This picture concerns us. Between life and death, one bird dives downward and another rises up, its wings spread in the pose of a martyr. It is a dead duck that is also on the verge of an ascension, lifted up. Homer wants us to see it as relevant.

...

Homer's *The Gulf Stream* (fig. 18) was exhibited alongside his painting of the searchlight on Santiago's harbor. It focuses on another derelict object: a mastless fishing boat off the Florida Keys, its sail in a pile on the battered deck. Faint red lettering across the boat's transom reads, "ANNA—KEY WEST." A Black man is adrift on the boat with nothing but a few stalks of sugar cane to sustain him. His boat has no tiller and is surrounded by sharks. In the background to the right, we see one of the waterspouts common over the Gulf Stream and, to the left, the bare shadow of a ship that may or may not eventually see the man and save him. We are made to feel the force of the foremost wave; also, that shark in the middle with its foreshortened head and open mouth angled out. This is another picture in which everything in it lies toward the surface, falling forward into our space. The horizon is itself an advancing wave.

Homer originally sketched *The Gulf Stream* in 1884 during the first of several trips to Florida, Cuba, and the Bahamas, and then revised it over the next fifteen years, so it is very much a culminating picture for him and appears in the only known photograph of the artist at work. He was fascinated by the Gulf Stream, particularly oceanographer Matthew Fontaine Maury's description of it in his famous book *The Physical Geography of the Sea* (1855), which Homer referenced as a source. In describing the Gulf Stream, Maury emphasizes the clash of two separate bodies of water—the Gulf Stream and the sea—each so distinctly marked in color you could trace their "line of junction" with your eye: the "indigo blue" of the stream from the Gulf of Mexico channeling through the dirty green of the Atlantic. "There is a river in the ocean," Maury writes, running northward past Florida in a warm, accelerating current more rapid than the Amazon and discharging heat all

FIGURE 18. Winslow Homer, *The Gulf Stream* (1899). Oil on canvas. Catharine Lorillard Wolfe Collection, Wolfe Fund, 1906. The Metropolitan Museum of Art, New York.

across the Atlantic. Sometimes one half of a boat "may be perceived floating in Gulf Stream water, while the other half is in common water of the sea," the line between them being so sharp because the waters are reluctant "to mingle," like water and oil. It is "one of the most marvelous things," Maury says, to see that narrow upward current, indigo and warm, against the cold downward draft from the North Atlantic. Maury explains, without getting the science exactly right, how opposing pressures running in different directions from the north and south, including waters at different temperatures and the currents and countercurrents of trade winds, create a reaction in the form of the Gulf Stream and also the waterspouts that appear frequently above it.[37]

In *The Gulf Stream*, Homer set out to paint how colliding waters of different colors and degrees produce atmospheric effects—"the subject of the picture," he says, being wholly "comprised in its title," *The Gulf Stream*, so that everything else in the picture is subsidiary to it. "I have crossed the

Gulf Stream *ten* times," Homer writes, "& I should know something about it," which also means for him that the man in the boat and the sharks are "outside matters" to the task of painting that great current in which indigo meets green. Homer says to his dealer, "The boat & sharks are outside matters; matters of very little consequence. *They have been blown out to sea by a hurricane*."

I think Homer means by this that the Black figure and boat mean very little to those elemental forces that show no regard for human life. But he also of course means what he says: that in the picture, too, they are "outside matters; matters of very little consequence" to the Gulf Stream. They are the compositional elements that draw our attention to the subject of a picture that is "comprised in its title." Everything else in the picture, including the Black man in the mastless boat and the sharks circling it, are "accessories" in Chevreul's sense, whose significance is figured by their contribution to the impact of the stream. The accessory dabs of red are there not to draw attention to the sharks, for example, or for any other purpose than to intensify and increase the interest of the blues and greens.

Pictures, for Homer, stage these encounters between colors; the harmonies and contrasts focus attention on the relations of each element within a reciprocal system, "fixing," as Chevreul puts it, "the attention of the spectator upon the physiognomy of the figures he would reproduce." *The Gulf Stream* thematizes this tension between colors, degrees, and values: the dramatic relation between elements *is* its theme and what matters. It focuses at the point of stress to show how interactions within environments make certain colors visible to us—all the adjustments, arrangements, and attunements that fix our attention on some figures over others.

So when Homer tells his dealer, in response to concerns of prospective buyers, "You can tell these ladies that the unfortunate negro who is now so dazed & parboiled, will be rescued & returned to his friends and home, & ever after live happily," he is not simply telling them that the Black figure in the painting is only a figure of their perception and that they can imagine whatever fate they want for him. They can imagine that that ship will rescue and return him to his friends and home. Nor does he mean, as one contemporary critic suggests, that Homer does not "give a damn what happened to the dazed and parboiled man."[38] Looking at this central figure in a picture that took Homer decades to finish makes that difficult to believe.

I think Homer is saying that in a painting like this the tension between colors and figures *is* what he also suggests it is in *The Life Line* and other works: that is, cultivated for its potentiality, for what it brings to consciousness and visibility and makes apparent. And what it brings to the attention and mind of the viewer in this particular case is a figure of color that has been compromised—a figure of color at risk (in the form of a castaway), unless somehow, in a series of ongoing adjustments, we can bring him home.

Homer knew from Maury that the Gulf Stream is more saturated than the waters surrounding it; as the semitropical stream surges north, cooling winds cause evaporation and increase its salinity. It is a place of rare concentration. Homer also read in Maury how waters from every quarter of the Atlantic and everything they carry "tend toward" the Gulf and its stream, so that bottles cast from across the Atlantic, as far as the coast of Africa or Cape Horn, seem to end up there. I see the man on his boat like these bottles, or like the driftwood or all the other "outside matters" and figures that Homer elsewhere draws out with nearly religious devotion, caught in the current. They are bobbing on the surface or popping out like that shoal of flying fish off the side of the *Anna* with their leaps upward, skimming the water. They are salient in this intensified place as if Homer wants to literalize here on the saltiest current in the sea the pun Emerson makes on salience as the "*sal volatile*," the smelling salts that will bring us to consciousness.

For James, the parts of our mental life that we select and perchance reflect on may be spoken of as a "current" within the "stream of thought."[39] There is the formless, extensive flow of objects and perceptions, and then there are currents running in tension with that flow. A current within the stream is James's metaphor for a punctuating moment that shapes experience through selection and attention. It is the moment in which "outside matters; matters of very little consequence" are momentarily held up. They get channeled or put to some purpose. James writes of a current in the stream of thought, but for Homer a current or stream within the sea is just as apt a figure for these moments of consciousness. What better than a picture of the Gulf Stream to show that things can be distinguished and particularly made out? To show how much might be floated. What better than this picture to recognize what greater concentration will yield up?

6

Communication, Translation, and Spirit

Jacques Derrida delivered his essay "What Is a 'Relevant' Translation?" in French in 1998 at the fifteenth annual seminar of the Assises de la Traduction Littéraire à Arles (ATLAS), an organization that works to promote literary translation. It was subsequently published in the organization's proceedings and then in English in *Critical Inquiry* in 2001 in a translation by Lawrence Venuti. Venuti explains in his introduction to the essay that the idea of "relevance" has been central to translation theory and practice since Dan Sperber and Deirdre Wilson's defining work, *Relevance: Communication and Cognition* (1986) and certainly since Ernst-August Gutt applied Sperber and Wilson's theory to the practice of translation in *Translation and Relevance: Cognition and Context* (1991).[1]

I will turn to Derrida and translation shortly (not to mention the "Spirit" in the title of this chapter that I obviously need to explain), but I should give an account of Sperber and Wilson first. I roughly described their theory of relevance in chapter 2 when discussing the "poetic effects" of "The Raven" and Poe's fascination with clues to meaning. I suggested then that Poe's poem is very much about how it raises the expectation of relevance and that satisfying this expectation of relevance is what guides the student's interpretive process as he listens to the raven *uttering* "Nevermore" (though at first it "little meaning—little relevancy bore").

. . .

The work of Sperber and Wilson falls within a branch of linguistics known as pragmatics, which is concerned with the effects of context on communication and with the meaning of utterances and what speakers mean by the words they say within the particular circumstances of saying them. It is possible for a speaker in different circumstances to mean different things by the exact same words. Irony is a good example of this, and Sperber and Wilson discuss it at length: if a speaker says, "It's a lovely day for a picnic" just as it begins to rain, those words will mean something significantly different than if they are said in sunshine. They'll mean even more if the listener knows that the speaker had warned of rain or resented the picnic or was frustrated after planning for it for so long or for reasons that exceed a straightforward day in the park. An ironic utterance is always "echoic" in the sense that what the speaker has in mind, including her attitude toward what she says, reverberates beyond the literal words she says, and these *implicatures* need to be recovered by the listener for communication to take place effectively.

Irony is, in fact, a very effective way of communicating insofar as it conveys a great amount of meaning with minimal effort. "It's a lovely day for a picnic" can say so much more than what is explicitly voiced by these seven words and without the speaker having to spell out at length how terribly this plan has gone. But it takes contextual cues for the listener to get what the speaker means and also, importantly, background information, including some sense of who the speaker is and what the speaker believes. Maybe it is a sunny day instead, but the speaker has just learned that she has lost her job, and only knowing this makes her irony clear. In any case, to understand her words is to have the contexts it takes to interpret her attitude toward them. It is to move beyond the literal meaning of the words to some intended meaning, to understand the words as clues to meaning that are nonetheless vague or incomplete on their own. Most utterances are rich and inflected; a speaker "manifests" more than a speaker says.

But for Sperber and Wilson, irony—and also metaphor, hyperbole, and other forms of figurative or literary language—requires no special interpretive or inferential skills; they see them as being on a continuum with almost all forms of communication. The way humans think and communicate their thoughts are usually underspecified and require a pragmatic process of "meaning adjustment" in particular contexts. Words and gestures typically fall short of their communicator's state of mind. "In many—perhaps most—cases of human communication, what the communicator intends to make manifest is partly precise and partly vague," the idea being that listeners always need to make inferences and to construct a suitable context for these words in their minds. Again, irony presents an extreme example of this, but relevance theorists insist that the interpretive work that irony takes applies to the most everyday uses of language as well.[2]

To draw out an example that Gutt provides, Mary simply says to Peter, "The back door is open." She might mean that Peter needs to lock it before he leaves the house, but she might mean something else entirely. She might mean that the door is unlocked and should be left unlocked for a guest who will be arriving without a key. Or maybe the situation is different and Mary tells Peter that the back door is open because the house needs to be ventilated after a fresh coat of paint. In any case, all Mary says is that "the back door is open," and the assumption is that that is all she needs to say. From this economy of words, Peter will figure out the best context for them and what prior information (the fact that a guest is coming; the fact that the house is newly painted) they require on his part and, finally, what Mary intends in this case. There is nothing unusual about the fact that Mary does not say more than she does. Good communication always expresses the most that it can with the least amount of effort.

We can see why scholars reflecting on a relevance theory of pragmatics liken its interpretive work to an "exercise in mind-reading," because it suggests that every effective communication requires the ability to attribute mental states to someone else. Pragmatics tries to figure out the puzzle of just how a listener manages to process language as the recognition of a speaker's intentions. It tries to figure out just how a listener knows what is relevant to understanding at a particular moment. "What is puzzling," for Sperber and Wilson, is just how "it works."[3] Pragmatics builds on the William James lectures that H. P. Grice delivered at Harvard in 1967 on the "logic of conversation" and that circulated widely in manuscript before appearing posthumously in *Studies in the Way of Words* (1989). Grice laid the foundation for an inferential model of communication as an alternative to the classical "code model" in which a communicator encodes a message into a corresponding signal (let's say, an utterance of seven words) which is then decoded by the addressee using an identical copy of the code (say, the dictionary definition of those seven words). Grice suggested that communication depends not only on coding and decoding in conventionalized ways but on the expression and recognition of concepts that go beyond the "linguistically encoded" meaning of words and that include a range of evidence and background information that exceeds an overt signal.[4] Suppose I wink at you as we listen to someone bragging in the most excruciating way. I am offering you a *piece of evidence* about my thoughts, but there is no code in place for reading it. I am sharing my boredom and really hope that you'll see what I mean with only a wink by connecting my signal with what you know about me and what I know about you and think we both know about this excruciating person. You see my wink, and I hope that you will read my mind.

This type of communication is what Sperber and Wilson call *ostensive* and involves the display of pieces of evidence about the communicator's intentions, beliefs, and feelings that are designed "to attract the addressee's attention and convey a certain *import*." Ostensive acts include speaking and writing, but forms of nonverbal communication, too—winking, nodding, waving, catching someone's eye, pointing, tapping, touching, moving in certain ways. Terence Cave and Wilson give the example of patting the seat next to you as an invitation to sit down. Ostensive acts leave it up to the addressee to infer what exactly the proposition is, and sometimes it is easy to make out and sometimes the import of the act is more complicated and involves an "*array* of propositions." Sometimes that act communicates not only a "message" but vague concepts, impressions, and attitudes "that may be broader or narrower than the encoded meaning." Maybe that act of patting the seat is an invitation to sit down that is also a form of inclusion or of reaching out and welcoming that importantly means so much more than the simple fact of an available seat. Or maybe patting the seat in this instance is a way of being territorial and asserting more space for yourself, though this wouldn't be the conventional use of that gesture.

So what exactly does it mean right now? Relevance theorists believe that considerations of relevance play a fundamental role in all communication however simple or complex; that every ostensive act raises expectations of relevance; and that the search for relevance "is a basic feature of human cognition, which communicators may exploit." They believe that both communication and cognition are governed by the search for relevance. Ostensive acts carry implicit suggestions ("implicatures"), and to understand them involves an inferential process that starts from simply attending to these acts (first they have to grab our attention and not be ignored) and results in a "plausible hypothesis" about their communicator's purpose in a particular context. But, as Cave and Wilson explain, "The inference process involved is not a deductive one, where the truth of the premises guarantees the truth of the conclusion, but an 'inference to the best explanation,' where the resulting hypothesis, however plausible and well evidenced, may still turn out to be false." The challenge is to understand how utterances and other communicative acts "provide effective pieces of evidence which (combined with contextual information) enable the audience to recognize the speaker's intended import."[5] These acts will only ever be clues to meaning that lead to hypotheses about meaning in the makeshift contexts of a conversation or a day in the park.

And how does an addressee arrive at the most plausible understanding of a communicative act, pragmatically speaking? With so many semantic or referential possibilities, how does an addressee know "to choose the right hypothesis from an indefinite range of possible hypotheses?" "What criterion does the hearer use to select the right propositional form?" The answer is that she looks for the best or most satisfying context for explaining an ostensive act to herself. Of all the possible explanations for that word, phrase, grin, groan, look, wink, gesture, movement, expression, only some will be relevant to her at this time. Only some will work. A wink at another time might mean something else entirely, but all that is irrelevant right now.

Sperber and Wilson suggest, as I mentioned earlier—in discussing them but also others before them thinking through the work of cognition—that human minds are organized so as to "maximise relevance." We pick up on some stimuli while filtering others out; we are able to notice what is worth our attention and to use that information practically to answer a question or solve a problem or to increase our power to understand and respond. Relevance "is to be assessed in terms of the improvements it brings" to an individual's "representation of the world" and, Sperber and Wilson say, our "perceptual mechanisms—and perceptual salience itself [the very fact that certain things are salient and come to our attention]—are relevance-oriented."[6]

Their main idea, insofar as they address questions of communication, is that every act of ostension "comes with a tacit guarantee of relevance" and that this fact makes manifest to an audience the intention behind it. Every utterance or communicative act starts out as a request for our attention, and this creates an expectation of relevance (the belief that it was communicated to us because we will care to hear it). In other words, we begin by assuming that whoever is communicating has a meaning in mind that, as Billy Clark describes in his book on relevance theory, "justifies the expenditure of effort involved in arriving at it, i.e. which provides enough cognitive rewards for it to be worth expending the mental effort involved in reaching it. . . . This could be understood as resting on assumptions about what it is rational for communicators to do and for addressees to expect. We might point out, for example, that it would seem less than rational for me to attract your attention and invite you to pay attention to something if I did not think it would be worth your while to do so."[7]

So, when we pay attention, it is with faith that the stimulus that attracts our attention is one in which we *can* have faith; that it will be worthwhile because it will lead to new meanings or understandings in this situation and increase our ability to think or act at this time. We only pay attention to things when we have the expectation that they will interest us, when they hold the promise that we will be able to care. "Relevant information is information worth having." This is not to say, as Sperber and Wilson point out, that the world is not full of bores who demand our attention but never reward it and who disappoint our expectations of relevance. But the assumption is that they are at least *trying* to be relevant, to address us in good faith and convey something worth knowing, and that being addressed will yield, in turn, "positive cognitive effects." The hope is that the effort it takes to process that utterance, gesture, or look will prove it to be relevant (or else we would never bother to process it at all), and we "try to select a context which will justify that hope: a context which will maximise relevance," increasing the connections we make and the understanding we gain as best we can. "It is around this expectation of relevance that our criterion for evaluating possible interpretations is built."[8]

Relevance is always defined in terms of an optimal balance between "processing effort" and "cognitive effects." That is, we want the greatest number of cognitive effects with the least amount of cognitive effort. The "first principle of relevance" for Sperber and Wilson has to do with this cognitive efficiency: "for an input to be relevant, its processing must lead to cognitive gains." The more cognitive gains, the more relevant that input is, and the more it justifies what it takes to process it. According to Sperber and Wilson, cognitive gains "are achieved when newly presented information interacts with a context of existing assumptions by strengthening an existing assumption, by contradicting and eliminating an existing assumption, or by combining with an existing assumption to yield a contextual implication (that is, a conclusion deducible from new information and existing assumptions together, but from neither the new information nor existing assumptions alone). The greater the cognitive effects, the greater the relevance will be."[9]

The sort of effects Sperber and Wilson are interested in is the result of this "interaction between new and old information" in which the new information strengthens old assumptions or provides evidence against them. A new stimulus is relevant to the extent that it interacts with knowledge and assumptions already available to the addressee. It is relevant to the extent that it *speaks to* the addressee, given what that person already thinks and knows, and bears on these prior assumptions either by reinforcing them or somehow changing them. The "cognitive gains" are the ways in which these new thoughts evolve: how new information weighs upon old assumptions, modifying these assumptions and then becoming part of the "gradually changing background against which new information is processed" and experienced as relevant or irrelevant in turn.[10]

But it costs the effort of imagination and memory to bring it all together (new information and existing assumptions)—to make this new information matter—and the greater the effort required to process anything new, the lower its relevance will be. If it is too vague, it will offer insufficient encouragement to us. We will lose interest in it before we understand it unless any extra effort is outweighed by an increase in cognitive gains. If the work of understanding proves to be difficult, it should be because the difficulty pays off and results in more ideas. It should be because the great amount of effort it takes to find those words meaningful will render them even more meaningful for the way we think.

Relevance is always a matter of degree. If I am to pay greater attention (if those words are to matter *that much*), then they will need to open up a wider range of implications. If those words are nuanced—if their implicatures are "weak" (meaning even less explicit about their intent than words usually are)—the more I will need to bring to them from my background and what I already know, the more their suggestiveness will activate and stretch my resources. The greater my "responsibility for constructing" their meaning, the more insight they will take from me, and the more those few words might be relevant to me.

Language can be very effective when its implicatures are weak and when just a few words leave so much to suggestion. The smallest stylistic difference can invite a disproportionate increase in cognitive effects—in the expectation, that is, of relevance. Here is a variation on an example Gutt gives of two ways of saying the same thing:

1. Mother to father: Fred has broken a window.
2. Mother to father: Your son has broken a window.

The second instance is less specific but conveys significantly more. The propositional form has not changed, but the simple substitution of "your son" implies what "Fred" does not: that he is his father's son and that, in his mother's mind, this very much explains the broken window. She intends his father to understand that she is thinking this—even as she is informing him that Fred broke the window—and also to feel responsible in some way. Example 2 demands a higher "processing effort" but has higher relevance in this context because it conveys more and has a greater effect on its hearer. It provides an example of what Sperber and Wilson call "focal stress," in which some syntactical or intonational device draws our attention to that aspect of the utterance that is most relevant insofar as it contributes the most to contextual effects. The simple shift in style not substance suggests the point that Sperber and Wilson make about language that is more complex than this: that "style arises . . . in the pursuit of relevance." Style is driven by the need to make certain "background" implications salient and manifest, to call attention to some contexts for understanding over others.[11]

This little example also speaks to the relevance of the conversers to each other, mother and father of Fred, by presuming a mutual intimacy and understanding, a shared context ("mutually manifest context") in which this tacit way of speaking means more than it says. The mother simply needs to invoke "your son" to suggest everything that might mean to them both about Fred but to almost no one else. "Optimal relevance," Sperber and Wilson say, "will leave implicit everything her hearer can be trusted to supply with less effort than would be needed to process an explicit prompt." Between the most intimate people, a moment of eye contact should do.

Sperber and Wilson are interested in literary language because it leaves so much implicit. With a minimal number of words, a poem especially can prompt an extraordinary process of imagining and creativity. Its array of "weak" implicatures—none strongly implicated—opens out to the most implications. It communicates not so much a message as "impressions" and emotions, and it has effects on a reader. While it may take effort to understand it, none of the effort is gratuitous, because, in a good poem everything counts as a clue to meaning. Everything is *effective* and "clue giving." Drawing on Sperber and Wilson, Cave describes a poem as "an ingenious gadget, or a small, compact box that delivers, when one opens it, an explosive cocktail of responses." The effort to interpret produces cognitive effects—the possible thoughts, feelings, and moods that resonate beyond the poem—while never losing their bearings in the highly specific context of the poem that sets the reader to work. In other words, any interpretation that emerges is still an extension of the properties the poem puts forth and appropriate to it in its careful choices of syntax, rhythm, and arrangement, in its style, which all impose, in Cave's words, "quite rigorous constraints on the range of readings that might be derived." One could speak, he says, of "a web or a cage of implicatures."[12]

To use the example of a metaphor that scholars now working in pragmatics often use (first discussed by Stanley Cavell in his essay "Aesthetic Problems of Modern Philosophy" [1965] and then by John Searle in his book *Expression and Meaning* [1979]): When Romeo says "Juliet is the sun," whatever assumptions about Juliet are being communicated, only some will be salient for the audience in this context. Searching for an interpretation of Romeo's words we obviously never consider that Juliet is literally a star or made of hot gasses. But, in this context, other, figurative, senses of *sun* might be less relevant too. Does Romeo mean that everything revolves around Juliet? Maybe. But this is the balcony scene of *Romeo and Juliet* and Romeo, seeing Juliet, asks "what light through yonder window breaks?" ("It is the east and Juliet is the sun!"), and so we focus on what we know are the special properties of the sun that also fit the context of the scene. We are searching for an interpretation consistent with the principle of relevance that rings the most bells. The assumption that becomes salient—the context that is "accessed" to yield the greatest contextual effects—is that seeing Juliet dispels the darkness for Romeo who is "sick and pale with grief." To him she is like a sudden light from heaven—so bright he imagines the birds will think it is dawn already and sing. Some assumptions are more salient than others, and these play the greatest role in the interpretative process. But these assumptions are also the most salient because they activate more implications and insights, more contexts, more connections on our part, a richer, fuller sense of Juliet, and of Romeo too.

Alastair Fowler writes in a review of *Relevance*, "perhaps Sperber and Wilson's greatest triumph is to have extended pragmatics to very weak implicatures—ambiguities, implications of implications, doubtful figures—of the sort that make up the richest part of conversation."[13] Of the sort that is literature too. Their theory of relevance suggests the ways in which language works on its audience as an "instrument of thought" and is finally not so different in its effects from Dewey's sense of how poetry works by "intension" rather than "extension"; how "it condenses and abbreviates, thus giving words an energy of expansion that is almost explosive." Who can count the ways that meaning might reverberate? An idea well expressed exposes a large "echo chamber" just where readers find themselves at the moment of reading. And if our circumstances change, the benefits of reading may change, and reading itself may alter the assumptions and beliefs that come to bear on future reading.[14] This echo chamber is no less resounding than that of Poe's student who assumes the raven means what it says and whose single utterance means as much as heaven and hell to him. For me, the surprising effect of what Sperber and Wilson imply is to see that it is a poem, of all things, that can stretch the potential for finding relevance, including new forms of relevance, as far as they can go.

...

To go back, finally, to translation. In his 1991 book, *Translation and Relevance*, Gutt proposes "relevance," as Sperber and Wilson define it, as a principle for translation in lieu of older ideas of "equivalence" or "faithfulness." Equivalence suggests a strict correspondence between an original and translation as if translating is a process of decoding, word for word. Gutt says that translators should ask instead what the communicator meant to convey and what an audience would have inferred and to preserve these "dynamics" in the translation. He is building on Sperber and Wilson's sense that reading and listening are always interpretive to some degree: that the audience infers what the speaker intends. But the problem for translation is that inferences are context dependent—we bring our own social and cultural knowledge and our own backgrounds to bear on what we infer—and the "receptor language audience" (the audience, that is, for the translation) is always different from the audience the speaker addressed. In a translation, words are "interpreted against a context different from the one intended by the communicator"—there is a "mismatch in context"—so, while the literal meaning of the words may transfer, their intent and their range of effects may not.

What tends to get lost in translation? All those "cognitive effects" that make a text relevant to its audience. Because communication is not simply informative but is expressive, the translator's challenge is to make the translation *adequate* or *appropriate* to the text's expressive purpose and to the *effects* it had and to the *impression* it made on its intended audience. The challenge is to preserve the sense of translated words as "communicative clues," giving priority not to equivalence but to whatever it is the text suggests is important so that the audience can pick up on these clues and find them important. It means preserving the point of a text's stylistic choices and "focal stress"—not the equivalent of the original but the most relevant equivalent of the original. This could result, Gutt suggests, in a translated version in which few words are "reminiscent" of the original.[15]

A pragmatic translation, then, subordinates "semantic resemblance to other kinds of resemblances." Translation is an interpretive act that aims for "interpretive resemblance." It can be faithful by seeing the original text in terms of its effects on its audience and by trying to recreate those effects for a very different audience. Gutt is looking for a way to preserve the communicative value of the exchange rather than the message verbatim. He wants the translated text to be full of implications for its new audience so that it might continue to matter to its audience in a new context. As William Frawley puts it, "Resemblance involves likeness of implications: two texts interpretively resemble each other if they key the same implicatures and explicatures, and so a translation is an equivalent of another text if it interpretively resembles the original text."[16] Instead of asking whether the translated text is *equivalent* to its original, Gutt asks whether it serves the same purpose, turning to instruction manuals as a straightforward case of a text that may sound very different in translation so long as it does its duty and gets the job done. The value of the translation comes in its relevance. The translator as communicator must know how to manage not just what the original text says but what it implies and also how the reader might work with it and use it.

In another of Gutt's many examples, he turns to a dialogue from Stendhal to ask how one might think about preserving the French distinction between *vous* and *tu*, which has no equivalent in English. How might *you* in English suggest the same kind of intimacy as *tu* in French? One translator chooses *thou* to represent Stendhal's *tu*, and yet that seems so anachronistic (so *ecclesiastical*); the effect is different and the implications are different, and this could give the wrong impression and even alienate the reader who doesn't want to deal with that *thou* and think it through.[17] Will the audience be able to infer the range of meanings from *thou* that *tu* makes available? Will it "key" the same implicatures? Will *thou* ring bells in the "cognitive environment" of this current audience? Will they feel its relevance at all?

. . .

Derrida's lecture "What Is a 'Relevant' Translation?" reflects on the problem of translating the single word *relevant* ("relevante" as he writes it in French and leaves in quotation marks). He believes the word (our English word!) is "forever untranslatable," because, in the first place, "one can't decide the source language to which it is answerable"—he is speaking in French about a loanword in French—and "therefore, in what sense it travails, *travels*" between sources and hosts. He wants his lecture to be a reflection worthy of this single word that he feels incarnates (as a "translative body") the process and problems of translation itself, and he chooses to include the word in his title precisely, he says, "because of its untranslatability, premeditating my crime in this way, conspiring to insure the apparent untranslatability of my title through a single word": *relevant.*

He says to his French audience that those familiar with English probably already understand the word "as a domestication, an implicit Frenchification [*francisation*] or—dare I say?—a more or less tacit and clandestine enfranchisement [*l'affranchissement*] of the English adjective *relevant,* which would have thus passed into our language with bag and baggage, with its predicates of denotations and connotation." "You might ask to what language the word *relevante* belongs." The adjective *relevant* is an English word that remains English in its usage and currency even as it is loaned to French, and yet, Derrida continues, the verb *relever,* from the same Latin origin, is French "through and through." The word also retains an "obscure Germanic filiation." It is the resonance between the English, French, and German (which Derrida also describes as the "happy coincidence" of the same word, assuming they are all the same word, operating between languages like this) that brings him back to what he calls a "modest but effective experiment in translation" in which he claims he has engaged "for more than thirty years, almost continuously"—namely, thinking through how the word *relevant* itself operates between different languages, "first between German and French, then more recently between English and French."[18]

He claims he has been tracing *all this time* how this very same word could have operated, "in a single language, between three languages," so that in any one language it seems to retain the sense and memory of the other two (with that sense "hovering above it, as an aura or halo"). As a loanword, it always "translates" or in any case puts "to *work* different words belonging to apparently different contexts in at least two other source languages," so that when Derrida himself sets to work to translate "relevante," he hears at once the various semantic possibilities already inscribed in this family of languages and in *his* language most of all. "Well, this word 'relevant' carries in its body an ongoing process of translation"—as he tries to show.

What an absolute "stroke of luck," he claims, that the same word that we might follow in transit from context to context like a "go-between" should also be the very word for "whatever seems pertinent, apropos, welcome, appropriate, opportune, justified, well-suited or adjusted, coming at the right moment when you expect it—or corresponding as is necessary to the object to which the so-called relevant action relates: the relevant discourse, the relevant proposition, the relevant decision, the relevant translation." A relevant translation would therefore be, quite simply, a "good" translation that does its job or its duty (all along he is punning on *travel/travails* to suggest how the word both travels and *works* pragmatically) "while inscribing in the receiving language the most *relevant* equivalent for an original, the language that is *the most* right" and "the *most* possible."[19]

A translation is always "an attempt at appropriation that aims to transport home, in its language, in the most appropriate way possible, in the most relevant way possible, the most proper meaning of the original text." Good translations should aim for economy as best they can. But when what needs translating has a wide range of implications that are not strictly translatable (say, any kind of poetic language), the translation that is the most *appropriate* often must do something more than appropriate word for word while staying as close as possible to the equivalence of "one word *by* one word," respecting verbal quantity. It must suggest the range of meanings and effects that rarely can be conveyed by a literal translation—and sometimes to preserve these effects, the translator will have to break with what he calls the "economic law of the word" (a translation that is word for word) to provide the most relevant translation and to bring these effects to the reader's attention.

So, to return, Derrida is trying to translate the word *relevant* as an example of what a "relevant" translation might be. He says the word represents "one of those words whose use floats between several languages (there are more and more examples of them) and that merits an analysis that is at once linguistic and sociological, political and especially historical." In this lecture, Derrida has entrusted it "with an exorbitant task. Not the task of the translator, but the task of defining—nothing less—the essence of translation." This one word, *relevant* "whose relation to French or English is not very certain or decidable" (and that also retains that "obscure German filiation" he goes on to describe), is being called on here to show what a "relevant" translation is and what every translation *should be* (it should be relevant!). This word of Latin origins—even though, again, he no longer knows "to what language it belongs, whether French or English"—has become, he says, "indispensable to me, in its uniqueness, in translating several words originating in several languages, starting with German (as if it in turn contained more than one word in a single one); on the other hand, this translative word has become in turn untranslatable for the same reason." His concern, then, is to find the most relevant translation possible for the word *relevant* and also to explain to us, or at least "submit for [our] discussion, the reasons for which," he says, "several times over the space of thirty years, I have judged relevant my use of one and the same verb, *relever*, to translate first a German word, then an English one."[20]

. . .

Derrida begins then in earnest with the second instance: the English word he translates now into French as *relever*. The word appears in Shakespeare's *The Merchant of Venice*, when Antonio defaults on his debt to Shylock and Shylock, in keeping with the terms of his loan, demands a pound of flesh in return for the money that Antonio cannot pay. Of course the exchange values are famously incommensurable (money or a pound of flesh), but Shylock swears that he will stand by his oath and not perjure himself, and so the only way out for Antonio is for Shylock to forgive the debt and renounce his due. Then "the Jew must be *merciful*," Portia says.

Mercy, Portia continues, is an act of grace. It is wholly gratuitous and cannot be extorted. "It droppeth as the gentle rain from heaven / Upon the place beneath." It comes from on high, transcending all laws of economy, sovereignty, and the courts (from "above this sceptred sway"). Mercy is a spiritual power beyond "temporal power"; a quality of divinity "enthroned" within the human heart:

> It is an attribute to God himself;
> And earthly power doth then show likest God's
> When mercy seasons justice.

It is the human power that most resembles God's power, and asking for mercy is like a prayer. Here, Portia is asking Shylock to assume this godlike grace. If his "mercy seasons justice," it will bless him as much as Antonio. (She is also already calling for this Jew to convert to Christianity, a price we know in the end he will pay.)

The English word that Derrida sets out to translate into French is "seasons" from Portia's line: "mercy seasons justice." He is offering an alternative to François-Victor Hugo's French translation of the word as "tempère" (tempers). Derrida acknowledges that Hugo's choice is not bad; Shylock's mercy would *temper* justice and the word *tempère* in French in fact means "to season" (*assaisonner*), as in to mix, to cause to change, to modify, or to affect a sense of quality. Derrida nonetheless proposes to replace Hugo's translation, "tempère," with another: he translates Shakespeare's "seasons" as "relève" instead: "quand le pardon relève la justice."

He offers several justifications for using *relever* in this way even if he says it does not seem at first to be answerable to (*relever de*) Shakespeare's usage, and yet for him it comes some way toward explaining what it means to be as *relevant* as possible and to offer the most relevant translation for words that are strictly, literally untranslatable. First, *relever* conveys the sense of cooking suggested by Portia's "seasons," the sense of enhancing taste, "while giving it *still more of its own taste,* of its own, natural flavor—this is what we call 'relever' in French cooking," he says. "Un plat relevé" is a seasoned dish, an elevated dish, and when Portia says mercy seasons (*relève*) justice, she means that mercy elevates justice, makes justice even more than just, according to the law.

Second, *relever* expresses elevation more generally, so that Derrida, in using it, is picking up on Portia's suggestion of how mercy *lifts* justice. Thanks to forgiveness, this is a kind of justice that transcends the ordinary justice of the law and crown. It is a higher justice, a godlike and spiritualizing justice—justice in the spirit of justice, raising and lifting itself above itself (*se relevant*). "Mercy sublimates justice," Derrida writes.

Finally, the justification for suggesting *relever* here as the most just—the most relevant and appropriate—translation for Portia's phrase returns Derrida to that thirty-year-old project of translation that he has been referencing all this time: a philosophical project that brings him full circle to the philosophy of translation that he again puts forth in this lecture around the example of *The Merchant of Venice*. He says that in 1967 he proposed the noun *relève* and the verb *relever* as the best, most economical (using a single word only) French translation for that crucial German word at the heart of Hegel's philosophy, a word "that the entire world had until then agreed was untranslatable—or, if you prefer, a word for which no one had agreed with anyone on a stable, satisfying translation into any language": *aufheben.*[21]

. . .

The verb *aufheben* and noun *Aufhebung* naturally have an entry in the wonderful *Dictionary of Untranslatables: A Philosophical Lexicon*, edited by Barbara Cassin, which claims that ever since the publication of the first volume of Hegel's *Phenomenology of Mind* in French in 1939, these words "have been revered as fetishes of the untranslatable." The debate "regarding these two words," writes the author of the entry, "is probably the most long lasting, the most documented, and the best known of all those that concern problems of philosophical translation." The "double meaning" of the verb *aufheben*, as Hegel describes it, meaning at once "to preserve" and "to abolish"—"to maintain" and "to cancel"—provides philosophy with one of its most important concepts and the key to "Hegelianism." It contains the idea of "transcending" a point of view without refuting it, of "carrying out a 'synthesis' while retaining the best part of the 'thesis' and 'antithesis' and at the same time 'opening' onto broader perspectives." *Aufheben* stands for what Hegel means when he describes the dialectical process by which consciousness evolves. Old and opposing ideas get taken up in the spirit of the new ideas that supersede them. Prior understandings give way to later understandings they nonetheless inform; they are gathered up as part and parcel of the developing thoughts that come to replace them.

Aufhebung is usually translated into English as *sublation*, but this word is only a placeholder in English for Hegel's word, which again has no equivalent in English. *Sublate* was an arcane term meaning to cancel, contradict, or deny (to "disaffirm the existence of"), especially within the field of logic. Only later, by the mid-nineteenth century, did J. H. Stirling and other translators of Hegel afford *sublate* that extra semantic sense of "preserve" or "include" (right along with "cancel") for the sole purpose of having a word in English to express the double meaning of *aufheben* in Hegel. They simply marshaled this word into the philosophical service of expressing in English how (to quote Hegel in English) "what is sublated is at the same time preserved; it has only lost its immediacy, but is not on that account annihilated."

So, again, Derrida tells us that thirty long years ago, he proposed the verb *relever* as the most relevant French translation of *aufheben*, and, though "the entire world had until then agreed [it] was untranslatable," the use of *relever* for *aufheben* now "has become irreplaceable and nearly canonized, even in the university, occasionally in other languages where the French word is used as if it were quoted from a translation, even where its origin is no longer known." The root *heben* in *aufheben* means "lift," and so does the verb *relever*. But Derrida says that he chose *relever* because even as it suggests (as we see from his discussion of Portia's phrase) the act of lifting, raising, or transcending, it also suggests the act of superseding what is transcended in the way that *un plat relève* changes the nature of the dish by elevating it. Thirty years ago, the verb *relever* allowed Derrida a way of retaining in a single word the "double motif of the elevation and the replacement that preserves what it denies or destroys, preserving what it causes to disappear." He likens *aufheben* to what is called, in the armed forces, the relief (*relève*) of the guard—a use that also is possible in English: to relieve, meaning both to raise something out of trouble or difficulty and to take its place.[22]

"Was my operation a translation?" Derrida asks. Certainly not "in the strict and pure sense of this word." But he hopes it preserves in French and English the "effect" of what Hegel calls the "speculative spirit" of the German language that manages to have words with the property of saying two contradictory things at the same time. This "speculative spirit" attaches itself to words like *aufheben* that are dispersed here and there by a "stroke of luck," and Hegel speaks of the "joy" of discovering words that can do so much. Derrida says he feels the same "stroke of luck" in coming upon *releve* (or *relevance*), a word which in its essence suggests for him an *Aufhebung*, a process of elevating and taking in or interiorizing and replacing all at once, just as mercy, according to Portia, "elevates, preserves, and negates [*relève*] justice [i.e., the law]." Mercy, in other words, supersedes justice and renders it null by preserving the "spirit" of justice only. It internalizes the godlike ideal of justice in order to transcend justice. It carries forward in human acts the eternal spirit or essence of justice even as it leaves the law at its word behind. For Derrida, Portia is saying that mercy would make the spirit of justice *relevant* in the particular and immediate case of Antonio.

Thirty years earlier, Derrida had translated the great philosophical movement of *Aufhebung* that Hegel describes as the "process of establishing relevance." Relevance preserves the value or spirit of what precedes in whatever follows and replaces it. "[Relevance] is also," Derrida says, "a translation," or all that "a translation might be *obliged* to be, namely *relevant*." Relevance promises the survival of the essence of the original, including the senses of meaning that have accumulated in the original, even as its form is left behind for new forms and iterations in new circumstances and as the occasion demands. Relevance as translation, like relevance as a philosophical principle, saves the spirit of the thing while superseding it in fact, which is why Derrida imagines relevance, in the case of mercy in Portia's speech, like some absolute or divine spirit (of justice) as it gets translated into other, more appropriate forms (of justice).

It is also why Derrida finally analogizes relevance to the idea of the

Resurrection (and not only because Portia herself associates the transformation relevance suggests with Christian conversion for Shylock [a *relève* that Shylock resists]). Relevance in translation guarantees "survival" by "losing the flesh during a process of conversion," by which Derrida, more simply, means that a relevant translation preserves only the spirit or value of the words while discarding their literal form:

> Isn't this what a translation does? Doesn't it guarantee these *two* survivals by losing the flesh during a process of conversion [*change*]? By elevating the signifier to its meaning or value, all the while preserving the mournful and debt-laden memory of the singular body, the first body, the unique body that the translation thus elevates, preserves, and negates [*relève*]? . . . The measure of the *relève* or relevance, the price of a translation, is always what is called meaning, that is, value, preservation, truth as preservation (*Wahrheit, bewahren*) or the value of meaning, namely, what, in being freed from the body, is elevated above it, interiorizes it, spiritualizes it, preserves it in memory.

Derrida really insists "on the Christian dimension": relevance as Resurrection. Aside from the fact that Hegel's *Aufhebung* is "explicitly a speculative *relève* of the Passion and Good Friday into absolute knowledge" ("one must never forget that he was a very Lutheran thinker"), the work of relevance—which is also always the work of the development of knowledge and consciousness—is best imagined as a resurrection in any case. It is the memory of "the body"—of that original form still untouched ("preserved in its grave")—while its ghost is resurrected, a spirit "that rises, rises again [*se relève*]," and speaks to us now.[23]

Alfred Schutz defines *relevance* as the "translation" of what otherwise is lost to us into the spirit of our own.

Nietzsche defines *translation* as resurrection: "Should we not make new for ourselves what is old and put *ourselves* into it? Should we not be allowed to breathe our soul into their dead body?"[24]

7

Relevance Is God

The Eternal Object

In *Process and Reality*, Alfred North Whitehead tries to explain how new objects of meaning and value emerge in the world. Announcing his debt from the start to James, Dewey, and Bergson, he sets out to isolate the occasions in which the potential for meaning becomes *an experience* of meaning—in which these "potentialities" are first felt and then actualized in the moment they fill a need or provide an "intensity of feeling" or "depth of satisfaction." There is always something out there that can serve as a "lure for feeling." The process by which a subject's feelings come together around this object, taking it in and realizing it for oneself, is what Whitehead calls the "creative process." It is the process, he says, by which an "unrealized abstract form," pulled out from the universal background, gains emphasis, value, and purpose and becomes an occasion for concern.

This process is not so different from the pragmatism in James and Dewey that, in Louis Menand's words, "hooks people up with their circumstances in ways they find useful." Their hooks go hand in hand with Whitehead's lures. For all of them, philosophy is about how novel ideas get made and connect us to aspects of the world that never would interest us unless somehow we come to believe in them—in their importance and purpose, that is. For Whitehead, the task of philosophy is to recover speculatively the "totality of things" we have not yet taken in—to understand that what matters is only what we are conscious of and "sensitive" to right now. In other circumstances, we might discover any number of the other things that have been "obscured by the selection."[1]

Those things "which shine with immediate distinctness, in some circumstances, retire into penumbral shadow in other circumstances, and into black darkness on other occasions." What comes to consciousness on one occasion "is only the last and greatest of such elements by which the selective character of the individual obscures the external totality from which it originates." But all other elements and entities have the *potential* to come into focus another time and to gather one's thoughts as objects of "subjective intensity." They might shine with distinctness too.

Whitehead has his very own idiom, so I will try to be clear: the elements that have been out there all along, but of which we were not before conscious—elements in that unrealized flux that forms the "eternal" background to experience but nonetheless have the potential to feel real and intensely meaningful on certain occasions—are what Whitehead calls the *primordial nature of God*. The creative advance of these elements into a feeling of "real concrescence"—the discovery of their presence and their admission into some real connection with oneself—is what Whitehead calls *God's purpose* or *God's consequent nature*. And the process by which these "eternal objects" come to consciousness as actual and felt objects—rising into importance and answering to some purpose and need at particular moments (their "ingress" into every actual occasion)—is the principle of *relevance*, according to Whitehead.

Relevance is God. Relevance is the feeling of being in touch with some share of the eternal. It is the entry or "ingression of an eternal object" into the particularity of the present at the very moment when it addresses a need. Relevance so often gets defined cosmologically, as we've seen (in Derrida, too, and in Emerson and James), but this makes sense most of all in Whitehead. "Relevance is always what Whitehead has associated with God," as Isabelle Stengers puts it. Whitehead is looking to philosophy to "disclose the very meaning of things," and relevance is about actualizing this potential to be meaningful. It is about the process of recovering on "actual occasions" something old, universal, enduring, or nontemporal, somewhere out there already or existing regardless of us, and of bringing these envisaged potentialities into new and immediate relation. It is the proposition of raising again into importance some idea or object from elsewhere or beyond the present moment for the purposes of the present moment. Whitehead calls it the "hold up"—and on these occasions, we bring some "eternal object" to bear on the specificity of the present because it intensifies our feelings and infuses a sense of meaning and satisfaction into the present. "God's primordial nature" is that storehouse of all the universals, truths, facts, and memories from which we select certain elements at certain times for their practical importance. We hold them up. "We confess their relevance," Whitehead says, "in thinking about them at all."[2]

The occasion in which these abstract entities come together and get constituted for us *as* valuable and take on "forms of definiteness" as part of our reality represents, for Whitehead, "God's immanence in the world." Relevance is the ingression of an idea or object from this "eternal," transcendent source of infinite possibility (from the "non-temporal generality") into the contingency of the moment. It is the admission of this entity into "effective feeling." When we take in something old, remote, distant, vague, abstract, or unrealized for its potential meaning and importance—when we come to realize and, most of all, have faith in its capacity to be meaningful—Whitehead says that we can practically call it "God."

Here is how he puts it:

> In what sense can unrealized abstract form be relevant? What is its basis of relevance? "Relevance" must express some real fact of togetherness among forms. The ontological principle can be expressed as: All real togetherness is togetherness in the formal constitution of an actuality. So if there be a relevance of what in the temporal world is unrealized, the relevance must express a fact of togetherness in the formal constitution of a non-temporal actuality.

Anything has the potential to be relevant. In theory, everything has "proximate relevance." And each of these things may be brought into relation to some degree, so Whitehead allows for "degrees of relevance, and for negligible relevance." He uses the term *prehend*—from *apprehend*—to stand for the perception and grasping that all experiences have of prior experiences, for the way that one freely selects from past actualities something to bear on the present, and for how this "fact of togetherness" creates new actualities in the present. Prehension is what allows for the possibility of new knowledge, for perceiving which "datum" is "relevant to the subject," and also for relegating "into irrelevance, or into a subordinate relevance" whatever is not assimilated just then in "the process of concrescence" (i.e., in the making of a new actuality adapted for the attainment of an end and satisfying in some way). But, again, anything might be pragmatically put to use on another occasion, which is why, to repeat that line from Whitehead that I mentioned earlier, there finally is no irrelevance, just "neglected modes of relevance."[3]

The "general potentiality of the universe must be somewhere" out there. "It retains its proximate relevance to actual entities for which it is unrealized" until it "reappears in subsequent concrescence," by which Whitehead means that "envisaged" potentialities are brought into new connections that make what was merely latent or potentially meaningful *actually* meaningful right now. He is interested in our "appetite towards" potential meaning, in the way some previously unrealized object can become a "lure for feeling" and also in how every lure is a "proposition." Some object out there, in other words, is "proposed for feeling." It may draw those who entertain it into a new relation to their world. There is a "penumbra of eternal objects," writes Whitehead, sounding just like William James on selective attention. Some people "admit elements from this penumbral complex into effective feeling, and others wholly exclude them. Some are conscious of this internal decision of admission or rejection; for others the ideas float into their minds as day-dreams without consciousness of deliberate decision; for others, their emotional tone, of gratification or regret, of friendliness or hatred, is obscurely influenced by this penumbra of alternatives, without any conscious analysis of its content." In other words, "the elements of this penumbra are propositional prehensions." They suggest the "potentiality of relatedness" to ourselves. They are "valuations determining the relative relevance of eternal objects" for a particular occasion, and our appetite for the satisfaction they promise means that we select them for that purpose. Relevance reflects the "decision of emphasis" that is "finally creative of the 'satisfaction.'" And when we decide that one of these universals—there all along—might satisfy a need or provide an answer—when we emphasize one of those "elements from the penumbral complex" and admit it "into effective feeling"—what had been "abstract" only can now express "a useful abstract for many purposes of life." "Such anticipatory feelings involve realization of the relevance of eternal objects as decided in the primordial nature of God."

Why does Whitehead turn the principle of finding relevance into a cosmology? Why does he call everything with the potential for being relevant "the primordial mind of God?" "From beginning to end of *Process and Reality*," Isabelle Stengers writes, "one invariant remains: the fact that if God's intervention is necessary, it is in order to think of relevance." In *Science and the Modern World*, the function of God is also "to ensure that mental decisions are 'relevant.'" Really everywhere in Whitehead's works, the divine experience brings us back "to the only invariant that ever defined God's role for Whitehead: relevance."

Whitehead writes, at the beginning of his essay "Immortality" (originally delivered at Harvard Divinity School), "It will be presupposed that all entities or factors in the universe are essentially relevant to each other's existence. A complete account lies beyond our conscious experience. In what follows, this doctrine of essential relevance is applied to the interpretation of those fundamental beliefs concerned with the notion of immortality." There is no irrelevance, just neglected modes of relevance, and each time we become aware of new relevance—of the way these neglected modes might be concretely brought in as elements of our lives and made to matter—we also become conscious of the potential importance of the world beyond ourselves and how infinite it is and how infinitely more might matter. "Importance arises from this fusion of the finite and the infinite." "The particular providence for particular occasions" is "the love of God for the world."[4]

What is religious aspiration after all but a sense that "there must be value beyond ourselves" and the belief that this sense of worth might be brought home to us with "enhanced intensity" and feel purposeful? Religion is "the doctrine of the varying relevance of potential forms," an infusion of the potential, abstract, or ideal into particular moments when it makes a difference. It fills the moments to which it belongs with new value and meaning. Religion is "an ultimate craving" for "acquiring this measure of connection." An enduring idea or object that we were not feeling before becomes possible. This possibility gets "picked out, held up, and clothed with emotion." Then "finally," writes Whitehead in *Modes of Thought*, "there is deity, which is that factor in the universe whereby there is importance, value, and ideal beyond the actual. . . . Apart from this sense of transcendent worth, the otherness of reality would not enter into our consciousness. There must be value beyond ourselves. Otherwise every thing experienced would be merely a barren detail in our own solipsist mode of existence." Some unrealized "eternal object" or truth all at once comes together for us and enters our consciousness, "for the kingdom of heaven is with us today."[5]

Relevance, for Whitehead, is "divine intervention." It marks the ingression into real experience of some "nonrealized sensum" that had been beyond experience but felt as a need. "Its ingression responds in a relevant way to what is felt as a 'lack.'" He illustrates his point with an example from

David Hume's *A Treatise of Human Nature* about a person who, having enjoyed perfect sight his whole life and been perfectly well acquainted with all sorts of colors and shades of blue has nonetheless missed one particular shade of blue, "which it has never been his fortune to meet with." Should all the different shades of blue that he knows be lined up in order in front of him on a color chart from deepest blue to lightest blue, "he will perceive a blank" where that one particular shade is wanting "and will be sensible that there is a greater distance in that place, betwixt the contiguous colours, than in any other." Hume suggests that it is possible for the man to supply the idea of that particular shade from his imagination without ever having seen it, the point being that ideas are not always derived from immediate impressions. But Hume also suggests that his example is so "particular and singular" that it is not enough to disprove the rule that ideas usually derive from our immediate impressions.

Whitehead disagrees with the singularity of the example and takes from it instead that new actualities almost always come to us like that particular shade of blue would; that "conceptual feeling" originates in a sense of need or lack in the basic data; that there are "eternal objects" (like a shade of blue) that seem as if they might satisfy this feeling because of their "germaneness to the basic data" and because their absence is glaring. "The gradation of eternal objects in respect to this germaneness is the 'objective lure' for feeling." Whitehead means by this that we select from all possible objects the one that seems most adequate to the occasion and most belonging to this instance of need; that our feelings are "'vectors'; for they feel what is *there* and transform it into what is *here*." In speaking of James on religion, William Lapoujade writes, "The flow of the stream of consciousness is oriented toward new meanings that increase the expanse of its field and its powers of thought." What is new is not the missing shade of blue itself but its "mode of ingression" or entry into our experience of the world, the way that what had been beyond us or elsewhere can help *here*. Conscious perception of it "is the feeling of what is relevant to immediate fact in contrast with its potential irrelevance." It is the "realization of the relevance of eternal objects" to actual facts on the actual occasions in which they are "felt as definite elements in experience."[6]

The question of exactly how any "eternal object" newly enters the world is, in Stengers's words, "crucial for Whitehead, since it is connected with that of relevance. . . . Novelty, in the cosmological sense, is always 'relevant novelty.'" "Therefore, whenever blue is 'missing,'" she continues, "God is not far, for God is precisely that thanks to which what has been realized is plunged into the possible, that thanks to which realization is not the last word." We bring the new element, that missing shade of blue, into our sense of reality. And insofar as this serves as a simple illustration for divine intervention, it is because it demonstrates how some timeless source can feel timely and immediate (that it can be "*what is best for that impasse*"). Its verification depends not on any kind of "truth" but on its effects and the difference it makes in its appearance and in the "subjective satisfaction" it provides for the person who entertains it. "For speculative thought," Stengers writes, "[God] is not associated with truth but with relevance." God is a way of thinking about the possibility of new forms of relevance that might help us in concrete ways.

God is relevance. He represents "the principle of concretion—the principle whereby there is initiated a definite outcome from a situation otherwise riddled with ambiguity." God stands for an absolute resourcefulness. Stengers writes,

> "God's power," corresponds to the correlative need to think of something beyond the blind, smothering facts, behind them and within them, to think in terms of the possible and not only of the probable. God is then the respondent to the ultimate ideal, and the quest without guarantees. Yet this purely factual world, thematized by the solitary consciousness, a world subject to routine, to the arbitrary, to relations of force, a world that is deaf to its complaint, to its appeal, to its hope, is the work of this consciousness. The religious feeling is thus an appeal to a transcendence capable of restoring what was first denied to the world by the solitary consciousness, *an appeal to the interstices in which new possibilities of relevance lurk.*

These new possibilities make their way into each concrescing (or evolving) occasion. There is not out there any memory or thought, sensation, fact, or shade of blue that cannot make itself felt, "moving onward and never perishing," advancing creatively—nothing that cannot at some time or another be appealed to for the possibility of new connections and comfort, for the meaning it might lend to the moment that takes it up for some reason. This is why Whitehead calls these elements "everlasting." The consequent nature of God is the way these elements, out there all along, pass into the immediacy of life so that we become conscious of them and the actual difference they make. They are no longer lost to us like a missing shade of blue. Whitehead says, "The image—and it is but an image—the image under which this operative growth of God's nature is best conceived, is that of a tender care that nothing be lost." Relevance saves. "It is the judgment of a tenderness which loses nothing that can be saved." It takes care of everything possible.

"To pray," W. H. Auden writes, "is to pay attention to something or someone other than oneself."

"Attentiveness," Walter Benjamin writes, is "the natural prayer of the soul."[7]

. . .

Relevance, for Whitehead, is a deus ex machina. What helps us appears from elsewhere right when we need it, though we never could see it before. Something eternal is brought into the contingent moment—it is "order entering upon novelty"—but this is not meant to sound any more metaphysical than the contrivance of a god dropped on stage by a crane, since, in Alfred Schutz's words,

> The experience of transcendence is part of everyday life. Man accepts as unquestionably true that the world existed before he was born, and will continue to exist after his death. He is convinced of the existence of a physical universe in its quasi timelessness and its expansion toward an outer limit, possibly infinity. Above all, however, he accepts the social world as a whole, including the large regions forever beyond his grasp and experience; and he accepts its historicity, its extensions into both the past and the future.

Sometimes we become aware of these remote realities lying beyond our immediate context, and we believe in the meaning and purpose of our awareness with each conscious thought, "just like the joint in a bamboo stem, tying together past and future in a single continuous present—what James calls 'specious present,'" as Lapoujade puts it. Sometimes these realities from other regions appear to us so that subconscious or previously invisible forces rise in our consciousness. "James says that we may call such unconscious forces God if we like. We do not take leave of the immanence of the flow of consciousness; on the contrary, we explore and expand it."

Visions enter. James calls this "invasive" experience. Dewey describes it as a process of "taking in," opening the mind to perception in a sort of fusion of the timeless with the new (revealing new and immediate worth in the old). "What was received as alien, has been recreated as private." The sense of personal connection with a possible timeless source of meaning beyond our immediate moment, enlarging our consciousness and increasing our power to think and act in the present, is very much the appeal of religious faith for James.[8]

In 1868 James wrote in a letter to his friend Oliver Wendell Holmes Jr., "If God is dead or at least irrelevant, ditto everything pertaining to the 'Beyond.'" God is one name for something lying outside of our reality—an unrealized possibility or an ideal—*made relevant* and alive to us in an actual moment. It is the experience of how, in our imaginations, "things unrealized in fact come home to us and have power to stir us," as Dewey puts it in *A Common Faith*. Dewey also calls these things by the name "of God, or of the divine," insisting that they are not ideas only or wholly abstract or supernatural. God represents the way that ideal values come to have an "undeniable power" over our thoughts and actions; the way they "supervene" or "enter profoundly" into human life.

Dewey says, "It is this *active* relation between ideal and actual to which I would give the name 'God'" and not to "rootless ideals, fantasies, utopias." This is because for Dewey the ideal alone (or pure supernaturalism) finally has something in common with atheism; both end up negating "God" by dislocating religious values from experience and by failing to relate to our personal needs. Both leave us isolated, in the "barren details of our own solipsist mode of existence" and without help, as Whitehead puts it. God is the name for any ideal that comes to be *realized* in its "hold upon humanity" and in the world that gives it coherence and solidity. "Suppose for the moment that the word 'God,'" Dewey says, "means the ideal ends that at a given time and place one acknowledges as having authority over his volition and emotion, the values to which one is supremely devoted, as far as these ends, through imagination, take on unity."[9]

"In any case, whatever the name" (whether "God" or the "Beyond" or the "ideal"), "the meaning is selective," Dewey continues. "For it involves no miscellaneous worship of everything in general. It selects those factors in existence that generate and support our idea of good as an end to be striven for. It excludes a multitude of forces that at any given time are irrelevant to this function." In the horizon of possibilities, "the 'divine' is thus a term of human choice and aspiration." Divinity is whatever our selective attention brings to the "top of consciousness" because of its power to be "relevant" to our lives. George Santayana writes in *Interpretations of Poetry and Religion* that, in Aristotle's conception of God, there is "no suspicion of irrelevancy," and the influence of Dewey and James is unmistakable:

> This God is not a mere title of honour for the psycho-physical universe, confusedly conceived and lumped together; he is an ultra-mundane ideal, to be an inviolate standard and goal for all moving reality. Yet he is not irrelevant to the facts and forces of the world, not the dream of an abstracted poet. He is an idea which reality everywhere evokes in evoking its own deepest craving and need. Nothing is so pertinent and momentous in life as the object we are trying to attain by thought or action.

God is what we find when we extract importance from an inchoate universe and bring it home, within our actual reach. "[God's] tenderness is directed towards each actual occasion, as it arises."[10]

Whenever we might feel that God is dead, we are neglecting to anticipate the potential for relevance on those occasions.

Unconcealment

The American painter Abbott Handerson Thayer was friends with William James, a fellow bird-watcher and the father of Thayer's favorite art student, William James Jr., who called him "Uncle Abbott." Thayer painted birdlike angels emerging out of backgrounds (fig. 19). We see their solid forms extrapolated from empty space. James writes that anyone with an inaptitude for faith would be "incapable of imagining the invisible," but Thayer's paintings are full of faith because "invisible impalpable things" always come into the picture. They advance into realization. The contours of darkened angel wings peel off the mottled backgrounds where they blend. In *A Winged Figure*, for example, we feel the pressure of the angel's urge outward. A figure is detaching from the ground. It is condensing, sculptural and thick, from pure atmosphere and stepping onto a pedestal. "Genius is not a lazy angel contemplating itself and things," writes Emerson. "It is insatiable for expression. Thought must take the stupendous step of passing into realization."

Thayer "worshipped Emerson," his youngest daughter Gladys writes in her reminiscences. In 1907 Thayer wrote, "I am 57 years old, and still Emerson stands to me as do all the eternal quiet things, the stars, the sky the drop of water, all things." In place of Shakespeare's "world of powers," Emerson

FIGURE 19. Abbott Handerson Thayer, *A Winged Figure* (1904–1911). Oil on Canvas. Gift of Charles Lang Freer. The Freer Gallery of Art, Smithsonian Institution.

was given "sight itself, as it were, so pure and all enveloping that it somehow instinctively postponed the seeing of the countless trappings with which life is resplendent . . . and just so does Emerson like Christ stand out *little* against the Eternal Quiet." Thayer kept a replica of Daniel Chester French's bust of Emerson near him for the last forty years of his life. In a photograph of the artist outside his home in Dublin, New Hampshire, you can see it perched on the porch (fig. 20). Thayer's third child was named after Emerson—Ralph Waldo—and when he died as a baby Thayer turned to Emerson's poem "Threnody," written in memory of his own son, Waldo, and to his other poems and essays for comfort. Over the years, Thayer especially seemed to find meaning in Emerson's essay "Spiritual Laws," calling it "my Bible" in a letter to William James's son in 1910. If you remember, "Spiritual Laws" is also the essay from which William James indexed passages in his notes under the heading *man a selective principle* and the primary source for his theory of "selective attention" that I have been describing all along. A man is "a selecting principle," Emerson says, "gathering his like to him, wherever he goes. He takes only his own, out of the multiplicity that sweeps and circles round him." "What attracts my attention shall have it, as I will go to the man who knocks at my door, whilst a thousand persons, as worthy, go by it, to whom I give no regard."[11]

The artist selects those things we normally would never be able to see or acknowledge and brings them "out of the multiplicity." They rise up from the far recesses of awareness. He hopes to give them our regard. "It is the secret of the world," Emerson writes,

> that all things subsist, and do not die, but only retire a little from sight, and afterwards return again. Whatever does not concern us, is concealed from us. As soon as a person is no longer related to our present well-being, he is concealed, or *dies*, as we say. Really, all things and persons are related to us, but according to our nature, they act on us not at once, but in succession, and we are made aware of their presence one at a time. All persons, all things which we have known, are here present, and many more than we see; the world is full.

The purpose of Thayer's pictures is always this un*concealment*. We are made aware of the presence of these subsisting things one at a time. Each angel is like the momentary "fixation" that Emerson describes when a memory, idea, or thought is "taken up" from the "unbounded soul of the world" and

FIGURE 20. Abbott Handerson Thayer standing in front of his home in Dublin, New Hampshire. Photograph. Nelson and Henry C. White research material (ca. 1851–1961). Archives of American Art, Smithsonian Institution.

given weight again. But "to make it available," Emerson goes on to say, "it needs a vehicle or art by which it is conveyed to men. To be communicable, it must become picture or sensible object."

The artistic act is the gleaming "incarnation" (the return) of something that was invisible and lost to us but now is being communicated in the picture. "It is the advent of truth into the world, a form of thought now, for the first time, bursting into the universe, a child of the old eternal soul, a piece of genuine and immeasurable greatness." From "all that mass of mental and moral phenomena" that have yet existed, writes Emerson, the making a matter "a subject of thought, raises it." It bursts into the world that brings it to light. "We behold it as a god upraised"; "And so any fact in our life, or any record of our fancies or reflections, disentangled from the web of our unconsciousness, becomes an object impersonal and immortal. It is the past restored, but embalmed." In the experience of a picture or sensible object that gathers that matter up, we have the feeling of being in touch with some piece of the eternal. And beyond this experience? That "enchanted statue," as Emerson calls it, will be "released again to flow in the currents of the world."[12]

In Thayer's paintings, the "enchanted statue" is almost always an angel, wings still tinged by the ambient colors of its surroundings. It is a brilliant object pulled from out of a deep background. Something that may have been lost to all eternity appears to us here. "The Angel," writes a contemporary critic of one painting, "is one of those visions which demands to be expressed, . . . a pictorial thought arising unbidden, something that is born inevitably and appears out of the night of vacancy." The job of the angel is *to appear*. In each case, Thayer is making a point about visibility and how such resplendent visions can come to us, even as he insists that these visions *came to him*: "all of a sudden I *saw my* picture," he says.

This angel is no allegory and no symbol. Nor is it religious in any usual sense, since Thayer spurned his Unitarian upbringing, calling "all labeled religions . . . obnoxious [and] savoring of hypocrisy and narrowness," according to his daughter Gladys. Thayer's angel is a perceptually phenomenological figure of unconcealment in honor of his idol Emerson. It is also in honor of James, to whom Thayer gifted a sketch of a partially realized angel who looks like she is emerging out of whole cloth.

Thayer's winged figures are emissaries or carriers of whatever he chooses to bring forward. They come out as if on a proscenium stage, which may explain the tableau-like quality of the figures, the prop-like contraption of halo and wings, the starchy costumes. Thayer's figures are attention grabbing. They "always demand attention," a reviewer says.[13] The one in *Winged Figure Seated upon a Rock* looks especially like she is on a stage set, perched on her articulated seat, while the treatment of the flat and decorative trees under the sliver of moon makes them seem like they are drawn on a backdrop (fig. 21).

I think the up-frontness of these angels suggests that you need to be

FIGURE 21. Abbott Handerson Thayer, *Winged Figure Seated upon a Rock* (1914). Oil on canvas. Gift of Charles Lang Freer. The Freer Gallery of Art, Smithsonian Institution.

attentive to something to make it perceptible at all. The angels manifest the sort of physical and metaphysical phenomena that James, in explaining how consciousness works, puts under the category of "perchings" as opposed to "flights." "Like a bird's life," James writes, the "wonderful stream of our consciousness" seems to be "made of an alternation of flights and perchings. . . . The resting-places are usually occupied by sensorial imaginations of some sort, whose peculiarity is that they can be held before the mind for an indefinite time, and contemplated without changing." The "resting-places" are the "substantive parts" of consciousness and the places of flight are the "transitive parts." Obviously Thayer is focusing on the substantive parts. The perching winged figures "can be held before the mind for an indefinite time, and contemplated." They have been dislodged from the cosmos that normally swallows them up. They are one reified piece of that whole cosmos crystallized in the frame of thought. When painting the rock for this seated figure, Thayer shouted out to Rockwell Kent, his then apprentice, "God said, 'let there be rock'—and there it was."[14]

"Elements which shine with immediate distinctness, in some circumstances, retire into penumbral shadow in other circumstances," in Whitehead's words. Thayer is attempting to recover in consciousness what has been lost in the shadows, to admit "elements from this penumbral complex into effective feeling." It is always important to realize that what Thayer brings forward so monumentally in these pictures for us to see are the things that are most meaningful to him. These pictures are monuments to what he has lost. The winged figure seated on the rock, for example, is a portrait of his daughter Gladys painted in memory of his wife Kate, who was hospitalized for depression and then died from tuberculosis in an asylum three years later without ever coming home. A Latin inscription on the rock translates as "Mother of my daughter! To you this monument." In *Winged Figure Seated upon a Rock*, Thayer is "[restoring] . . . the *vague* to its psychological rights," to return to the language of James.

The painting was based on an earlier painting titled *Stevenson Memorial* in memory of another one of Thayer's favorite authors, Robert Louis Stevenson, whose books he read with his children (fig. 22). It shows that very same winged figure (that later became Gladys in memory of Kate) on a tomb-like boulder meant to represent the Samoan mountain on which Stevenson is buried. Years later, *Stevenson Memorial* became the model for the memorial to Kate. It was brought out again for a new use, the old in a newer iteration and in satisfaction of new needs. Both memorials may be

FIGURE 22. Abbott Handerson Thayer, *Stevenson Memorial* (1903). Oil on canvas. Gift of John Gellatly (1929.6.127). Smithsonian American Art Museum.

thought of as "perchings" for the winged figures that Thayer wants us to hold before the mind for an indefinite time. They are "resting-places," as James would say, where the most "transitive" of souls are here *taken up* as if with wings and raised, then raised again.

I think that Thayer believed that painting is about this process of *taking up* figures in the idiom of Emerson and James. Another reflection follows from this: given Thayer's relationship to James and his son (and more on this in a moment), it is difficult for me to see all the halos in some form or another in every Thayer painting without remembering how important this word, *halo*, is to James. It is James's word throughout *The Principles of Psychology* and elsewhere in his work, and it is his word in these decades if it belongs to anyone. When James talks about the "fringes and halos" of perception, he means the "nascencies of cognition," the faint awareness or vague sense that there is much more out there than we see right now. "Every definite image in the mind" has a "halo or penumbra, that surrounds and escorts it," suggesting the relations to it near and far, the associations and meanings that hover over and around every definite image. They may come into focus still:

> Every definite image in the mind is steeped and dyed in the free water that flows round it. With it goes the sense of its relations, near and remote, the dying echo of whence it came to us, the dawning sense of whither it is to lead. The significance, the value, of the image is all in this halo or penumbra, that surrounds and escorts it—or rather that is fused into one with it and has become bone of its bone and flesh of its flesh; leaving it, it is true, an image of the same *thing* it was before, but making it an image of that thing newly taken and freshly understood.

For James a "halo" stands for how any figure, subject, or thought takes on an aura. Let's call it a *significance.* Our very thoughts and words may be "fringed," a "whole sentence bathed in that original halo of obscure relations, which, like an horizon, then spread about its meaning." These halos of relation—"inarticulate perceptions, whereof the objects are as yet unnamed"—may finally become clear, emerging from obscurity like the burnished halo that coalesces around Thayer's seated figure on the rock. It is no longer so immaterial. It is very material and, in the picture, Thayer takes that halo and makes it "distinct and comparatively abiding." He seems to be saying that what would have remained an "obscurely felt relation" beyond one's reach is now, in the figure of Gladys in loving memory of Kate, a *significant other*.[15]

In a letter to an art critic who asked him to explain the meaning of one of his angels, Thayer replied, "How you set me talking! As to what my pictures mean, you see now, exactly. I want the image of one I worship to become visible for all time to this world—*voilà tout!*"[16]

Hide and Seek

For Thayer, it always comes back to figure and ground. The questions he wrestles with are about visibility and why some things are noticed while others are ignored. He was known later in life not only for his paintings of angels but for his theories of animal coloration and, in particular, his controversial idea "that *all* animal markings, no matter how conspicuous, serve the purpose of concealment." In 1896 he published "The Law Which Underlies Protective Coloration," based on a talk he gave on Harvard's campus at a meeting of the American Ornithologists' Union, exploring how the surface colors and patterns of animals evolved to make them invisible in their surroundings. With the later publication of a lavishly illustrated book, *Concealing-Coloration in the Animal Kingdom: An Exposition of the Laws of Disguise through Color and Pattern* (1909), nominally written by his son Gerald, Thayer became the first to articulate a theory of how protective coloring conceals animals in plain sight.

Critics doubted his science and methods, most famously Theodore Roosevelt, who called Thayer a "lunatic" and published a 110-page refutation of *Concealing-Coloration* in the *Bulletin of the American Museum of Natural History*. Roosevelt had his own ideas about animal visibility based on the extensive time he had spent shooting game in Africa (his own book, *African Game Trails*, takes on Thayer in its appendix). Some Darwinians thought Thayer's theory of assimilation to natural environments was flawed for downplaying sexual selection as the cause of an animal's appearance. But other scientists found Thayer's theory of what soon would be called "camouflage" compelling. Importantly, so did philosophers and psychologists, including Edward B. Titchener at Cornell, who studied phenomenology within experimental psychology and wrote at length, as I mentioned, about the structure of attention (arranging it into "foreground and background," "focus and margin") and also about attentional capture or what happens when a new object pops into focus. In chapter 4, I discussed his idea of how consciousness picks up on "relevant" things while ignoring "irrelevant" ones. Needless to say, Thayer's animals are not meant to be picked up on.

In a review of Thayer's work on "concealing coloration," Titchener writes that critics "have failed to realize that conspicuousness is solely a matter of relation to background; that black is conspicuous against white, and white against black, but that neither is conspicuous in and for itself." Nothing, in other words, is intrinsically noticeable. The ability to notice anything, to see it at all, depends entirely on context and the viewer's perspective and whether, from that perspective, the contours of any particular figure emerge from its hidden ground. Thayer's critics, in other words, "have forgotten that there may be a vast difference between the conditions under which they see an animal and the conditions under which he is present, in nature, to his enemies or victims; so that his conspicuousness to human eyes may be altogether irrelevant."[17]

A peacock, for example, would seem to be conspicuous under any circumstances, but Thayer attempts to show that its spectacular patterning works as protective or "obliterative coloration" just where concealment is most needed (fig. 23). The peacock's neck is leafy green when looked *down at* and sky blue when looked *up at*, "so that it tends to fit itself exactly" to the background of predators high and low. What is more, the peacock's iridescent colors and shimmering ocelli are the "perfect color-notes" of its shifting background. They disrupt the form of its silhouette against the flickering light of the sun-dappled forest, giving the impression that the peacock is not there at all. The iridescences also create a "bewildering play and movement of his colors." They "hold the attention" of the viewer on dancing spots of colorful light just long enough for the animal to slip away beneath them. In other words, the "occasional effects" of color and shading depend on an animal's movement against a particular background from the vantage point of its predators at "crucial moments." At the moment of life and death, the illusion of invisibility will be most complete and the peacock will seem as if it is "vanishing into air."

Peacocks, flamingoes, and other gorgeous birds "reveal the simple fact, which seems never to have been noticed, that these traditionally 'showy' birds are, at their most critical moments, perfectly 'obliterated' by their coloration." Flamingoes, when seen in the day from above, as *we* might see them, are as "showy" as can be. But in the early morning or early evening, during the feeding times of their aquatic predators (alligators, anacondas), "they are wonderfully fitted for 'vanishment' against the flushed, rich-colored skies" (fig. 24). Thayer paints red flamingoes and roseate spoonbills

FIGURE 23. Abbott Handerson Thayer and Richard S. Meryman, *Peacock in the Woods* (1907). Oil on canvas. Gift of the heirs of Abbott Handerson Thayer (1950.2.11). Smithsonian American Art Museum. Reproduced in *Concealing-Coloration in the Animal Kingdom: An Exposition of the Laws of Disguise through Color and Pattern* (New York: Macmillan, 1909), frontispiece.

glowing against the red and rosy hues of sunset and dawn so that they "look like a real sunset or dawn, repeated, on the opposite side of the heavens." The principles of obliterative coloration, he writes, "work together to render the creature's actual surface unrecognizable as the surface of any object

FIGURE 24. Abbott Handerson Thayer, *White Flamingos; Red Flamingos; The Skies They Simulate*. From *Concealing-Coloration in the Animal Kingdom: An Exposition of the Laws of Disguise through Color and Pattern* (New York: Macmillan, 1909), plate 10.

or objects of the immediate foreground, causing it to pass for *an empty space through which the background is seen*."[18]

Thayer wants us to see how a bird can become pure background. At the same time, he insists that it takes not the natural scientist but the artist to demonstrate exactly how light and shade and color can work to make objects appear in foregrounds and disappear into backgrounds. In his review of *Concealing-Coloration,* Titchener—who, again, spent his career studying foregrounds and backgrounds—agrees that questions of visibility and invisibility should be settled at last by "the student of color, the artist and the psychologist."

Thayer's book is filled with renderings of "background-picturing on obliteratively-shaded birds" that he painted from photographs of birds or stuffed birds and with collages of cutout birds pasted onto pictures of forests, fields, marshes, and ponds. Birds disappear into habitats that are pictorially adjusted for local light and time of day. We see how shallow water or deep water creates different visual effects on the surface of the bird swimming in it. Or sometimes Thayer shows birds against "more distant 'backgrounds'" of twigs, branches, and tree trunks crisscrossing in stretches of diffused light.

The feathers of the ruffed grouse, for example, match the chiaroscuro and variegated patches of the forest in a way that makes the bird "almost certain to coalesce perfectly with its background" (fig. 25). The ruffed grouse's silhouette becomes impossible to trace. The patterning of its feathers can "cut to pieces" its solid form and the overall effect is the eye's "failure to recognize it as a solid object of any kind, seeming, if [the eye] rests on it at all, to see *through it to what is beyond.*" The eye does not see the bird's surface as the surface of any object; the ruffed grouse will pass as empty space through which the background is seen. "Nature has, as it were, used the bird's visually unsubstantialized body as a canvas on which to paint a forest vista."[19]

Paintings of animals with dark backs and white underbellies show the effects of "counter shading," in which the animal is dark where it faces up toward the sun and light where it normally is in shadows below. Every artist knows that shading around a light, uniformly colored object puts that object in relief and gives it solidity; countershading reverses this effect. It "flatten[s]" the object when it is seen from certain angles, creating the illusion of a "hole," or negative space. An animal with countershaded skin, fur, or feathers can look "at most like a flat plane interposed between its background and the observer." So from the perspective of predators chasing from behind and below, the white rump of an antelope or the white tail of a rabbit will match the brightness of the sky. It will suggest a "sky-picture" from certain viewpoints, causing an actual animal to look like nothing in itself and "to pass for an *empty space,*" while the "spectator seems to see right through the space really occupied by an opaque animal."

"Only an artist, perhaps, can rightly appreciate the profound and per-

FIGURE 25. Gerald H. Thayer, with Abbott Handerson Thayer, *Male Ruffed Grouse in the Forest* (1907–1908). Watercolor on paper. Metropolitan Museum of Art, New York, Rogers Fund. Artokoloro / Alamy Stock Photo. Reproduced in *Concealing-Coloration in the Animal Kingdom: An Exposition of the Laws of Disguise through Color and Pattern* (New York: Macmillan, 1909), plate 2.

fect realism of these background-pictures worn by birds and other animals," Thayer says. The artist, with his tricks, can even recreate these disappearing acts before our eyes, which is just what Thayer did when he arrived for that talk at Harvard in 1896 with a bag of sweet potatoes, oil paints, brushes, and wire. He suspended three potatoes on wires a few inches above the dirt road and rubbed them with dirt, so that they would be the color of the road, and then painted white on the underside of the two end ones. When viewed from a little distance, the two end ones disappeared from sight, while the middle one stood out in strong relief. Thayer explained that birds and mammals with white undersides or hindquarters are protectively colored to counteract the effect of shadows that otherwise, as the case of the middle potato proves, makes objects "abnormally conspicuous." An account of the event later published by the Fourteenth Congress of the American Ornithologists' Union reported that when witnesses questioned whether the invisibility could be entirely due to a little white paint, Thayer took his brush and painted white the bottom of the middle potato, too, and—just like that!—"the middle potato at once disappeared from view." "The effect was almost magical," the report says. Then Thayer took two more potatoes and painted them green, except for underneath which he painted white, and he suspended them by wire above the green grass and this obliterated any sign of *their* presence against that new background. In *Concealing-Coloration*, Thayer continues to display these kinds of optical effects as the magic of an artist who is able to make things appear and disappear. There are the images demonstrating how animals in their surroundings are, in Thayer's words, "magically obscure," and then images revealing for us (*voilà tout!*) the silhouettes of the animals we miss when their patterned skins "*blot out their foreshortened bodies against the sky*."[20] The paintings in the book themselves are veiled by protective sheets of diaphanous tissue that must be lifted in order to reveal them.

"Our book presents, not theories, but revelations," the introduction says. Thayer believes that all paintings work on the principle of hide-and-seek, which is why he writes that the model for his theory of animal coloration "belongs to the realm of *pictorial art,* and can be interpreted only by painters." It belongs to the "optical principle" that "there *can be no such thing as INTRINSIC conspicuousness* since things show or don't show wholly according to whether you look at them against a contrasting background or one that they match."

In all his paintings, Thayer manipulates the effects of light and shade to conjure figures out of the empty space containing them in rhythms of seeking and finding against contrasting and matching backgrounds. His figures remind me of the logic of the figures in the empty room of William Merritt Chase's painting titled *Hide and Seek* that play right at the thresholds of where they might be seen, like the girl in front who is peaking past the diaphanous curtain (fig. 26). (When certain things that have lapsed from in-

FIGURE 26. William Merritt Chase, *Hide and Seek* (1888). Oil on canvas. Acquired 1923. The Phillips Collection, Washington, DC.

terest or consciousness "surge up," James writes, "we have a peculiar feeling that we are 'warm,' as the children say when they play hide and seek; and such associates as these we clutch at and keep before the attention.")

Or else the figures play at the thresholds where they might go unseen: the other girl is falling out of focus and about to be hidden completely in the background. She has what Thayer describes as the "ghostly elusiveness" of his own figures at the *crucial moment* in the act of disappearing. It seems like it would be easy enough for her to melt right now into the uncongealed ground against which she seems to float. But I can also imagine (with Thayer) that, from the angle of the girl who pursues her from behind, her white dress would line up against the luminous sliver from the light source ahead, causing her "solid form to pass for an *empty space*." I can see how the figure already appears to be a "background picture," vanishing into her background and dissolving before our eyes. One imagines seeing right through her, like a mirror on the wall (just like the mirror to the left) for the girl in front, her mirror-image, who is looking.[21]

Look how paint can perform the games of visibility. For Thayer, the artist's knowledge of how things come to be seen and unseen under particular circumstances—of what rises into the consciousness of the viewer—is always a matter of final importance. It is often actually a matter of life and death, which is why in 1912 Thayer drew on his theory of protective coloration to explain how the invisibility of the white iceberg to the officers on the *Titanic* sank the ship and killed 1,500 lives. From the viewpoint of the sailor on watch, the iceberg would have been obliteratively countershaded, appearing to merge with the sky just as the white rump of an antelope merges with the sky (counting *as* sky) from certain angles. "Here is a thing that people don't realize," Thayer says, "viz., the psychological law that makes circumstantial evidence so formidable and vicious. Our busy brains go no further than to ascribe all phenomena to whatever cause is the commonest cause of such phenomena. White, as a rule, is too bright to be anything in the scene but *sky*, therefore whenever we see it where sky is to be expected we incline to *count it sky*."

During World War I, Thayer worked to apply his theories of protective coloration and countershading to conceal naval ships from German submarines and to create patterned military uniforms that would disrupt the silhouettes of Allied soldiers and help them blend into their surroundings. The French military obtained a copy of *Concealing-Coloration* and learned to paint disruptive "camouflage" patterns on military equipment and even horses. Thayer wanted to convince Britain to adopt his methods as well, and in 1915 he sent photo collages of figures in different habits against different backgrounds to the American artist John Singer Sargent, who had been appointed as official war artist to the British government. (In the collages, the soldiers in monochromatic uniforms naturally stand out most.) Thayer tells Sargent that he could make the British armed forces an "absolute replica of cabbage patches, emerald green fields, bare brown earth, poppy fields, etc., all so fresh and bright as to be indistinguishable! . . . and save thousands of lives." So Sargent arranged for a meeting with the War Office, and Thayer sent him in advance a sketch for a prototype of a sniper suit that could "entirely efface the soldier" in a pattern of bright yellow, red, and green blotches.

Thayer's model for the design of the military uniform was William James's very own hunting coat, gifted posthumously to Thayer in 1910. Thayer had worn it constantly until it was covered with blotches of bright paint. James's son recalled his father's "familiar garment on the back of my dear old 'Uncle' Abbott," watching it "grow shabbier and more and more covered with paint as time went on." In her account of the coat, Hannah Rose Shell describes it as Thayer's "sartorial second skin, practical for painting in the studio and trekking through the outdoors alike."[22] Onto William James's paint-blotched coat, Thayer attached colorful fabric swatches and strips of painted rags, which altogether disrupted the contours of his own silhouette even more than the splatters of paint alone as he went trekking around Dublin. Apparently, Thayer wore the coat while writing responses to Roosevelt and other critics of his work on protective coloration.

When, with Sargent's help, Thayer finally arranged to meet with the British secretary of war—who happened to be Winston Churchill at the time—he brought William James's coat with him to London. And when, having made himself sick with anxiety, Thayer did not make the appointment with Churchill after all, sailing home instead, he left an instructional note for Sargent along with a suitcase full of demonstration material that included James's coat with the colorful rags and swatches pinned to it. Sargent delivered the suitcase to the War Office, where its contents had some influence in uniform design and in the camouflage patterns that the British painted on tanks, although the office completely rejected the idea of soldiers carrying with them strips and swatches of different brightly colored cloth to pin to their uniforms as their surroundings changed. "This was evidently the last appearance of my father's brown coat," writes William James Jr. years later.

One of Thayer's students, Homer Saint-Gaudens, son of the sculptor Augustus Saint-Gaudens, served as a captain in the United States army's camouflage unit and later founded the American Camouflage Society in 1916. He recalls how he and fellow artists convinced military officers that they were "wizards who could hide them in any emergency." They replicated for the officers Thayer's old demonstrations at Harvard of countershading potatoes and suspending them with wire over dirt roads, then viewing them at a little distance.[23]

Thinking of Thayer in James's coat, I guess it makes sense to say that the lessons and uses of protective coloration is the work of the artist in the habit of the pragmatist. He understands that our perception—what we notice and disregard—depends on our circumstances at urgent moments and just as much on our point of view. Trekking in his bequeathed coat around Dublin, Thayer *takes up the mantle* of James in calling attention to the thresholds of awareness and to the utility of selective attention during difficult times. He knows why certain things cannot be seen. He knows how to keep them hidden to protect them or how to confer recognition when that could save them instead.

From his house in Dublin, Thayer could see Mount Monadnock, which appears in several of his paintings, with its distant snowcapped peak (fig. 27). "So call not waste that barren cone / Above the floral zone, / Where forests starve: / It is pure use," writes Emerson of Monadnock's peak in his poem "Monadnock," which Thayer knew well. Thayer made good *use* of that white peak, which "God aloft had set" and which functions in his paintings like the tip of the iceberg from the watch below, concealed against the clouds: a sky picture. The mountaintop face matches the sky it disappears against, an exercise in concealing coloration. (Thayer even drafted a painting of Monadnock on the back of page proofs for *Concealing-Coloration.*) In the foreground, dark masses of unresolved snow patches and trees lay heavily on the surface in the indirect light of either sunrise or dusk. They also conceal parts of the mountain, subsuming the tonal range in its close surroundings, while the blurred edges of the muted forms keep spatial depth to a minimum. Monadnock dwells in this atmospheric landscape, eternally serene behind a veil of trees.

But Monadnock needed to be saved. It was threatened by real estate and commercial development aimed at tourists and seasonal residents with summer homes. Thayer worked hard as a community activist in Dublin to combat development and also pollution and especially to prevent the installation of electric lighting along the roads. If Dublin was not going to lose its "Presence, those trees," he needed to bring its pristine nature to attention.

In *Monadnock Angel*, Thayer painted the distant mountain as a revelation (fig. 28). The white peak now appears as a white winged figure, the point being that it *appears*. No longer countershaded, its shape is shaded into relief, around the arms, legs, feet, and head and between every fold. No longer a "sky-picture," the figure's brilliant coloring contrasts with the sky from this angle so that it stands out sharply. The figure of the mountain is materialized from afar and brought right into the foreground. It is an angel larger than life. The hope is that the mountain might become something for

FIGURE 27. Abbott Handerson Thayer, *Mount Monadnock* (ca. 1918). Oil on panel. Purchased with funds provided by Cecile Bartman. Los Angeles County Museum of Art.

the residents of Dublin to believe in even as developers were disregarding it completely. As Thayer writes in a draft of an angry letter to prospective homeowners who were trying to build houses on Monadnock, "The one meaning of Jesus Christ is that nothing belongs to anyone who cannot make the highest use of it." What is a godhead, after all, but something brought into our thoughts and prayers at the crucial moment?[24]

Thayer's animals always need to be invisible, but his figures need to be seen. Many of his "figures," as I have been suggesting, seem to be in the process of becoming visible, like the winged figure he gave to William James or the figure in *Woman in Green Velvet* that may be the closest Thayer ever

FIGURE 28. Abbott Handerson Thayer, *Monadnock Angel* (1920–1921). Oil on canvas. Gift of an anonymous donor (1930.17). Addison Gallery of American Art, Phillips Academy, Andover, MA / Art Resource, New York.

FIGURE 29. Abbott Handerson Thayer, *Woman in Green Velvet* (1918). Oil on canvas. Gift of Mrs. Arthur H. Savage. Addison Gallery of American Art, Phillips Academy, Andover, MA / Bridgeman Images.

came, as Kevin M. Murphy puts it, "to transposing one of his cutouts of a soldier in a camouflaged uniform to an idealized female subject" (fig. 29). It is a painting for which, for all the blending and countershading—around the soft edges of the left shoulder, for example, where the woman in green recedes into the brush—the decision finally seems to be to bring her out with integrity. "Watch this being!" Thayer says to the critic who asks about the meaning of angels, "Thou wilt surely see, now and then, the being . . . come forth and be fully in sight." The figure in green velvet finally appears to be a visitation, too, with her halolike headband and the feathered atmosphere around the brush like two apparating wings. The priority is on her presence. The "holes" in this image where we lose sight of the form of the figure in the weeds make us conscious of the fact that she finally manages to come forth, an angel.

Critics write about how insistent Thayer seems to be on purity in his "idealized" pictures of women as virgins and angels; also, in his antimodern resistance to the vulgarity and showiness of commercial life and to overt displays of women especially. He called popular artists who sexualized women in art "whore painters"; "Art is worship, and there's the end of the subject," he says. The son of a doctor who specialized in infectious diseases and had a "morbid fear of germs," Thayer developed such a deep fear of contamination, especially after Kate died from tuberculosis, that he kept his children at home in Dublin and homeschooled them. He had his family sleep outdoors year-round in New Hampshire in lean-tos in order to breathe pure, fresh air.[25] There is no doubt that his spiritualizing pictures are transfigurations of a modern world that he found to be filthy and foul, like the muck in which the animals are concealed until he lifts them out.

Yet I think the question of "purity" in the paintings of angels is best addressed not as a "sublimation" of desire or of real bodies in any way but as an effort to abstract out of life's muddle what Thayer calls a "crystal type." Purity, in Thayer's paintings, is clarity, a sort of extract, requiring on Thayer's part the work of lifting out figures that essentially were lost in the big picture, laid in the ground. "Had not the term 'pure' been so often abused in philosophic literature," Dewey writes, "had it not been so often employed to suggest that there is something alloyed, impure, in the very nature of experience and to denote something beyond experience, we might say that esthetic experience is pure experience. For it is experience freed from the forces that impede and confuse its development as experience." Thayer suggests that the experience for the viewer his effort brings about is no longer muddled (or muddy) but concentrated. The angel is what we get when we extract an essence (something quite essential) from the wide universe and concentrate it in the vivid matter of a painting. Everything else is left behind, in the background, and then an angel appears as if by magic, disentangled from the gross, the aggregate, "purged of what is irrelevant." "Disentangled from the web of our unconsciousness," it "becomes an object impersonal and immortal." What was beyond us, Emerson says, "has a new value every moment to the active mind, through the incessant purification." "Instantly, it is raised, transfigured; the corruptible has put on incorruption. . . . In its grub state, it cannot fly, it cannot shine,—it is a dull grub. But suddenly, without observation, the selfsame thing unfurls beautiful wings, and is an angel of wisdom."[26]

Gladys Thayer writes that her father "liked as slogan" another line from Emerson, this time from "Self-Reliance": "I shun father and mother and wife and brother, when my genius calls me. I would write on the lintels of the door-post, *Whim*. I hope it is somewhat better than whim at last, but we cannot spend the day in explanation." This happens to be Stanley Cavell's favorite line in Emerson's essay and maybe the line he emphasizes more than any other in all of Emerson's works and in his philosophical response to Emerson. Now I know that it was Thayer's personal slogan too. It speaks to the elevation of the whims we follow and to Emerson's hope that they may be better than whims at last. Cavell explains it like this: "something which is of the least importance, which has no importance whatever but for the fact that it is mine, that it has occurred to me, becomes by that fact alone of the last importance; it constitutes my fate." The substitution at work in the passage is this: what Jesus required of the person who follows him (to "hate father and mother," from Luke), Emerson requires of himself in following his interests. And just where, in Deuteronomy, we are told to inscribe the name of God on the lintels of our doorposts and on our gates, Emerson writes the word *Whim* instead. In place of God we have Whim. We have only what interests and occurs to us, but always with the sense that its occurrence—the fact of a connection that makes it come to mind—means that it is *important*, by this fact alone an article of faith. Gladys explains that the "slogan" from Emerson meant for her father those moments of "perfect harmony" between individuals who otherwise never can manage to come together, like the "fluctuating rapport . . . of two clocks which every so often will seem to be ticking in absolute unison, then separately so slight though definite the difference in their tempo."[27] Those brief moments of coalescence are whimsical. They are but for the grace of God.

"Whatever does not concern us is concealed from us." There are things always around us of which we are never aware, but in these intensified moments—when attention isolates the experience of an object from its background—the effect is the enlarging of consciousness. Emerson, James, and Whitehead all believe that the value of "God" is in the way in which whatever form God takes "expands our mental horizon"; we come to believe in the reality of things that simply were invisible to us before. Each one of these things is "the advent of truth into the world . . . a child of the old eternal soul, a piece of genuine and immeasurable greatness."[28] God is a figure for how importance or significance is revealed to us at the necessary moment. Thayer's angels are not about any ideals in particular (let alone ideal womanhood or ideal nature). They are about the way in which ideals come to us, seemingly out of the blue—like a whim or like angels bearing messages.

8

Resurrection and Reconstruction

Henry Ossawa Tanner is best known now for his painting *The Banjo Lesson* from 1893 (fig. 30). In a talk Tanner delivered that same year to the World's Congress on Africa, he said he was drawn to paint Black subjects because of the newness of the field and the desire "to represent the serious, and pathetic side of life among them" and not "the comic, the ludicrous side," and it is on the basis of pictures like this that the African American philosopher Alain Locke writes that Tanner "vindicated the Negro artist beyond question of shadow of doubt." If only, Locke continues, Tanner had stuck to these "at home folk types" instead of turning to religious paintings, he might have been "the founder of a school of American Negro art," but, finally, there are only a couple pictures along these lines.

An "old Uncle Ned" type, as the reviewers called it, gives a young boy a banjo lesson.[1] The figure was familiar from minstrel shows, with his banjo, his hat and pipe on the floor at one side, and pots and pans on the other. But in 1893 this is also a scene of Reconstruction, and Tanner, the son of a former slave, has recast the old type in new light. He gives us a bright moment of cultural transmission in which a new generation, figured here as the child, takes up for itself something back of it. The aims and ideals of *The Banjo Lesson* derive from the ways in which this reconstructive act sustains and organizes the experience of the new relations brought out for us in the picture. For example, the painting leaves me with the impression that some things (the hat, pipe, and frying pan) have been *put down* for now, while the banjo is *taken up* for the lesson, dusted off. There are many objects in

FIGURE 30. Henry Ossawa Tanner, *The Banjo Lesson* (1893). Collection of the Hampton University Museum of Art, Hampton, VA.

this ensemble that seem to mimic the distinct form and slant of the banjo: the pipe's bowl and stem, for one, and the iron frying pan with *its* handle that is especially banjo-like, and even the plate beside the pitcher with *its* handle. All these rhyming forms suggest to me that the banjo is simply an object among objects in the room except that now it has been given priority by being picked up while the others are set down, even as the young boy is *picking up* the banjo—which is just what it means to take lessons (to pick up something)—and, of course, in this lesson the boy is learning *to pick* the banjo; the sunlight on his tensed fingers is highlighting this.

The idea of the picture seems to *be* that we can pick up the banjo—meaning, take it up and make good on it, which is also what Locke means when he says that art as the expression of a racial past can "redeem" it, or what Dewey, born the same year as Tanner and influenced by Locke, means when he says that the past can be "reconstructed" with respect to its "relevancy in a much changed human situation." It can be taken up in a way that can retain "'actuality' in a world whose main features are different." Certainly the figures in Tanner's picture are taken "up from slavery"; like his friend Booker T. Washington, Tanner cares a lot about uplift in ways we will see.[2] In a scene of culture and pedagogy, these figures have been elevated (lifted) by Tanner's respectable articulation, but they are also on the high ground, with the floor planks tilting up as they recede like a stage above the sunken hearth at the right. It gets more vertiginous the more I look, with the high point of view and cutoff ceiling compressing the scene unlike any usual genre painting, and then with the figures pressing down on that pitched floor that projects right out of the picture toward us.

The focal point of this interior is the sounding board of the banjo. Sounding board is the term for what gives the banjo its loud full sound and resonance. A sounding board is also a platform for getting ideas out. And, since Tanner was the son of an African Methodist Episcopal bishop, he also knew that a "sounding board" is the name for the circular board placed above a church's pulpit; from the pulpit, a sounding board would have projected his father's voice. When I think that Locke claimed the moment had come when African American artists, no longer feeling the need to be representative and speak "for the Negro" to a white audience, could now "speak to their own and try to express"—that art at this time might be "racially expressive" rather than racially representative—then this seems like an expressive picture to me.[3] The objects Tanner takes up in the tight room express—meaning (and we have seen this before), they *press out*, express or *press forth* as if from some internal pressure. What is inside comes out. The radiant light attaches itself to the man, child, and banjo from who knows where?—the implied window to the left and the fire at the right are not nearly enough of a source, as reviewers noticed, to warrant the flash of light that detaches these figures from their background, solidifying them at their edges. They now look to be punched through opaque material, so that the light behind them, working like a light projector, really brings them out even as it reveals them. That halo of light makes this scene of Reconstruction look more like a resurrection.

In "Negro Youth Speaks," published in his famous anthology *The New Negro*, Locke describes how the long interval in African American art between early folk art and contemporary art was an "awkward age, where from the anxious desire and attempt to be representative much that was really unrepresentative has come." He says that in the decades before the Harlem Renaissance, Black artists saw their role as representing socially acceptable types—the countertypes to racist stereotypes—in an idiom of "cautious moralism and guarded idealizations." Artists portrayed African Americans, just released from slavery, as respectable and cultured (as "creature[s] of moral debate") in "art that was stiltedly self-conscious, and racially rhetorical rather than racially expressive." So, Locke writes in his essay "The New Negro,"

> for generations in the mind of America, the Negro has been more of a formula than a human being—a something to be argued about, condemned or defended, to be 'kept down,' or 'in his place,' or 'helped up,' to be worried with or worried over, harassed or patronized, a social bogey or a social burden. The thinking Negro even has been induced to share this same general attitude, to focus his attention on controversial issues, to see himself in the distorted perspective of a social problem.

Artists and intellectuals "felt art must fight social battles and compensate social wrongs; 'Be representative': put the better foot foremost, was the underlying mood." But now, with the moment of the publication of *The New Negro*, "there has come the happy release from self-consciousness, rhetoric, bombast, and the hampering habit of setting artistic values with primary regard for moral effect—all those pathetic over-compensations of a group inferiority complex which our social dilemmas inflicted upon several unhappy generations." The writers in the anthology, Locke says—including Langston Hughes, Jean Toomer, Zora Neale Huston, Claude McKay, and Countee Cullen—have "stopped speaking for the Negro—they speak as Negroes. Where formerly they spoke to others and tried to interpret, they now speak to their own and try to express." Freed from the burden of either reproducing "stock figures" or directly countering them, these artists, by "acquiring ease and simplicity in serious expression, have carried the folk-gift to the altitudes of art. There they seek and find art's intrinsic values and satisfactions." This is what Locke also finds to be prescient in Tanner's *The Banjo Lesson*: the "revitalization" of a folk type in "some revised and reconstructed form."

Locke tells us that artists of the Harlem Renaissance are using art as the means of self-expression and not for polemics or race debate, that "race for them is but an idiom of experience, a sort of added enriching adventure and discipline, giving subtler overtones to life, making it more beautiful and interesting, even if more poignantly so." In other words, race for them is "but an idiom" of the sort of experience that art best realizes. We are meant to understand that art that is not necessarily about social protest might be art in which we can find "intrinsic values and satisfactions" and that what Locke means by this is to celebrate a sort of art that is freed from the necessity of engaging with social issues or responding to the history of oppression in terms defined by that history.[4]

How do we *pick up* on what could be valuable in cultural types, and in heritages, traditions, and backgrounds? Can we make new use of ossified forms, "which prejudice and caricature have overlaid?" Can we reevaluate in order finally to appreciate what otherwise would be "dead letters to our eyes?" Can we connect these old, dead forms meaningfully to a new way of life so that they offer up "a deepening rather than a narrowing of social vision"—so that, as Locke puts it, "out of a deeper penetration into each, a new relevancy comes"?

W. E. B. Du Bois famously criticized Locke for pursuing what seemed to him to be art for art's sake. Du Bois calls it his "search for disembodied beauty" and saw *The New Negro* as depoliticized and an ineffectual response to Reconstruction and the urgent need to organize Black labor. In a review of Locke's anthology and later in his essay "Criteria of Negro Art," Du Bois insists that Black arts should pursue the goal of political liberation, the "pertinent and pressing problem," instead. "All Art," he says, "is propaganda and ever must be, despite the wailing of the purists. . . . I do not care a damn for any art that is not used for propaganda. But I do care when propaganda is confined to one side while the other is stripped and silent." Locke responds to Du Bois by saying, "My chief objection to propaganda, apart from its besetting sin of monotony and disproportion, is that it perpetuates the position of group inferiority even in crying out against it. For it lives and speaks under the shadow of a dominant majority whom it harangues, cajoles, threatens or supplicates. It is too extroverted for balance or poise or inner dignity and self-respect. Art in the best sense is rooted in self-expression and whether naive or sophisticated is self-contained."[5]

Art is not insurrectionary. But I think it would be wrong to say that, for Locke, art's "self-containment" or "intrinsic values," as he puts it, speaks to anything like the autonomy of art or an aesthetic retreat from life or even a politicizing of aesthetics suggesting that art transcends life. What Locke actually says is that the ways in which race can be realized in art will make *life* "more beautiful and interesting." So to understand the intrinsic value of art for Locke, we need to understand the value of making life interesting, as if life is not already interesting, or as if value depends on life being interesting rather than, say, equitable and just. But first it would help to know what Locke means by "value." It also would help to know what Locke means by "adventure" (as when he says that race for artists is "a sort of added enriching adventure") since, after slavery, after Reconstruction, it really is not clear that race should be more of an *adventure* than it once was.

Value and the Range of Appreciation

It strikes me how much Locke sounds like Henry James in that letter to H. G. Wells I keep mentioning in which James says, "It is art that *makes* life, makes interest, makes importance, for our consideration and application of these things, and I know of no substitute whatever for the force and beauty of its process." What precedes this line is, again, James's claim that so far from "literature being irrelevant" to life and "to its being made as interesting as possible," he regards it "as relevant in a degree that leaves everything else behind." Locke was the editor of *The New Negro* and also a literary critic who worked for "a sharpening of critical discrimination" and "the appreciation of new forms" of literature and art in his own essays for *The New Negro* and elsewhere. But Locke was above all a philosopher who spent his academic career developing theories of value and of cultural pluralism. He was influenced by William James as an undergraduate at Harvard and also at Oxford where, as the first African American Rhodes Scholar, he heard James's Hibbert Lectures that became *The Pluralistic Universe* and informed his own theories of pluralism.[6] He studied under Hugo Münsterberg (whose work on attention I mentioned in chap. 4) first at Harvard and later in Berlin. After being appointed to the faculty at Howard University and returning to Harvard for his PhD, he worked with Ralph Barton Perry, whose own book on value theory, *General Theory of Value: Its Meaning and Basic Principles Construed in Terms of Interest*, would have lasting value to him.

But possibly the greatest influence on Locke was the British pragmatist F. C. S. Schiller, who directed his thesis at Oxford and who, once again, believed that the truth of an idea comes down to the interest we take in it and to its relevance in human affairs. If you remember, it is Schiller whom Dewey credits in a eulogy with inventing the philosophy and "principle of relevancy." On the back of Schiller's first invitation to Locke to join him for tea, Locke writes, "This is a great day—when I met Schiller—the whole prospect of my work and life seemed different."[7] Du Bois may accuse Locke of promoting art that is irrelevant to Black lives, but Locke's idea of the value of art points back to nothing less than the principle of *relevancy* that changed the prospect of his own life from the day he met Schiller.

In Locke's defining essay, "Values and Imperatives," he writes that he is looking for some middle ground between "objectivism" and "subjectivism"—between the idea of universal value, discoverable by "the colorless, uniformitarian criterion of logic," and value measured by the "atomistic relativism of a pleasure-pain scale." We should think of value instead as a feeling, attitude, or orientation *toward* something, in reference to something, which is why Locke says that we should speak of a "value reference" rather than a "value claim." So Locke is, first of all, "de-throning our absolutes" in the study of values (axiology) as well as in all philosophies. It seems to him that all philosophies "are in ultimate derivation philosophies of life and not of abstract, disembodied 'objective' reality; products of time, place, and situation, and thus systems of timed history rather than timeless eternity." There is "no fixity of content to value," and what is valuable to me may not be valuable to you—and yet, he says, we do not want "completely individualistic and anarchic relativism" and "we must take care not to exile our imperatives, for afterall, we live by them."

There are no absolute values, but unless philosophy can give some account of *normative* values, the imperatives and "ultimates" we live by, then we are left with "philosophic nihilism" or else "bloodless behaviorism," but without any value at all, according to Locke. "Man does not, cannot live in a clueless world." We may not have absolute values, but there is no getting past the absolute power of the values we have and how these tend to be the normative principles within the group or society in which we live and with which we identify and that "rightly or wrongly hypostasizes [these principles] as universals for all conditions, all times and all men." Locke is interested in just how normative values evolve but also in their functions and possibilities even if they are just an operative way out of the dangers of value absolutism or of value anarchism. "To my thinking," he says, "the gravest problem of contemporary philosophy is how to ground some normative principle or criterion of objective validity for values without resort to dogmatism and absolutism on the intellectual plane, and without falling into their corollaries, on the plane of social behavior and action, of intolerance and mass coercion."[8] We cannot wish our way out of imperatives. We do not want them to be absolutist, dogmatic, or coercive. And yet we *will* have ends and live by them, and these ends meet a purpose and need. They are like "ideals" for Dewey or like "God" for James, Whitehead, and Dewey too.

Values, for Locke, are necessarily attitudes and modes of feeling and not Kantian judgments of preference and not logical either, "for they pertain to psychological categories." They are unpredictable and constantly changing; they nonetheless shape human experience and human consciousness. Concepts of value and worth exceed the fields of truth discoverable by reasoning and scientific methods: "to the poet, beauty is truth; to the religious devotee, God is truth." Values are "not grounded in types or realms of value, but are rooted in modes or kinds of *valuing*," and Locke hopes most of all to understand how we come to value something new and to conspire with others for the priority of one value over another and also how our values define our relationships and loyalties to the social world. He is looking at "the genesis of values and their relations to the objects of desire to which they refer, to the value-feelings which accompany them, and the *valuation-processes* and value-judgments by which they are reached" within the realms of aesthetics, metaphysics, ethics, religion, and beyond economics (to which I'll return).

But value theory, Locke says, has been long neglected in philosophy in favor of the objectivity of description and empiricism on the one hand and "idealisms" and analytical logic on the other. In the essay "Value," he writes, "Value is one of the last of the great philosophic topics to have received recognition, and even now the *Encyclopaedia Britannica* has an article only on economic value. Its discovery was probably the greatest philosophical achievement of the 19th century, but opinions on the subject are not yet crystallized." The limited reflections on value usually began with the distinction between "fact" and "value" and between "description" and "appreciation" and with the belief that consciousness of value always follows on consciousness of fact. Value represents a "reaction upon fact"; it is "an attitude assumed toward fact" and a weighing (appreciation or depreciation) of fact in relation to one's interests, feelings, desires, purposes, and needs. It follows, Locke argues, "(1) that a certain subjectivity, or, better, a relation to personality, is inherent in all values; (2) that value arises out of the mind's practical attitude, when it reacts upon stimulation . . . (3) that values are something super-added upon the other qualities of objects by the mind, in order to express their relation to its purpose and acts, and do not inhere in objects *per se*." Values, then, are as "subjective, variable, and personal" as can be, and yet they also get "objectified and projected into objects, when these are regarded as valuable objectively and *per se*, or when the 'validity' of actual valuations and of existing values is called into question. Hence 'superpersonal' or 'over-individual' and even 'eternal' and 'absolute' values are recognized by many philosophers."[9]

To clarify: the sense of value that we feel when we appreciate a good deed or a just decision—or a prayer, painting, poem, or sunset—derives from forms and qualities of feelings in the experience of it and the consciousness of these feelings and our appreciation of the experience. The feelings include exaltation, ecstasy, salvation, acceptance, consistency, equilibrium, repose, and satisfaction, according to Locke. But these "feeling modes" are different for different value types (moral value, ethical value, aesthetic value, religious value, or logical value), although sometimes the feeling modes also break out of their value genres so that a logical proof becomes "beautiful" or a landscape becomes "divine." Each value situation suggests an "emotionally mediated form of experience" and may be judged, as more or less valuable, by how appropriate it is to these emotions and how much of our interest it excites. We confer value on a situation through our interest and the quality of our feelings for it, but it is also the case that the types of value that we confer, in our *valuing* and appreciation, are *types*—"normatively stamped." There are "generic types of value"—Locke even calls them *stereotyped values*—that over time and in certain contexts come to define our interests and the quality of the experiences we recognize as having value. We assign value to our personal experiences from the normative categories of value that recognize these interests and typify them into social and cultural values that are taken as given, natural, or necessary. These typified values become the common "background"—that is, the set of plausible a priori ideas of value—against which our own feelings of value and importance figure. These values are what we actually mean when we talk about our cultural and social backgrounds.

Again, Locke emphasizes how value, beyond economic value, "is one of the last of the great philosophic topics to have received recognition" and that by the early twentieth century, philosophers had only just begun to move beyond the Kantian *impasse* that certain important beliefs (in freedom, in moral absolutes, in God) could be postulated for purposes of action but never scientifically proven as objects of knowledge. In "Value," Locke tells us that after Kant, philosophers, almost exclusively in Germany, had studied how knowledge itself is conditioned by our interests and desires and also our belief in the "prospective value of the objects of our cognitive endeavors"; how values cannot be divorced from existence but "arise in the mind as reactions" to facts in the world and as a way of showing that "personal experience is not deducible from metaphysics, but *vice versa*." The rise of pessimism and the influence of Schopenhauer questioned the value of life as a whole while drawing attention to how values are lost, found, and still sustained. And Nietzsche famously took on a "transvaluation" or "revaluation of all values" and of all moral standards according to individual and creative measures of valuing.

In the English-speaking world, Josiah Royce familiarized the distinction between "description" and "appreciation" in his book *Spirit of Modern Philosophy* (1892). (Royce had been Locke's favorite professor as an undergraduate at Harvard, and he chose Harvard again for graduate school in order to continue working with Royce, but Royce died just before he arrived.) Locke says that since Royce, the dominant investment in idealism has been unfavorable to discussions of value except for the pragmatists who "recognize the presence of valuations in cognitive processes" and "tend to regard all values as relative, primarily in the particular situation which is valued, and declare the existence and efficacy of values to be plain, empirical facts." Ralph Barton Perry, Locke's dissertation advisor, defines value as any "object of interest" and argues that, without the mind's selective attention to objects of interest and concern (an idea he takes from James), it would be a world without value. This is why Perry sets out to define the origins of "interest" and "modes of interest" by writing a *General Theory of Value: Its Meaning and Basic Principles Construed in Terms of Interest*. He wants "to see under what conditions anything *becomes* an object of interest and *acquires* value."[10]

Thus, Locke writes about the history of the concept of value in order to situate his own work within this genealogy that includes Nietzsche, pragmatism, and his mentors and to advance the idea that, in his words, "value is conferred upon an object by a personal attitude towards it." Like Perry, Locke tries to understand the circumstances under which anything at all manages to acquire value, but he is also concerned with how values find expression in the social, cultural, religious, academic, or legal institutions that inform our attitudes and interests in turn. He is fully aware of how, in economic terms, maximizing value is a "non-Marxian principle" of profit. But he also says that "the curtailing of the struggle over the means and instrumentalities of values will not eliminate our quarrels and conflicts about ends, and long after the possible elimination of the profit motive, our varied imperatives will still persist. Economic classes may be absorbed, but our psychological tribes will not thereby be dissolved." Since there may be "monopolistic attitudes and policies with respect to ends and ideals just as well as monopolies of the instrumentalities of human values," Locke is choosing to focus on the values conferred by attitudes and interests apart from the profit motive, which is not to say that, within the Marxian principles he grants, these social, cultural, and religious values, for example, cannot participate in the profit motive. But he is acknowledging, too, that the focus on economic value alone has obscured other ways in which theories of value can account for the qualities of those ends and imperatives that will always drive our sense of importance and will never go away so long as we continue to act with and feel we need a purpose.

It can be confusing how value is always both an expression of individual emotion and interest and a normative principle to which individuals subscribe, but I think Locke is taking seriously the pragmatist belief in the way beliefs or feelings become "plain, empirical facts," a part of our reality. If an object has been consistently valued in a particular way, "its value adheres to it" and it seems "intrinsically valuable." If objects have obtained social recognition as valuable, they "come to rank as objective values." Values acquire objectivity in such a way that our personal valuations look like "a mere recognition of an already existing value." Values are not "superpersonal" or categorical, but they tend to function this way, so that the qualities that our immediate apprehension of an object reveal carry a "formal claim to universality," and our personal values usually happen to turn out to be the uncontested values of our social or cultural group. It is not that Locke believes in the truth of normative values, but he knows that everyone treats normative values as if they were true, which is why he writes, in "A Functional View of Value Ultimates," that he prefers "a functionalist theory of value" that explains just how values based in our personal feelings and interests become normative values (ethics being the most obvious example of this); how they serve as practical constants and "sustaining imperatives of their correlated modes of experience; nothing more, but also nothing less." "It should be possible," Locke argues, "to maintain some norms as functional and native to the process of experience, without justifying arbitrary absolutes, and to uphold some categoricals without calling down fire from heaven."[11]

But, again, to maintain that norms may function *as* intrinsic to the process of experience is to suggest that the values we assign to experiences are not intrinsic at all but serve the function of imbuing an experience with meaning at one time or another. We have a plurality of values and a plurality of value norms and, for Locke, value theory provides the basis for the critical and comparative study of these norms and how they might function differently and also how other values might at other times become new norms and new "ultimates." Here is what Locke says:

> There is no warrant of fact for considering values as fixed permanently to certain normative categories or pegged in position under them or attached intrinsically by nature or "essence" to that mode of valuation to which they may be relevantly referred. Only in our traditional stereotyping of values is this so: in actuality, something in the way they are felt or apprehended establishes their normative relevancy.[12]

The question for Locke seems to be what difference it makes to any of us to acknowledge these modes of valuation. His "functional view of value ultimates" is ultimately a perspective on these ultimates (the values that seem so absolute) in order to ask, in each case, whether they are relevant right now. And if, in each case, we feel and apprehend their relevance to be practically constant and sustaining, then Locke says these normative values should be seen as having "normative relevancy" and nothing more, but also nothing less.

The question, then, is whether these types or "stereotypes" can serve our purposes and whether we might recognize something valuable in any of them and, only if so, might they be considered "valid," since validity is never indisputable but simply "a high or generally recognized and practically indisputable degree of value." Locke's sense of value is so similar to Schiller's sense of "relevance" as to be practically indistinguishable from it. I am thinking especially of when Schiller writes, "To say that relevance means subjectivity merely means that it is conceived not as a quality residing in the thing thought of *per se* but only in its relation to us; *it lies in its value for us and in our attitude towards it.*" Relevance implies "the right to select the *humanly valuable* part"; "such selection, of course, means *preference* and *choice* and *rejection* of the irrelevant," and we have the right to make such selections "if we have the right to believe in the value of our thinking; for all our thinking does in fact select."

But individual values, for Locke, are also always mediated through social categories and types, so what Locke says, following Schiller, is that the stability of values "is always to some extent a fiction, because it is never absolute, and because there are no eternal values, none that endure unchanged and untransformed by new valuations forever." At any point stability is "always more or less a construction for methodological purposes, like the extraction of stable objects out of the flux of happenings," and what we extract "seems to lie in that peculiar selective preference for certain culture-traits and resistance to certain others which is characteristic of all types and levels of social organization."[13] In other words, certain cultural traits and social categories are taken as facts for the purpose of assessing their value; some, in Locke's words, "bulk large because they are attended to and selected." Others, of course, we may not appreciate at all.

In *Normative Discourse* (1961), Paul Taylor describes how we put different "value systems" into practice when different "needs and interests arise." We select which values work and are "relevant" to our way of life and find that some value systems take precedence over others because they better bring about the "ideals" of our way of life:

> In summary, to commit oneself to a way of life is to subscribe to certain principles. These principles are of two types: principles of relevance and principles of relative precedence. When we subscribe to a principle of the first type, we *decide* which value systems shall be relevant to a certain kind of situation and which shall not. In choosing a way of life we *make* a given system relevant or not relevant to a given situation. Similarly, when we subscribe to a principle of the second type, we *decide* that one value sys-

> tem shall take precedence over another in a situation where they conflict and to which they both are relevant. In choosing a way of life we stipulate the relative precedence of our value systems. Thus we cannot answer the question why a certain value system is relevant or why it takes precedence over another. We can only say that these simply are the principles to which we subscribe in virtue of the fact that we are committed to a particular way of life.

"On Locke's account," Leonard Harris writes, "axiology always entails a normative dimension." But which normative values and normative types may be relevant and useful to our way of life, and which may be called into question as invalid, depends very much on our ability to "revaluate" standing values. Locke focuses his philosophical attention not on particular values per se but on values "as apprehended"—that is, on the cognitive work of perceiving values and how they come to be "relevantly referred." How do new values emerge into consciousness? How might we arrive at the feeling that there are better forms of value out there if only we can appreciate them—that these better values might "have some quite vital and relevant connection" to ourselves?[14]

"Change the attitude," Locke says, "and, irrespective of content, you change the value-type." Changing attitudes is finally the project. But how completely difficult is this when our attitudes are so *normative*, so categorically set and stereotypical? We suffer from the inhibitions and dogmatisms of habit that Locke calls "value bigotry." He wonders how we will ever free ourselves from bigotry to find new connections and relevance to our lives. He wants new loyalties—"value loyalty" rather than "value bigotry"—arising from shifting attitudes and orientations, because social "sub-groups" are always also "psychological sub-species" divided by "the basic difference in their orientation toward their common values." So, Locke is proposing what he calls an "affective theory of valuation" in which every value is a "feeling-attitude" and every "changed feeling-attitude creates a new value."

What releases us from our bigotries, dogmatisms, and absolutisms, from our "ideologies," as Locke sometimes calls them? Simply this changed feeling-attitude. Liberating us from "superficially imposed standards," it brings new forms "within the range of appreciation." It is the "perceptual recognition" of values belonging to someone else, "revealed or developed in experience as *better*," becoming "*the new good*, shifting to the position of normative acceptance or urgency formerly occupied by older value content."[15] The revaluation of values creates new norms.

. . .

Locke was a philosopher of value, and he was also an art critic and a literary critic. In a chapter titled "Existence, Value, and Criticism" in *Experience and Nature*, Dewey writes that because of the sense of "the evanescence and uncertainty of what used to be called ends but are now called values, the important consideration and concern is not a theory of values but a theory of criticism; a method of discriminating among goods on the basis of the conditions of their appearance, and of their consequences," because "values are as unstable as the forms of clouds." Locke imagined, with Dewey, that the theory of values at the heart of his project very much serve as a theory of criticism as well. Criticism is not "a matter of formal treatises, published articles, or taking up important matters for consideration in a serious way," Dewey says. Criticism occurs instead "whenever a moment is devoted to looking to see what sort of value is present; whenever instead of accepting a value-object wholeheartedly, being rapt by it, we raise even a shadow of a question about its worth, or modify our sense of it by even a passing estimate of its probable future."

Locke's criticism in *The New Negro* and elsewhere is devoted to recognizing how these moments of recognition occur—to appreciating how art, literature, and other forms of expression are particular modes of "apprehending" values. Criticism's purpose, which for Locke is ultimately the social and ethical purpose to which I return, corresponds to an enlarging of consciousness and to the new feelings that come with appreciation and the "expansion and emancipation of values" that he suggests follows from these. The call for "perceptual recognition" is always an ethical call. Its point is that "widening of the range of appreciation" through acts of selective interest—to take in these alien forms we had never appreciated and that had never interested or concerned us as part of our reality and as relevant to us right now. These forms are "revised and reconstructed," Locke says, because they take on new kinds of significance in our experience of them. And "if value is conferred upon an object by a personal attitude towards it, it is clear that all objects can be valued by being included in a valuation-process." It is clear that objects that had not "obtained social recognition" might "come to rank as objective values." In a period of Reconstruction, Locke calls this work of recognition "constructive criticism."[16]

A further suggestion from Dewey reminds me of Locke and also of Whitehead's claim that there is no irrelevance, just neglected modes of relevance: "Irrelevance exists, but it is relative and specifiable. An idea or emotion is irrelevant not as such, through and through, but because it is a version of the meaning of events which if it were differently edited would be relevant to actions *in* the world to which it belongs." Writing of Locke's theory of values, Charles Molesworth explains that the corrective to "value absolutism" lies in demonstrations that values are rooted in emotions that make the objects, events, and ideas that were alien to us "pertain to us." Molesworth also draws attention to the way that Locke concludes his essay, "Values and Imperatives," by slipping in "with little fanfare" the idea that "the model or source of the various valuing scales—in other words, the value beneath all other values—was best thought of as esthetics." Aesthetic value for Locke is *the* model for how value works in all other realms of value. "There will be no sudden recanting of chronic, traditional absolutisms" and "no huge, overwhelming accessions of tolerance," but Locke still manages to stake his philosophy in his faith that art can have a "greater influence than any other phase of relativism upon our conception and practise of values." Whatever values a work of art professes, it calls for "a revolution in the practise of partisanship in the very interests of the values professed."[17]

This has all been a roundabout way of saying that when Locke talks about conferring value, he is also talking about relevance. And when Locke speaks of "intrinsic value," he means, so far from art being autonomous and irrelevant to the interests of life, it might be relevant in a degree that leaves everything else behind.

Perceptual Recognition

Tanner, as I mentioned, is best known now for *The Banjo Player*, but until a couple decades ago, this first internationally acclaimed African American artist was primarily known for religious paintings of scenes from the Gospels. In his painting *The Pilgrims of Emmaus*, two disciples and the resurrected Christ are seated at a table with a loaf of bread and a platter of grapes in the interior space of a home (fig. 31). There is no discernible source of light except the luminosity of Christ's face and the halation around it. The two disciples at the table all at once realize that the figure with whom they have been traveling all along and breaking bread is actually *God*. It is the moment of revelation, an evanescent instant when something that had gone

FIGURE 31. Henry Ossawa Tanner, *The Pilgrims of Emmaus* (1905). Oil on canvas. (RF1977-334). © RMN-Grand Palais / Art Resource, New York. Photograph: Hervé Lewandowski.

unrecognized suddenly and intelligibly appears. "With that their eyes were open and they recognized him" (Luke 24:31). The special illumination of the moment—Christ vanishes just after—is reflected in the glowing faces of the two disciples and in the overall glow and also in the arch of the back wall that recapitulates Christ's halo, as if to suggest that this painting, too, is a manifestation.

Locke thought that Tanner, in turning to religious subjects like these, did not do enough to make Black art relevant and to give it recognition, and maybe not. But we can say at least that recognition mattered enormously to Tanner. His paintings show how something phenomenally comes to consciousness even as Christ *comes to* the disciples at the table. In *The Two Disciples at the Tomb*, we see nothing but a scene of recognition as Peter and John, looking into Christ's tomb and finding nothing there, realize that Christ has been resurrected (fig. 32). The viewer is brought close to John's illuminated face; we feel that we accompany him in kneeling at the thresh-

FIGURE 32. Henry Ossawa Tanner, *The Two Disciples at the Tomb* (1906). Robert A. Waller Fund. Art Institute of Chicago.

old. This is the "fulfillment of the promise made to them," the realization of God's presence in the material world and the expectation of God's return. In *The Pilgrims of Emmaus*, about one of the first appearances of Christ after the resurrection, Tanner focuses on the very moment the disciples pick up on the fact that God has materialized at supper. What is consciousness raising, after all, but showing how something yet unrealized comes to matter, taking shape in a way that is imminent right here and now and toward which we decidedly turn? Another way of describing this awareness—that something all of a sudden becomes significant (in the way that a fellow traveler in this picture becomes God)—is to say that it is brought home to us, just as Christ is *brought home* in the domestic space of Emmaus or how Tanner's reviewers praised him for "[setting] forth incidents" in the gospel stories that "come home to the spectator." Henry James, whom Tanner visited at his home in Rye, writes that "the extraordinary is most extraordinary in that it happens to you and me, and it's of value (of value for others) but so far as visibly brought home to us."[18]

When you study Tanner's paintings, writes his son Jesse Ossawa Tanner, "you keep discovering new things about them—a new form is revealed, a new star seems to shine, a new shadow stretches out—in a word, his pictures are very much alive. A Tanner can do more than give you enjoyment, it can come to your rescue."[19] We see these surprising appearances in *Angels Appearing before the Shepherds*, where a transparent choir of angels drifts toward Bethlehem (fig. 33). Because they are painted so thin, like the atmosphere from which they emerge and also the smoke from the shepherd's fire (the message they come bearing is more like a smoke signal), we may not discover right away that angel with the halo that coalesces in the lower left corner, desublimated, as it were. Why did it take so long to notice? It expresses itself by confronting us directly. The more you look at a picture, the more there is to it; images emerge from the images. We should encounter every work with the expectant belief that these activated spaces will open us to more revelation, to perpetual novelty. We might remember how William James describes religious faith as anything that, enlarging the field of consciousness, lets visions enter.

In *The Disciples See Christ Walking on the Water*, the disciples have lost their bearings (fig. 34). The composition is cropped just above the horizon line so that the sea, which mirrors the cloudy sky, fills the background and there is no clear horizon. The picture is mostly all reflection, with the moon outside the picture and only visible on the choppy surface of the water. We

FIGURE 33. Henry Ossawa Tanner, *Angels Appearing before the Shepherds* (ca. 1910). Oil on canvas. Gift of Mr. and Mrs. Norman Robbins. Smithsonian American Art Museum.

have a nocturne, a moonlit mist, the soft focus of nebulous reflections. And then, in the distance to the left, we can squint and just make out a shroud of light, a vertical phantom. It is a revelation! Tanner paints a brilliant vision hovering above a darkly moving drift, the sheer disclosure of a resurrected figure against a foggy background. And, when it appears, the apostles see its potency and dynamic connection to their lives in the boat. A praying apostle reels back. The faint outline around another in the stern suggests that he is shaken. We see, in so many of Tanner's pictures, an image of some depth like this and then that "focused apparency." A new horizon opens up. A new perception on the horizon brings forth all the value there can be. If

FIGURE 34. Henry Ossawa Tanner, *The Disciples See Christ Walking on the Water* (ca. 1907). Oil on canvas. Gift of the Des Moines Association of Fine Arts (1921.1). Des Moines Art Center Permanent Collections.

you wait, then something comes to the surface, like Christ walking on the water, and the mind attends to it with maximum power. To experience its appearance is to become conscious of this imminent process. Jesse Ossawa Tanner seems to understand all of his father's pictures on the principle of this painting: we see the appearance as the apostles do; a form is resurrected and shines out or stretches in front of us. When Jesse says that these paintings can come to our rescue, he means that there is something redeeming about the hide-and-seek impulse they share, even as the disciples, tossed by the boat in the waves, know right away that they are saved.

How exactly can pictures save? The logic seems to be this: that what was invisible, hidden, or unfigured, what we thought or never knew was lost, comes to light and takes on substance like never before. Within a perceptual field this is described as the figure-ground effect that I discussed earlier at length: a figure detaches itself from what is observed vaguely or not at all as a matter that is capable of being looked at empirically. Rescued from obscurity, it expresses a separate identity—an objective identity. It is not hard to see how a picture like *The Disciples See Christ Walking on the Water* is fraught with background, and how out of this background comes some final, decisive expression. Let's call it an incarnation. Given the brilliance with which it emerges, it seems to follow that the kind of attention we are showing it is special. We could say that it comes to figure.

I think this is what Tanner means when he suggests that a successful painting is a statement of faith: "I paint the things I see and believe." Or when he claims that he believes sincerely in religious sentiment in religious pictures but also that he has never seen religious sentiment in a picture that did not also have artistic qualities. This is also what Laurence Buermeyer, theorist of aesthetic experience and contributor to *The New Negro*, means when he says that he thinks great art is only possible when the feeling expressed is "religious" in the sense of revealing or bringing forth something of ultimate importance. "It is a question whether the intensity of feeling, the freeing of the mind from everything irrelevant, which is essential to the greatest art, is possible except when the feeling expressed is religious in character," he says. "The artist is inspired to do his utmost only if he feels that what he is showing is that which is best worth showing. If this is true, if the greatest art is always religious art, secular art of the first rank is only the art of a religion that has not yet found recognition and a name."[20]

For Tanner, almost anything might be religious art. The most prosaic, everyday moments might be revelatory, as when he tells an anecdote of riding in a "jiggling, ill-lighted omnibus in Paris" one evening and being "struck with the beauty of the effect around me." He sees from inside the ill-lighted bus "figures dimly lighted with a rich cadmium" and, through the windows, "the cool night with here and there a touch of moonlight." But then Tanner doesn't want to paint the interior of a bus, so he paints an episode from the Gospels instead. "*Judas Covenanting with the High Priests* is the result," he says. The painting, unlocated now but visible in a photograph, shows Judas receiving thirty pieces of silver from the high priests in exchange for identifying Jesus to them. The figures face each other on wooden benches perpendicularly set against framed windows and, though we cannot in the photograph see the glowing light of the interior against the cool night, I guess we can begin to imagine how it looked inside an omnibus. Maybe we should see the painting as a betrayal of the reality of a Paris omnibus ride in the form of a picture of Judas's betrayal instead. It seems like the transfigurations of the painting are *either* a betrayal or else a disclosure of the effects of cadmium light inside an omnibus as a moment of faithful illumination. "What is called the magic of the artist resides in his ability to transfer these values from one field of experience to another."[21]

So while Tanner may not have done his share, in Locke's opinion, to raise awareness of Black art or the specific relevance of a life of adversity to art, Tanner does seem to have faith in Locke's idea that the function of art is to bring some aspect of life to attention as having value, having relevance, with the momentary "freeing of the mind from everything irrelevant." Tanner suggests that a painting with artistic qualities can instill conviction in the reality "of things not seen" through some intensity of feeling that brings their realized presence into our objective reality. A reporter visiting Tanner's studio writes, "Hence every picture is instinct with religious emotion. And this is of such a nature that it thrills also the spectator and rouses within him the faith, hope, and love which were first kindled in the heart of the artist. If 'the end of art is to deepen and intensify the sense of life,' that purpose is here fully realized." Most of all, Tanner knows that our sense of life will deepen and intensify when the pictures that bring to light the aspects of life they select interest us. Religious art is "interesting" art, he suggests, whereas art without religious sentiment is an "uninteresting, inartistic production" with little to appreciate.[22]

In other words, Tanner keeps faith with the idea that Locke calls "art pluralism" and defines as "a growing liberation" of values: the bringing of new forms and figures within the range of appreciation. A painting will pick up on things of which we were unaware as valuable but that come to bear on us now by their emphasis in works of art. In this way, art finally provides "as good an example as we can find of what democratization can mean in a value field." When Locke tells us to "recall how suddenly the Negro spirituals revealed themselves" after being suppressed for generations under stereotypes, "secretive, half-ashamed," or how an African heritage is now *revealing itself* in African American art, he is suggesting, in Monroe Beardsley's words (more on Beardsley later), that "something fresh is added to the world; something like a miracle occurs" when certain unknown, lost, or alien things are resurrected and make an appearance. And I think that Tanner, like Locke, wants us to see that art is especially good at these appearances—at making something that was nonapparent to us, or past us somehow, appear, like magic (like miracles)—building out the matter so that new objects of attention really emerge. Jesse says his father was a "great mystic" who "felt influences which the common mortal does not perceive, his pictures reflect this perception."[23]

. . .

Look at how the shrouded figure in Tanner's picture of a Moroccan archway emerges and comes to light, only just distinguishable from the background (fig. 35). Look at how other figures from Tangiers, in *Street Scene, Tangiers*, emerge from gates, more vertical shrouds of light at the threshold of a visible world (fig. 36). They are figured just the way Christ is figured as an iridescent shaft on the surface of the water, only now these figures are North Africans in kaftans appearing from a distance. "There should be a glow," Tanner says, "which indeed consumes the theme or subject." Between 1897 and 1912, Tanner took trips to Morocco, Algeria, Palestine, and Egypt and produced pictures like these in which sheathed figures come into focus against a whitewashed building or the sun-bleached entrance to the Kasbah. Sometimes the light is so blinding from inside a passage looking out that the figure under the archway between the high walls almost dissolves in the motes of dust and heat against the painted surface of the mud-packed walls. But they are not dissolving. They are surfacing, like the figures Locke praises in the poems of the Belgian poet Émile Verhaeren that appear in the process of being "realized and revealed." Locke says, "By welding his figures to their backgrounds, like Rodin scarcely freeing them from the rock, he gains his essential purpose, which is to exhibit in an art free from conventional illusion and sentimental over-emphasis, the underlying vitalism of the universe." Out of these deeper penetrations "a new relevancy comes."[24] In Tanner painting's, the viewer is always engaged in extrapolating this essence out of its surround.

These flashes of figures from Morocco are issuing out, and the tilting perspective of the pictures, like that of *The Banjo Player*, sliding forward

FIGURE 35. Henry Ossawa Tanner, *Moroccan Scene* (ca. 1912). Oil on canvas. Gift of the Mahdah R. Kniffin Estate (1971.30). Collection of the Birmingham Museum of Art.

into our space, seems to suggest the way that whatever culture it is they express *comes down to us* in this moment of transmission. The arches above remind us of the vaulted ceiling in *The Pilgrims of Emmaus* and of Tanner's halos everywhere else. They remind us that these otherworldly figures—these spectral exposures from other worlds—are revelations too.

While living in Paris in 1919, Tanner painted a cenotaph build in memory of French soldiers who died in World War I (fig. 37). It was hastily installed

FIGURE 36. Henry Ossawa Tanner, *Street Scene, Tangiers* (ca. 1912). Oil on panel, unframed. The John Axelrod Collection—Frank B. Bemis Fund, Charles H. Bayley Fund, and The Heritage Fund for a Diverse Collection (2011.1840). Photograph © 2022 Museum of Fine Arts, Boston.

beneath the Arc de Triomphe and dramatically illuminated at the evening ceremony that Tanner depicts in *The Arch* with a crowd in back and a widow and child closer in to the left and two veterans in blue uniforms to the right. How do we bring to mind what we have lost or never actually knew to begin with? How do we appreciate whoever this may be? Another incandescent white form appears beneath an arch, another version of the glowing vertical forms brought out from beneath the arches of Tangiers. Another take on the resurrected Christ brought home to his disciples in Emmaus. There is a

FIGURE 37. Henry Ossawa Tanner, *The Arch* (1919). Oil on canvas. Gift of Alfred W. Jenkins (32.10). Brooklyn Museum.

radical outsideness to what comes to our attention. In the selective operations of art, Dewey says, "material to which it is alien enter consciousness."

"Thus 'art' in the general sense which I require is any selection by which the concrete facts are so arranged as to elicit attention to particular values which are realisable by them. For example, the mere disposing of the human body and the eyesight so as to get a good view of a sunset is a simple form of artistic selection. The habit of art is the habit of enjoying vivid values." These are Whitehead's terms, but they seem to me to apply well to Tanner. We might think of an artwork as offering for us "the direct perception of the concrete achievement of a thing in its actuality. We want concrete fact with a high light thrown on what is relevant to its preciousness."[25] Tanner's paintings are concerned with eliciting attention to particular values that are realizable whenever an object is selected and arranged in such a way that we might dispose ourselves toward it. He is throwing a highlight on whatever is of the essence. He wants us to enjoy its value, and not "miss" its preciousness.

When the sociologist Eviatar Zerubavel speaks of the work of "attentional socialization" or of attention itself as a "sociomental act," he is referring to the way our particular social and cultural groups (our "attentional communities") "determine what we come to regard as relevant" and what we continue to relegate to the background. The point is that the effort to draw attention elsewhere, to change our sense of perceived saliency so that what is unperceived in the background comes to the foreground and gets recognized instead is always social and ethical work. I understand the call to attention to be no more an evasion of politics in Tanner than it is in Locke but very much the precondition of new relations, since what we tend to notice and ignore determines what we come to regard as valuable. What we come to notice, in turn, brings to consciousness the persons, relations, and structures of relations that we had taken for granted, since our normative values (made typical or stereotypical in socially approved forms of awareness) mean that we normally take our world for granted beyond question. But, on occasion, maybe while looking at a painting, we are made to see something questionable and strange; from the norms of our disattention, it raises our attention. It is the apprehension of something as remote, foreign, or otherworldly as a dead soldier or as a North African if you are living in Paris or New York. The qualities of real things are drawn out and reconstructed in a form (maybe the form of a painting) that "adds, to the values actually present in the reality, a whole range of others which the artist transfers from remote realms of experience." "There must be value beyond ourselves," says Whitehead. "Otherwise every thing experienced would be merely a barren detail in our own solipsist mode of existence." In Tanner's paintings the phenomenological moment of recognition is always the resurrection of importance beyond our solipsistic mode and independent of us. This is why so many of his paintings show the revelation of God, as if to agree with Whitehead that "we owe to the sense of deity the obviousness of the many actualities of the world" never obvious before.[26]

Relevance is usually associated with political awareness, and imagining that relevance might arrive in the disclosures of religious pictures taken from the Gospels is no exception to this, though in no form of messaging

Du Bois would approve. The artists and writers who first thought about the phenomenology of relevance always imagined how important theories of consciousness and recognition would be for reconstructing the political world. This is why the sort of perceptual work that Tanner's paintings (or Thayer's or Homer's paintings) invite is ultimately taken up by sociologists like Zerubavel who write about historical shifts in "what we tend to notice and ignore" and about the ways in which the marked and unmarked (notable and unnotable) parts of our phenomenological world render certain persons invisible as well. There are those who may not "gain even the minimum attention required to feel that [their] presence has been acknowledged," so that they are "nonpersons" or "background persons," like extras in films or like all the Black persons behind the scenes or in the background who historically understand "that they should act so as to maximally encourage the fiction that they aren't present" in what the sociologist Erving Goffman describes as a *social invisibility*.

Attentional norms do more than simply suggest what we might see as distinguished; they actually determine what we come to regard as historically significant and worth keeping in mind. How to keep something in mind is, for sociologists, a sociological question, though the fact that the flow of consciousness can be oriented toward new realities and that perception can enlarge so as to bring even more to mind was first taken up by artists and philosophers alike. Alfred Schutz, whose reflections on relevance form a part of his "phenomenology of social relations," believes that social problems always involve a struggle for recognition under threat in a particular social world.[27] How does perception evolve when it is always shaped by the institutionalized norms of social groups that themselves are the "natural conception of the world taken for granted" and go unquestioned as a way of life?

For Schutz, whom I discussed in chapter 4, changing the social structure means changing a belief in what counts as relevant, moving from one relevance structure to another so that a "relevance structure which demarcates a *particular* domain of typification is no longer taken for granted beyond question but becomes questionable itself." Schutz wants to know how new subjects become "thematic" or rise into attention that we might regard what we never think about and so that whatever it is we normally regard without thinking becomes "an open concept to be rectified or corroborated by supervening experience." How do new subjects come to be relevant and meaningfully felt? Other "provinces of reality" are within reach of our "paramount reality," and Schutz thinks that in the "transition from one to the succeeding states of consciousness" (and from one "province of reality" to another), we move beyond our prejudices and typifications that freeze relations and are never the same as when we started. Finding relevance will change us even as it makes new subjects intelligible and appreciable to us.

When the radical abolitionist John Brown was condemned for his raid on the federal armory at Harpers Ferry, Henry David Thoreau appealed to his readers: "Do yourselves the honor to recognize him. He needs none of your respect." When there has been, in Robert Pippin's words, a "breakdown in the possibility" of "intersubjective intelligibility," we confer value through attention. We can widen the range of our recognition, and we also can restrict the range as Thoreau famously does, in "Civil Disobedience," when he chooses to ignore any government that supports slavery. The state says, "Recognize me; and the simplest, the most effectual, and, in the present posture of affairs, the indispensablest mode of treating with it on this head, of expressing your little satisfaction with and love for it, is to deny it then." "I cannot for an instant," he says, "recognize that political organization as *my* government which is the *slave's* government also."

For Locke the "politics of recognition" that Thoreau suggests is always mediated by that "last of the great philosophic topics to have received recognition": *value*. And he always understands the discovery of value perceptually, on the model of an unconcealing of figures that are raised into relief, like an encased Rodin figure pulled out of the block. Or on the perceptual model of an artist drawing out a figure from the background, so strikingly we feel compelled to turn to it, that Locke also calls "reconstruction."[28]

Our Backgrounds

In Tanner's *The Resurrection of Lazarus* (fig. 38), a figure comes out of the ground. We see Lazarus coming to consciousness within the crowded cave as he gets raised up in his luminous white shroud as Christ, standing beside the grave, commands (from John 11:43), "Lazarus, come out!" "Lazarus, come forth!" In the back among the mourners, a single Black figure is linked to Lazarus in the way that he is also draped in white and *comes out* for us while the other figures surrounding him blend in browns. The man's face and open eyes are illuminated by an unseen light and shine from within the dark cave's opening. An article on Tanner from 1902 says of the painting, "There was race in it, a quality that one critic avers to be new to Biblical

FIGURE 38. Henry Ossawa Tanner, *The Resurrection of Lazarus* (1896). Oil on canvas. (RF1980–173). © RMN-Grand Palais / Art Resource, New York. Photograph: Hervé Lewandowski.

painting." We know that Tanner painted a self-portrait as Lazarus for another painting that is now lost, and certainly the story of Lazarus's resurrection could be seen as relevant to an understanding of Black lives during Reconstruction. Invoked on pulpits, it suggested the promise of a vital life after the social death of slavery in the way that Frederick Douglass, speaking to the neglect of Black liberation in these decades and the cultural amnesia of Lost Cause racism writes, "The assumption that the cause of the Negro is a dead issue is an utter delusion. For the moment he may be buried under the dust and rubbish of endless discussion concerning civil service, tariff and free trade, labor and capital . . . but our Lazarus is not dead."[29]

The story of Lazarus also can be seen as relevant to the kind of cultural work that makes certain figures and forms relevant even as they uplift you, like a Tanner painting, according to his son. The old man at the head of the grave who is helping to lift up Lazarus—his arm tensed with the weight of the head—was not originally there. In most paintings of Lazarus, like Rembrandt's *The Raising of Lazarus* to which Tanner's painting was compared, the figure rises up magically at God's command. But Tanner added the old man, in the garb of an Old Testament prophet, as if to draw attention to how Lazarus is *picked up* in the painting and all the serious effort it is taking to pick this figure up and out of the ground. Insofar as Lazarus also functions as a figure for Tanner, we might say this is a pick-me-up too.

The painting was a great success when it was shown in the Paris Salon of 1897 and, soon after, the French government purchased *The Resurrection of Lazarus* to hang beside James Abbott McNeill Whistler's *Arrangement in Grey and Black, No. 1; or, The Artist's Mother* in the galleries at the Musée du Luxembourg (fig. 39). The French government had bought Whistler's picture in 1891, the year that Tanner arrived in Paris, although he would have seen it on display a decade earlier at the Pennsylvania Academy of Fine Arts while he was a student there. When Tanner returned home to visit his family in Kansas City after the Paris Salon, he painted *Portrait of the Artist's Mother* of his mother Sarah Elizabeth Miller Tanner. She is closely adapted from Whistler's famous painting, sitting in profile on the rocking chair with her scooped form stretched horizontally across an arrangement of muted and modulating tones in thin washes of paint. The raised perspective means that Tanner also looked up to his mother.

Tanner's painting is after Whistler, except that in 1897 it is hard not to see that it picks up on his own painting of Lazarus too. Sitting on an incline, ensconced, with her back and arms supported and head supported and face glowing from a hidden light, *Portrait of the Artist's Mother* recalls the picture hanging alongside Whistler's picture in Paris as well as Whistler's picture (fig. 40). The luminous white sheet spreads forward from Sarah's shoulder in liquid folds, like Lazarus's burial cloth. The reddish-brown tones resemble those of *The Resurrection of Lazarus* much more than Whistler's arrangement of cool blacks and grays. They also recall Rembrandt's *The Supper at Emmaus*, which served as Tanner's model for his painting of Lazarus (much more than for his own painting of Christ at Emmaus). Rembrandt's resurrected figure rocks back in profile on a chair and looks abstractedly into the mellow space of the home. This means that Tanner's portrait of his mother

FIGURE 39. James Abbott McNeill Whistler, *Arrangement in Grey and Black, No. 1; or, The Artist's Mother* (1871). Oil on canvas. (RF699). © RMN-Grand Palais / Art Resource, New York. Photograph: Jean-Gilles Berizzi.

is an adaptation of Whistler's portrait figured as a resurrection and also figured as a moment of recognition, since the point of *The Supper at Emmaus* is the surprising appearance of the resurrected figure before the disciple who, with eyes opened, from Luke, "recognized him."

Once more, the word *relevant* derives from the verb *relevate*, whose meaning is to pick up or to raise, so to make something relevant is to raise it. But, actually, to re-levate, with its prefix *re-* meaning again, is to raise it or take it up again, on another occasion. So, some subject—let's say, the

FIGURE 40. Henry Ossawa Tanner, *Portrait of the Artist's Mother* (1897). Oil on canvas. Partial gift of Dr. Rae Alexander-Minter and purchased with the W. P. Wilstach Fund, the George W. Elkins Fund, the Edward and Althea Budd Fund, and with funds contributed by The Dietrich Foundation, 1993 (EW1993-61-1). Philadelphia Museum of Art.

gospel story of Lazarus—gets picked up in another context on another occasion (let's say the occasion of Reconstruction), and if it comes to matter in this new light, it is relevant, but otherwise it is irrelevant. Locke knew from Schiller that finding relevance always depends "on the purpose and needs of the moment." It is about seeing value in figures that would not otherwise figure at all the way that Locke describes the "act of experiencing figures . . . not in isolation but contextualized within a reciprocating movement of perception, conception, and valuation." It seems to be the phenomenal work of Tanner's paintings to do this kind of figuring out. Figures "continually come into view and appeal to our interest," so that, now relevant, "our earlier lines, having grown irrelevant, are then dropped."[30] New values are called into play when a figure from the background is brought up and rendered perceptible. Here, an essential part of Tanner's background, in the form of his mother—with her own background of slavery in Virginia—is brought forward appreciably (reconstructed even from Whistler's already clichéd form) and given recognition.

And then, the following year, Tanner paints another mother at home sitting on the soft folds of a white sheet spilling light, her lit face again turned in to the left, only this time he calls it *Annunciation* (fig. 41). The Archangel Gabriel appears at the moment of divine conception as a shaft of fulgent light. The figure is glazed with yellow, then scraped down to reveal the white abstraction of an angel shining out from underneath. The angel is so brilliant it almost looks like a neon tube installed on the wall. Of course by this point, we have seen this florescent beam on many other occasions. In *Reconstruction in Philosophy,* Dewey writes, "Taken in its full concreteness, [an experience] yields no instruction, it throws no light. What is called abstraction means that some phase of it is selected for the sake of the aid it gives in grasping something else." The angel here throws the light that gives relief to the tender portrait of Mary in her foreshortened room with its tipping floor.

Tanner had just returned to Paris from a trip to Egypt and pictures Mary as a young North African "of the poorer classes" beneath an interior arcade.[31] The angel announces this moment of incarnation, the advent of something new and tender in the world. It projects what is coming to us. It calls it out. But the focus all along is on the disposition of the figure of Mary, who seems to have been "roused from sleep to meet the mysterious announcement" on the edge of her unmade bed. She is just getting up. It the phenomenological moment of becoming conscious of the significance of what is coming to her, of self-consciousness. We, too, are meant to see this appearance as transfiguring.

...

There have been plenty of critics of Locke when he claims, for example, to want to "redeem" the idea of race through the creation of a Black culture, holding onto the sense of a shared background and heredity. It is not just that the traditions he calls "African" and "folk," and means to adapt for formal and stylistic innovation, risk reproducing "culture types" of Blackness and primitivism rooted in a long history of racist discourse that sees

FIGURE 41. Henry Ossawa Tanner, *Annunciation* (1898). Oil on canvas. Purchased with the W. P. Wilstach Fund, 1899 (W1899-1-1). Philadelphia Museum of Art.

primitivism as aesthetically desirable. It is also that Locke argues that the concept of race itself has pragmatic use while also always acknowledging that race remains the concept of an entrenched, white power. Locke's "strategic essentialism," to use Gayatri Spivak's term, means that he believes that "race as a unit of social thought is of growing importance and necessity" for the solidarity and group consciousness of Blacks, if only finally as a "forerunner . . . of that kind of recognition [Blacks] are ultimately striving for, namely, recognition of an economic, civic, and social sort." Locke "repudiates the older biological and historical doctrines of race" and the "fallacies" of thinking that race creeds and racial essentialism imply: belief in the purity of race, for example (he calls it the "biological fallacy") or belief in the ontology of race (the "fallacy of the permanency of the race types"). "Physical race or 'pure race' is a scientific fiction," he writes: "biologically, it is irretrievable, if ever possessed—historically, it is an anachronism, being attributed to national not racial groups, and then only to justify the historical group sense—politically, it is mere policy or subterfuge of empire." But Locke still maintains, in essays such as "The Concept of Race as Applied to Social Culture," that "in some revised and reconstructed form, we may anticipate the continued even if restricted use" of the idea of race, and of culture based in race, "as more or less necessary and basic concepts that cannot be eliminated altogether."

What is the function of a Black heritage on the way to Black liberation? Why should the idea of a heritage come to matter at all? One can imagine how little Du Bois, for one, would keep faith with Locke's sense of how "race pride" might "[rehabilitate] the race in world esteem from that loss of prestige" that followed from the fate of slavery. However the flowering of a Black culture in Harlem might hope to address the ideologies of racism, it could never address those "ideologies as historical forces" preventing the emergence of a Black labor movement and consigning Blacks to the reality of poverty and racial violence.[32]

But Locke was a critic and theorist of value, and the "perceptual recognition" of a culture mattered to him. "It does not follow," he writes, "that if the Negro were better known, he would be better liked or better treated. But mutual understanding is basic for any subsequent cooperation and adjustment." What Locke means by subsequent adjustment is complicated but includes, for a start, the way in which "the Negro mind has leapt, so to speak, upon the parapets of prejudice and extended its cramped horizons. In so doing it has linked up with the growing group consciousness of dark-peoples and is gradually learning their common interests."[33]

Locke writes, "In dealing with race and culture we undoubtedly confront two of the most inevitable but at the same time most unsatisfactory concepts involved in the broadscale consideration of man and society. There is the general presumption and feeling that they have some quite vital and relevant connection." But as to the nature of this connection or as to why race and culture should ever be relevant to each other no one can agree. At least Locke confirms, as the basis for any discussion, that the terms *race* and *culture* are not constants, not even paired variables, nor are they organically or causally connected, "though they have at all times significant and definite relationships." What Locke finally wants to suggest is that culture takes race not as essential or real but as the operative trait of a "vital common background." "Race operates as a tradition, as preferred traits and values" that over time and because of historical circumstances and also often "by accident" become a normative set of shared traits and values that a distinctive group takes for granted. "Race accounts for a great many of the specific elements of the cultural heredity, and the sense of race may itself be regarded as one of the operative factors in culture since it determines the stressed values which become the conscious symbols and tradition of the culture." The shared experience of a group "under social pressure" suggests that the memories and traits associated with that group determine its cultural emphasis and its sense of importance, "the stressed values which become the conscious symbols" it lives by.[34]

Thus, a shared experience based in race determines the normative interests and values that are taken for granted and become the background against which individual interests and values emerge. These are, again, the practical constants and sustaining imperatives of their "correlated modes of experience; nothing more, but also nothing less." Every new encounter and every new experience gets valued or devalued in light of these reminiscences. But the revival of a past is never literal, since we only ever remember what interests us and because it interests us; those selective interests are the "stressed values" that become the "conscious symbols" of a heritage. Our sense of our backgrounds is built up from nothing but these interests, "some deposit of the meaning of things done and undergone" in Dewey's words, and then these "funded and retained meanings . . . constitute the capital with which the self notes, cares for, attends, and purposes." These selected memories form "the background upon which every new contact with surroundings is projected" and then valued as being to the purpose and worth our care or as notable or not. "Yet 'background' is too passive a word, unless we remember that it is active and that, in the projection of the new upon it, there is assimilation and reconstruction of both background and of what is taken in and digested."

Locke believes that culture does the salutary work of *activating* a "background," of bringing out whatever remains out there. This is why it can help to think about Locke alongside Tanner's paintings, which work very hard to make us aware of the factors that constitute a background and of the way that something distant stands out. What is perceived or brought to consciousness always will be, as Dewey writes, "characterized by marked luminosity" and "charged with value."[35] Our cultures are very much about these acts of stress, emphasizing the qualities of things that are certainly behind us, keeping them visible as conscious symbols over time and in evolving contexts and circumstances. Culture raises them. But actually what Locke suggests is that culture raises them again. It restresses those "stressed values" of our backgrounds and traditions in another context, on another occasion—let's say a folk tradition in the context of 1930s Harlem—and if that tradition is appreciable for the value it adds to this new context, then we say that that tradition is relevant, and if it does not serve to widen the range of appreciation, then we say that it is irrelevant. In that case, our backgrounds can be left behind—just backgrounds.

But, as Locke writes, if that cultural work instead has "broadened base perceptibly" through its new use of past forms, then it will have served toward "appreciative understanding of alien art forms and idioms" that "were dead letters to our eyes previously." It will have raised these dead letters again for us. "The old, the 'stored,' material is literally revived, given new life and soul through having to meet a new situation." This material enhances the present moment with a new meaning that does not exactly belong to the present or the past either but to the "reconstructive" consciousness of those renewed forms of which we are suddenly focally aware. Art provides these encounters between old and new in which the readjustment in consciousness feels—this is Dewey again—like a quick, unexpected "fit" between the old and new or like a "harmony which in its bright abruptness is like a flash of revelation; although in fact it is prepared for by long and slow incubation." We might visualize this flash in the meeting of the old and new like one of Tanner's electrifying flashes from beyond this immediate world.

Locke knows, as Tanner does, that any expansion of perception works on the gestalt principles I have been describing all along: to recognize something is a matter of cognition that depends on its relation to different backgrounds, surroundings, and objects. "Gestalt psychology," Locke says, "has demonstrated the factual reality of a total configuration functioning in perceptual recognition, comparison and choice." In calling perceptual recognition a "total configuration," Locke means that it takes all the interacting aspects of an experience for perception to work, including the play of figure and background but also the particular situation of the experiencers and everything those persons bring to it from their prior experiences, memories, and backgrounds. As Ernest D. Mason puts it, "In short, the configurative complex of the perceptual field is for Locke that of experiencerexperiencing-figure-within-background. . . . That is to say, perceptual recognition is, as Locke tells us, the act of experiencing figures (objects, events, situations, persons) not in isolation but contextualized within a reciprocating movement of perception, conception, and valuation."[36]

Can we have any revelation about ourselves without a sense of our backgrounds? Can we appreciate others without an awareness of theirs? Locke would say no. We never perceive in isolation; our perceptions are contextualized against the backgrounds that set new experiences in relief and that, acting upon these contexts, make those experiences alive and visible in turn. Locke thinks about culture on the horizons of a phenomenology that sees the African American or Black heritage as the otherwise inert background that gets activated when it is brought forward and into contact with new experiences in the moment. A tradition enhances the present with intensified interest and value but also gets "reconstructed" (Locke's word and Dewey's, too) in light of the present in which it shines. When Locke says, for example, that "obviously there is much" in Frederick Douglass, "both of word and deed, which is vital and relevant to this present generation and to our world of today," he means that the past significance of Douglass's life is "not to be superceded except by some revised version of itself." The appreciation of Douglass's life intensifies when we bring it into contact with the twentieth century if our attention to what we thought we knew and took for granted can make it matter still.

What do we take up and what do we leave behind? Henry James says that for the artist, what it always comes back to

> is this attaching speculative interest of the matter . . . the how and the whence and the why these intenser lights of experience come into being and insist on shining. The interest of the question is attaching . . . because really half the artist's life seems involved in it—or doubtless, to speak more justly, the whole of his life intellectual. The 'old' matter is there, re-accepted, re-tasted, exquisitely re-assimilated and re-enjoyed—believed in . . . for re-assertion of value, perforating as by some strange and fine, some latent and gathered force, a myriad more adequate channels."

Locke believes in picking up on the old matter that is there. He believes in the process of finding relevance, which is, once again, the concept he brings to his study of African American culture from his study of theories of value; "what is called the magic of the artist resides in his ability to transfer these values from one field of experience to another."[37] Locke's value theory concerns "this attaching speculative interest" of old, stale, stereotyped, alienated forms for new experiences of the vitality that was lost. The force of the re-attaching, of the exquisite re-assimilation, and most of all the felt contact when these old, hardened types are taken in, is what re-asserts their value. For the reader or viewer who re-enjoys them, they will be charged with vast significance. They will feel like what it means to perceive in an open-ended way, expanding the horizons of appreciation. The alternative remains ignorance of these other types, their irrelevance, and the loss of plurality into sameness.

. . .

Locke had a fraught relationship with Albert C. Barnes, the American chemist, art collector, writer, and founder of the Barnes Foundation in Merion, Pennsylvania, who nonetheless did a great deal to bring African and African American art to public attention. With the millions he earned from developing Argyrol, a drug for treating gonorrhea, Barnes built an important collection not only of European paintings—including many by Renoir, Cezanne, Picasso, and Matisse—but also of American and African American artworks and probably the best collection of African art outside of Africa at the time. He installed them all at the Barnes Foundation, an educational institution dedicated to the teaching of art appreciation across races and classes and also to the art education of the Black workers at the Argyrol factory, who were exposed to rotating exhibits of paintings on the factory floor and required to take daily seminars on the works of William James and John Dewey.

Locke wrote an essay, "A Note on African Art," based on Barnes's collection. Another essay, "The Legacy of the Ancestral Arts," drawing on African sculpture in the collection, appears in *The New Negro* along with Barnes's own essay, "Negro Art and America," and a series of reproductions from the foundation galleries. For Locke, the collection provided the opportunity for "contact and interaction" between African art and African American art, between African art and European art, and between "primitive" folk forms and the high modernist forms that appeared to absorb their principles of abstraction, technical inventiveness, and stylized design.[38] In Barnes's galleries they all hang together in ensembles that bring these incongruous works into relation in tight, symmetrical groupings that Barnes was known to readjust in the middle of the night when new patterns and relationships occurred to him. The viewer is meant to see how lines and shapes resonate across the works, rhyming with each other and their surrounding space: recumbent figures, rounded backs, curves of breasts and thighs, the angles of elbows and spread legs, undulating lines, pyramids, blocks of color, grids, things that look like halos. Locke's anthology honors this idea of fortuitous interactions and how expressions can take on the color, form, and value of other local expressions and the perceptual adjustments new contexts require. The anthology also celebrates how the trends of migration brought southern Blacks into the integrated space of New York and how the energy created by the impact of cultures and traditions meeting and dynamically adjusting in a new context produced the cultural expression that is *The New Negro*, including its own appreciation for all the African and folk traditions that Barnes brought in. To appreciate artists, the anthology suggests, is to know their contacts.

Barnes was an irascible millionaire with a famous temper whose gatekeeping of the important collection of art he had the means to buy up could compete with the efforts of Locke and others to articulate the importance of these cultural traditions for themselves. Barnes accused Locke of taking the ideas he had communicated during Locke's visits to the foundation for his own essays on the legacy of African art, though Locke always credited the work of the foundation. Still, Barnes may have done more in these years to advance the cause of art appreciation, not only through the collection itself and what it brought to light but through the foundation's educational curriculum and outreach and his own publications on the perception of art, derived almost entirely from his close friend, John Dewey, whose idea it was to start the foundation. Dewey served as the first director of education at the Barnes Foundation, contributing to its many publications; during his time in Merion, he refined his own ideas of aesthetic experience while talking with his friend in the presence of his ensembles of art. Dewey dedicated *Art as Experience* to Barnes, "in gratitude."

Those ensembles are meant to interest us. When you step across the threshold into any room, they are surprising and weird. In one, a small painting by Renoir hangs directly above a wood relief of the crucified Christ, which hangs above a case of African masks and figures carved in wood, ivory, and bone (fig. 42). This vertical axis is flanked on each side by Picasso portraits and, further out, by Modigliani portraits, each of which hang symmetrically beneath watercolors by the American painter Charles Demuth of circus acrobats, light as air, kicking or doing a handstand. A Dutch bel-

FIGURE 42. Ensemble view, south wall, Room 22, Philadelphia (2012). © 2020 The Barnes Foundation.

lied flagon rests on top of the case of African masks just below the crucifix, which looks like it could slip right in. Interspersed among the paintings are ordinary metal objects: a pewter ladle, door pulls, a chest lock at the top. Barnes arranged for compositional balance and resonance across a wall, always adding bits of metalwork that pick up on the curves, silhouettes, and angles of the pictorial forms: metal keys, keyhole escutcheons, iron hinges and double hinges, furniture handles, door pulls, calipers, hooks, locks, scissors, spoons, spatulas, pastry cutters, dough scrapers, andirons, candlesticks, carpenter squares, weather veins. They activate the spaces between the artworks, putting them in relations to each other, like the plus signs Barnes included in instructions for installers: "New Rosseau [*sic*] balances other Rousseau, woman + church." They are oriented and sometimes bent or combined to correspond to a march of diagonals or to echo the rhythm of S-curves or V-shapes across the canvases. In one case, a double hinge and keyhole escutcheon combine to create a human form whose open arms and wide stance directly invert the folded arms and closed legs of the sitter in the Chaim Soutine painting beneath it. In another, a ladle and two hinges mimic the head and pyramidal torso of the sitter in a seventeenth-century portrait by Frans Hals. Barnes wrote, "the motives, such as arabesques, patterns, etc., discernible in a picture have their analogue, sometimes a very close one, in the iron work."[39] They also relate to the forms of the antique decorative arts he added in: the backs of Windsor chairs, the handles of coffeepots, the motifs on a Pennsylvania German chest.

There is no clear logic to the arrangements, at least in any art historical sense of lineage, though some pieces are old and some are new, some are folk art and some are high art, and there are clear lines of influence built in. But with Barnes's mix of industrial arts and decorative arts and the assembly of major works from across periods and traditions, all we can really say they share is their condition for hanging together, which either comes to us or not. It is simply that they have all been raised at once—as a kind of proposition—and that they finally seem to add up in the way that Barnes's plans for installers with his plus signs add up. They contrive to hang together, and the challenge to us is somehow to pull out the principle of configuration and "to bring up [the] quality," in Barnes words, by which we can understand why they should all hang like that. Some essential shared quality is selected and brought out in each work in light of its surroundings. That quality is something like what Locke calls a "form-quality" that depends on the whole experience in context—the gestalt—but certainly would be lost in isolation.[40] The fact of the ensemble should make these qualities that we ordinarily would miss intelligible. And every single element of the ensemble, even the most adventitious metal scrap, helps and has contributive value. It is related and not irrelevant. It bears on everything else and may even provide the clue to the quality that the rhythm of lines and shapes suggests. It may be the iron hinge that hinges it all together. That handle could give us a handle. The pulls pull us in. The hooks hook us. The key may be the key to it all! You get the picture. The key unlocks all the qualities you get out of it.

Again, Barnes changed his arrangements, sometimes in the middle of the night, moving a Renoir, swapping a Cezanne. He studied unfamiliar works he did not understand or like at all until he saw something valuable in them at last. Maybe they would work in a different context, so he reattached them to a different sort of ensemble that would stress the new value he saw. The new context might bring out a warmth or coolness, shallowness or depth, the feeling of density or space that relies on the surprise of the way otherwise unrelated pieces come into contact. The new encounters could allow for the shock of fresh discoveries, of novelty. They could bring into existence more relations; aesthetic insight could be the means to further aesthetic insight. Barnes believed, in Dewey's words (from a piece he adapted for the *Journal of the Barnes Foundation*), that the measure of the best works is in their "capacity to attract and retain observation with satisfaction under whatever conditions they are approached"—so Barnes kept changing his approach. The "'eternal' quality of great art" meant there is always more to it if only we are patient enough. We should look until we see something. A good work will be "indefinitely instrumental to *new* satisfying events." It "affords continuously renewed delight" or else it "turns in time to the dust and ashes of boredom."

Barnes said he was trying to "see as the artist sees," which he understood as the ability to be fully interested in "something which is real independently of us, as when we speak of interest in music." "The artist gives us satisfaction by seeing for us more clearly than we could see for ourselves. . . . His interests compel him to grasp certain significant aspects of persons and things of the real world which our blindness and preoccupation with personal and practical concerns ordinarily hide from us." There are all sorts of interesting things that never should interest us. "Persistence of effort is the indispensable condition of real interest." So Barnes studied paintings to learn to see precisely what it was about the world the artist had grasped in them, and then he tried to exhibit them in such a way that we might grasp it too.

"Art is a fragment of life presented to us enriched in feeling by means of the creative spirit of the artist," writes Mary Mullen, who taught a class in art appreciation at the foundation and often collaborated with Barnes. The artist, Barnes says, "illuminates the objective world for us." Art is an expression of the artist's reaction to life and not something apart from life. The artist, "stirred by some specific aspect of the world, reacting with his whole personality—his senses, habits of perception and interpretation, imagination, emotional attitudes and muscular adjustments—is impelled to extricate, to draw out from the object of his emotion the particular set of qualities and relationships that called forth his response, and to reincorporate them in a form of their own, in the process of which the work of art comes into being." Out of the "sum total of our actual sensations," the artist selects something for emphasis and attention, disregarding everything else, and brings it out in such ways that enhance and prolong the perceptual experience.[41]

For us to find the picture interesting, Barnes always continues along these lines, "we must understand . . . what the distinctive aspects of reality are in which the artist is interested, how he organizes his work to reveal and organize those aspects, the means which he employs, and the kind of satisfaction which rewards his efforts when they are successful." In other words, we have to be in a position to appreciate what the artist first appreciated and "only in the light of such an understanding can any one build up the habits of perception and background in himself which will give him admission to the world of esthetic experience." Aesthetic experience is, after all, the life lesson from Dewey that Barnes is trying to teach at his foundation and in his seminars and galleries. He wants to help viewers have an aesthetic experience by cultivating in us the habits of perceiving what the artist once perceived and also a "background," or store of interests (or interestedness), that compels us to see, in the midst of everything we could see, whatever it is that will be most meaningful and satisfying—Barnes calls it "specifically relevant"—on any occasion. But "the ordinary observer has never really learned to see," he says.

Finding relevance, for Barnes, is the key to artistic perception and to experiencing the ensembles that he kept reconfiguring to bring certain qualities to the fore. Barnes writes, with Violette de Mazia, "Every perception . . . involves selection from among the many qualities of an object, of those relevant to our interests, and the amplification of such qualities by appropriate meanings stored up in our minds by past experience." The feelings and experiences that allow for the appreciation of art get built up over time and provide the resources for further appreciation. It is the appeal to these feelings, Barnes writes, "that confers significance and establishes a principle by which the essential can be distinguished from the trivial or irrelevant." The more background experience I have, the more interests I bring to the art, the more I notice and care, the more I find that it is relevant to me. This experience includes my past exposure to art and my likings and dislikings that may have nothing to do with art. It also includes the cultural traditions I have and the cultural traditions I am taught. These create "standards of appreciation which are confirmed and deepened by further experiences."[42]

In most art education, Barnes writes, the viewer comes away with some understanding of the conditions for making a particular picture and a sense of the competence with which it is made and of the biography of the artist, but these are not the "key to the understanding" of a picture. If a viewer supposes that "the only alternative to chaos . . . is authority" in the form of "academicism," then the viewer "comes away with no impression specifically relevant to what he has looked at." The alternative to the chaos is not any authoritative knowledge but the ability to look at a picture and get something out of it. The alternative is a built capacity to disentangle what is "characteristic or essential in experience from the adventitious or irrelevant material" in which it is set. But this takes time. It takes an education, in fact.[43] The hope is that we can learn from artists and their works how to let our interests draw out something essential, truly integral, from the most adventitious, inscrutable mix of images and objects not made by logic or laws, having little to do with us or each other, cooked up with spatulas and spoons, and yet, if we can manage to see it, hanging together.

What do we get when a painting of a Gospel story by the African American artist Horace Pippin hangs together with not only his other paintings of Black rural life in the South but also a postimpressionist picture of a Massachusetts harbor by Maurice Prendergast and a portrait of a half-clad young woman by the Bulgarian Parisian painter Jules Pascin plus a spatula, two door pulls, andirons, a miniature drop-leaf desk, and more (fig. 43)? I cannot really say. But there are things to notice that are offset in this context—for example, the bright white paint in Pippin's *Christ and the Woman of Samaria* announcing the two figures in this scene of recognition (the woman of Samaria recognizes the resurrected Christ while drawing water for him at a well). The white paint picks up on the white paint Pippin used for the aprons and sleeves of the figures giving thanks or eating in the Southern rural interiors of his other pictures. We are invited to recognize how these quotidian "folk" figures are being transfigured along the lines of the drawing out for Christ, whose dark complexion is also now, in relation, more visible against the blocks of white paint.

What else? We are invited to recognize how these pictures we might otherwise take for fairly flat are dramatically tilted and foreshortened, just like Pascin's tactile portrait of the young woman who looks like she could tip into our laps. The stones surrounding Pippin's drinking well have exactly the same shape and thrust as that young woman's seat. And, with the Prendergast, the succession of contrasts of line, color, and mass that, in Barnes's words, give rise to "a series of interlocking rhythms . . . comparable to that of a Bach fugue," draw attention to how elements in all the other pictures

FIGURE 43. Ensemble view, east wall, Room 12, Philadelphia (2012).

also work to bring out certain lines and points over others, at certain times, contrapuntally. We see how much Pippin's lilac-pink horizon in *Christ and the Woman of Samaria* picks up on the "horizontal lilac-pink river bank" by Prendergast's harbor that Barnes says "may be considered as a motif in the fugue." But that, too, is only the bright backdrop for the way other forms and figures get built out in layers one on top of the next in keeping with

Pippin's own method of painting, which he describes as "work[ing] my fore ground from the back ground. That throws the back ground away from the fore ground. In other words bringing out my work." Pippin's *Christ and the Woman of Samaria* was probably based on the famous African American spiritual, "Jesus Met the Woman at the Well," or so Barnes thought in setting it over these other pictures he also thought of on the principle of music. Pippin's older and folk forms are brought out in light of contemporary expressive images; we are asked to take our cues from the woman of Samaria and to recognize a resurrection. In the ensemble, they suggest what Dewey means when he talks about "the revelation of meaning in the old effected by its presentation of the new."[44] On top of it all, a metal door knocker resonates with the shape of Pippin's well and Pascin's seat. It is held up by a hinge whose birdlike form evokes the Holy Spirit.

. . .

In *The New Negro*, Locke illustrated Countee Cullen's famous poem, "Heritage," with reproductions of four African masks from Barnes's collection. This is the famous first stanza of Cullen's poem:

> What is Africa to me:
> Copper sun or scarlet sea,
> Jungle star or jungle track,
> Strong bronzed men, or regal black
> Women from whose loins I sprang
> When the birds of Eden sang?
> *One three centuries removed*
> *From the scenes his fathers loved,*
> *Spicy grove, cinnamon tree,*
> *What is Africa to me?*

The speaker recalls a Black heritage that, three centuries removed, is so alienated it is difficult to say that it is his. What is it to him? A point of origin so mythical it is Edenic; so trite he sprang from its loins. The stock images of royalty and jungle heat, of cinnamon and spice, are exactly the sort of "alien" forms Locke describes as "dead letters to us previously," if only the speaker could revive them here. But what is Africa to him?

Locke worked closely with Cullen on different versions of the poem and in the third stanza of the last version, published later, Africa is the contents of a "book one thumbs / Listlessly, till slumber comes."[45] "Unremembered are her bats / Circling through the night, her cats / Crouching in the river reeds." Why bother to bring them up? The book of Africa is boring. It is hard to feel interested in a world so distant and gone, to keep alive any sense of its reality. What is the point of holding on to an African ancestry in the midst of life in New York? "What is last year's snow to me?" asks the speaker. "Last year's anything?" As he addresses an implied listener in the room in which he lies, Africa takes the form of the snakeskin coat the (presumably male) lover wears: "Silver snakes that once a year / Doff the lovely coats you wear." It is a dead imported sort of skin. It is nothing but a habit, a put on. It is only a cover for the secret of what is so intimately alive to him in his room instead, "Lest a mortal eye should see; / What's your nakedness to me?" He knows the dead idiom of skin will always manifest more than his sexuality, his interests and orientations.[46]

And "so I lie," he says. And so he lies on the bed, apathetic, spent in other ways, trying to think of a world that does not exist for him. And so he *lies*, conjuring up distant, foreign images out of the African blue, "wild barbaric birds / Goading massive jungle herds." He puts his thumbs in his ears to hear only the sounds inside his head and his pulse inside his skin and to imagine a blood tie that feels as vital as that pulse. And as the poem moves from refrain to refrain—"What is Africa to me?"—it begins to feel like more to him than it was, less "removed." It actually becomes all he can think about and feel, shutting out everything else, so that he finds "no peace . . . no slight release."

It is not unlike the effect of the raven for the speaker in his room, also nearly napping while reading a book, a century before. The refrain captures his attention. The question gives rise to a series of possible answers that give no peace. He will keep asking the question until it answers to him, responds to the call, until, by sheer force of concentration, this African heritage that is not his in any discernible way comes home to him like the raven in the room. He will keep asking until it feels relevant to ask. Not what Africa is, but what it is *to him*.

And so the speaker internalizes the rhythm of that refrain. He takes it in and takes it to heart, and his own pulse feels like the drums, and his body moves to the beat of jungle feet treading out a jungle track. The beat of the "feet" join the patter of the real rain outside and he is compelled to match that "weird refrain" with his own rhythms and, of course, with the feet and measures of the poem,

While its primal measures drip
Through my body, crying, "Strip!
Doff this new exuberance.
Come and dance the Lover's Dance!"
In an old remembered way
Rain works on me night and day.

The sound of the rain "works on" him and calls up some repressed ancestral force that was too forgettable to matter but now cannot be kept down because it matters too much. In an old remembered way, it gives vivacity to a past that was lost to him, and now he can "Strip!" and "doff this new exuberance" rather than doffing a dead skin. The feeling of new attachment produces this second erotic image in the poem since what he feels is the sensuous thrill of a change in perception, a sudden awareness where he had been "listless" and half asleep, the sense of immediacy where there was so much distance. And this new consciousness of something of which he was unaware awakens in him a self-consciousness too: of his own body and attractions, of the way he is moving, of the way he is moved by something that was strange, illegible, "outlandish," but that means something to him now in the most visceral way. It had been buried or suppressed, but now he can keep it up. It is a "Lover's Dance," and as Dewey says about new forms of contact, "that appetition is there."[47] This strange encounter is a coming together. Whatever the image of Africa is to the speaker, it is a consummatory experience in his poem.

Of course, whatever the image of Africa from three centuries ago is to him is strictly speculative. How it is that Africa should make anything matter at all right now is an open inquiry. There is "no construction that does not raise the question of 'how it holds together,'" and there is no pursuit of "relevance" that should not be described as an "adventure." Looking for relevance or what anything means *to me* suggests the openness to "embark on an adventure," with *adventure* deriving from the Latin *adventurus*, as Martin Savransky puts it, "which signals an exposure to that which is about to happen, that is, an investment in the possibility of an event, where the latter becomes associated with a sense of a difference that matters." It points to the realization of old ideas *as* new and the willingness to be exposed to them and to take them seriously rather than listlessly and without heeding them. But exposure always involves a risk: because of the enormous gap between now and then; because there is no obvious point or sense to it; because of the imaginative leap in the dark it takes to bring forward something stale *as* significant; because this may not work as the drums and rain finally "work on" the speaker of the poem.

In the poem the effort to make an African heritage matter to African American life in New York feels like nothing less than a jungle adventure out of a book, lions crouching in the reeds. What we get most of all is the feeling of the thrill of exposure (figured here as sexual exposure). We get the energy that comes from the collision, and the adjustment in consciousness, and the spark this creates, like the "spark" Dewey describes "when old and new jump together, like sparks when the poles are adjusted."[48] It is like the spark or "ember" that appears at the end of Cullen's poem that would "*set / Timber that [he] thought was wet / Burning*," unless the speaker smothers it, quenching his pride, as he puts it.

What smothering it would bring, as the last stanzas suggest, is finally a full assimilation to an American life and, in particular, to a Christian life since the speaker insists on telling us of his "conversion": "I belong to Jesus Christ, / Preacher of humility; / Heathen gods are naught to me," he says. It would require quenching his pride, leaving behind any importance he would make of his heritage. (What is Africa to me? Naught to me, he says.) Yet still, "*Not yet has my heart or head / In the least way realized / They and I are civilized*," because life still might be filled with the adventure of these inheritances, and because a poem might be a good place for exposing us.

I think the answer to the question that keeps driving Cullen's poem is, finally, something like what Locke means when he says (in that line I quoted a while back) that race for this younger generation of artists and writers "is but an idiom of experience, a sort of added enriching adventure and discipline, giving subtler overtones to life, making it more beautiful and interesting, even if more poignantly so. So experienced, it affords a deepening rather than a narrowing of social vision." The younger generation, he explains, "has thus achieved an objective attitude toward life." In other words, the experience of race provides them with *objects* of interest; old, typified, alienated forms forming a background that may not actually be theirs get "remembered" and brought into contact with new ideas and expressions. These objects are revived for the potential they have for "working" outside of their tired, familiar uses and for the satisfaction they give elsewhere. In *The New Negro*, "Heritage" appears in a section titled, "The Negro Digs Up His Past." It comes up, like Lazarus from the grave.

The speaker in the poem may now "belong to Jesus Christ," but he also "in his heart" plays "a double part . . . Wishing He I served were black." So he calls up those "Quaint, outlandish heathen gods / Black men fashion out of rods." He calls up gods that are naught to him in the light of Christ, who then takes on their "dark despairing features" and their "dark rebellious hair": "Lord, forgive me if my need / Sometimes shapes a human creed." His venture into the unknown assimilates the present to the past while bringing about a reconstruction of the past: God translated back into the solid terms of human and emotional pertinency, heathen gods brought up as Christ. "The junction of the new and old," Dewey writes, "is not a mere composition of forces, but is a re-creation in which the present impulsion gets form and solidity while the old, the 'stored,' material is literally revived, given new life and soul through having to meet a new situation. . . . Things retained from past experience that would grow stale from routine or inert from lack of use, become coefficients in new adventures and put on a raiment of fresh meaning."[49]

The speaker says, "*One thing only must I do: / Quench my pride and cool my blood*," lest I make a spark. "*Lest the grave restore its dead.*" Lest the book of Africa should be something and not naught to me, just like the book of Aristophanes or Hafiz was relevant "to me and mine" to Emerson. Lest there should be resurrection, and reconstruction too.

9

The History of Fallacies / The Sophistry of Criticism

1

In 1866, British painter Albert Moore titled a painting *Pomegranates*, but it is hard to see why since the pomegranates are mostly hidden in a bowl on the cabinet, and, in any case, the woman at the right is eating cherries (fig. 44). The cherries dangle from her hand like the tassels on the tapestry behind her. The woman resembles the wall hanging in other ways: up against the wall in fabric and low relief, and, of course to us, she is a wall hanging insofar as she is not a woman but a painting. Everything in the picture reinforces its decorative surface: the foreshortened figures reminded critics more of the convexity of a Greek vase painting than an easel painting because, by 1866, Moore had rejected the principles of perspective and the illusions of spatial depth. Against a flat grid, the women, bowl, and pomegranates fulfill a strict geometric logic built around the circular folds of orange and pink drapery on the women's rounded backs and the curved arcs of white wall paint in rhythmic relation to the orange and white spirals on the cabinet.

Moore helped to define the Aesthetic Movement in Britain and the United States by insisting on the values of chromatic patterning rather than on narrative and naturalistic content. Moore's close friend was J. M. W. Whistler, who insisted, after all, that *Arrangement in Grey and Black, No. 1* (fig. 39) is not a painting of his mother but an arrangement in gray and black, especially when critics confounded it with emotions and virtues foreign to it: Puritanism, patriotism, love, and the like. "To me," Whistler says, "it is interesting as a picture of my mother; but what can or ought the public

FIGURE 44. Albert Joseph Moore, *Pomegranates* (1866). Oil on canvas. City of London Corporation. Art UK, Heritage Digital Ltd.

to care" about that. And yet the critics, Whistler says, kept weighing in on the painting so "that the moment may not be lost, and the *àpropos* gone for ever."[1] And so the critics of Moore's paintings kept retitling them to refer to the historical subjects within them—*A Greek Lady*, *A Roman Lady*—but Moore dissociated his works from any nuance of historical or sentimental meaning (which are *gone forever*), because his paintings were "no more 'about' the women on whom we instinctively focus" than about the pomegranates we may have otherwise overlooked.

Compare Moore's pomegranates to the pomegranate in Dante Gabriel Rossetti's *Proserpine* (fig. 45), a painting retelling a Greek myth—Proserpine eats a pomegranate in Hades and so is condemned to spend half her life in Hades—where the fatal fruit at the center is the cause of her fall and also its mythological symbol, just as the ivy branch behind her "may be taken," says

FIGURE 45. Dante Gabriel Rossetti, *Proserpine* (1874). Oil on canvas. Presented by W. Graham Robertson, 1940. © Tate.

Rossetti, "as a symbol of clinging memory." The patch of light may be taken as her glimpse of earth from below, and her dress, like spilling water, as the turning of the tides for her.[2] And in case we have not made it all work quite like this, Rossetti includes an explanatory poem at the top of the painting to ensure it all fits and coheres.

Maybe Moore called his painting *Pomegranates* to encourage us to see it more as a still life—a visual arrangement of things offered up, like pomegranates on a cabinet—instead of a painting about looking deep for something beneath the pomegranates, as the woman down on her knees does, or even about women as sensuous as pomegranates, full and pink, dangling their cherries in front of us. But it remains the case that a painting that is neither about the pomegranates nor the women who are not eating them—a painting for which the pomegranates may be entirely irrelevant to its meaning despite its title—nevertheless *lifts* the pomegranates into our attention through its title and also, purposefully, onto the cabinet at its center. When the content that is lifted into attention is fitting or apropos to the context in which it is lifted—when it has some bearing on that context of some relationship to itself—then we say that *this* content (this pomegranate) is relevant and, of course, when it has no bearing and does not fit, then we say that it is irrelevant. In the field of logic, something that, when it arises, appears to be relevant but finally is not is called a "fallacy," and sometimes a "red herring"—which draws us back to the very *fishy* vehicle of the pomegranates in Moore's painting.

And in case it seems like *this* painting does not bear on what follows, I promise to make it fit in the end.

No one cared very much about red herrings before the nineteenth century. I should qualify this: no one cared very much about red herrings between the medieval logicians who revived Aristotle's treatise on fallacies, *On Sophistical Refutations* (as *De sophisticis elenchis*), and the British logician Richard Whately, who in his 1826 book, *Elements of Logic*, brought fallacies back again into the logical curriculum. Within twenty years there were nine editions of Whately's book and many reprint editions in Britain and the United States, but probably its greatest influence was on John Stuart Mill, who based his 1843 work, *A System of Logic*, on Whately's *Logic* and included a full volume on the fallacies in it. Before Whately, the history of the study of fallacies involves "a series of waves of anti-Aristotelian attempts to get rid of the subject altogether," a history in which, with few exceptions, a whole discipline of learning became dormant in part because it seemed illogical to study invalid forms of logic in which the conclusions do not follow from the premises. Whately was one of the first of many in this period to insist that logic was a formal science—he inspired the direction of pioneers of algebraic logic who saw no difference between logic and mathematics—but errors by definition are undisciplined, and even Mill admits that things "which are not evidence of any given conclusion, are manifestly endless, and . . . cannot be made the groundwork of a real classification." Could it ever be logical in a book of logic to include mistakes? Truth may have its norms, but "there *is* no such thing as a classification of the ways in which men may arrive at an error," writes the logician Augustus De Morgan, as if to confirm why Jeremy Bentham writes earlier that "from Aristotle down to this present day, on the subject [of the fallacies] . . . all is a blank."[3]

But then sometime around this time studies of inadequate reasoning began to appear in their own right, including Bentham's *The Book of Fallacies*, published posthumously in 1824 and written, he says, in order "to do something in the way of filling up this blank" that he describes. Others, including Alfred Sidgwick in *Fallacies: A View of Logic from the Practical Side* (1883), write about the many forms that fallacies can take, in which arguments become inapplicable and beside the point through appeals to sentiment and prejudice instead of logic, or through shades of departure from the question, or else by begging the question and simply postulating what needs to be proven in the first place. "Why does opium occasion sleep?—Because it is soporiferous" (the example is Bentham's).[4]

When Bentham claims that there is little precedent for the formal study of fallacies, he does not mean that no one talked about deviant thinking, especially when it set out to persuade or mislead. In *The Advancement of Learning* (1605), Francis Bacon had laid out four classes of argumentative errors or "idols" that lead us astray and have their roots in human psychology and behavior. John Locke created a class of "*ad*-arguments," in *An Essay Concerning Human Understanding* (1690), that later gave rise to a class of "*ad*-fallacies" involving personal attacks (*ad hominem*) and other irrelevant appeals: for example, *ad verecundiam* (the appeal to authority) or *ad ignorantiam* (the appeal to ignorance, which assumes that a conclusion is true just because it has not yet been proven false). Locke had read the *Port Royal Logic* of 1662 by Antoine Arnauld and Pierre Nicole of the Port-Royal Abbey in France, which includes a section titled "Sophisms: The Different Ways of Reasoning Incorrectly" and may be the one true exception to Bentham's sweeping claim that between the Aristotelians and the nineteenth century, on the formal study of fallacies, "all is a blank." But Bacon, Locke, and others were finally empiricists who distanced themselves from Aristotle's logic and the scholastic tradition. They insisted that the errors they found were not fallacies within syllogistic arguments but rather arguments "that men in the reasonings with others do ordinarily make use of" and that derive from or else play to false beliefs, prejudices, superstitions, bad temperaments, and social and political pressures.[5] People, after all, may be influenced by all sorts of specious things that never pretend to be logical.

What is largely lost, in other words, between twelfth-century medieval theories of the fallacy based in Aristotle and the fallacy's nineteenth-century return is an interest in how sophistical arguments shadow logic and embarrass it by resembling it. Fallacies are different from lies: they seem like logic and take after it. They bear many of the signs of reasonable argument. They appear to be sound while leaving us with the irresistible feeling that they plainly are not. Fallacies are "the shadow of illogic that logic carries with it," writes D. Vance Smith. They move along just like arguments do but take us back to where we started (circular reasonings), or they work to divert and lead us astray (red herrings). As mistakes of logic, in other words, fallacies are not lies but not exactly nonsense either because they continue to "[have] reference," in Mill's words, "to the positive property which they possess of appearing to be the evidence." Fallacies have reference to the truth they merely appear to be. From Aristotle, who first categorized them, through Mill and others who revived them as a field of formal study, fallacies have been defined by this condition of *appearance*. Not the opposite of truth, but the appearance of truth—truth's apparition or "phenomenon," says Smith.

"A catalogue of the varieties of apparent evidence which are not real evidence, is an enumeration of Fallacies," according to Mill. Fallacies are those things that, not being valid, "are susceptible of being mistaken" for valid. They are not so much illogical as paralogical. People inexperienced in logic may mistake the appearance for the reality and thus be deceived by a bad refutation. They may be surprised or dazzled "by some beautiful appearance" of logic that is only a trick of logic. And so nineteenth-century logicians wrote textbooks to teach us how to recognize these appearances. The student of logic might learn to see that fallacies are not logic but fictions of logic that always also (in their "supreme confidence trick," as Terence Cave describes it) make us conscious of how the trick works.[6]

In *On Sophistical Refutations*, Aristotle identifies the fallacy (or sophism) of *ignoratio elenchi*, which translates as the "ignorance of refutation." Aristotle's point is that there are refutations that may appear to be logically valid but nevertheless ignore or fail to address the question. But when in 1826 Whately writes about *ignoratio elenchi*, following Aristotle, he renames it the "Fallacy of Irrelevant Conclusion" because, he says, "the Conclusion is not the one required, but irrelevant." And this is what we still call the fallacy today—the fallacy of the *irrelevant conclusion*—and this is what Mill called the fallacy, too, though the translation is really not so apt itself.[7]

Aristotle meant for the fallacy of *ignoratio elenchi* to refer specifically to cases in which arguers think they have proved one thing but have at best proved something else, in which, in the nineteenth-century's terms, "the journey has been safely performed, only we have got into the wrong train." But Aristotle also says, as Mill does millennia later, that we might consider every last logical fallacy there is—including appeals to emotion and appeals to authority—as covered by *ignoratio elenchi*, too, since, for Mill, all fallacies are beside the point and reasonings that are strictly "irrelevant" to the purpose at hand.

Fallacies are "nothing to the purpose," says Bentham.[8] By the nineteenth century, studying fallacies became a way of judging not the consistency of an argument but its fit or application to the needs of the occasion. Now one could be asked to test arguments to see whether they sufficiently stand up and work or could be made to work within the contexts to which they refer. By the nineteenth century to think about the value of an argument—to think about its "truth for" getting where we need to go (on some *train* of thought)—was to think about its relevance or irrelevance.

. . .

Formal logic in the nineteenth century, including algebraic logic, was context free. As the science of the laws of thought, it was concerned with deductive arguments and valid inference and the principles that determine validity. The nineteenth century quantified the syllogism, representing a priori concepts in abstract equations and expressions instead of in ordinary language. They shaped its variables as numbers and symbols. The content or matter of these expressions mattered less than their own internal relations and consistency, which is why Mill calls deductive logic the "Logic of Consistency" while claiming that his own logic is the "Logic of Truth." Formal logic is about deciding whether a particular case is consistent with an a priori principle or premise; Mill asks us to test instead whether the principles are in accordance with—*just for*—the particular cases we observe.

And when the rules no longer apply—when, for example, we discover new facts and need to adapt what we had known to what we know now—then we make new premises. We start with facts and then come up with a context or law to explain them. We uncover, that is, the meaning of the things we experience by discovering some principle by which they seem to work and fit. But there are no universal and invariable laws, so we need to keep testing and justifying the fit, and sometimes we have to change our principles so that our understanding can unfold and evolve. There are no general truths, just standards of truth we hope to meet in time.[9]

When Mill, Sidgwick, and others reintroduced the idea of fallacies into logic—in a practice that is now called "informal logic"—they set out to recognize the sources of logical *inconsistency*, all the openings, holes, and voids they could find within the weave of a proposition and QED. Returning to *On Sophistical Refutations*, they also returned to the logic of the sophists for whom logic was practical and workable—not about metaphysical proofs and demonstrable laws but about opportune moments (or *openings*) in current affairs. Sophistry is a "radical principle of occasionality." If the sophists deceived, if their logic persuaded when it never should have, it was because they first proposed, and caused others to admit, that logic can be shifty like this: that the power and value of ideas might come in fact in their adjustability and applicability to real occasions and that arguments can be made to work for the interests, moods, and demands of a moment. The sophists represent a challenge to logic because, as Barbara Cassin explains, they are "not in pursuit of truth or dialectical rigor but merely opinion, seeming coherence, persuasion, and victory in oratorical joust." The sophists also represent a challenge to any principle of ontology because they seek refuge in the kinds of meanings that take shape occasionally or accidentally at just the right moment. "If one makes use of the standard of being and truth in order to judge the teaching of the sophist, it must be condemned as pseudophilosophy: a philosophy of appearances and a mere appearance of philosophy."[10]

The sophists believed that the value and use of the way we argue is context bound and that the same language in a different context can be put to different purposes. Language might even mean different things at the exact same time if we pay attention to its effects: to tone, inflections, accents, irony, sarcasm, and all the possibilities of ambiguity. This is why Cassin suggests that sophistry falls "outside the principle of noncontradiction," making us aware of "the slippery nature of any proposition of identity." A statement might have a range of contextual effects that go well beyond its semantic purpose. There is almost always something left over to make out.

Hence the philological passion of the sophists, "which considers that all of eternity may not be enough time to understand a sentence adequately." Our words are never only or necessarily what they are or had been.

Speaking of sophistical arguments, F. C. S. Schiller writes that verbal contradictions "arise out of the fact that old words have to be used as vehicles of new meanings and transform and supersede their traditional meanings. . . . Such contradictions, when they appear in actual contexts, are like Mahaffy's famous Irish bulls, 'always pregnant.' They are challenging, picturesque, and paradoxical ways of enunciating novelties of thought." This is also why sophistry is capable of changing our minds. It takes widely accepted ideas we think we know or else never bothered to think about and recasts them in a new light. It plays, in Cassin's words, the "choice of prevalence . . . over being." It contrives "new types of obviousness." Sophistical reasoning introduces a spirit of "crisis" or an opening (from the Greek *kairos*, meaning "the opportune moment") into the security of formal logic and preexistent proofs.[11] A statement may seem to be one thing by design, but *in effect*—that is, in the real moment in which we hear or read it—it may chance an opportunity too.

. . .

The difference between sophistical logic and formal logic is what Schiller calls "a conflict ultimately between the spirit of adventure and the craving for security." "The logic of adventure is fed throughout the ages by the growth of knowledge, and draws its justification from the need of understanding it." This "spirit of adventure," introducing an opening in the closed system of logic, is also what Schiller defines as the search for "Relevance" in logic, especially in his book *Logic for Use: An Introduction to the Voluntarist Theory of Knowledge*. Its defining chapter, titled "Relevance," begins,

> If logicians had been able to start with a clean slate, instead of puzzling over the palimpsests of 2000 years, they could hardly have failed to recognise the existence and importance of Relevance much sooner and more explicitly than they have done. As it was, they never discovered it, and the central doctrine of the most prevalent logic still consists of a flat denial of Relevance and of all the ideas associated with it. For it represents knowledge as based upon, and aiming at, all-inclusiveness instead of at selection of the relevant.
>
> But, of course, the blindness of logicians did not prevent the practical man from needing the notion of Relevance. . . . Thus Relevance is a shining

> example, not only of the imperious way in which practical need acts as a stimulus to theoretic progress, but also of the slowness of theorists to learn from experience. For its theory is still rudimentary, though practically the conception is too valuable not to be in constant use under a variety of names, English being the only language equipped with a complete and adequate vocabulary for it. Although it has not yet found its way into the dictionaries of philosophy, even logicians find themselves constrained to use it, in a covert and confused way, though they are still far from recognising it as one of the primary notions in our actual reasoning, and from being willing to discard the traditional theories which conflict with it.[12]

Later Schiller writes, "Relevance is Risky: Hence the peculiar *honesty* and straightforwardness of the appeal to Relevance, which involves no sailing under false colours. It lays no claim to 'cogency' or 'formal validity' any more than to exhaustiveness. It does not play for safety first, but avows that it takes a *risk*." Of course, what Schiller is describing as "*honesty* and straightforwardness" is nothing but the shiftiness that marks the turn from formal logic to sophistical forms of reasoning. Still, in recognizing the "existence and importance of Relevance," the honesty, for him, comes in admitting that logic is always partial like this. Logic brings to attention aspects of truth that may be considered less truthful by other standards and on other occasions. The straightforwardness comes in not trying to cover up the fact that "damns [Relevance] in the eyes of every formal logic," that sometimes logic is only the name for the "truth" that seems likely to solve a problem or advance an inquiry right now. Relevance is not systematic like the formal logic that flatly denies it and all ideas associated with it. It is not self-evident, but the momentary *appearance* of self-evidence, a kind of makeshift formulation or workable cogency pulled not from classical systems of proofs but from well outside these systems or elsewhere.[13] Relevance, Schiller says, has not "found its way into dictionaries of philosophy," and yet even logicians feel the need to use it, without a vocabulary for it, without ever admitting that what they think they should never need is predicated on their faith in it as well. I will return to why in a moment.

This pragmatist philosopher, whom Dewey credits with discovering the "principle of relevancy," takes his humanist dictum directly from Protagoras, the fifth-century sophist who said, "man is the measure of all things." Schiller often called himself Protagoras's disciple, and Protagoras appears throughout his books, which include *Plato or Protagoras?*, a critical examination of Protagoras's speech in which the answer to who wins is clear.

Schiller insists that Protagoras did not deny all truth when he declared that "truth was relative to man" and that "every man had his own truth," but rather that his statements are "the truest and most important thing[s] that any thinker has ever propounded." Protagoras was not against truth but rather "a pluralist about truth, not a monist, and still less a nihilist." He brought in a great deal that "intellectualism would like to leave out, a great deal it has no use for, which it would like to extirpate, or at least to keep out of its sight."

"Relevance startles Formal Logic," Schiller says, by welcoming what is foreign to it and by suggesting that even formal logic is not exhaustive, especially where it pretends to be. There is something real beyond it that it tries very hard to keep down ("out of its sight"). Even the absolute truths to which formal logic makes its claim are finally cherry-picked for the satisfactions they give and for the difference they make at the right moment. If we are to be honest, all logic is a search for relevance that draws on the sense of crisis and insecurity in the logic of the sophists that Cassin calls a "consequential relativism." For Schiller, logic is only honest if it admits that the value of the way we argue depends on our immediate situation and that there always will be new and unprecedented situations requiring different forms of logic and claims to relevance. "No proposition is universally true, i.e. true on all occasions for all purposes, and in all contexts, not even this one," Schiller writes.[14]

This may all seem self-evident to us now, but it wasn't self-evident to Schiller or to any of the philosophers or logicians he says could not manage to recognize the existence and importance of relevance for that two-thousand-year gap he describes—and it certainly wasn't self-evident to Bentham or Sidgwick before Schiller. When we talk today in literature departments about gaining relevance—or else argue for the contemporary relevance of Shakespeare, Rabelais, or Emerson—we do not normally think of our arguments as sophistry. But the idea of making Emerson a useful object of our attention—of appropriating Emerson for present purposes (and finding him *apropos*)—relies on a claim for Emerson's suitability, and on an adjustment of the value and meaning of his words to our particular context, that can only be logical in a sophistical world.

. . .

The original name of the *Port Royal Logic* is *The Art of Thinking*, itself signaling a new approach to logic that had been seen as the art of reasoning, but not exactly *thinking*, which is not the same thing. We might see the *Port*

Royal Logic as the beginning of a classroom pedagogy in "critical thinking," one that, by the nineteenth century, was also beginning to understand logic to be a discipline not unrelated to psychology. The *Port Royal Logic* was taught at colleges throughout England and the United States well into the nineteenth century; the 1818 English edition served as the standard logic textbook at Oxford and Cambridge. The *Port Royal Logic*'s two sections on fallacies ("Sophisms: The Different Ways of Reasoning Incorrectly" and "Concerning Faulty Arguments Advanced in Public Life and Everyday Affairs") include many of the fallacies in syllogistic reasoning that Aristotle discussed but also examples of mistakes in reasoning in civil and ordinary life that extend well beyond the scope of traditional logic. In Aristotle, the treatment of fallacies appears as an appendix to the discussion of reasoning in *Topics*; the fallacies in *On Sophistical Refutations*, in other words, are classified as "other" to the topics of logic proper, appearing as a deviation from the norm and a remainder at the end. But in the *Port Royal Logic*, the discussion of fallacies figures centrally as part of a new understanding of the topics and discipline of logic itself, whose aim is not only good logic in formal arguments but also good behavior in public affairs.

For Arnauld and Nicole, mistakes in logic may follow from all sorts of human and social causes and occasional circumstances that are external to the principles of formal argumentation. There are fallacies that result from bad habits, self-love, servile submission to human authority, and especially a failure to pay attention. These are all mistakes that we make in ordinary life rather than the mistakes we make in "science" or formal proceedings, and the *Logic* finds them to be both more numerous and also more dangerous, since they represent not only errors but (moral) faults and blindnesses. The *Logic* thus marks a shift from the view of sophisms as logical tricks for dialecticians to something more like sins.

Arnauld, Nicole, and the members of the Port-Royal Abbey were radical Catholic reformists (Jensenists) whose target was the Catholic hierarchy and particularly the Jesuits, whose "Jesuitical" or casuistical reasonings they saw as the dazzling trick of conservative power in the church during the rise of an absolute monarchy in France. Their book of fallacies is faithful to the Aristotelian and scholastic traditions, but it also shows where logic might be less pedantic, more deeply involved in human affairs, and where close attention to the variability of reasonings and persuasions that fallacies make apparent also marks the entry of logic into politics and life. Some scholars even suggest the *Port Royal Logic* can be seen as an early attempt to link studies of logic to the sort of studies of attention within psychology and phenomenology that come much later, in the nineteenth century, and that I discussed in chapter 4. The book suggests that logic someday might even help us think our way out of an institutional crisis, if only we can learn to pay better attention.[15]

When Bentham, Mill, and the rest returned to the logic of fallacies "in speaking of Aristotle's collection of fallacies, as a stock to which from his time to the present no addition has been made"—a topic which Bentham, again, says it "seemed not too early in the nineteenth century to take up . . . on the ground of morality"—they were committing themselves to knowing the sources of error, and especially the feelings and intentions, that enhance or restrict the application of knowledge in particular contexts. For Bentham, who applied logic to politics and legislative debate, all fallacies are irrelevances that impede the progress of the present. In *The Book of Fallacies*, he describes them as the ideas from elsewhere (the past, for example) that, like adamant "lumps," are unadaptable and inconsequent to the occasion. In Parliament, they are appeals to authority (*ad verecundiam*) or appeals to precedent (*ad antiquitatem*) that obstruct new legislation by legislating from beyond the grave. Or else they are appeals to popularity (*ad populum*) that support the status quo and not reform.

Sentimentalism, even in the form of respect for custom and history, is an affective fallacy, like fear of change: "whatsoever be the measure in hand, they are, with relation to it, irrelevant." Fallacies of distrust and suspicion, drawing attention away from the measure in hand to impute the motives or character of the man proposing it, are intentional fallacies and also "irrelevant." "If the measure is a good one," Bentham says, "will it become bad because it is supported by a bad man? If it is bad, will it become good because supported by a good man? . . . if the measure is beneficial, it would be absurd to reject it on account of the motives of its author." Then, of course, there are the red herrings, the fallacies of artful diversion and delay, which turn aside from the measure in hand "the affections and attention of those whom you have to deal with." "In the character of an irrelevant counter-measure, any measure or accidental business whatever may be made to serve, so long as it can be made to preoccupy a sufficient portion of the disposable time and attention of the public men on whose suffrages the effectuation or frustration of the measure depends."[16]

(By 1830 or so, when members of Congress on the floor of the US House of Representatives artfully delayed a measure, they were "called to order for irrelevancy," so that "irrelevancy" instead of "order, order" became a common charge in the rules of order on the House floor. John Quincy Adams was often called to order "for irrelevancy" when speaking out against slavery because "reading and commenting on such matters" was "out of order" and "not pertinent to the question before the House" in the years of the Gag Rule prohibiting discussion of antislavery petitions.)

It is the idea of irrelevances as political diversions that led British reformer William Cobbett to coin the term *red herring* to begin with in the 1807 *Weekly Political Register* in which he tells the apocryphal story of how, as a boy, he had used a red herring—which is really a preserved kipper—as a decoy to deflect the hounds of competing hunters chasing after the hare he also was chasing. Thus the "political red herring," as Cobbett calls it, is a metaphor for deflecting parliamentary attention from the purpose at hand.[17]

For Bentham, our logic, which is our thinking, is "an instrument for the application" of the principle of "utility," so red herrings and other fallacies, "by means of their irrelevancy . . . consume and misapply time, thereby obstructing the course of progress of all necessary and useful business."[18] "Nothing to the purpose," fallacies are contrivances for leaving things undone. They are inefficient. They are, by nature, unprogressive and illiberal. They are irritants that cannot be assimilated and reconciled to the needs of the present. And Bentham's own ingenuity comes in making something, really anything, that is not defined by progress and utility—in making all of history especially—irrelevant by making it illogical.

. . .

For Mill, too, the rules of logic should speak to ingenuity and progress, which is why he writes that "the task of finding the rules of logic is of the same type as the legislator's." It is of the same type as the judge's and jury's, too, and so it turns out that problems of "irrelevance" and "relevance" also came to predominate legal concepts of evidence for the first time around this time. Again Bentham took the lead with his five-volume study, *Rationale of Judicial Evidence*, edited by Mill and published posthumously in 1827. Bentham's volumes are considered to be the first extensive treatment of evidence law in Anglo-American law, which also knew itself at the time to be the only legal tradition among Western legal traditions that needed principles of judicial evidence in the first place. Evidence law, as Alex Stein explains, is "a peculiarly Anglo-American phenomenon. It is not recognized as a branch in most European continental countries." In most European systems, evidentiary rules were scarce; they typically included standards and burdens of proof and rules controlling the presentation of proof in order to promote efficiency and fairness in trials. Judges had the primary responsibility for investigating and adjudicating a case and could enforce adherence to these standards, which were often based in a numbers system, according to which specific numbers of witnesses were required for certain kinds of cases, with the relative weight of each witness measured and represented by numerical values. But in Britain and the United States, by the beginning of the nineteenth century, the work of fact-finding and of judging the use and value of evidence became much more involved. The old quantifiable system of legal proof was replaced with what was called "free proof" or "freedom of proof," understood as free and unrestricted access to facts and information. Legal fact-finding was now shared, for every case, among increasingly contentious lawyers, who gathered, sifted, and prioritized competing evidence; also the judge, who adduced their competing versions of the facts and laws for the jurors; and finally the jurors, who were asked to determine what all of it meant. So while we can trace the beginnings of modern evidentiary law back to sixteenth- and seventeenth-century Scotland, what we know now as the legal concept of evidence was not actually in operation until just around the time Bentham writes his foundational study of it (with few notable treatments of judicial evidence until just a couple decades before then).

While trials invited considerations of evidence from the moment there were juries, it was not until modern criminal trials, conducted by lawyers, that there seemed to be a need for new understandings of how to prevent prejudice and error from influencing the jury, even as the judges, who used to do more of this work themselves, became relatively passive. In the courts, there was a move away from oath-based testimony primarily toward the admission of more circumstantial evidence and also adversarial examinations and cross-examinations of witnesses. Not an oath to God, but the "truth-detecting efficacy of cross-examining lawyers," as John H. Langbein puts it, would be a safeguard against deception and the measure of probative value at a moment in which the courts also began to articulate the beyond-a-reasonable-doubt standard of proof. In other words, it seemed to take new powers of reasoning and new competence both to argue for and be persuaded by what *counted* as proof beyond a reasonable doubt, since jurors were left to inquire more for themselves and since there was a preponderance of evidence that needed to be weighed as more or less meaningful without recourse to strict exclusionary rules so much as common sense and the ability to pay attention.[19]

Bentham believed in aggressive cross-examination as the most effective system for exposing all the "mendacity-serving information" that lawyers use to obstruct due process. But lawyers, judges, and juries also needed more guidance now on what should count as evidence and on the applicability of facts and testimony to each particular case. They needed new principles for excluding certain testimony and circumstantial evidence from consideration, because all kinds of things might be legally admissible that are not logically probative but brought in to deceive or distract instead ("under the spur of sinister interest," Bentham says). In 1806 the legal scholar W. D. Evans commented on the recent need for the court "to require an explanation of the motive and object of the questions proposed, or to pronounce a judgment upon their immateriality." Indeed, our popular sense of a dramatic courtroom in which adversarial lawyers keep interrupting to object to the antics of other lawyers ("Immaterial!" "Hearsay!" "Leading question!") dates from this time, and these practices get reinforced with the rise of court reporting and the printed reports and proceedings that brought them to attention after 1790. These courtroom objections were occupied much less with legal admissibility than with deciding what part of the enormous mass of admitted facts and testimony should be *logically* excluded. In other words, the legal concept of evidence was driven from the start by logical determinations of irrelevance.

Like his principles for parliamentary procedure in *The Book of Fallacies*, Bentham's principles for judicial procedure and proof provide the "opportunity of separating what is pertinent to the cause from what is irrelevant." Legal argumentation should be an "instrument of distinctness," he says, but it too often involves an "indefinite accumulation of irrelevant matter, and consequent increase of indistinctness" for the purposes of deceiving and winning a case. One can see, for example, from the nature of the circumstantial evidence used in past cases, how much the "ingenuity" of lawyers has aimed to find "arguments which, the more obscure and irrelevant they were, would be but the more difficult to be refuted." So we need to learn to look for loopholes in legal arguments that are dangerous because, appearing to be sound but finally unsound, they encourage false inferences or else bring in evidence that is beside the point and cause "that of preponderant collateral inconvenience in the shape of delay, vexation, and expense: placing to the account of useless delay and vexation every proposed interrogation, that, in the judgment of the competent judge, is either *irrelevant* or *superfluous*." "But, for the detection of mendacity, no question that can contribute any thing, can be irrelevant," but we first have to know how to detect sophistical arguments in court and how to think about what evidence is worth considering and what should be discounted because it is "capable of being exaggerated by prejudice and hasty reasoning."[20]

All along Bentham was never actually in favor of binding evidentiary laws and worked to abolish the so-called exclusionary rules that formally determined the types of evidence that may be admitted in a trail. He called instead for the application of the same kind of logic in court that he applied to parliamentary debate, because, for Bentham, the question of evidence is not a question of rules of law but of right thinking in each case. It takes value judgments based on an ability to recognize what matters to the matter at hand or else serves as an obstacle to reason and progress, and it requires constant adjustments in thinking as new facts and arguments are brought forward in an ongoing trial. Determining evidence suggests a mental operation of sorting on the part of the jurors especially, who also need to weigh all manner of things that are decidedly extrinsic to law: human motives and intent, emotions and passions, the particular circumstances in which the facts unfold, the backgrounds of the witnesses. It requires the sort of critical determinations of relevance and irrelevance that Bentham's handbook on fallacies can teach.

Evidentiary theory, though introduced by Bentham, did not become influential until decades after the posthumous publication of *Rationale of Judicial Evidence*. When it finally became a field of study, it was based not on principles of law but of logic. Specifically, it was based on the principles of "relevancy," first articulated in that turn away from formal logic I described as a mental and *attentional* process of selecting among all of the available facts. Legal scholars began to recognize that the veracity of "proffered testimony" and circumstantial facts is often not at issue so much as whether these facts really should bear on consideration of a case; also whether they all hang together, as "facts in issue," to produce a verdict. So, in the first major theory of legal evidence after Bentham, the British judge James Fitzjames Stephen insisted on using the language of "relevancy" in determining evidence while also sharply distinguishing between those facts that may be proved to be true and those facts which, if true, are relevant. In *Digest of the Law of Evidence*, based on his *Introduction to the Indian Evidence Act* of 1872, he writes of "the ambiguity of the word evidence (a word which sometimes means testimony and at other times relevancy)," suggesting that testimony and relevant testimony are not the same thing. There are "primary facts" and there are "evidentiary facts" (referring to Bentham's distinction between all the *facts* as such), and Stephen's *Digest* is concerned with the general principles that regulate the relevant facts (or the "facts in issue"). He argues that the question of which of the facts might turn out to be evidentiary in a trial—"the relevancy of facts to facts in issue"—is not actually determined by the rules of law but by "the common course of events" and by "the process of induction." It is a theory of evidence, he adds, that "does not greatly differ from Bentham's, though he does not seem to me to have grasped it as distinctly as he probably would if he had lived to study Mr. Mill's Inductive Logic."

Sometimes the court rejects testimony because it is irrelevant, but sometimes it rejects testimony even though it is relevant because of some legal technicality or policy. This is why Stephen asks us to understand the difference between "relevance" and "admissibility" and why he, and others after him, insist that the principle of relevance is an "extra-legal" concept.[21] The American legal theorist James Bradley Thayer defines evidence that is "relevant" as "logically probative" in contradistinction to "legally admissible," though he also sets out to establish the legal principle by which, "unless excluded by some rule or principle of law, all that is logically probative is admissible." In *A Preliminary Treatise on Evidence at the Common Law* (1896), Thayer writes,

> There is a principle—not so much a rule of evidence as a presupposition involved in the very conception of a rational system of evidence, as contrasted with the old formal and mechanical systems—which forbids receiving anything irrelevant, not logically probative. How are we to know what these forbidden things are? Not by any rule of law. The law furnishes no test of relevancy. For this, it tacitly refers to logic and general experience,—assuming that the principles of reasoning are known to its judges and ministers, just as a vast multitude of other things are assumed as already sufficiently known to them.

We misunderstand the nature of relevance if we imagine that there can be a "mechanically determinative" law of it because relevance involves probability not certainty and, as J. L. Montrose puts it, "Relevance is relative; there is no relevance in the air." Also, "The categories of relevance are never closed: it is impossible to say *a priori* that fact A is not relevant to fact B." So, while relevance is for Thayer too an *extralegal* affair and cannot possibly depend on any hard policy, "it is, nevertheless, necessary for courts to judge whether tendered evidence is relevant or irrelevant." And "since courts of law are human institutions, it is possible for them to err. Judges may find that tendered evidence is relevant when the better judgment is that it is irrelevant, and, vice versa, they may find that such evidence is irrelevant when the better judgment is that it is relevant."

The relations between empirical facts are always so indirect and unclear, and everything depends on circumstances: one kind of fact may be relevant in one set of circumstances and irrelevant in the next. The jury is called on to study the material it gets and to "compare a great body of facts and ideas," but the function "of observing its implications, and the effect of one part on another, of comparing and inferring" does not belong to the law alone but to the principle of "relevancy,—an affair of logic and experience." The "purpose in hand" is never merely that of ascertaining and setting forth facts; litigation brings in a contest of facts and how, for the purposes of ever deciding, "part of this mass of matter is excluded" and part of this mass of matter is grasped does not have "to do merely with ideal truth, with mere mental conceptions," says Thayer. The principle of relevance works "in an atmosphere, and not in a vacuum; it has to allow for friction, for accident and mischance. Nor is it, like natural science, occupied merely with objective truth. It is concerned with human conduct, and all its elements of fraud, inadvertence, wilfulness, and uncertainty." It derives not from any idealism about truth or justice but from a combination of "logic and experience," of inductive reasoning and empiricism, which also accounts, in Thayer's mind, for relevance's absence "in all other than English-speaking countries," since he sees it as deriving from English-language philosophies of inductive reasoning and empiricism. But neither is relevance "an affair of logic and experience" alone, because, unlike all other reasoning, "yet a thousand practical considerations come in to shape it." It must be handled under different conditions and under exigencies that are so practical, such as the time that is allowed to any particular case and limitations on the number of witnesses and the opportunities for cross-examination. It must be conducted in light of an adversarial contest that always has a "personal element," requiring "not merely a consideration of what is just, in general, but of what is just as between these adversaries." It is "determined by its purely practical aims and the necessities of its procedure and machinery," but also in the company of a jury, with *its* personalities and peculiarities, always in danger of being misled and different every time, while all along also promoting justice and the existing governmental order and legal system, which may be more or less just. Facts are to be put together in a meaningful way through a "great multitude of decisions, emerging day by day" and having, finally, "so little to do" with the law "which they are professing to declare." The process has its own logic, deriving from the competition of arguments and beliefs and from the extraction from all of it of the most probable truth in the "decisive moment."[22]

John Henry Wigmore, the American legal scholar best known for his book *The Principles of Judicial Proof, As Given by Logic, Psychology, and General Experience and Illustrated by Judicial Trials* (1913), developed a "chart method" for diagramming and teaching forensic arguments based on the mental process of sifting through a mass of evidence to "enable us to lift into consciousness and to state in words the reasons why a total mass of evidence does or should persuade us to a given conclusion, and why our conclusion would or should have been different or identical if some part of that total mass of evidence had been different." The chart was a teaching tool for representing legal propositions and their relations to each other and the inductive conclusions these relations implied. For Wigmore, understanding evidence requires the "logical (or psychological) process of a conscious juxtaposition of detailed ideas, for the purpose of producing rationally a single final idea," but, of course we know now that *any* "logical" process that sets out to "lift into consciousness" one coherent idea from "a larger number of ideas"—any logical process attendant on a psychological process of "attention" like this—actually requires an understanding of sophistical reasoning. So Wigmore's chart method drew on Bentham and Mill and especially on Sidgwick's *Fallacies: A View of Logic from the Practical Side*. It includes Venn-like attempts to capture syllogisms in diagrammatic form, but it also uses an array of arrows to represent relations between propositions and to suggest that, in everyday arguments (rather than formal logic), several propositions might be "chained together" in ways we could never predict.[23]

Of course the "skill in thinking about evidence" that allows us to lift into consciousness some mass of facts as relevant finally cannot be systematically taught in colleges and law schools for the same reason there cannot be systematic rules for determining the exact evidence in every case: it requires a perpetual construction of the sense of what counts in the midst of a trial and in the crisis that unfolds in the moment. It takes the appearance or phenomenal impression of logic under these circumstances, like the image of a chain of arrows abstracted out of a mass of facts. It represents not logic but an opening or loophole within the disciplines of logic and law filled with accidents and friction. Most of all, it requires a willingness to expose oneself to mistakes, to the facts out of the mass of them all that are *mis*-taken when they should have been excluded. Fallacies may especially lead to truth.

. . .

Schiller returns to the sophists because, long before the time of "skilled lawyers," they understood that "what is relevant to an inquiry is variable, and varies as the inquiry proceeds. The discovery of any truth is always a process which *moves away from* the *data* it started with, and transforms, corrects, and revalues them." In both *Logic for Use* and *Our Human Truths*, published posthumously, Schiller suggests that all that is needed to render "logic workable is to admit the conception of 'relevance,'" but this also takes admitting that "the 'facts' argued from" must be relevant and "cannot, therefore, be merely 'given,' but must be selected from a much larger mass of irrelevant, alleged, and illusory 'facts,' as *facts-for-the-purpose-in-hand*. This process will involve acts of choice, preference, and valuation." We need to admit, in other words, that every claim of truth treats "as irrelevant all the contents of phenomena over and above" that claim; that any facts from which we argue are just the ones that "rise into consciousness" as relevant for making that claim right now. "Thus for any human purpose we consider only part of the total truth, of the thinkable logical whole, nay, even of what is before the mind, the *psychological* whole, viz. the part which seems to us likely to further our inquiry and to solve our problem." The claims for truth necessarily confess that they are disputable. "For once," Schiller says, "we abandon the assumption that aspiration to the totality of truth is an infallible guarantee, and rest our title to truth on a selection of the relevant part, we admit that the *value* of any selection may be questioned. Selections other than those we prefer are thinkable, and others may prefer them. They will differ, therefore, from us in drawing the line between the relevant and the irrelevant, and in accepting what is to be accounted 'truth.' And it is possible that they are right." But it is possible that there are alternatives, because in every case we make up our minds about which "truth" is best and "truest" for us in this case. This is the "risk" built into relevance, which nonetheless holds on to the right to choose what is "plainly a part." It admits that our thinking is driven onward by the urgency of a need and that to think is to take what we need for it. It is the voluntaristic "right to exclude the irrelevant and to attend to and select the relevant" and then to call *this* logic and human reason. Schiller wants us to be honest about the purposiveness of thought and not try to abstract from it, since thinking is always a "thinking for" our needs and not in a vacuum and self-justifying, but "inspired by interest." "All actual knowing is in fact knowing by persons for personal ends; but for reasons which are never publicly avowed this all-important fact is utterly slurred over and ignored in the traditional logic."[24]

Relevance always consists in "getting to the point," which is not the truth, but the "'truth' desired." So it follows, Schiller continues, "that, the better the reasoning, the more rapidly will it contract the relevant, and the straighter will it go to the point. As for the irrelevant, it will mean that portion of the total truth which lies outside the sphere of relevance: and it is plain that any influence it exercises will be pernicious; it will only side-track and thwart the inquiry." Successful thinking does not discriminate between the true and the false but "between the true and relevant and the true but irrelevant," between *the point* of thinking and everything that is beside the point right now. Fallacious thinking is "pernicious" because it picks the wrong emphasis, sometimes by emphasizing too much. It makes thinking feel so meaningless, like there really is no point. But the concept of relevance assures us that there can be *a point* to our thinking and that "we have the right to rid ourselves of the rubbish that blocks our path, the right to select the *humanly valuable* part, the right to desist from vain attempts to include everything in a whole which could only be a chaos." We should "not plead guilty to any *intellectual* shortcoming by way of inattention or omission or failure to include" all we might have included. We can justify the selection "by ascribing it to conscious, willed, purposive, and rational *concentration* upon *the point*."

Anyway, what is the point? From a whole world of truths, we think to extract something meaningful and "essential," something *humanly valuable*. We think to discover an object that is worth it. The fact of what we discover "moves us" not because it is "disinterested and dispassionate, but because it is near and dear to our hearts." When we feel a truth to be "a value and worth achieving," *this* is relevance. Relevance is the "*personal* side of knowing." It announces itself as belonging to "a logic of values." "We can prefer the *valuable* to the *valid*," Schiller says.[25]

Theories of value themselves have origins in this principle of logic, admitting fallacies, that Schiller links to the concept of relevance and that much later comes to be called "informal logic" (being other than formal logic). This is why Alain Locke, value theorist and Schiller's student, writes about the need for a "recognition of logic as a science of values," entailing

> a radical revision of the antitheses between fact and value, existence and "value," the "theoretic" and the "practical." If all "truths" are values, there can be no absolute separation of the practical, the sphere of value, from the theoretic, the sphere of facts. Facts, being the objects of truths, must all imply values, and it must be vain to search for any existence which is wholly free from valuations.[26]

Thinking is, as Dewey describes it in his own *Essays in Experimental Logic*, "knowledge-getting" and "far from being the armchair thing it is often supposed to be." The reason it is far from an armchair thing is because it is never "an event going on exclusively within the cortex or the cortex and vocal organs" but instead "involves the explorations by which relevant data are procured. . . . It comprises the readings by which information is got hold of, the words which are experimented with, and the calculations by which the significance of entertained conceptions or hypotheses is elaborated." There are so many facts out there, but then there are "truths of fact" that signify "that they are taken as the *relevant* facts of the inference to be made." By this Dewey means that they are *taken* and not *mis-taken*, since there are always far more facts than we need, and "the worthlessness of this sheer accumulation of realities, its total irrelevancy, the lack of any way of judging the significance of the accumulations, are good proofs of the fallacy of any theory which ascribes objective logical content to facts wholly apart from the needs and possibilities of a situation." A proposition, Dewey writes, is always a "judgment of value." It is the expression "of an individual's way of thinking" and of the "interests that induce the individual to look this way rather than that."

"Propositions are lures for feelings," Whitehead says. They are the selected "truth" we "entertain" for the possibly that they just may be of value. "The interest in logic, dominating overintellectualized philosophers, has obscured the main function of propositions in the nature of things. . . . A proposition is 'realized' by a member of its locus, when it is admitted into feeling."[27] Logic, in other words, is realizing the "value" to ourselves of what we know. For Dewey, Schiller, Locke, and Whitehead, too, logical thinking is the art of stating or making explicit what we have "to deal with next amid all the surrounding and momentarily irrelevant circumstance," as Dewey puts it. "It eliminates everything which in spite of its immediate urgency, or vividness, or weight of past authority, is rubbish for the purpose in hand. It enables one to get down to business with just that which (presumably) is of importance." Being of utmost importance or essential right now, "it is no wonder," Dewey writes, "that these logical kernels have been elevated into metaphysical essences."[28] (Remember that Whitehead goes so far as to call each relevant proposition an aspect of "God.")

Logic is a "judgment of value" and not about finding truths but about finding them to be "good" and treating them in a certain way, "hanging on" to them and "dwelling upon" certain points and not others. "In this sense," Dewey says, "the word *logical* is synonymous with wide-awake, thorough, and careful reflection—thought in its best sense . . . *Thoughtfulness* means, practically, the same thing as careful attention; to give our mind to a subject is to give heed to it, to take pains with it." What we have to reckon with is not the problem of how to think in the abstract but "How shall I think right *here and now*? Not what is the test of thought at large, but what validates and confirms *this* thought?" To think is to deliberate on the value of facts for our purposes, attending carefully to these while ignoring the rest. The ones we find relevant, we say are only logical, while the many facts and bypaths of thinking that are set aside as irrelevant, we call "false" and "logically repugnant."

Emerson writes, "I want not the logic, but the power, if any, which it brings into science and literature; the man who can humanize this logic, these syllogisms, and give me the results." Like Schiller, Emerson wants a humanistic logic, our *human* truths. There are no "truths" without a sense of appreciating them *as* truths, of bringing them forward, while it remains logical to think that every alleged fact contains the proposition, the possibility, of some value if only it gets raised at the right time. It actually is *psychologically* impossible, Locke suggests, to arrive at any sense of truth without imagining that this process is "permeated throughout by values, *viz.*, a purposive endeavor to attain an end ('good') by a choice of the 'right' means, which implies selective attention, preferences for what seems valuable."[29] If we ever should speak of the "validity" of the thinking process, as opposed to its value, it only could be because the thinking is isolated from its historical circumstances and material contexts. But then, of course, it will have no relevance, no point. It would not be right thinking but the sort of crooked thinking that only appears to be systematic—some idea or set of facts or observations that are mis-taken as essential and that Locke, like Schiller, associates with isolationism, absolutism, and dogmatism instead.

People with prejudice, for example, are thoughtless and the opposite of Dewey's sense of "wide awake," naturally conscious of very little. Their thinking is stiffened and blocked, filled with all that accumulated "rubbish" that cannot evolve or be applied to living situations. They are inattentive. When Locke says he uses logic as a method for finding "truths," he means "valuable" truths that are "struggling into being, which others do not as yet see or recognise." But those who reason without value are guilty of fallacies at every turn. Racism especially involves a set of logical fallacies we can learn to recognize and expose much like all of those fallacies that Bentham understands to be obstructing thought and impeding reform in government. Locke writes of "The Biological Fallacy" (arguing for racial purity), "The Fallacy of the Permanency of Race Types" (arguing for racial essentialism), "The Fallacy of the Masses" (treating peoples in terms of false aggregates), and many other fallacies that reveal these "race creeds" to be dogma: not logic but the appearance of logic. As arguments, they are without any value as such.

...

By framing the philosophy of "relevance" with Protagoras in mind, Schiller is building on what he sees as possibilities for new applications of logic that are relevant to political and human affairs and for logic that is flexible, portable, and honest about the appearance of truth it temporarily makes. The sophists believe that the political as such lies in this constant competition of claims and in the way some claims prove better than others and more persuasive. Language for them is always a political and social faculty, speaking to choice and the effort to gain consent and to bring others around to claims of value and importance in the face of new competing claims. The sophists played "time against space," Cassin writes, logology against ontology, the exigencies of the moment against enduring and absolute truths, and somewhere in the midst of this "plural condition," they see the political as their effort to speak to truth for a time. Cassin focuses on the sophists' pedagogical role especially in teaching Greek citizens how to think critically about arguments; "the apprenticeship begins," she says, quoting Protagoras, "as soon as the child 'pays attention' or 'understands what is being said to him.'"[30] Political virtue begins with an understanding of the claims that words make and the values they bring to attention as they court agreement in the name of better claims, a better life, and the democratic transformation of politics, even if they *are* sophistry: the public appearance of truth and not universally valid. Even if they only appear to be "just"–*just for*—this critical moment.

In "Truth and Politics," Hannah Arendt writes that "to look upon politics from the perspective of truth . . . means to take one's stand outside the political realm," where, by truth, she means an objective truth. Arendt's distinction between political life and private life owes to her sense of Protagoras in Plato's *Sophist* and to sophistical arguments as Aristotle describes them. She defines the specificity of the political realm through sophistical speech that is adapted to the moment and occasion even if she finally is aware of the political dangers of hypocrisy that sophistry comes to represent. The political realm is constituted in the arguments that court public consensus by seeming meaningful, however true or not they may be at different times. Arendt says that sophistical logic is the groundwork of attending to the city in the name of the virtuous and "good," except that she recalls that, in Greek vocabulary, "good" really means "good for" or "fit"—*good for* the people living in the city, *good for* us and *good for* now. The highest idea of politics "is that of fitness," of being able to articulate a public that is "a place fit to live in" and to apply our actions to it. The political is the realm of the *relevant*: "Wherever the relevance of speech is at stake, matters become political by definition, for speech is what makes man a political being." And so, in *The Human Condition*, Arendt defines the public as the *appearance* of civic virtue that only a sophist could manifest,

> since our feeling for reality depends utterly upon appearance and therefore upon the existence of a public realm into which things can appear out of the darkness of sheltered existence, even the twilight which illuminates our private and intimate lives is ultimately derived from the much harsher light of the public realm. . . . There, only what is considered to be relevant, worthy of being seen or heard, can be tolerated, so that the irrelevant becomes automatically a private matter.

This is not to say "that private concerns are generally irrelevant." Arendt insists that "there are very relevant matters which can survive only in the realm of the private," for instance love, which gets extinguished the moment it is displayed in public or used for political purposes. It is simply that what "the public realm considers irrelevant" is beside the point in *public* life, although it may be of utmost relevance to other realms, other parts of life—for instance, wherever people love each other (but why should anyone else care?). It is even the case that sometimes "what the public realm considers irrelevant can have such an extraordinary and infectious charm that a whole people may adopt it as their way of life, without for that reason changing its essentially private character." There are "small things" that become "charming" precisely because they are outside of the public realm and loom extraordinarily large as the objects of our "care and tenderness": perhaps a "chest and bed, table and chair, dog and cat and flowerpot." These modern enchantments are often the objects of poetry or part of the art of living charmingly and well rather than greatly ("the *petit bonheur* of the French people"). The public realm "may be great," Arendt says, but "it cannot be charming precisely because it is unable to harbor the irrelevant."

Still, the point remains that everything that is charming and irrelevant to the public is not objectively irrelevant or "generally irrelevant" and actually may become or be "very relevant matters" of true importance to others elsewhere. The possibilities of the public take shape out of a world in which these distinctions of relevance are made from our plural condition and in the very acts and words that make only certain things "appear out of the darkness of sheltered existence" as worthy of "being seen and heard" in public right now.[31] The political is the sophistical claim that in a relativist world of shifting values, the collective should pay attention at this moment to *this* proposition that is being raised into relief (to offer us relief, to relieve us). The political is simply where we come together to argue for new relevance.

. . .

I have one last comment before I get back to Albert Moore and his pomegranates, like red herrings, lest you think that was completely pointless.

The fallacy of formal logic for Schiller comes in the coerciveness of its claim to validity. It presumes to speak of universal truth, but there are always "alternative universals," and so the lie of formal logic is that it is a "provisional ideal" passing for *the* ideal. It is a version of truth raised out of phenomena and possible facts and then hung onto and treated in a certain way. But "an infinite regress lay artfully concealed," because if we look further we can see that these "exhibited universals" are all "entangled in 'matter'" they artfully ignore. For every claim of absolute truth, there are "all the contents of phenomena over and above the universal we are seeking to apply to them" even as we keep insisting that "though they appear to *be* much more than bare universals they *mean* nothing more." Formal logic is the part extracted out of the whole and then treated as if it were the whole experience. Its universals hide the fact that they really are personal selections substituting for universals while disregarding everything else.

Formal logic in Schiller is what William James in *Pragmatism* calls the "rationalist's fallacy" (an idea he owes to Schiller). The rationalist who believes that truth is just "the system of propositions which have an unconditional claim to be recognized as valid" commits the fallacy of "extract[ing] a quality from the muddy particulars of experience." Finding it "so pure when extracted," he contrasts it "with each and all its muddy instances as an opposite and higher nature." The rationalist who also believes that "truth is a name for all those judgments which we find ourselves under obligation to make by a kind of imperative duty" commits the fallacy of thinking that "life transacts itself in a purely logical or epistemological, as distinguished from a psychological, dimension, and its claims antedate and exceed all personal motivations whatsoever. . . . There never was a more exquisite example of an idea abstracted from the concretes of experience and then used to oppose and negate what it was abstracted from." Dewey calls this "the fallacy of selective emphasis" of which the "intellectualist fallacy" is the worst instance, being a thin account of human truth that tries to leave all human purpose, desire, and interest out of it. "For Logic," Schiller writes, "has always hitherto assumed that *all* facts have to be considered, and philosophy has always professed to aim at the inclusion of the whole; both therefore *are bound to deny the existence of irrelevance*, at any rate for their purpose." Thus logic has "lost its way in the swamps of Irrelevance, by reason of its vain pursuit of the whole."[32]

"The notion of relevance relieves universals of these embarrassments," Schiller says. It acknowledges that every universal is a "construction." Logic is not formalist, but the proposition of new forms pulled out of "muddy particulars"; not static ideals, but extracts or essences that seem so ideal in the act because they are "near and dear to our hearts." Since universals are just "selections of relevant aspects, fashioned as instruments for operating on the flux of happenings, and taken out of larger wholes for our various purposes, our selections will naturally vary with the purposes they serve." There are no wholes, merely sophistical wholes that entertain competition. Selective emphasis is inevitable wherever reflection occurs, so let us call thinking what it is and not conceal its operation and the reasons why we are "entitled to ignore whatever contents of the real are irrelevant to our purpose." The relevant "stands out of a chaotic whole as a *selected* extract, and raises the general problem of our right to make such extracts."

This is why Schiller believes that all those other terms that pass as synonyms for *irrelevant*—in languages other than English, too, like *nihil ad rem*, *unwesentlich*, *sans importance*, *senza concludenza*, but also *immaterial*, *unessential*, *unrelated*, *does not matter*, even what he describes as the use of *irrelative*—are all inferior to *relevant* because they are all "*objectivist* phrases, which try to render the object responsible for the guidance of the thought." These terms suggest that there is something "indispensable to the existence of each thing" that renders it what it essentially is and is not, but only the terms *irrelevant* and *relevant* admit that what we take as essential "expresses not only the *relation* to purpose, but also the *value for the purpose*." Let us announce the deception, Schiller says. Let us admit the fallacy by owning that what we take or leave as "truth" is a "sheer bit of human favouritism," "fashioned as instruments for operating on the flux of happenings" and holding back chaos.[33] Truth is the art of appreciating what we choose to hang onto only because we find it to be meaningful and good.

2

If the pomegranates in Moore's painting *Pomegranates* are a red herring, then for us, the red herring seems more like a premise. It shapes the formal logic of the painting and indeed of almost all of Moore's paintings from this period. These are "academic" paintings that refuse to be contextualized and seem unsuitable for moral or social analysis but that conceptually attach themselves to a single, impertinent detail brought to our attention from somewhere among the liquid patterns and lines of fabric.

Take, for another example, the painting Moore calls *Beads*, presumably suggesting that it is *about* a string of beads, so we look very hard to find them (fig. 46). There, on the floor in the far left corner (*left* in the corner) we hardly notice them but still try to account for them because at last we have found the beads in a painting called *Beads*. But then Moore painted another picture that is formally identical to *Beads* except for its scale of colors and tints, and he calls it *A Sofa* instead, because now presumably the sofa and not the beads is what mattered to him (fig. 47). And the beads? They still abide in the picture. Like the raven, they still are sitting, *still* are sitting, but little relevancy bore (in this version, *nevermore*).

FIGURE 46. Albert Joseph Moore, *Beads* (1875). Oil on canvas. National Galleries of Scotland (NG 1019).

FIGURE 47. Albert Joseph Moore, *A Sofa* (1875). Oil on canvas. Private Collection. Bridgeman Images.

FIGURE 48. Albert Joseph Moore, *Apples* (1875). Oil on canvas. Private Collection. © Christie's Images / Bridgeman Images.

Then, Moore painted a picture called *Apples,* because here two apples happen to appear on the floor, all the way in the right corner (fig. 48). Now *they* bear no message. They do not mean what apples might mean in relation to languorous women. They do not mean what the apple means in the painting of a languorous woman by Rossetti that includes an apple, or what the apple certainly means in another painting by Rossetti of Venus tempting with an apple (fig. 49). Instead, Moore's paintings always seem, in the words of one critic, to "dramatize the irrelevance" of the subjects that are nevertheless brought to our attention and that serve as vehicles for Moore's more abstract experiments in color and arrangement, subtly modulated blues warming to greens and browns in apples, fabrics, and fans, also the toes and hands of figures pointing in radiating lines like fans.[34]

The painting *Reading Aloud* has a title that is uncharacteristically descriptive for Moore of a narrative event (fig. 50). We obviously are invited to say that this painting is *about* reading aloud and the determinative relationship the picture seems to create between the book being read at the left and the figure listening at the right. The figure at the right who is holding her head on her hand seems to frame her ear in the act of listening. But then,

FIGURE 49. Dante Gabriel Rossetti, *Monna Pomona* (1864). Watercolor and gum arabic on paper. Presented by Alfred A. de Pass, 1910. © Tate.

FIGURE 50. Albert Joseph Moore, *Reading Aloud* (1884). Tempera on paper on canvas. Art Gallery and Museum, Kelvingrove, Glasgow, Scotland. © CSG CIC Glasgow Museums Collection / Bridgeman Images.

in a painting that Moore calls *An Open Book*, that exact same figure of the woman on the right in *Reading Aloud* gets lifted just as she is into another frame on another occasion, and now we have to shift the ground on which the book (this time, set on the bench) might relate to the woman with her head on her hand (fig. 51). She isn't listening now. Is she thinking about the book she just heard? In this picture, the book's relationship to the figure is not just causal, if it ever had been (causal, I mean, as reading aloud is to listening). Now the connections between the book and woman are more figurative maybe: the book resting on the bench looks a little like the form of the woman who rests there, too, also on her back and spine. The interlaced leaves on the woman's garment fan out in flaps and folds like the fanned leaves of the book. Is *she* an open book?

And then there is another painting that takes a figure from *Reading Aloud*—not from the right this time but from the sofa—and lifts *it* again just as it is into another frame on another occasion (fig. 52). Moore calls it *Red Berries*. *Red Berries* is not about reading aloud, though the same figure of the woman who is elsewhere reading aloud remains. We can guess that *Red Berries* is about the red berries that now swell into plump existence as the

FIGURE 51. Albert Joseph Moore, *An Open Book* (1884). Watercolor.

vehicle of a metaphor for the painting—the little irrelevances that impishly divert from the central figure and her act but somehow manage to change the whole logic of the image so that everything seems to follow from their rounded, lustrous forms. For me, the ripe, red berries justify the woman's flushed red face set against the sprigs of foliage on the pillow or the way the contours on the wall seem palpably to swell and almost burst. If the painting is *Red Berries* then it is ripe for this kind of thing. Or maybe the red berries in

FIGURE 52. Albert Joseph Moore, *Red Berries* (1884). Oil on canvas. Painters / Alamy Stock Photo.

the picture are just red herrings, dramatizing the irrelevance of the subject brought to our attention—red herrings, or Moore's trick.

What makes for the evidence for making sense of a painting or—thinking back to "The Raven"—a poem, when so much of what we have to go on seems circumstantial? How does the content of a Moore painting bear its "truth"? To ask this is only to want the arrangement of each picture to become intelligible to me in some way so that the time I spend with it feels worthwhile, worth the effort it takes, and so that I do not feel that I have been led astray. These pictures proceed by logical starts and turns. The stray elements have recurring roles, and every time I look I am being asked to trust that the elements are put to some purpose or overall effect even if their success only comes in their "logical irrelevance," as I. A. Richards calls it, and if that finally *is* the point. Or are they all red herrings? Moore suggests that reading requires the work of fitting snippets into the bigger picture, letting them fall together. The important part of our taking them all in would be that we should take them *as* aspects, as visibilities to be kept in mind if we can manage to discover them at all. The "stray suggestion," as Henry James puts it—here in the shape of berries, apples, strings of beads on the floor—can have "the power to penetrate as finely as possible."[35] Each is a curiosity and there to keep our interest fresh, but only if we think we can do something with it, see it as being *for* something, some sense, even as its being given the floor, as it were, seems inassimilable or as irrational as a raven.

After all, the elements will lose our interest if we lose faith in "the neat action of their own weight" to hang together as a picture or a poem, a concrete experience. If we lose faith in them as needed. So we get the sense that Moore is guiding our perception, helping us see how all these things get reeconomized in each instance, leading to the sum of what happens when we take them into focus, and not leading us astray, left dangling like cherries on a stem. The pictures invite us to convert the facts into revelations with the logical finish being that each picture is finally a proposition for getting hold of something and raising it in a particular way. The proposition is that all these aspects "may be translated into one 'thought,'" which is what we call "the 'point,'" says Paul Ricoeur; that the berries, apples, and beads *can have* a point. That is, on every occasion the elements suggest that together they are putting on the appearance of an experience, that they are, to use Ricoeur's term, a *configurational arrangement*.[36] It would be the experience of a work of art only (an appearance only), and never definite and certainly not self-evident or foreclosed in any way, but rather the feeling for some inferential point from which there might be judgment. It would be the feeling for how all these little charming things can, with some process of appreciation, add up and come to matter, a certain moment of recognition that they might be promising and relevant in some way.

And "in this way," writes Whitehead, "details hitherto undiscriminated or dismissed as casual irrelevances are lifted into coordinated experience." It never happens in the "safe advance" of dogmatic readings but suggests "another type of progress, namely the introduction of novelty of pattern into conceptual experience." The gathering of details into a moment of real clarity—a crystallization—should always be toward a "new vision" and new sorts of significance. It should be an "adventure." But there may be details that cannot be gathered in and plenty that will not be understood to be contributive, and part of the logic of looking, at least where art's "value" is at stake, is recognizing what might not work as well.

Laurence Perrine defines poetry as "the art of the totally relevant": in other words, a poem that succeeds "is a verbal construct of which every part has manifold relations to every other part, and of which no part could be changed or shifted without weakening the whole. Not only is every part relevant to the meaning of the whole, it is totally relevant: That is, it is held in its place in the poem not by one bond only, like a picture hanging from a nail, but by many bonds, like the solar system." This is only to say that for critics like Perrine, there can be an expectation on the part of the reader that each part has "a reason for its being as it is and not otherwise," and this reason can be explained in some satisfactory way that accounts for the part in light of everything else (that lets it count): why, for example, those beads left in a corner are implicated in the painting.

The verb *implicate*, as David Bohm suggests, means to "enfold" or "fold inward," like the folds and pleats of fabrics and fans that resonate in the rhythm of Moore's frames. To read these manifold things is not to fit pieces into a whole mechanistically but to reckon perceptually with how they hold their own and yet reverberate throughout what Bohm calls the "implicate order." It is "to 'feel out' what may be the relevant new features," bringing attention to how they hold together beautifully, so that in a poem, for example, every word "takes color from the company it keeps and gives color to the company it joins." The high concentration of words yoked together like never before in a compressed space suggests that they will work with each other and count, that the "words, like chemical elements, have valences for each other and will hook on together." There can be a "controlled explosion" of meaning, but only when they are packed tight in a space that leaves out everything inessential and incapable of "touching off a spark."[37] It is all *controlled* because, although (to recall the language of relevance theory) the poem has an inexhaustible array of implications, these are only made possible by the logic that this moment conditions. It is a point that Moore playfully makes by retaining his elements just as they are while lifting them into new orders on new occasions, in the meantime expanding our sense of how a string of impertinent details can be continually implicated and made to fit.

Of course there are always the facts from without that cannot be folded into the experience of the work on a particular occasion, when trying to make them fit amounts to the critical fallacies we have come to know well. The "value" of a work, writes Richards in *Practical Criticism*, "cannot be demonstrated except through the communication of what is valuable" in it, and this requires "navigation" on the part of readers, "the art of knowing where we are wherever, as mental travellers, we may go." And *this* requires having "*the mental condition* relevant to the poem," by which he means being oriented and disposed toward whatever it communicates and being interested enough to see what happens. It also requires removing any impediments to experiencing it in earnest: those critical "fallacies" that do not bear on the "worth" of the poem to the reader, including all "doctrinal adhesions" and "general critical preconceptions" as well as too much "sentimentality," which raises "a question of the due measure of response."

"Relevance," Richards says, "is not an easy notion to define or to apply, though some instances of irrelevant intrusions are among the simplest of all accidents to diagnose." These include "mnemonic irrelevances" that interfere when a reader is reminded of some personal moment and then distracted by the "emotional reverberations from a past which may have nothing to do with the poem." There are also "irrelevant associations and stock responses" that precede any understanding of the poem and make prior demands on it. "Ideas, handed to us by others or produced from within, are a beguiling substitute for actual experience in evoking and developing our responses." Most are "irrelevancies," he says. "Stereotyped reactions" are a "withdrawal from experience," unless, of course, the stock response is actually the appropriate response to a "stock poem" that itself is absent of any original character (there are plenty of them).[38]

Richards was interested in the relationship between psychology and criticism, how any reader becomes aware enough of a work to get something out of it, and he was ready to admit that "every interpretation is motivated by some interest." His book *The Meaning of Meaning*, written with C. K. Ogden, followed on a symposium he attended in 1920 called "The Meaning of 'Meaning'" in which F. C. S. Schiller debated Bertrand Russell on the nature of meaning and the "intimate connexion between meaning and value" (with British idealist philosopher Harold Joachim responding). Richards's sense of the internal relations and complexity of a poem (as a logical construction) may derive from Russell. But he seems to have taken from Schiller his own sense that the meaning of a poem depends on the perspective and "mental condition" of its reader. That meaning requires a judgment of value and an articulated criticism. Understanding how a poem works can also help us understand how the mind always works "through inhibition" that lets us sort through evidence for judgment and avoid confusion and chaos ("we cannot indulge one mental activity without inhibiting others," Richards says). That is, he seems to agree with Schiller that we find meaning by suppressing some things while selecting and emphasizing others according to our interest, our sense of importance, and the need for a response that is "appropriate to the situation." Meaning follows from this perceptual work of identifying fit or "misfits," relevance and its limits. In his contribution to the symposium, Schiller writes about the "apparent paradox that meaning should be most intense when it is most obstructed," likening it to the way "the strength of a current is revealed when it eddies over the rocks that obstruct its course." "Thus what philosophers are wont to call 'thought' is essentially a phenomenon of obstructed perception"; "it is natural enough, therefore, that cases of obstructed expression should yield the purest and intensest consciousness of meaning."[39]

When W. K. Wimsatt and Monroe C. Beardsley defined the intentional fallacy and the affective fallacy in essays on the fallacies in the 1940s, they were warning readers against "the irrelevant excursion, the disproportionate development, the feeble conclusion" that result in "failures of meaning." Returning, as they say, to Aristotelian logic for their principles of critical thinking, the fallacies they name interfere with their own "propositions," which simply demand that a work *works* and that it operates to "produce an end." (That end is not very unlike "a vote by a jury or a senate," Wimsatt says.)

The intentional fallacy attempts to derive the standard of meaning from the psychological causes of words. It looks past a poem for evidence of intentions that are not "effective" in it. But the poem is the only "adequate evidence" we ever have in front of us, and "critical inquiries are not settled by consulting the oracle." The affective fallacy attempts to derive the standard of meaning from the psychological effects of words. The reader indulges in sentimentality or self-interest rather than seeing the poem as an *object* of interest. As a result, the poem becomes less *interesting*, because poetry is "a discourse about both emotions and objects, or about the emotive quality of objects," and so any emotions that are not "correlative to the objects of poetry" are not part of the "matter dealt with." These personal feelings do not tell us nothing—they tell us a lot about ourselves in ways that may be important for other purposes in other contexts—but they have little to do with critical judgment of the poem. They most of all fail to help us see how the poem can be an instrument for getting hold of other, complex feelings not realized in its absence or how the poem "objectively" might matter to us. For Wimsatt and Beardsley, these fallacies admit "irrelevant" and "inadequate" evidence that contribute nothing to critical understanding, which can only succeed when "all or most of what is said or implied is relevant" and when "what is irrelevant has been excluded, like lumps from pudding and 'bugs' from machinery."[40] They want readers and critics simply to demand that the poem work and to be needful in relation to it, to let it be meaningful and practical for new understandings and never the occasion to validate what we already feel, think, or know.

Beardsley writes, "effective thinking is thinking that succeeds in getting from known truths to truths that are as yet unknown." The line is not from his work on "practical criticism" but from his work on "practical logic," which closely follows, especially in the way it comes together a few years later in his textbooks *Practical Logic* and *Thinking Straight* on the art of "effective thinking." As a logician, Beardsley is actually credited with pioneering what comes to be called "informal logic," and he naturally draws in his textbooks on forms of logical thinking that had been returning to the logic of the sophists since Bentham. His exercises in arguing and communication read a lot like Bentham's own *Book of Fallacies* and include just as much on the importance of "critical reading (or listening)" to make sense of political affairs and to decide what to believe, when "our eyes and ears are assaulted by a bewildering and frightening torrent of words." Thinking is how we learn to cope and *choose*, he says: "When experience surprises or disturbs us, we have to 'make up our minds.'" He tells us that we "*should* be looking carefully for mistakes." We especially should be looking for appeals to feelings that "narrow attention" and result in prejudice or "capsule thinking," because these are "vicious half-truths" that deliberately "leave out of account some other relevant facts" (he calls them the "fallacy of *oversimplification*"). We should also learn to recognize appeals to feelings that "shift attention" and "get thinking off the point" so that we lose track of our sense of purpose. These include *ignoratio elenchi*, "directed toward proving some irrelevant conclusion" and any "red herring" or "fallacy of distraction" devised "to get people away from the point at issue to another point, which they feel is somehow relevant but which is really not relevant."[41]

Informal logic sets the terms for Beardsley's theory of criticism and, also, his theory of aesthetics in his book *Aesthetics: Problems in the Philosophy of Criticism*, in which the question for the reader is not what is "true" in a work of art but what is "'true *to*' it" and in which criticism is always about evaluations that are "logically relevant and persuasive" given the preponderance of *evidence*. We think about aesthetic objects in order "to decide with what attitudes and expectations" they are "best approached, if we wish to get out of them what is most worth getting." Thinking about art issues in a "claim to truth" and the "method of doing it may in a broad sense be called 'logic,'" but Beardsley knows there can never be a strict or formal "logic of explication," since the very notion of critical explication simply involves "getting as much meaning" out of a poem or painting as possible. The critical claim to truth is only a claim to value, so what he proposes, sounding like Schiller, are "criteria of relevance" for getting the most out of a work that we can and for appreciating it as best we can. And what this requires is, first of all, the acknowledgment that in every experience of a work of art, we have made a choice. We have chosen to give it our attention as a possible answer to the problem of value and to hold it out in a "temporary" way because it promises to be satisfying and filled with meaning; because it gives "an air of being more than it seems to be at first glance" and this makes it interesting; because it invites an "intense awareness." The aesthetic object "segregates itself for perception from its environment; it takes on individuality," Beardsley says. It is "regarded as a whole," or "almost a whole, because it is fairly detachable." We treat it *as if* it were an individual entity, real and self-contained, since the experience of the work "stands out to a certain degree for attention, or makes its presence known, so to speak, in comparison with other areas." For it to be *an* experience, it must be "bounded or framed in some way, marked out for perception from its background, so that what is within its boundaries can constitute a limited picture-plane."[42]

Beardsley's idea of aesthetic experience is based on Dewey's writings on "value theory," experimental logic, and aesthetic experience from *Art as Experience* and elsewhere. He credits Dewey with the ideas that shape his own sense of an aesthetic experience as "a segment of experience in general that is demarcated from the rest by its high degree of unity." This unity consists in "its being pervaded by a single individualizing quality"; also, in the way this quality gets intensified in a work of art by "its consummatory character (impulses aroused in the experience being carried to completion within it), its continuity (the passage from stage to stage without gaps and dead spots, so that each stage carries within it the past and the future), its rhythm (a controlled dynamism, or ordered change), its cumulativeness (a progressive massing of materials), its shape (or dominant kinetic pattern), its concentration of energy." Beardsley's claim is that art feels like an experience that can "hang together" or is coherent to an unusually "high degree." It is also "an experience that is unusually complete in itself." So once, or rather *if*, we grant that a work of art is some segment of experience, standing out from everything else for attention—like "one crowded hour of glorious life" offering up "immediately, and richly, the best there is in life"—then, Beardsley says, we can think about what is and is not *relevant* to this experience and what intensifies it and makes it meaningful or lessens it.

"The world of the work" under consideration, he says, "detaches itself, and even insulates itself, from the intrusion of alien elements." Certain things are not "fitting" to the work of "assembling, or feeling out, the admissible" possibilities for it and the way "it means all it *can* mean, so to speak." If we believe that a painting, for example, "play[s] with a sense of ideal possibility"—that it tries to "bring into existence new universals, never exemplified in any particulars before those particular paintings"—then we can wonder how we are guided by its "logical and physical possibilities." How exactly the "heterogeneous but interrelated components of a phenomenally objective field" hang together as a "concrescence of patterns" that give the work a sense of significance—of *plenitude*. "It seems to me," Beardsley says, "that what I find in aesthetic objects I find nowhere else, and I go to them looking for qualities they alone afford." In each case, we can see that a work's "thickness" is compatible with "precision and control" and incompatible with "looseness, vagueness, flabbiness, or wildness." We can understand how to value a poem by accounting for "the greatest quantity of data in the words" within it or for how many parts play their part within the density and "total web of relation." These parts join together to concentrate our attention, detaching and isolating the experience from the background while leaving in the background everything that is, in Dewey's words, "irrelevant to the matter of experience artistically organized." "What is to be interpreted in a text is a proposed world, a world that I might inhabit," Ricoeur says. It is the "world of the work." But as Alfred Schutz reminds us, it is only one world—one "province of relevance" among other provinces of relevance and meaning—and we soon enough move from one province to another or leap between them.[43]

Before Beardsley and Wimsatt, and before Richards, in the time of Moore, critics already were drawing on sophistical logic to understand what constitutes the evidence for making sense of a poem or painting, the point being that discovering what is relevant to critical judgment can help us appreciate that object and see its value. "The problem," Beardsley writes, "is to provide an adequate criterion of relevance" or "to set the bounds of relevance for critical reasons." The desirable effect is a coherent understanding of the work (what then gets crystallized or else burns for us "with a hard gemlike flame").[44] In 1885 English scholar Richard G. Moulton called for an "inductive criticism" that could help readers "get a closer acquaintance with their phenomenon," so as to appreciate without prejudice (which is a "barrier to appreciation"). He quotes Emerson in an appeal to readers to "experience" a work and to be open to the "reversal of critical judgments by further experience."[45] In *The Modern Study of Literature* (1915) , Moulton provides examples of "inadmissible" facts to the "intrinsic study of literature" that block this experience in some way: "Let it be conceded," he says, "that the main thing is to get into contact with the literature itself. But we are not in real contact with the literature if, displacing theory by subjective criticism, we are letting traditional ideas of others come between us and what we read. We are not in contact with the literature."

And so Moulton names all the "fallacies" that interfere with the possibilities of appreciation: the "author fallacy" (which asks whether the poet "really meant" everything we get out of a poem) and the "fallacy of mechanical induction" (which attempts to apply formal, inflexible logic and principles to a work that will never fit a scheme) and the "fallacy of the moral" (which confuses finding a "lesson" in the work with interpreting the work). There is the "allegorizing fallacy" (in which a work is given allegorical significance that has no claims to be an allegory); the "fallacy of kinds" (which adheres to the idea of old forms in the face of new forms); the "fallacy of the superior person" (which attempts to make a literary work square with the views of the critic who thinks he "has a philosophy more advanced than the philosophy of the literature he is studying"). All these and many more are "irrelevant" to understanding, deriving from static and unfounded ideas. They do not put us in "the most favorable position for intimate contact with the literature." This is not to say that aspects of biography or history, for example, should not be considered in interpretation but "that ideas imported from outside must find some point of attachment in the text of the work that is being interpreted." Moulton wants us "to be able to see the part in its relation to the whole," never mechanically, but as the way of "piercing through the haze of non-significant particulars to the elements of life closely relevant to principle."[46]

And before Moulton? There was Poe, of course. His own criticism explains how something as irrelevant as a raven can be implicated in a poem that burns as bright as its subject's fiery eyes, but only if we concentrate. (Poe probably learned about relevance and irrelevance from reading Mill's logic; in "A Blackwood Article," he even jokes about committing an *ignoratio elenchi*, "a nice little Latin phrase, and rare too.")[47] I won't repeat here what I said in chapter 2 but simply draw attention one last time to Poe's sense of the relation between the formal constraints of "The Raven" and the dawning of relevance: those on-the-spot adjustments that make irrelevant words so fitting, and then the enjoyment of the "fitness" and the clearness that comes from seeing how it all holds together (like a "crystal," Poe says). Something that was apropos of nothing achieves "a unity or totality of interest" that is marked out for perception. But the reader has to be willing to carry all the words into a unifying idea, to undergo the process of construction that lets everything be *interesting* and directly contribute, leaving no touch of the experience irrelevant that might help. "Some features, that at first sight seem extraneous, belong in fact to expressiveness," Dewey says in *Art as Experience*. "For they further the development of an experience so as to give the satisfaction peculiar to striking fulfillment."[48]

At the same time, there will be false starts and stops until the reader finds a logic that appears to work. Ideas will be put aside and excluded until that point when he manages to come right up against his object ("Straight I wheeled a cushioned seat in front of bird, and bust and door"). Then the reader will no longer look for meaning in contexts and sources beyond the raven because the only logic for the raven will be *in* its poetic expression—the currents and undercurrents of meaning that impart density and fullness to an object beheld within the insulated space that is as necessary to its effects as "a frame to a picture," Poe says. We are reminded in "The Philosophy of Composition" that by the end of the poem we finally get the first metaphorical expression of the poem: the bird's beak is only in the reader's heart metaphorically; not the bird, but the bird's "form" is on his door. ("'Take thy beak from out my heart, and take thy form from off my door!' / Quoth the Raven 'Nevermore!'") From this moment the reader regards the raven as emblematic: Poe writes, "the intention of making him emblematical . . . is permitted distinctly to be seen." The impertinent raven has been removed from its usual surroundings and held up on a bust of Pallas, and the intensive effect on the reader is something like the experience of a work of art. The raven is meant to be, along with everything else it appears to be, an emblem for the poem "The Raven" and apropos of nothing but the effects of reading "The Raven." It finally demands to be recognized as a poem.

And the apples, and the beads? It turns out that they are little emblems too. The orange beads, you see, provide the tonal key to the chromatic scale of the painting that goes by the name of *Beads*, a painting based in the orange of the beads and then—and Moore was as scientific about this as Winslow Homer was—orange's complementary color on the color scale, which is blue. The terms of this chromatic equation are actually laid out geometrically in the carpet at the figures' feet, which is woven with alternating bands of the chromatic complements, orange and blue. These terms seem to be a kind of master plan. They are, as it were, the figure in the carpet.

The painting *Apples* is named after the apples and not the beads because now the picture takes its shape and logic from the greens and blues of the apples, a chromatic arrangement that is also represented in the rug. As one of Moore's friends writes, "Each of his scientific pictures is a little problem of color. The problems are plain enough, as each picture generally contains some little emblem and strip of matting or carpet which is at once the proposition and Q.E.D." At once the proposition and QED—the *quod erat demonstrandum*—meaning that which we set out to demonstrate has been exactly restated in the demonstration. The apples are the painting that is *Apples*—just as the raven is the poem that is "The Raven"—a demonstrative logic that is as self-contained or circular as the circles and curves throughout the painting *Pomegranates*, which are just like the pomegranates on which the picture is based. Moore's art gives us the *appearance* of self-evidence in the formal or logical sense: art prima facie. What had been irrelevant about the painting—here, the pomegranates—achieves its distinctiveness and sensuous shape "not by irrelevance of local texture" but by something that Wimsatt, speaking of a poem, actually calls its "extra relevance or hyperrelevance": the interrelational density of things taken in their fullest, most emblematic character in art. Supercharged with significance, a poem, like a painting, has "an iconic solidity." It "takes on something like the character of a stone statue or a porcelain vase."

Maybe even like the porcelain vase in *Pomegranates* that Moore bases on a fifth-century Greek vase in ways the sophists would appreciate (fig. 53). Like the fifth-century Greek vase in John Keats's poem on a Grecian urn, it is a "well wrought urn."[49] In art things can be brought together and made to

FIGURE 53. Albert Joseph Moore, *Pomegranates* (1866) (detail).

fit in ways we never could imagine in other contexts. But it is its own context. There are others to divert us.

. . .

In his great study *Recognitions: A Study in Poetics*, Terence Cave charts the history of recognition scenes in literary plots from Oedipus through Freud and in literary theory from Aristotle to Barthes, where the device of recognition is always, as he calls it, a "scandal." An implausible contrivance happens to bring about the shift from unawareness to knowledge: that Oedipus has killed his father and married his mother; that Odysseus, though disguised, has come home; that Prince Amerigo and Charlotte were, let's say, shopping together before they claimed to have met. A messenger, a birthmark, a casket, a dropped handkerchief, a golden bowl, the accidental discovery of an accidental scar, a necklace—or, yes, sometimes a string of beads: in every case it is a trivial, coincidental accessory or token left aside but on which the whole plot of recognition comes to depend. The idea of the recognition scene first appears in Aristotle's *Poetics*, where he calls it *anagnorisis*. The device of *anagnorisis*—say, the golden bowl that gives Prince Amerigo away—is at once contingent and essential to the formal integrity of the plot since it resolves a sequence of unexplained occurrences in what appears, in retrospect, to be a logical outcome (of course Prince Amerigo and Charlotte had known each other). The golden bowl always sitting there on the mantle now brings about an astonishing consciousness of the way in which, to the characters in the narrative and to us, it insists adamantly on the causes and effects that brought it there.

But *anagnorisis* is not a moment of logic. It is the appearance of logic, a false logic. In *Poetics* Aristotle calls it a "paralogism" or pseudologic, in which the trick is passed off and the reader is fallaciously induced to recognize the truth of the antecedent from the fact of the consequent—the fact, again, that the golden bowl is sitting there, like the fact that a raven may be perched above a door.[50] The bowl and the raven do not imply everything we think they imply within their motivated narratives unless we are willing to grant the validity of their contrivance to begin with, and then obsessively infer from there. These devices, after all, are completely unlikely and specious and, as Cave shows, historically scandalous, because as artists' tricks and lies, they make a whole narrative turn on an arbitrary bowl or a handkerchief that happens to drop, where the contingent clue seems to obey the causal laws of logic and philosophy. They are tricks for rendering plausible a highly implausible sequence of events, or red herrings—in which charades of action can follow from inconsequential things—and yet, for Aristotle, they are intrinsic to the way art works, even, we could say as Cave does, a signature for fiction as a whole. To admit the fallacy is to admit the logic of art.

In *The Golden Bowl*, Prince Amerigo and Charlotte go "hunting in London" for "some little thing with a charm" and find the golden bowl. The antiques dealer, having lifted the bowl from its box, leaves "the important object—for as 'important' it did somehow present itself—to produce its certain effect," but the shoppers do not buy it. Neither one of them could give it to the other because there would be no "logic" in it, no point. "Where's the logic?" Charlotte asks. And, when the Prince laughs, she says, "But logic's everything. That at least is how I feel it. A ricordo from you—from you to me—is a ricordo of nothing. It has no reference." A ricordo from him to her is apropos of nothing because there can be no valid connection between them. That little thing would never *mean* anything, since there will never be an admission in anyone's minds, including theirs, that they had "gone together," as Maggie Verver later puts it. As a gift it would mark this diversion as an "occasion." It would be a way of treating the golden bowl "as if it were important," but, again, there will be no projecting of any relations, no "signally attaching proposition" (to use James's words from a different context) that would make this act a logical act, since the Prince is already engaged to marry Maggie. In any case, the golden bowl, which is crystal, has an aberration, a crack. With enough pressure its exquisite crystal form will shatter to pieces.

Later, when Charlotte and the Prince go to Matcham—"We must see the old king; we must 'do' the cathedral"—their day of diversions feels, the Prince says, "like a great gold cup that we must somehow drain together." And Charlotte reminds him "apropos of great gold cups" of "the gilded crystal bowl in the little Bloomsbury shop" she once thought about offering to him before his marriage to Maggie. So that now at last, the little discounted bowl, for Charlotte at least, gets attached to this adventure, the "occasion" of the trip to Matcham in which the affair between Charlotte and the Prince finally is consummated ("I feel this an occasion," he says).[51] The bowl that was a ricordo of nothing is finally apropos of the occasion and treated meaningfully, since the relations between Charlotte and the Prince are finally established and real.

It is the truth of these relations that the golden bowl finally brings to

Maggie Verver's consciousness, since the bowl by the sheer contrivance that Cave describes ends up on Maggie's mantelpiece after she finds it in the same curiosity shop. She had been looking for a gift for her father, a great collector, having long realized that finding any worthwhile object, with all of his own constant rummaging in shops, "was by a rigorous law of nature a foredoomed aberration." She discovers the aberration and buys the bowl, which she later learns is unsound when the dealer comes to her house to tell her about the crack he had failed to disclose before. Seeing photographs of Charlotte and the Prince, he also discloses that he happened to make their acquaintance in the shop earlier over the same article. After which Maggie, whose "imagination" in usual daily life "was clearly never ruffled by the sense of any anomaly," suddenly knew herself "in presence of a problem, in need of a solution for which she must intensely work." A "new perception bristled for her." She becomes conscious in a "flash" of a "mass of vain things, congruous, incongruous," of accumulations "never as yet 'sorted,'" but there all along. These include the Prince's "expression" toward her when he returns from Matcham, first of too much tenderness and then of dismissal when he figures out that she is unsuspecting. All along she had been unaware of the nature of the "aspect and arrangement"—the basis of the way they were "all four arranged," including her father (now married to Charlotte), and of how "Amerigo and Charlotte were arranged together" and she was "arranged apart"—until "the first shock of complete perception." But now the "odd intimations," the dim perceptions of anomalous things, "were to come back to her—they played through her full after-sense like lights on the whole impression." "Objects took on values not hitherto so fully shown," with that aberrant bowl figuring as especially *important*, since it suggests how Charlotte and the Prince had "originally gone together." It is crucial to the recognition of the way that everything—the expressions and behavior, the arranging—"fitted immensely together," the way that she and her father especially had been arranged. "That cup there has turned witness," Maggie says to Fanny Assingham, "—by the most wonderful of chances."[52]

Maggie draws attention to the gilt cup, on the cluttered mantelpiece of ornaments and accessories, of which Fanny before "hadn't taken heed," but sees at last has been lifted up on a stem on an ample foot in the central position "to allow it the better to show." This accessory, turned witness, gets admitted as *evidence*. "It has everything [to do]," with the problem at hand that Maggie is making out. "The question was obviously not of its intrinsic value," as Maggie puts it, especially when it cracks in pieces, but its "other value is just the same": that of the crystal's having given Maggie the "truth" about Charlotte and the Prince that it *crystallizes* and makes so evident. "Then it all depends on the bowl?" Fanny Assingham asks (though in the configuring now happening we learn that so far as Fanny herself was so squared, "she had become an image irrelevant to the scene"). Certain persons and things recede to the background while these other things Maggie had never thought to see until this *achieved hour* gain value and "loomed, to her sightless eyes, on either side of her, larger than they had ever loomed before."

In the prefaces to his novels, James describes the art of fiction as the result of a process of "foreshortening," like the anamorphic foreshortening in pictures (especially Hans Holbein the Younger's famous painting *The Ambassadors*, for which James may have titled *The Ambassadors*). By "foreshortening," James means "the craft of selection, omission or commission" in which a given picture of life brings forward certain objects and values exaggeratedly, so as to render them "both rich and sharp, that the mere procession of items and profiles is not only, for the occasion, superseded, but is, for essential quality, almost 'compromised.'" In the "[boiling] down so many facts in the alembic," the "produced appearance, should have intensity, lucidity, brevity, beauty." Something will be extracted from the scene, and brought out in the new placement, while what is left will be (scenically) left behind, "superseded" and "almost 'compromised.'" These, he says, are the "terms of literary arrangement": they work "under the law of mere elimination" and "the simple device of more and more keeping down" so as to raise the prospect of a "precious truth." Of course, it takes a "certain factitious compactness." It requires cropping a scene by that process of selection "for foreshortening at any cost, for imparting to patches the value of presences, for dressing objects in an *air* as of the dimensions they can't possibly have." "We recognise the character of our interest only after the particular magic." The discovery of new significance comes in the distortions for emphasis and the shifting of the relations and values within the little ensemble so that certain things intelligibly come to attention and grow in importance. By this process, we can make interest, make importance where there was none.[53]

Maggie, conscious of how she had been "arranged" (one of the many "miracles of arrangement" in the midst of which she says she lives), sets out to readjust the picture. It becomes a question of creating a different effect with the same elements, differently placed. She "showed something of the glitter of consciously possessing the constructive, the creative hand." She is by now in fact the central consciousness of a novel in which she hadn't figured much at all, and there will be a new "logic of the 'scene'" and "the entire succession of values that flower and bear fruit." It will be a different sort of *hanging together*, on new principles of weight and admissibility. She will establish a "claim" to the Prince's attention and "the fruit of his attention to her couldn't help being a sense of the growth of her importance," an intensification of interest. The Prince has "never been half so interested in you as now," Fanny tells her. "But don't you, my dear, really feel it?"

What was dismissed will come to matter and feel relevant on the fallacious logic of the golden bowl and of everything else in the book that takes on "a sharpness of importance," just as Charlotte had early on been a "quite irrelevant presence" to Maggie's father and then in an instant the "predominance of Charlotte's very person, in her being there exactly as she was" gave *that* "truth a sort of solidity of evidence." Naturally the solidity of evidence shifts with the taking on of importances later and the rest falling away, so that Maggie, not Charlotte, ultimately seems "'foreshortened' . . . to within an inch of her life," as James describes characters elsewhere. She get clarified and distilled so that to Charlotte she finally appears "like some holy image in a procession, and left precisely to show what wonder she could work under pressure." Maggie is shown as mattering, demonstrating through the whole second half of the book the creative work of squeezing out essentialness and value. And when, at the end—"the whole scene having crystallised" for Charlotte, who has been squeezed out and has lost her place—she sees how Maggie and the Prince "fairly 'placed' themselves" among all the "decorative elements" that are "required aesthetically by such a scene" in which "their contribution to the triumph of selection, was complete and admirable." The constructive logic of the scene (the mise-en-scène), brings forth new value through the efforts of concentration and focus, of the very consciousness that gets made. The Prince, keeping Maggie close with her face right before him and his hands on her shoulders, his whole act enclosing her so that she is dramatically foreshortened from this angle of vision, says, at the very last, "I see nothing but *you*."[54]

When, in *The Ambassadors*, Lambert Strether took the train to the countryside outside of Paris, "it had been the only adventure of his life in connexion with the purchase of a work of art," since he set out to see something that would remind him of a Lambinet print that "had charmed him, long years before." The whole rambling day, "he really continued in the picture—that being for himself his situation," that everything got fitted to the way "the frame had drawn itself out for him." The rustle of the willows, the tone of the sky: "Not a single one of his observations but somehow fell into a place in it; not a breath of the cooler evening that wasn't somehow a syllable of the text. The text was simply, when condensed, that in *these* places such things were, and that if it was in them one elected to move about one had to make one's account with what one lighted on." When he happens to see Chad Newsome and Madame de Vionnet there "in a boat of their own"—in that contrived scene of recognition that is also a "scandal" because Strether understands at last the nature of their affair and the "deep, deep truth of the intimacy revealed"—his first impulse still is to take them in as part of the picture and its overall effect. "It was suddenly as if these figures, or something like them, had been wanted in the picture, had been wanted more or less all day, and had now drifted into sight, with the slow current, on purpose to fill up the measure." The "wonderful accident" of their happening to be there and appear means that Strether "had within the minute taken in" at once "that he knew the lady" *and* that her "parasol, shifting as if to hide her face, made so fine a pink point in the shining scene."[55]

This way that Strether, as James says of himself in writing *The Ambassadors*, always "accounted for everything," so that "'everything' had by this time become the most promising quantity," is very much what he has been doing all along in Paris. He wanted to "make the moment an occasion," to feel an aspect of life distilled into the concentrated experience of it, to take in everything *as if* it had "contributive value." As he tells Little Bilham, "it's a mistake not to." He is there to recall Chad home to Woollett and the family business; Mrs. Newsome has asked Strether to carry out this favor with the assumption that it will be the fulfillment of the duty on which marriage will follow. But Strether also goes to Paris to recover other relations, remembering when he gets there, for example, the wife who died when he was young and the son who may not have died at school if only his father had not "given himself to merely missing the mother" and neglected him. Strether "had wanted to put himself in relation, and he would be hanged if he were *not* in relation." What happens then in Paris is that the substance of what would otherwise be missed and perceptually lost emerges for him as a "concrete presence . . . full of reality." The "beauty of the constructional game," as James calls it elsewhere, "was to preserve in everything its especial value for *him*." It always "rested, all so firm, on selection," Strether tells himself at the end. The idea was to find himself in the presence of a moment (it would be "only for a moment") as intelligible and full of significance as a picture in which "everything directly contributed, leaving no touch of experience irrelevant." And this would make for what Strether calls that "lift" he aims to get from Paris, the raising of new interests, new importances in connection with himself, the *reconstruction* of old connections, too, "re-accepted, re-tasted, exquisitely re-assimilated" ("he wasn't there to dip, to consume—he was there to reconstruct"), and all along the readjustment of the sense of values for total effect. Of course in the end Strether recognizes that Chad is not worth the effort. With Chad it takes too much effort for too little effect to maintain the romance, the lift it gives, and, as Strether goes to visit him in his apartment—before that decisive turn when we know Chad will return to Woollett to make money in advertising—Strether has to take the stairs all the way, "the lift, at that hour, having ceased to work." All along "there had been simply a *lie* in the charming affair." And yet knowing that it was all an illusion, a deceit, is, as James writes, "just my demonstration of this process of vision" and how it only ever works.[56]

The logic of Strether's "adventure," in other words, is the way it proceeds with the same "force and logic" as the discovering of the subject of the novel itself that James describes in his preface: it "puts on . . . the authenticity of concrete existence." In this, James continues, "resides surely much of the interest of that admirable mixture for salutary application which we know as art. . . . [Art] plucks its material, otherwise expressed, in the garden of life—which material elsewhere grown is stale and uneatable. But it has no sooner done this than it has to take account of a *process*"; and this "process, that of expression, the literal squeezing-out, of value" is its affair too. The full process, as James says of the contrivance that brings Strether to Paris, is, "if not involved by strict logic then all ideally and enchantingly implied in it."[57]

The figure for this logic that is not strict logic and how it can be made to work in the novel is Maria Gostrey, the figure James famously calls "the most unmitigated and abandoned of *ficelles*," simply the contrivance on which a dramatist depends. A *ficelle* is an artifice, a trick or deceit (literally, from French, the "string" or "thread" attached to the puppet). In the novel Maria Gostrey represents the "deep dissimulation" of a "connexion." She meets Strether throughout but cannot be said ever to have a real relation to him—even with the final proposal of marriage that Strether declines—only the contrivance of a relation, whose "function" is to make apparent a certain logic for what happens to him. Sometimes this means providing for the exposition of "certain indispensable facts," so that dining with Strether in London or conversing in Paris allows for so much background information to be "treated scenically," that is, expressed efficiently and compactly. But the contrivance is more important than this; indeed, James tells us that Maria Gostrey "achieves, after a fashion, something of the dignity of a prime idea." She is, from an early stage, necessary to "the very form and figure of 'The Ambassadors.'"[58]

She is the figure for James's effort, as he says, "to project imaginatively, for my hero, a relation that has nothing to do with the matter (the matter of my subject) but has everything to do with the manner (the manner of my presentation of the same) and yet to treat it, at close quarters and for fully economic expression's possible sake, as if it were important and essential." Maria Gostrey is, what James calls, that "signally attaching proposition": the proposition of a relation that gives the *appearance* of a relation that is treated *as if* it were important and essential. It is, of course "artfully dissimulated, throughout . . . with the seams or joints of Maria Gostrey's ostensible connectedness taken particular care of, duly smoothed over, that is, and anxiously kept from showing as 'pieced on.'" It is a "false connexion" made to "carry itself, under a due high polish, as a real one."

Go*strey* is the *stray* suggestion that James describes—"the stray suggestion, the wandering word, the vague echo"—whose "virtue" for the novelist "is all in its needle-like quality, the power to penetrate as finely as possible." She suggests "the intensity of suggestion that may reside in the stray figure, the unattached character, the image *en disponibilité*." She is the *form and figure* for making a stray suggestion suggestive of interest, suggestive of importance by bringing it into relation with oneself. The "prime idea" that dignifies her presence is the ability of such a contrived connection, appearing as a real one, to make possible certain expressions unimaginable without it, "to express as vividly as possible certain things quite other than itself." But, James adds, since "all art is *expression*, and is thereby vividness, one was to find the door open here to any amount of delightful dissimulation."

With Maria Gostrey, Strether is more aware of the "elements of Appearance" than he had been for a long time. She is all along a "charming associate of his adventure," the "signally attaching proposition" of a meaningful experience in which everything is contributive and nothing lost, straining, as only she can help make happen, "to a high lucidity and vivacity." It is simply that she has been there to see him through, with her "smelling-salts," as James puts it (or her *sal volatile*, as Emerson had put it—her *saliency*). "'But through what?'—she liked to get it all out of him." "Why through this experience," Strether says. Never speak, she reminds him, "as if my part were small." She is the figure for the proposition of a relation inside a logic that is not a strict logic, but "enchanting[ly] implied" in it. One would never say it is valid. She is an acknowledged sophism, a "put on" and a thread of artifice, brought in from out of the blue with her only "function" being the "lively extractor of [Strether's] value and distiller of his essence." She stands not for any truth in particular but for the sudden, artful appearance of truth or reality and, in the hour that now passes, she can help him find something worth the effort it takes, against his mis-takes and the unreality of everything he misses. James invents a figure for "the office of expressing *all there is in* the hour," holding the rest in abeyance, "creating for his . . . mind," like everything else brought in on the occasion, "even in a world of irrelevance the possibility of a relation."[59]

10

News and Orientation

"Reading the morning newspaper is the realist's morning prayer. One orients one's attitude toward the world either by God or by what the world is. The former gives as much security as the latter, in that one knows how one stands." This aphorism about the morning newspaper appears in a fragment Hegel wrote in his "Wastebook," being the English word that he chose for describing the collection of loose-leaf notes he kept between 1803 and 1806 while teaching at the university in Jena. The next year Hegel completed *The Phenomenology of Spirit* and left his university position to become the editor of a local newspaper, the *Bamberg Zeitung*. His career at the newspaper was short, only a year and a half, before returning to the academy, but during that time it was a way of extending philosophy in the academic sense into what Kant calls "philosophy in the worldly sense"—of getting his bearings in the movements of daily life and of knowing in relation to this life how, as he puts it, "one stands."[1]

In the American painter Helen Turner's *Morning News* from a century later the ritual of reading the morning paper is just like a morning prayer (fig. 54). What the reader sees in the creases of the newspaper's folds is the sign of the cross bathed in the light of the window. In an impressionist painting, this at least is the impression they make. The matter of the daily news is abstracted into the symbol of the spirit of the world that unfolds before the reader at the breakfast table. Who knows what she reads about this time? In a painting from 1915 it is probably the war, since the red robe that flows sensationally from the black-and-white sheet seems there to suggest that "if

FIGURE 54. Helen M. Turner, *Morning News* (1915). Oil on canvas. Collection Zimmerli Art Museum at Rutgers University, Jersey City Museum Collection, gift of Nellie Wright Allen (2018.032.048).

it bleeds it leads." But all that pours off. This is a morning prayer that sublates the grisly facts of current events into a window through which the spirit of the times translucently shines through. The paper's crossed folds most of all resemble the mullions of the window etherealized in the sunlight behind it as if to say that the grid of a paper is most like the panes of a window.

By the nineteenth century, newspapers, often called "The Spirit of the Age" or "The Spirit of the Times," claimed to represent the free and comprehensive unfolding of information that brought the world within the reader's field of vision. A newspaper, writes American minister Henry Ward Beecher, "is a window through which men look out on all that is going on in the world." Only when reading the morning paper became a ritual of daily life could it be a reflection of the moment one was in, which is also to say that the nineteenth century saw its own evolving character reflected in the perpetual advance of the news. The newspaper "is, and is to be . . . the circulating life blood of the whole human mind" (*Springfield Republican*, January 4, 1851). Like Hegel's "reconciliation" of mind with world, it was the duty of the dailies to bring "the *Course of Event*s to bear on the progress of every individual," and so it comes as no surprise that Hegel continued to love the newspaper long after his career as an editor in Bamberg. We might say that the newspaper is not only one place where, in Hegel's words, "the writing of history and the actual deeds and events of history make their appearance simultaneously" but where "they emerge together from a common source": the self-recording, self-narrating "spirit of the times" as it is realized in the everyday life of the newspaper.

Thus, Hegel's devotion to newspapers speaks to the ways in which a philosophy of mind becomes the expression of the world-historical context that the newspaper manifests and records every morning and then, increasingly, in late editions and extra editions that succeed the earlier editions throughout the day. "The skilled and faithful journalist, recording with exactness and power the thing that has come to pass," writes James Parton in 1866, "is Providence addressing men." Who would ever want to bury himself in academic thought "when the movement of *his own* time at every turn sweeps him up and carries him onward?" Friedrich Schelling once asked of Hegel. The morning papers are the signs of the times that Hegel—an armchair philosopher who "never left the shores of the continent" and yet wrote a "Philosophical History of the World"—could nonetheless observe in the advances of Napoleon or the revolutions in Haiti, but only by way of the press. Newspapers "bear us along with them, abreast of the rapid flood of passing events," says American editor George Lunt in 1857; to resist "may seem to some little better than rank heresy to the spirit of the age and its main instruments of thought."[2]

For Hegel, historical change is not simply a consequence of transformative events but follows from the way they are recorded and narrated to the world. That "history" means both events that happen and the form they take in writing is a profound coincidence for a philosopher who sees the progress of his times as depending, at least in part, on a self-conscious understanding of how consciousness evolves. Change is a recursive process that is intensified by reading stories of change, which is why the nineteenth century could have faith that its newspapers were the expression of the "world spirit" that emerges, as Hegel would say, when "the writing of history and the actual deeds and events of history make their appearance simultaneously." Hegel must have seen in newspapers—especially as their reporting of events became more comprehensive and immediate—one more means of communicating "the spirit of the age as the spirit present and aware of itself in thought." The newspaper, Parton continues, "connects each individual with the general life of mankind, and makes him part and parcel of the whole." Newspapers now registered the progress of the present for their readers, who could understand their own acts of reading in turn as "part and parcel" of, and relevant to, its progress. In other words, what the nineteenth century learned from the newspaper was that reading—indeed the act of reading it suggested as a daily practice—was nothing less (and maybe nothing more) than a reflection of the moment they were in. To read was to keep up with the times and to find one's place within them. If the goal of the press, according to one newspaper's motto, is "to shew the very age . . . its form," then perhaps the "new shape of knowledge" in the age of news is the "self-consciousness" Hegel feels when he "orients" his attitude toward the world every morning at breakfast.[3] At least when reading the newspaper, he says, "one knows how one stands."

What does it mean to orient one's attitude toward the world? By the end of the nineteenth century, the newspaper had not been the subject of much philosophy unless we take seriously those editors and newspapermen I have cited (James Parton, George Lunt, and the rest). And why not? The pragmatist and sociologist Robert E. Park writes in 1923 that the newspaper editor "is the philosopher turned merchant" by "making information about our common life accessible to every individual at less than the price of a telephone call." But, he adds, "as a matter of fact we do not know much about the newspaper. It has never been studied." When the newspaper is studied at last by Park, who first studied Hegel in classes with John Dewey at the University of Michigan, he claims, "I studied philosophy because I hoped to gain insight into the nature and function of that kind of knowledge we call news" and also into "the philosophical aspects of the effects of the printed facts on the public." Park studied Hegel and then wrote the circular for a prospective newspaper called *Thought News* that would show how philosophy can "finally secure the conditions of its objective expression" in a newspaper. The bringing together of news and philosophy would give philosophy its social bearings or, as William James puts it, "relevancy in universal affairs," since "any philosophy which annihilates the validity of the reference by explaining away its objects . . . leaves the mind with little to care or act for." Park thought *Thought News* "would help to make the movement of history intelligible, because only philosophy could transform 'happenings' into 'typical facts,' and only the events of daily life could make philosophy 'real' and relevant." But it was never funded. Dewey said it was too far ahead of its time to be funded. But when, as I say, Park writes about the news at last in essays such as "The Natural History of the Newspaper" and "News as a Form of Knowledge" after decades of academic work, he finally says of it at the close of the nineteenth century exactly what Hegel had said of it at the start of the century: "News performs somewhat the same functions for the public that perception does for the individual man; that is to say, it does not so much inform as orient the public." He also says, "The function of news is to orient man and society in an actual world."[4]

. . .

The Orient, as we know, is the *east*—etymologically, it is the direction of the sunrise—and "to orient" something is, in its first sense, to place something or to arrange it so as to face the sunrise. In English and German, it is a religious word and refers to the act, for example, of building a church on an east–west axis, with its main alter at its eastern end, or of burying persons with their feet in the direction of the eastern horizon. So when Hegel says that the newspaper orients us like a morning prayer, he is suggesting that the newspaper gives us our sense of direction each day—rather, it aligns us with this direction—like an alter with the morning sun.

The first penny daily was Benjamin H. Day's *New York Sun*, and its masthead was a sunrise (fig. 55). In 1833 the *Sun* changed the history of the news

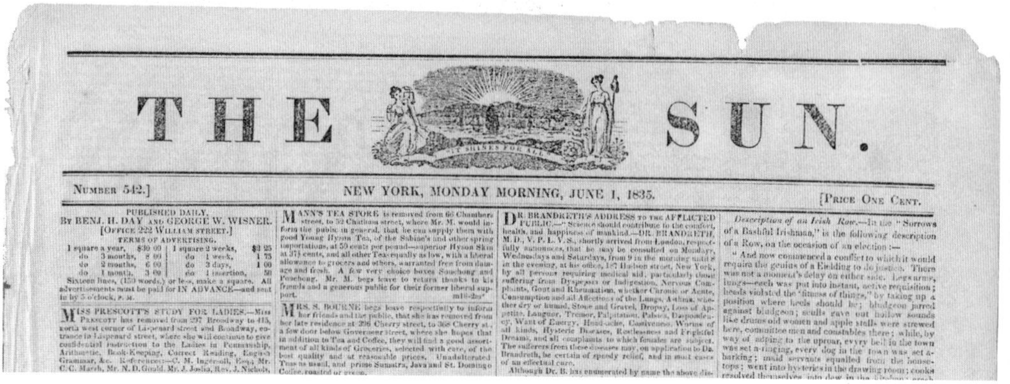

THE SUN.

"IT SHINES FOR ALL"

NUMBER 542.] NEW YORK, MONDAY MORNING, JUNE 1, 1835. [PRICE ONE CENT.

PUBLISHED DAILY,
BY BENJ. H. DAY AND GEORGE W. WISNER.
[OFFICE 222 WILLIAM STREET.]

TERMS OF ADVERTISING.

1 square a year,		$30 00	1 square 2 weeks,		$2 25
do	3 months,	8 00	do	1 week,	1 75
do	2 months,	6 00	do	3 days,	1 00
do	1 month,	3 00	do	1 insertion,	50

Sixteen lines, (150 words,) or less, make a square. All advertisements must be paid for IN ADVANCE—and sent in by 5 o'clock, P. M.

MISS PRESCOTT'S STUDY FOR LADIES.—Miss PRESCOTT has removed from 297 Broadway to 415, north west corner of Lispenard street and Broadway, entrance in Lispenard street, where she will continue to give confidential instruction to the Ladies in Penmanship, Arithmetic, Book-Keeping, Correct Reading, English Grammar, &c. References:—C. M. Ingersoll, Esq.; Mr. C. C. Marsh, Mr. N. D. Gould, Mr. J. Joslin, Rev. J. Nichols,

MANN'S TEA STORE is removed from 66 Chambers street, to 52 Chatham street, where Mr. M. would inform the public in general, that he can supply them with good Young Hyson Tea, of the Sabine's and other spring importations, at 50 cents per pound—superior Hyson Skin at 37½ cents, and all other Teas equally as low, with a liberal allowance to grocers and others, warranted free from damage and fresh. A few very choice boxes Souchong and Pouchong. Mr. M. begs leave to return thanks to his friends and a generous public for their former liberal support. m18-2w*

MRS. S. BOURNE begs leave respectfully to inform her friends and the public, that she has removed from her late residence at 396 Cherry street, to 368 Cherry st., a few door below Governeur street, where she hopes that in addition to Tea and Coffee, they will find a good assortment of all kinds of Groceries, selected with care, of the best quality and at reasonable prices. Unadulterated Teas as usual, and prime Sumatra, Java and St. Domingo Coffee, roasted or green.

DR. BRANDRETH'S ADDRESS TO THE AFFLICTED PUBLIC.—"Science should contribute to the comfort, health, and happiness of mankind.—DR. BRANDRETH, M. D., V. P. L. V. S., shortly arrived from London, respectfully announces, that he may be consulted on Mondays, Wednesdays and Saturdays, from 9 in the morning until 8 in the evening, at his office, 187 Hudson street, New York, by all persons requiring medical aid, particularly those suffering from Dyspepsia or Indigestion, Nervous Complaints, Gout and Rheumatism, whether Chronic or Acute, Consumption and all Affections of the Lungs, Asthma, whether dry or humid, Stone and Gravel, Dropsy, Loss of Appetite, Languor, Tremor, Palpitation, Palsies, Despondency, Want of Energy, Head-ache, Costiveness, Worms of all kinds, Hysteric Diseases, Restlessness and Frightful Dreams, and all complaints to which females are subject. The sufferers from these diseases may, on application to Dr. Brandreth, be certain of speedy relief, and in most cases of an effectual cure.

Although Dr. B. has enumerated by name the above dis-

Description of an Irish Row.—In the "Sorrows of a Bashful Irishman," is the following description of a Row, on the occasion of an election:—

"And now commenced a conflict to which it would require the genius of a Fielding to do justice. There was not a moment's delay on either side. Legs arms, lungs—each was put into instant, active requisition; heads violated the 'fitness of things,' by taking up a position where heels should be; bludgeon jarred against bludgeon; sculls gave out hollow sounds like drums old women and apple stalls were strewed here, committee men and constables there; while, by way of adding to the uproar, evyry bell in the town was set a-ringing, every dog in the town was set a-barking; maid servants squalled from the house-tops; went into hysterics in the drawing room; cooks resolved themselves into dew in the kitchen; ...

FIGURE 55. Masthead, *The* [*New York*] *Sun*, Monday Morning, June 1, 1835.

by making *the news* itself—that is, the succession of daily events rather than political commentary—the chief object of the morning paper and then, by charging a penny and shifting to a steam-powered press, reaching a mass audience so that, as the *Sun*'s motto says, "It shines for all." In Edgar Degas's painting *Dancer Resting*, the dancer is reading the morning paper (fig. 56); if she were a compass rose, her newspaper would point east toward the heat source represented by the stove. The picture suggests all the rapid movement of a ballet class—the spontaneous rhythm of pastels struck carelessly across a floor that tilts beneath the dancer's feet and the quick lines of horizontal newsprint bleeding, like more newsprint, into a fluttery tutu—but this dancer has stopped for a moment to read the newspaper and taken a stand. Is it too much to suggest that, in the terms of this ballet, she has assumed the fourth position, like the "fourth estate"—as Thomas Carlyle called it—to which she turns when she stops and stands? (Maybe. But Degas, working at this time in England and America, turns out to be a great phenomenologist of the news, as we'll soon see.) Magritte's man with a morning newspaper has the same orientation east toward a similar incandescent stove in a painting that is otherwise about a succession of impressions, like subsequent prints from the same inky plate (fig. 57). It is about disappearance too. The everyday picture is unsettling—it is, in fact, *surreal*—because the man and the newspaper vanish by the second frame, but also because in the repetition of the images there is, in each case, the slightest, sideways displacement. Our point of view keeps changing just perceptibly enough to disorient us when the paper is gone.

FIGURE 56. Edgar Degas, *Dancer Resting* (ca. 1879–1880). Pastel and black chalk. Art Heritage / Alamy Stock Photo.

FIGURE 57. René Magritte, *Man with a Newspaper* (1928). © 2021 C. Herscovici / Artists Rights Society, New York. Oil on canvas. Presented by the Friends of the Tate Gallery, 1964. © Tate.

Orientation in the secular sense, in the sense that Hegel and Park use it to describe the secular religion of the newspaper, is a nineteenth-century concept coming into its own. It simply did not exist before this moment, which makes Hegel one of the very first to see how the religious practice of positioning a church or a coffin might be applied to other efforts to put ourselves in right relation to our surroundings and to make our attitude relative to them. Hegel probably derived his sense of orientation from Kant, whose 1786 essay "What Does It Mean to Orient Oneself in Thinking?" (itself based on Moses Mendelssohn's *Morning Hours*) describes how we arrive at our most abstract thoughts, even thoughts of God, in much the same way we orient ourselves geographically. "In the proper meaning of the word," Kant says, "to *orient* oneself means to use a given direction (when we divide the horizon into four of them) in order to find the others—literally, to find the *sunrise*. Now if I see the sun in the sky and know it is now midday, then I know how to find south, west, north, and east. For this, however, I also need the feeling of a difference in my own subject, namely, the difference between my right and left hands." If, that is, I find the sun in the morning, then the intuitive sense of difference I have between right and left will let me find everything else (the south, west, and north) or get my bearings in relation to the sun. "Thus," Kant continues, "even with all the objective data of the sky, I orient myself *geographically* only through a *subjective* ground of differentiation" (through, again, my intuitive feeling of right and left).

Then Kant extends this concept of the process for orienting oneself (in relation to a single object or point, then subjectively feeling one's way) to suggest that it works *mathematically* for any physical space. "In the dark," for example, "I orient myself in a room that is familiar to me if I can take hold of even one single object whose position I remember" and then navigate right and left. And it works not merely in any physical space but in thinking in general, which Kant refers to as "that immeasurable space of the supersensible, which for us is filled with dark night." In this way, I can orient myself *logically* and get my bearings. And the reason why we need to take hold of *one reliable object* when we think and then feel our way from it, like homing pigeons or like Charles Darwin's mice with dead reckoning in the dark, is that otherwise our thoughts get disoriented in that immeasurable space of the supersensible. Our thoughts become impertinent—or inapropos—to the object or task at hand. Without this object and our tendency to use it, we stray, in Kant's words, into "merely impertinent inquisitiveness," playing with "figments of the brain."[5]

"No particular results" but "only an attitude of orientation, is what the pragmatic method means," writes William James. It is the attitude of turning to face whatever arises and of adjusting ourselves to it and holding steady. It suggests a process of moving and feeling our way toward that object (or objective) on the horizon that gets us where we need to go. Joan Richardson writes that "James came to experience himself as a needle on a compass, constantly oscillating, drawn by the very force of the earth itself suspended in its magnetic field, feeling 'infinitesimal attraction . . . yield[ing] to a current so feeble as can be felt only by a needle delicately poised.'" All of our past experience "orients us towards the future," James says, our stores of memories and formed dispositions, tendencies, and interests, so that this aspect of cognition is as somatically felt as it is finally intellectual too. It is "the integrated exercise of body and mind," as Richard Shusterman puts it in *Pragmatist Aesthetics*: "As dancers, we understand the sense and rightness of a movement or posture proprioceptively, by feeling it in our spine and muscles, without translating it into conceptual linguistic terms." We know where to turn, says Ross Posnock, "by relaxing the will to know it and letting instinct and feeling guide us."[6]

For Dewey consciousness of the world will always rely to some extent on a "universe of non-reflectional experience" and on "a context which is non-cognitive and which holds within it in suspense a vast complex of other qualities and things that in the experience itself are objects of esteem or aversion, of decision, of use, of suffering, of endeavor and revolt, not of knowledge." Thus, the opening up of some experience for its promise for us—at least for those "(like myself)," he says, "who believe thoroughly in pragmatism as a method of orientation as defined by Mr. James"—means first orienting the contents of our own experience (residing deeply in our tendencies and interests) toward this object out of all possible objects and places to turn. It means having a *feeling* for just where to turn and marks a genuine beginning "to the determination of the meaning of objects, the intent and worth of ideas as ideas, and to the human and moral value of beliefs." It is "not unlike the movements of a person entering a dark and unfamiliar room, littered with he knows not what, conscious only of a need to find a resting place. The inquiring, groping and testing continue until what is found answers the specific purpose in view, enters into the required relationship with what has gone before." To perceive is to find the *standpoint* from which one is mentally adjusted and oriented dynamically (forward and outward) toward the world. Dewey says it is like "the turning toward light of the body as a whole, like the heliotropism of plants." Whitehead describes it as "a tropism to the beckoning light—to the sun passing toward the finality of things, and to the sun arising from their origin," with this turning, as if to west and east, being also, for him, the beginnings of speculative thought: the possibility of something new just up on the horizon.[7] For Hegel, that one object that continually arises from out of the dark night—so that every day we feel compelled to turn to it for the beginnings of consciousness and world awareness—is the morning newspaper.

. . .

We appear to be living, Park writes, from day to day, in the "specious present" because news as a form of knowledge is not concerned with the past or future but with the most sensible present while being by nature a perishable commodity. In Washington Irving's "Rip Van Winkle," nothing speaks to the archaism of eighteenth-century society more than the fact that the men of the village gather to debate an "old newspaper." By the nineteenth century, old news was a source of amusement that Thoreau, for example, plays on when he chooses to read the scraps of newspaper in which his "dinner of bread and butter" is wrapped. There are, Thoreau says, things to "relish" in the fragments of the "Daily Times" that make their way to the woods, but the absurdity of his "appetite" for them is also the sign of his distance from the world "in which the events that make the news transpire." As media historians observe, the daily papers of the 1830s marked a turn away from the weekly partisan and trade papers that provided content to audiences of subscribers who shared political and public interests and whose discussion of their interests formed the basis of the deliberative public sphere that Jürgen Habermas famously ascribes to the eighteenth century. Now the dailies competed for mass readership that demanded its information at accelerating speeds and shared, if nothing else, an investment in the commodity of *news* itself, which became central like never before to both the business and culture of newspapers. For the first time the news, instead of political or editorial comment, became the primary object of the newspaper, so when Charles A. Dana, another editor of the *Sun*, writes that "a newspaper without news is no newspaper"—or when Parton writes that "the word *newspaper* is the exact and complete description of the thing"—it is not redundant or even self-evident, because the *news* is what was new. Newspapers "bear us along with them," writes Lunt, "abreast of the rapid flood of passing events."

If in 1800 readers might find five to twenty items in a four-page paper—mostly long political essays that ran for more than a page and continued from one issue to the next—by midcentury, a typical four-page paper contained thirty-five to forty items about the day's events. Stories were now "items" or "articles"—like merchandise—and editors knew that they were read in inverse ratio to their length. Editors devoted their resources to extensive newsgathering operations, employing carrier pigeons, boats, competing rail lines, the pony express, and, after 1846, the telegraph and wire services, while readers measured the efficiency of papers by "[counting] the number of items they contained" (where "the paper that had the largest number of items was the best paper"). Newspapers rivaled one another for timeliness with "extras" and "late editions"; the invention of the steam-powered cylinder press made multiple editions of daily papers cheaper and more profitable; and reporters specialized to provide comprehensive and expert coverage on a wide range of "beats." "There is," writes the editor of the *Springfield Republican* in 1851, "a great deal more news nowadays than there used to be," suggesting how the world itself seemed essentially more eventful as the horizon of what could be known expanded across networks and new transportation and communication technologies and as the telegraph and wire services especially intensified the timely transmission of the news.[8]

As newspapers began to prioritize the coverage of events over the discussion of ideas, the competition for readers came to depend less on the deliberative public life that followed from their content and more on the ability of the news itself to give shape and meaning to communities that emerged in response to the fact that something happened somewhere and not very long ago. The cycles of such "simultaneous consumption" as Benedict Anderson writes, impart to reading newspapers in the nineteenth century the character of a "mass ceremony"; by recognizing the regularity with which the news was always new and changing, readers were "continually reassured" that their modern world was visibly rendered in habits they could learn and make their own. The diminishing time lag between distant events and their appearance in the newspaper came to pattern daily rituals of urban culture, especially as "extras," hawked by newsboys on the streets, made it possible for crowds of readers to track unfolding stories with the sensation of real time while preserving the sequential flow of new developments. Reading newspapers was a practice of historical engagement with the present moment as it emerged and then inevitably receded. Thus, what Anderson calls "the obsolescence of the newspaper on the morrow of its printing" is a crucial aspect of its power to keep readers coming back for more news when the old became irrelevant. As early news gave way to breaking news, newspapers encouraged the belief that time itself is dynamic and superseding and that our reading is significant to the degree that it keeps pace with the progress of the current moment. What happens latest matters most since news as a form of knowledge is perishable and can only exist in the present moment. "Where there were no news-boys," says Thoreau, "I did not see what they would do for waste paper." "NEWS," writes a Providence, Rhode Island paper as early as 1814, "pours in upon us so fast."[9]

In Degas's *A Cotton Office in New Orleans*, painted during his stay in New Orleans in 1873, the pressure of the present—of being, that is, *in* the moment of this picture of cotton merchants—is represented by the open newspaper at its center (fig. 58). Because the framing of the painting cuts off our view in the middle of what should be the middle ground—because our vantage point seems sometimes very high and sometimes low and the lines of sight do not converge where they should—everything gets crowded into our immediate field of vision. The furniture is abruptly cropped; our peripheral vision is restricted as if limited by a frame like the window frame for the door's transom at the top left. We are boxed into the immediate picture in a painting that also happens to be, as critics point out, surprisingly small. In fact, it is just about the real size and dimensions of the *New Orleans Daily Picayune* that the seated figure reads at its center. Émile Zola, who did not like this tableau of American commerce and cotton, with its literalness and its "bourgeois range," as another critic puts it, also said that it altogether reminded him of a plate from an illustrated newspaper. Within the grid of windows and boxes, Degas frames one crowded, fragmentary moment with a newspaper. The picture is stuffed full, including the stuffing on the table (Degas said his head was full of "a lot of stuff" when he painted it), and then those fifteen black-and-white figures more or less dealing with the stuff. It all presses down on a tilting, vertiginous floor so that the man with the newspaper—also the man in front whose legs are chopped off at the lower edge—seem like they are positively in danger of sliding out of the picture. To return to the paper from Providence, they "[pour] in upon us so fast."

Degas painted a picture of being in the precarity of a moment with a

FIGURE 58. Edgar Degas, *Interior of the Cotton Bureau in New Orleans* (*A Cotton Office in New Orleans*) (1873). Oil on canvas. Scala / Art Resource, New York.

newspaper. It also is a picture of his own family's cotton brokerage business in New Orleans. His uncle, who owned the office, is the figure sitting in the front with his legs cut off, and his brother, René Degas, who worked in his uncle's office, is reading the *Daily Picayune*. In 1873 the market crashed, and the family firm did not survive it. The cotton business had changed too much during Reconstruction; with the rise of sharecropping and the trading of cotton futures in large exchanges, and with the decline in demand for American cotton, too, old brokerage firms like this became obsolete. Degas's uncle in the front really has been *cut off* because the liquidation of the firm had been announced on February 1, 1873, in the *Daily Picayune*, just before Degas painted the picture. His brother, René, might in fact be reading the fatal announcement in the *Picayune* right here. So, the firm was being liquidated. On the wall at the right is a framed seascape of a downed Confederate ship. Because of the disequilibrium of the picture, the whole picture even takes on the quality of a seascape or else a sinking ship, bow down, careening forward (in that "sea of cotton," as Degas called the stuff on the table).[10]

These figures have lost their bearings. For all the structural anchoring against frames within frames, windows, doors, shelves, boxes, this business is about to fall off the grid. In newspaper lingo at the time, everything that would manage to fit into the pages of an issue was called the daily "budget," but in this office in New Orleans the budget is blown. The uncle wears a funereal suit. His wife has just died—and, as Christopher Benfey reminds us, an empty chair will always be a symbol of mortality—but it is also the case that in an age of modernity, in Baudelaire's words, "we are all in mourning for something." The uncle is "classing" the sample cotton—that is, classifying it for its resiliency—but the work seems so wistful because his cotton is failing. Right around this time, his cotton would even have stopped being the *stuff* of newspapers, since the dailies, including the *Picayune*, shifted from printing on paper made of cotton to paper made of wood pulp, which is to say that the newspaper in the picture, with its obituary for the business, also reminds us that the Degas family cotton is not now a paper asset. Scraps of old paper are about to spill out of a circular bin in the foreground. We imagine that today's *Picayune* will join the waste in there tomorrow.[11]

Robert E. Park was both a sociologist and theorist of the newspaper and also the theorist and popularizer of the idea of "succession." It is a term he called an "ecological concept" and that he borrowed from plant ecology. He used it to describe an irreversible series of events in which each succeeding event is more or less determined by the one that precedes it. New things emerge from old things and take their place, followed by some equilibrium and then more succession, and, for Park, the nature of these changes in society—say, in the market or the city or even the history of communication—are identical in form with the sort of changes that plant and animal ecologists at the time called "succession" in nature. Studies of succession are concerned not only with the form that change takes but with the circumstances that precede, accompany, and follow change and that act on the living things that adapt and evolve in response. In short, studies of succession are natural histories. So, when Park writes "The Natural History of the Newspaper," or when he says elsewhere that "the function of news is to orient man and society in an actual world," he means that the daily newspaper represents both the principle of ecological succession, like nothing before it, and the instrument by which we understand our "own relations to the movement of life."[12] It is the means by which we keep adapting to our changing surroundings, like the tropism of plants toward the sun as it moves through the day.

We did not speak of *orienting* ourselves until the mid-nineteenth century. In fact, the concept of *orientation* is as new to the nineteenth century as the concept of *news* itself. Orient is what we need to do when there are too many directions in which to turn, too many points of view relative to our surroundings and in succession—and what replaces mere "point of view" is the truth and surety of orientation, which, as Kant suggested (well before the word came to mean what it does), begins in some a priori feeling, a tendency toward a particular point or object that keeps us focused. Certain objects or stimuli in an environment stand out and gain apparency. They have meaning for us—and they become relevant to us—because our orientation puts them there, and then we consciously or unconsciously tend toward the interests enshrined in our orientation. We survey the field and then orient ourselves so as to focus on some object of practical and pragmatic concern from this perspective while excluding objects of less concern. But these orientational discriminations depend on our disposition and the feeling that accompanies the act of taking a stand: the feeling for right and left, for example, and how we like to lean, and then the relating of this basic feeling in orientation to some larger frame of reference. For natural scientists, this is how living, evolving things adjust to environmental conditions and relate or habituate themselves to the immeasurable space outside themselves (it is the primary encounter of the subject with the world). For pragmatists, it is how we gain knowledge as we navigate an expansive world and try to locate our place within it. Dewey describes every "new conception of the world" as a "new mental orientation." From the projective force of our past experiences and habits, our orientation "shapes our expectancies" and individual consciousness of the objects we experience, and it lets us act toward them in a directed way.[13] It centers our consciousness and indicates the sort of focalism or attention we give to a situation. What we turn to has *attentional importance* and always also involves a process of selection, pointing us toward some objects and not toward others, east and not west, so that one knows, remembering Hegel, how one stands.

When Park, after working for years as a newspaper reporter, returned to academic work so that he "could describe the behavior of society, under the influence of news," he went to Harvard to study philosophy and psychology with William James. While earning his MA there and before moving to Germany for his doctorate, Park was most influenced by an essay James read out loud in class before it was published, "On a Certain Blindness in Human Beings," in which he says (in a line I have mentioned before), "Wherever a process of life communicates an eagerness to him who lives it, there the life becomes genuinely significant . . . wherever it is found, there is the zest, the tingle, the excitement, of reality; and there *is* 'importance' in the only real and positive sense in which importance ever anywhere can be." He also says, "Life is always worth living if one have such responsive sensibilities." The essay includes a long passage from Walt Whitman, whose procession of images, one succeeding the other, while crossing Brooklyn ferry or walking up Broadway, are for James the very best example of "the intense interest that life can assume" when one is responsive like this. "To be rapt with satisfied attention, like Whitman, to the mere spectacle of the world's presence, is one way, and the most fundamental way, of confessing one's sense of its unfathomable significance and importance."[14]

By the time Whitman wrote the first edition of *Leaves of Grass* in 1855, he had edited or coedited ten newspapers and contributed to over twenty, calling his early journalistic career the "gestation-years" on "which everything else rests" and "the period . . . out of which *Leaves of Grass* rose." Whitman describes his poem to Emerson as part of a national literary movement that includes "the three thousand different newspapers, the nutriment of the imperfect ones coming in just as usefully as any the story papers . . . the one-cent and two-cent journals" and other forms of "active ephemeral myriads" of print that, for him, link the urge toward currency in writing with the ceaseless democratic progress of America: "All are prophetic;" he writes, "all waft rapidly on. I see that they swell wide, for reasons. I am not troubled at the movement of them, but greatly pleased." The inventorial impulses of Whitman's poem, with its ecumenical mingling of events—street fights, suicides, sudden illnesses, riots, criminal arrests—resemble a newspaper page, where the principle of organization is just "all the news that's fit to print" (as the *New York Times* called it by the end of the century) from one moment in time. Whitman's inclusion of "these one and all" sounds, for example, much like Dana's claim that the *New York Sun* "was not too proud to report" whatever "the Divine Providence permitted to occur." The preface to the first edition of *Leaves of Grass* was set in columns like a newspaper, and one might say that Whitman's famous decision to leave his name off the title page was also in sympathy with the newspapers, which published largely without bylines. The cleaner title page, as Ed Folsom suggests, also speaks to Whitman's training as a newspaper compositor who was deeply invested in visual design; indeed, in its wide spacing and modern typeface, the title page visually recalls the changes Whitman made to simplify the look of the *Brooklyn Eagle*, which appeared, as he puts it, with a "clean face" ("as clean and neat as a newly washed child") soon after he began to edit it. If there was, in Whitman's words, an "incisive directness" to the 1855 edition, we might say that the simplicity of a title page without an author's name on it aspires to the kind of accessible transparency of the poet who claimed to do nothing but "flood himself with the immediate age," or of the nineteenth-century newspaper that claimed to be, in Whitman's words, "the mirror of the world."

Each of the eight editions of *Leaves of Grass* absorbs and builds on prior editions, like the "extras" and "supplements" Whitman says he bought throughout the Civil War and after ("we got every newspaper morning and evening, and the frequent extras of the period"), so that his poem grew and unfolded successively over time. It may be no surprise that Whitman, who saw the newspaper as a model of progress, also liked Hegel, for whom, in Whitman's words, "the whole earth . . . with its infinite variety" was slowly becoming known to us through "the endless process of Creative thought, which, amid numberless apparent failures and contradictions, is held together by central and never-broken unity—not contradictions or failures at all, but radiations of one consistent and eternal purpose; the whole mass of everything steadily, unerringly tending and flowing." ("Do I contradict myself?' writes Whitman in "Song of Myself." "Very well then I contradict myself.") At least this is how Whitman's poem also tends over decades, taking in more as it goes, new facts and events, by combining the old with the new so that it preserves what it also replaces, but always, in Dewey's words, with "an end in view, with express consideration of which it selects." "The mind at-tends," Dewey writes; "it is stretched out towards something." At one point in the poem Whitman speaks of "the long stretch of my life."[15]

We discover the world in which we live to be "visibly expanding about us as the perspective of our practical interests and actions lengthen," writes

Park in his essay, "Morale and the News." The mind comes to attend to something that comes to us by way of the news from the "outer limits of our world" and that feels "immediately important that something needs to be done about it." "For news," Park says, "is not something new merely, it is something important; and it comes to us with an urgency that requires action, even if no more than a change of attitude or the reaffirmation of an opinion." How we come to take in something new *as* important is what "news as a form of knowledge" means to Park, especially in the way it requires a change of attitude or reorientation every morning.

In "News as a Form of Knowledge," he draws on James's distinction in *The Principles of Psychology* between the two forms of knowledge he describes: "knowledge of acquaintance" and "knowledge-about." "Acquaintance with" suggests the sort of knowledge one acquires in firsthand impressions in which we come to know things "through the responses of our whole organism," as we know the things "in a world to which we are adjusted." "Such knowledge," Park writes, "may, in fact, be conceived as a form of organic adjustment or adaptation, representing an accumulation and, so to speak, a funding of a long series of experiences. It is this sort of personal and individual knowledge which makes each of us at home in the world in which he elects or is condemned to live." "Knowledge about," by contrast, is a rational and systematic coming to terms with the "flux of events." "It is based on observation and fact but on fact that has been checked, tagged, regimented, and finally ranged in this and that perspective." And Park's point is finally that news exists on a continuum between these two forms of knowledge, in "a location of its own," as it reaches "the persons for whom it has 'news interest.'" It seeks to put things in their proper place and relation, but only right now or for the moment. It is news so long as it has "news interest," and it ceases to be news "as soon as the tension it aroused has ceased and public attention has been directed to some other aspect of the habitat or to some other incident sufficiently novel, exciting, or important to hold its attention." Its primary goal, then, in such a wide world of events, is not to provide knowledge about events in the way that history, for example, makes sense of them but, more fundamentally, to capture our attention so that we orient our consciousness toward what it holds.

The promise of the news, as we look to it each morning, is that it will hold our interest and feel important to us, which is why we continue to have that orienting response and engage with it ritually every morning, like a prayer at an altar. Hugo Münsterberg, with whom Park also studied at Harvard, understands the newspaper headline, just as he understands the close-up in a film, as "[objectifying] in our world of perception our mental act of attention": think of a clerk who "buys a newspaper on the street, glances at it and is shocked. Suddenly we see that piece of news with our own eyes. The close-up magnifies the headlines of the paper so that they fill the whole screen. . . . Any subtle detail, any significant gesture which heightens the meaning of the action may enter into the center of our consciousness by monopolizing the stage for a few seconds." Deeply involved in a phenomenology of attention, the news, putting us into contact with our surroundings as we try to make our way, is much like philosophy itself is to James: "an aid to navigation," as Joan Richardson puts it. Again, Park insists that the news performs "somewhat the same functions for the public that perception does for the individual man; that is to say, it does not so much inform as orient the public, giving each and all notice as to what is going on."[16]

. . .

Degas called his painting of the cotton office a "naturalist" picture because, as a contemporary commentator on Degas suggests, the modern individual in his paintings is observed in "all aspects of the environment in which he evolves and develops. . . . We will no longer separate the figure from the background." *A Cotton Office in New Orleans*, in other words, is a kind of natural history. Its plant is cotton.

Degas avidly read natural histories by Darwin and others, often illustrated with pictures of birds and other animals in their habitats (fig. 59); like those pictures, his painting from New Orleans shows a kind of radical randomness. Its dispersed figures in their surroundings seem interested in the cotton more or less or not at all. The picture has all of the aspects of a chaotic and atomized crowd; its business is laissez-faire and, on the diagonal, there is a sense of imminent movement and flux. But it is also the case that, when the stuff of the picture becomes the stuff of the newspaper in the picture, as René Degas reads about the family business, for example—also as the cotton becomes the material of the newspaper pages themselves, maybe for the last time—we gain some perspective. All that fluff ends up in a rationalized space. It is held against a grid-like layout of columns and boxes, like the framework of mullions we see here. In the picture, it is hard not to see how the paired heads of men in hats seem almost serial.

News as a form of knowledge, Park writes, provides the impressions of

FIGURE 59. Alfred Edmund Brehm, *Winter Time*. From *Bird-Life: Being a History of the Bird, Its Structure, and Habits, Together with Sketches of Fifty Different Species*, trans. H. M. Labouchere and W. Jesse (London: J. Van Voorst, 1874), 603.

a world "to which we are adjusted" and to which we turn our attention, and "such knowledge may, in fact, be conceived as a form of organic adjustment or adaptation." When Park says, once again, that news does not so much inform as orient the public (though we had always assumed that news informs us), and that, in doing so, it functions for the public in just the way that perception does for the individual man, he means that news gives us the same kind of defined relationship to firsthand impressions or qualia or data (which is Park's word) that our senses do when we try to find our way in the dark. Its very business is to draw attention to some things and not to others in the wide universe in which we would otherwise lose our bearings and where there is no longer a single or self-evident context for determining how we stand. The question that concerns Park's studies of the newspaper "is not what constitutes the validity of knowledge—of a statement of principle or of fact—*but what are the conditions under which different kinds of knowledge arise*" (italics mine) even as those impressions or facts get "checked, tagged, regimented, and finally ranged in this and that perspective."[17]

"Everything is relevant if its relevance can be invented," writes Frank Kermode, "even the scattered informations of the morning newspaper."[18] By 1860 the revisualization of the newspaper "as territory," in the words of media historians, reflected the priority accorded to the most "relevant" events of the day and the need to orient its readers toward them. Newspapers not only made coverage of daily events their primary purpose but also began the practice of organizing their events for readers within a visual hierarchy of information that suggested the items that were most significant to know. In earlier newspapers, black ruled lines between texts were either nonexistent or ran mainly as horizontals, separating, for example, one ad from another. But now newspapers were organized on the principle of columns with vertical ruled lines between them. The number of columns increased (from two up to four, five, and eight by 1852), and, within the columns, items became more clearly grouped with subject heads, digests, and ad separators so that the divisions in content enhanced the sense of the grid. In the earlier nineteenth century, items appeared one after another with no mechanical or logical division and no ordered sequence. But now headlines—the new and outstanding feature of a newspaper—announced the most important items and drew the eye toward them. An increasing number of columns grouped items together, and subject heads and other labels used bolder typefaces to orient attention amid denser displays of text. Each item was now established with relation to the whole of the page, and the force of each item was due to the visual effect of headlines and heads in decks and banks (often descending in size and heaviness from the top to bottom bank). And while newspapers at midcentury often continued the tradition of placing the latest news on page two (with less timely matter on the outside pages in case ink smudged in delivery), the "extra" editions of newspapers began the practice of making the front page the incarnation of the news itself, with the headline, that epitome of news, bound up with the use of the first page, so that, by the end of the century, most newspapers would look like the "extra" had looked. (The *North American* of May 11, 1846, was glad to announce, "The Late and Highly Important News from the Seat of War Will be Found on the First Page.") The headline that broadcasted the top story increased in size and width until it migrated across columns and finally, as a "banner," across the whole of the front page.

By the end of the century the abstract, ordering geometry of the newspaper's design is finally inscribed on the succession of news from day to day and throughout the day in the form of the "grid" it comes to be called just in time for a modern era. And over this time, within the "grid," newspaper writing also came to adapt its own techniques for producing the effect of relevance, with stories employing the "inverted pyramid" of the news "lead" to formalize the packaging of facts in descending order of importance. Where earlier reports proceeded inductively, often withholding the most pertinent details of events while supplying their context, journalists began instead to condense the most pertinent facts of their accounts into the "lead" of the story—also in order to "catch and preserve the 'points'" and "fit the budget" (in the lingo of the papers)—so that by the last decades of the century, readers could know everything they needed to know right away without completing a story. In fact, editors believed that readers, with a pair of scissors, could cut a story after the first paragraph if the story was sufficiently *on point*. "Nowhere," writes Robert Park, "has Herbert Spencer's maxim that the art of writing is economy of attention been so completely realized." Eventually, the first paragraph of a news story comes to be called the "orientation."[19]

In Degas's more impressionist pictures, the cotton takes the form of tutus, white bits of pulp distributed across a pitched floor. The dancers, like the

FIGURE 60. Edgar Degas, *Ballet Rehearsal on Stage* (1874). Oil on canvas. Musée d'Orsay, Paris. The Artchives / Alamy Stock Photo.

fluff pieces in a second picture of the cotton office, are being tested for their "resiliency" (figs. 60 and 61). In one painting, they try to keep time with a violinist, who is keeping up with "the times," because there is—what else but?—a newspaper folded in his hat reminding us how fleeting these moments can be (fig. 62). On the barre in the back, a dancer is just hanging on. The girls' gauzy forms are almost always emerging or receding in these pictures, tripping forth from the wings of the stage or just dropping into view feetfirst from a spiral staircase, and then careening off in bunches around a bench or back into the wings offstage. For one moment only, they'll be *en pointe*.

Degas painted pictures of *succession* most of all. Dancers appear, then

FIGURE 61. Edgar Degas, *Cotton Merchants in New Orleans* (1873). Oil on linen. Gift of Herbert N. Straus. Harvard Art Museums/Fogg Museum.

disappear; their episodic placement sometimes suggesting the replication of the same girl in serial moments across a studio or stage. Degas also revised his paintings so many times and over so many years with so many successive, subsequent repositionings of outstretched arms or legs that, in the infrared photos, the figures often look like they're fluttering. Rilke remarked on what he called the "fluttering mood" of Degas's pictures: little dancers with the "sadness of birds who have lost their wings" arching their backs or yawning and hopping along on fragile legs. They are little "naturalist" figures, fragilely balanced in the spray of their outstretched feathery skirts in white, orange, yellow, and blue. Occasionally Degas's little waxed

FIGURE 62. Edgar Degas, *The Dancing Class* (ca. 1870). Oil on wood. H. O. Havemeyer Collection, Bequest of Mrs. H. O. Havemeyer, 1929. The Metropolitan Museum of Art, New York.

dancers were displayed in glass boxes, like naturalist specimens, and, again, we know that he cast some of them in images inspired by the illustrations of birds and other animals he saw in Darwin.[20] The dance pictures, too, are habitat pictures.

In *The Ballet Class* of 1880, a woman reads the newspaper in the midst of the commotion of a class (fig. 63). The newspaper tells us that we are *in the moment*, maybe even being oriented to it, and because she seems to follow the newspaper with the same attention with which the man behind her follows the dancers, I cannot help but think that the painting is suggesting a parallel between the two, the dancers and the news (with the man and the woman at the same angle to the picture plane, his tonsure rhyming per-

FIGURE 63. Edgar Degas, *The Ballet Class* (1880–1881). Oil on canvas. Philadelphia Museum of Art, purchased with the W. P. Wilstach Fund, 1937 (W1937–2-1).

FIGURE 64. Edgar Degas, *Dancers Practicing in the Foyer* (1880). Oil on canvas. (MIN 1903). Ny Carlsberg Glyptotek, Copenhagen / Ole Haupt.

fectly with her hat). These pictures of dancers seem to work, that is, on the principle of the newspapers in the pictures. Our eyes are drawn to all the places where they are on point. In the ecology of these media, the things in flux, all the little qualia, make it onto the grid and then fall off the grid. Balletic moments are framed in the columns—always columns—that come to serve, in Degas, too, as the central compositional device (figs. 64 and 65). They are the emphatically stationary element among the clouds. They hold the stuff that fits within their windows. Each frame of the fluttery movement is emblematically "held in some kind of para-logical suspension," as Rosalind Kraus describes the sudden sense of appearance we get within the panes of a grid in art.[21]

FIGURE 65. Edgar Degas, *The Dance Class* (ca. 1873). Oil on canvas. Corcoran Collection (William A. Clark Collection). Courtesy of the National Gallery of Art, Washington.

The little dancers are devoted to movement. For us, they are the quickened impressions of impressionist pictures that come and go. They are lifted into our attention, but only momentarily, like the dancers that emerge in *Dancers Climbing a Staircase* (fig. 66). To make something relevant is, one last time, to lift it into attention, with the word *relevant* meaning "to lift" or to raise or raise up. To make it relevant is also to put it into *relief*, especially insofar as it is possible for it to relieve something else by succeeding it, by doing the job for it in its spirit. This is, again, why Derrida renders Hegel's crucial concept *aufheben* in French as the verb *relever* and in English as *relevance*; it is the concept Hegel uses to describe the process by which consciousness evolves. A new perception is always relieving, superseding the

FIGURE 66. Edgar Degas, *Dancers Climbing a Staircase* (ca. 1886–1888). Erich Lessing / Art Resource, New York.

last—just as the dancers in the pictures proceed to go on as others come off. They are "entering into the center of our consciousness by monopolizing the stage for a few seconds" only. One after another in succession they become the momentary focus. They are always *on point*. And when they emerge and appear to me stretching up in the spotlight of the ballet? Well, it is always *relevé*! In a specious present, living from day to day, I feel them turn toward me; I turn toward them, knowing not their resilience, but maybe just a little, to return to Park, the conditions under which knowledge arises.

FIGURE 67. Edgar Degas, *Two Dancers in the Studio* (ca. 1875). Vital Archive / Alamy Stock Photo.

Acknowledgments

Sometimes it takes a while to appreciate what you have all along and how much of it turns out to be relevant. The understanding of how things come to contribute and bear is, for me in many ways, the point of this book. I am grateful to my colleagues in the University of California, Berkeley, English department for their encouragement and for helping to keep the work of writing and teaching so vital after a lapse of time: Charles Altieri, Oliver Arnold, Dan Blanton, Mitch Breitwieser, Ian Duncan, Anne-Lise François, Steven Goldsmith, Amanda Goldstein, Kevis Goodman, Dorothy Hale, Steven Justice, Jeffrey Knapp, Kent Puckett, Sue Schweik, and especially Stephen Best and Colleen Lye. Victoria Kahn told me what might be interesting early on and offered suggestions that made this book better. My warm thanks to Samuel Otter for his thoughtfulness and guidance; "let me make a clean breast of it here, and frankly admit," there are few people I've relied on so much.

Knowing that Alan Thomas was expecting the manuscript kept me at it and held me steady while making it feel like it mattered against the odds. I am grateful for his discernment and friendship over these years and for bringing my ideas into relief; also, for the fun and charge of looking at pictures. It has been a pleasure to work with Randolph Petilos again and the editors and staff at the University of Chicago Press, who remain exceptional in their care. I benefitted greatly from Carl Steven LaRue's sharp copyediting and from Marta Steele's help with the index.

The anonymous readers for the Press provided welcome directions at different moments. Gregg Crane read generously and openly, and I am so thankful for his advice. Ross Posnock buys books without knowing why and then waits for them to mean something; this book owes a lot to his models of patience, honesty, and enough irreverence to appreciate rightly and well. I continue to learn more from Alexander Nemerov than I have acknowledged about finding salience where it wasn't apparently.

Colleagues, friends, and students in C19: The Society of Nineteenth-Century Americanists have sustained me over the years of writing this book; others, near and far, also invited me to share parts of the book in progress and offered crucial suggestions or clarifications or else warmth and cheering along the way. They made this book feel worth the attention I gave it: Rachel Adams, Branka Arsić, Sara Blair, Hester Blum, Christopher Castiglia, Russ Castronovo, Amanda Claybaugh, Joshua Clover, Raúl Coronado, Peter Coviello, Jennifer Fleissner, Barbara Fuchs, Matthew Garrett, Nicholas Gaskill, Susan Gillman, Teresa Goddu, Jonathan Grossman, Daniel Hack, Christopher Hanlon, David Henkin, Michael Jonik, Maurice Lee, Robert Levine, Christopher Looby, Michael Lucey, Christina Lupton, Jerome McGann, Mark McGurl, Michael Meranze, Dana Nelson, Sianne Ngai, Mark Peterson, John Plotz, Lloyd Pratt, Erik Redling, Joseph Rezek, Nancy Ruttenburg, Jonathan Sachs, John H. Smith, William Warner, and Cindy Weinstein. Helen Deutsch has been a support throughout; I feel lucky for her friendship and for the continuing friendship and conversation of the colleagues I dearly miss at the University of California, Irvine, especially Jayne Lewis, Irene Tucker, and, kindred spirit, Rodrigo Lazo.

My thanks to audiences at C19 and other conferences and at the following venues and events, who responded to this book in progress and improved it: Mahindra Humanities Center, Harvard University; University of California, Santa Barbara; Columbia University; Martin-Luther-University, Halle-Wittenberg; the inaugural symposium of the British Association of Nineteenth-Century Americanists at University of Sussex; "Rise of the News" at The Huntington Library; Interacting with Print Research Group in Montreal; University of Leeds; "Working Knowledge: Thinking through Culture, 1780—1820" in Ottawa; Rothermere American Institute, University of Oxford; Courtauld Institute of Art; and "Milieus of Minutiae" at the Institute for Cultural Inquiry, Berlin. Thoughts toward chapter 9 first appeared in the introduction to *Fallacies*, a special issue of *Representations* (Fall 2017), and a portion of chapter 10 draws on material published in "Literature and the News," *Oxford Handbook of Nineteenth-Century American Literature*, edited by Russ Castronovo (New York: Oxford University Press, 2012). I am thankful for the permission to include them here and to the contributors to *Fallacies* for helping me clarify ideas that are central to the book, though they appear very late within it.

I am grateful to the Andrew W. Mellon Foundation and to the Division of Arts and Humanities at the University of California, Berkeley, for subsidies toward this book's publication and the reproduction of its images.

This book is for Mark Goble, whose love and brilliance make interest, make importance every day; and for beautiful, sparkling Edith, *as sweet as sweet can be*: relevant "to me and mine, to nature and to the hour that now passes."

Notes

Chapter 1

1. Stephen Crane, "The Open Boat," in *Prose and Poetry* (New York: Library of America, 1996), 891, 894, 897.

2. Crane, 890. See also "Stephen Crane's Own Story," 875–84.

3. See especially Bill Brown's "Interlude" on "The Open Boat" in *The Material Unconscious: American Amusement, Stephen Crane, and the Economies of Play* (Cambridge, MA: Harvard University Press, 1996), 103–24; on Crane, see also Patrick K. Dooley, *The Pluralistic Philosophy of Stephen Crane* (Urbana: University of Illinois Press, 1993), and David Halliburton, *The Color of the Sky: A Study of Stephen Crane* (New York: Cambridge University Press, 1989).

4. Crane, "The Open Boat," 885–86, 889, 895, 897, 909.

5. John Dewey, *Human Nature and Conduct* (1922), in *The Collected Works of John Dewey*, ed. Jo Ann Boydston, *The Middle Works, 1899–1924*, vol. 14, *1922*, ed. Patricia Baysinger (Carbondale: Southern Illinois University Press, 2008), 128; William James, *The Principles of Psychology* (1890; New York: Dover, 1950), 1:402. I am taking Dewey's phrase, "momentarily focal," from his discussion of "consciousness" in *Essays in Experimental Logic* (Chicago: University of Chicago Press, 1916), 6. He writes, "'Consciousness,' in other words, is only a very small and shifting portion of experience. The scope and content of the focused apparency have immediate dynamic connections with portions of experience not at the time obvious. The word which I have just written is momentarily focal; around it there shade off into vagueness my typewriter, the desk, the room, the building, the campus, the town, and so on."

6. William James, "On a Certain Blindness in Human Beings," *Talks to Teachers on Psychology and to Students on Some of Life's Ideals*, in *Writings, 1878–1899*, ed. Gerald E. Myers (New York: Library of America, 1992), 844.

7. Crane, "The Open Boat," 899, 902, 907, 909.

8. Henry James to H. G. Wells, July 10, 1915, in Henry James, *A Life in Letters*, ed. Philip Horne (New York: Penguin Books, 1999), 555.

9. John Dewey, *Psychology* (1887; 3rd. rev. ed. 1891), in *The Collected Works of John*

Dewey, Early Works: 1882–1898, vol. 2, *1887*, ed. Jo Ann Boydston and Fredson Bowers (Carbondale: Southern Illinois University Press, 1967), 19.

10. See especially W. James, *The Principles of Psychology*; Robert B. Brandom, *Perspectives on Pragmatism: Classical, Recent, and Contemporary* (Cambridge, MA; Harvard University Press, 2011), 8.

11. John Dewey, "F. C. S. Schiller: An Unpublished Memorial by John Dewey," ed. Allan Shields, *Transactions of the Charles S. Peirce Society* 3 (1967): 51–54.

12. F. C. S. Schiller, "Relevance," *Mind* 21, no. 82 (April 1912): 153–66; F. C. S. Schiller, "Is the Distinction between Moral Rightness and Wrongness Ultimate?," in *F. C. S. Schiller on Pragmatism and Humanism: Selected Writings, 1891–1939*, ed. John R. Shook and Hugh P. McDonald (Amherst, NY: Humanity Books, 2008), 354; Ferdinand Canning Scott Schiller, *Logic for Use: An Introduction to the Voluntarist Theory of Knowledge* (New York: Harcourt, Brace, 1930), 75–94.

13. Jacques Derrida, "What Is a 'Relevant' Translation?," trans. Lawrence Venuti, *Critical Inquiry* 27 (Winter 2001): 177. See also Lawrence Venuti's introduction to Derrida's essay in the same issue of *Critical Inquiry*, 169–73.

14. Abraham Flexner, *The Usefulness of Useless Knowledge* (Princeton, NJ: Princeton University Press, 2017), originally published in *Harper's Magazine* in 1939; Wallace Stevens, "Description without Place," *The Collected Poems of Wallace Stevens* (New York: Vintage Books, 1990), 344. Stevens copied into his commonplace book Henry James's line to H. G. Wells, quoted earlier, "It is art that *makes* life." Wallace Stevens, *Sur plusieurs beaux sujects* [*sic*]: *Wallace Stevens' Commonplace Book*, ed. Milton J. Bates (Stanford, CA: Stanford University Press, 1989), 77.

15. Schiller, *Logic for Use*, 77. See also David Bohm's discussion of the verb *to relevate* as a lifting into attention "so that the content thus lifted stands out 'in relief'"; David Bohm, *Wholeness and the Implicate Order* (1980; London: Routledge Classics, 2002), 42.

16. William James, "Pragmatism's Conception of Truth," in *Pragmatism: A New Name for Some Old Ways of Thinking*, in *Writings, 1902–1910*, ed. Bruce Kuklick (New York: Library of America, 1987), 575.

17. Henry James, *The Golden Bowl* (1904), introduction by Gore Vidal, notes by Patricia Crick (New York: Penguin Classics, 1987), 433; Henry James, *The Art of the Novel: Critical Prefaces by Henry James*, introduction by R. P. Blackmur (1934; Chicago: University of Chicago Press, 2011), 335–36; Henry James, "The Art of Fiction," in *Literary Criticism: Essays on Literature, American Writers, English Writers*, ed. Leon Edel and Mark Wilson (New York: Library of America, 1984), 53; W. James, *Pragmatism*, 508. I will discuss "acts of attention" at length later, but I take my sense of it here especially from William James's chapter, "Attention," in W. James, *The Principles of Psychology*, vol. 1.

18. H. James, *The Art of the Novel: Critical Prefaces by Henry James*, 128, 340.

19. Crane, "The Open Boat," 902–3. The lines are misquoted from the English poet Caroline Norton's "Bingen on the Rhine," suggesting perhaps an imperfect memory on the part of the correspondent (or author). The poem is undated but was probably composed in the 1840s. It appears in an American imprint as early as 1854 in *The Undying One; Sorrows of Rosalie; and Other Poems* (New York: C. S. Francis, 1854) and was anthologized for grade school elocutionary exercises in *McGuffey's Fifth Eclectic Reader* (1857) and in subsequent editions and elsewhere. See David H. Jackson, "Textual Ques-

tions Raised by Crane's 'Soldier of the Legion,'" *American Literature* 55, no. 1 (March 1983): 77–80.

20. Crane, "The Open Boat," 903. I return to this sense of an "impersonal connection" later in the discussion of Ralph Waldo Emerson.

21. Alfred North Whitehead, *Modes of Thought* (New York: Free Press, 1966; first published 1938 by Macmillan [New York]), 14.

22. John Dewey, *The Influence of Darwin on Philosophy and Other Essays in Contemporary Thought* (1910; Bloomington: Indiana University Press, 1965), 68; Crane, "The Open Boat," 902–3.

23. John Dewey, "Events and Meanings," in *The Collected Works of John Dewey*, ed. Jo Ann Boydston, *The Middle Works, 1899–1924*, vol. 13, *1921–1922*, ed. Barbara Levine (Carbondale: Southern Illinois University Press, 2008), 279; Thomas M. Alexander, *John Dewey's Theory of Art, Experience, and Nature: The Horizons of Feeling* (Albany: State University of New York Press, 1987), 200. I am referring here to the last line of the story in which the narrator says that the survivors "felt that they could then be interpreters"; Crane, "The Open Boat," 909. Here is Dewey at greater length in "Events and Meanings": "Meantime think of how much more interesting a world it will be to live in, even for yourselves, if only composed and articulate meanings are assigned to the happenings amid which we live. . . . Thinking about events and celebrating them in tone and color and form might become more important than being an event . . . For you will have developed a frame of mind which gives meaning to things that happen; and to find a meaning, to understand along with others, is always a contentment, an enjoyment. Events that have no attributed meanings are accidents and if they are big enough are catastrophes. By sufficient preliminary conversation you can avert a catastrophe. For nothing is a catastrophe which belongs in a composed tale of meanings" (279).

24. Laurence Buermeyer, *The Aesthetic Experience*, 2nd ed. (Merion, PA: Barnes Foundation Press, 1929), 40; John Dewey, "The Reflex Arc Concept in Psychology," in *The Collected Works of John Dewey*, ed. Jo Ann Boydston, *The Early Works, 1882–1898*, vol. 5, *1895–1898* (Carbondale: Southern Illinois University Press, 2008), 101.

25. The study, written between 1947 and 1951, was meant to be part one of a five-part work to be titled *The World as Taken-for-Granted: Toward a Phenomenology of the Natural Attitude*, but which Schutz never completed. The study was published posthumously as a book: Alfred Schutz, *Reflections on the Problem of Relevance*, ed. Richard M. Zaner (New Haven, CT: Yale University Press, 1970). Schutz was an Austrian sociologist and phenomenologist who immigrated to the United States in 1939, just before the Nazi occupation. He continued to write almost exclusively in German, but his study of "relevance" was drafted in English. The quote here appears on page 16 and refers to the French philosopher Vladimir Jankélévitch's book *L'alternative* (1938).

26. Alfred North Whitehead, *Process and Reality: An Essay in Cosmology*, ed. David Ray Griffin and Donald W. Sherburne (New York: Free Press, 1978; first published 1929 by Macmillan [New York]), 9, 78, 184–85; see also, Alfred North Whitehead, *Adventures of Ideas* (New York: Macmillan, 1933); see, for example, Isabelle Stengers, *Thinking with Whitehead: A Free and Wild Creation of Concepts*, trans. Michael Chase (Cambridge, MA: Harvard University Press, 2011), 14, 18–19, 495–96; Martin Savransky, *The Adventure of Relevance: An Ethics of Social Inquiry*, foreword by Isabelle Stengers (London: Palgrave Macmillan, 2016). Savransky also draws on Dewey, Whitehead, and Stengers to try to answer "the question of what relevance is, where it comes from, and what its

implications might be for the ways in which practices of knowledge-making in the contemporary social sciences are imagined, organized, and carried out" (31).

27. Buermeyer, *The Aesthetic Experience*, 15.

28. Savransky, *The Adventure of Relevance*, 38; Alain Locke, "Values and Imperatives," in *The Works of Alain Locke*, ed. Charles Molesworth (New York: Oxford University Press, 2012), 456; William James, "What Makes a Life Significant," *Talks to Teachers on Psychology and to Students on Some of Life's Ideals*, in *Writings, 1878–1899*, ed. Gerald E. Myers (New York: Library of America, 1992), 861.

29. Stanley Fish, "The Uses of the Humanities, Part Two," *New York Times* (January 13, 2008); Martha Nussbaum, *Not for Profit: Why Democracy Needs the Humanities* (Princeton, NJ: Princeton University Press, 2010); Geoffrey Galt Harpham, *The Humanities and the Dream of America* (Chicago: University of Chicago Press, 2011). See also Stefan Collini, *What Are Universities For?* (London: Penguin, 2012).

30. Stanley Fish, "Will the Humanities Save Us?," *New York Times* (January 6, 2008); see also *Save the World on Your Own Time* (New York: Oxford University Press, 2008); Helen Small, *The Value of the Humanities* (Oxford: Oxford University Press, 2013); Sam Ladkin, Robert McKay, and Emile Bojesen, eds., *Against Value in the Arts and Education* (London: Rowman and Littlefield, 2016); Maurice Blanchot, "Preface: What Is the Purpose of Criticism?," in *Lautréamont and Sade*, translated by Stuart Kendall and Michelle Kendall (Stanford, CA: Stanford University Press, 2004), 6.

31. F. C. S. Schiller, *Logic for Use: An Introduction to the Voluntarist Theory of Knowledge* (New York: Harcourt, Brace, 1930), 77–78; F. C. S. Schiller, "Relevance," in *F. C. S. Schiller on Pragmatism and Humanism: Selected Writings, 1891–1939*, ed. John R. Shook and Hugh P. McDonald (Amherst, NY: Humanity Books, 2008), 613–14; John Dewey, *Art as Experience*, in *The Collected Works of John Dewey*, ed. Jo Ann Boydston, *The Later Works, 1925–1953*, vol. 10, *1934*, ed. Harriet Furst Simon, introduction by Abraham Kaplan (Carbondale: Southern Illinois University Press, 2008), 17; Laurence Perrine, *The Art of Total Relevance* (Rowley, MA: Newbury House, 1976), 10.

32. Alfred Schutz and Thomas Luckmann, *The Structures of the Life-World*, vol. 1, trans. Richard M. Zaner and H. Tristram Engelhardt Jr. (Evanston, IL: Northwestern University Press, 1973), 183; Whitehead, *Modes of Thought*, 74; *Process and Reality*, 346, 350. Whitehead actually associates the term *relevance* with "God," but I will get to this later.

Chapter 2

1. Edgar Allan Poe, "The Raven," in *Poetry and Tales*, ed. Patrick F. Quinn (New York: Library of America, 1984), 81; "The Philosophy of Composition," in *Critical Theory: The Major Documents*, ed. Stuart Levine and Susan F. Levine (Urbana: University of Illinois Press, 2009), 68.

2. Poe, "The Raven," 83, italic emphasis mine. Throughout the book I return to the idea of "consciousness as a matter of threshold," as Gilles Deleuze puts it. "In each case we would probably have to state why the threshold is marked where it is." Gilles Deleuze, *The Fold: Leibniz and the Baroque*, trans. Tom Conley (1993; Minneapolis: University of Minnesota Press, 2004), 88.

3. Poe, "The Raven," 84, 86.

4. Poe, 84; Jerome McGann, *The Poet Edgar Allan Poe: Alien Angel* (Cambridge, MA: Harvard University Press, 2014), 133.

5. Poe, "The Raven," 83; Alfred Schutz, *Reflections on the Problem of Relevance*, in *Collected Papers V. Phenomenology and the Social Sciences*, ed. Lester Embree (New York: Springer Sciences, 2011), 107.

6. Poe, "The Raven," 85. I am drawing here on Terence Cave's applications of relevance theory, especially the work of Dan Sperber and Deirdre Wilson, in ways that will be clarified shortly. The idea of thought that is "grasped on the wing" derives from Cave; see, for example, Terence Cave, *Thinking with Literature: Towards a Cognitive Criticism* (Oxford: Oxford University Press, 2016), 4.

7. Poe, "The Raven," 83, 84–85; Cave, *Thinking with Literature*, 151; William James, *The Principles of Psychology* (1890; New York: Dover, 1950), 2:298, 299, 316, 322.

8. Edgar Allan Poe, "The Mystery of Marie Rogêt," in *Poetry and Tales*, ed. Patrick F. Quinn (New York: Library of America, 1984), 534. A later version of these lines appears in Edgar Allan Poe, "Doings of Gotham [Letter VI]," *Columbia Spy* 15, no. 10 (June 29, 1844): 3.

9. Poe, "Mystery of Marie Rogêt," in *Poetry and Tales*, 534.

10. Edgar Allan Poe, *Eureka* (1848), ed. Stuart Levine and Susan F. Levine (Urbana: University of Illinois Press, 2004), 14; John Stuart Mill, "Of Induction," in *A System of Logic, Ratiocinative and Inductive*, in *Collected Works of John Stuart Mill*, ed. J. M. Robson (Toronto: University of Toronto Press, 1973), 7:284.

11. Edgar Allan Poe, "The Purloined Letter," in *Poetry and Tales*, ed. Patrick F. Quinn (New York: Library of America, 1984), 690.

12. Mill, "Of Induction," 7:294. Mill is arguing against William Whewell's theory of induction: "Dr. Whewell maintains that the general proposition which binds together the particular facts, and makes them, as it were, one fact, is not the mere sum of those facts, but something more, since there is introduced a conception of the mind, which did not exist in the facts themselves" (294).

13. Poe, "The Purloined Letter," 692.

14. Carl G. Hempel, *Aspects of Scientific Explanation and Other Essays in the Philosophy of Science* (1965), cited in David N. Stamos, *Edgar Allan Poe, "Eureka," and Scientific Imagination* (Albany: State University of New York, 2017), 261; Poe, *Eureka*, 39; see also David N. Stamos on "eureka moments" and "intuitive leaps," in Stamos, *Edgar Allan Poe*, 11, for example.

15. William Whewell, *The Philosophy of the Inductive Sciences, Founded Upon Their History: A New Edition* (London: John W. Parker, 1847), 2:36, 41, 48, 51, 671; William Whewell to Richard Jones, October 31, 1832, as cited in Laura J. Snyder, *Reforming Philosophy: A Victorian Debate on Science and Society* (Chicago: University of Chicago Press, 2006), 24; see also William Whewell, *Astronomy and General Physics Considered with Reference to Natural Theology* [Bridgewater Treatise III] (London: William Pickering, 1833); Edgar Allan Poe, review of "L. H. Sigourney—H. F. Gould—E. F. Ellet," in *Essays and Reviews*, ed. G. R. Thompson (New York: Library of America, 1984), 877; Poe, *Eureka*, 98.

16. Poe, *Eureka*, 5, 7, 15–16, 24, 96; Edgar Allan Poe, "The Colloquy of Monos and Una," in *Poetry and Tales*, ed. Patrick F. Quinn (New York: Library of America, 1984), 450; George Bush, review of *Eureka*, by Edgar Allan Poe, in *The New Church Repository*, ed. George Bush (New York: John Allen, 1848), 1:508–9, as cited in Stamos, *Edgar Allan Poe*, 73; Stamos, 535.

17. Poe, "The Purloined Letter," 684, 691, 695–96.

18. Carlo Ginzburg, *Clues, Myths, and the Historical Method*, trans. John Tedeschi

and Anne C. Tedeschi (Baltimore: Johns Hopkins University Press, 1989), 115; Edgar Allan Poe, "The Murders in the Rue Morgue," in *Poetry and Tales*, ed. Patrick F. Quinn (New York: Library of America, 1984), 411, 414; Poe, "Mystery of Marie Rogêt," 506, 511, 534, 536, 550, 553.

19. Ginzburg, *Clues, Myths, and the Historical Method*, 101, 103–4, 107, 124–25; the line about "minor details" is Freud speaking of an "art-connoisseur" probably based on Moretti in "The Moses of Michelangelo" (1914), as quoted in Ginzburg, *Clues, Myths, and the Historical Method*, 99; Ginzburg, 103.

20. Ginzburg, *Clues, Myths, and the Historical Method*, 96, 114; Poe, "Murders in the Rue Morgue," 412; Franco Moretti, "The Slaughterhouse of Literature," *Modern Language Quarterly* 61, no. 1 (March 2000): 223; Arthur Conan Doyle, "The Hound of the Baskervilles" (1902), in *The Complete Novels and Stories*, introduction by Loren Estleman (New York: Bantam Classic, 2003), 2:46.

21. Poe, "Mystery of Marie Rogêt," 507, 526, 553; Doyle, "Hound of the Baskervilles," in *Complete Novels and Stories*, 2:45–46.

22. Poe, "Mystery of Marie Rogêt," 544; Doyle, "Hound of the Baskervilles," in *Complete Novels and Stories*, 2:24.

23. John Dewey, *How We Think* (Boston: D. C. Heath, 1910), 10–11, 13, 91, 104–5, 120, 193.

24. Dewey, *How We Think*, 103, 105–6, 114.

25. I discuss "interest" much more in the next chapter and will return to all the figures discussed here. Albert C. Barnes, "The Roots of Art," in John Dewey, Albert C. Barnes, Laurence Buermeyer, Mary Mullen, and Violette de Mazia, *Art and Education: A Collection of Essays*, 3rd ed. (Merion, PA: Barnes Foundation Press, 1954; first published 1929 by the Barnes Foundation), 52; Dewey, *How We Think*, 105; I am deriving the terms here from Bruno Latour, "Why Has Critique Run Out of Stream? From Matters of Fact to Matters of Concern," *Critical Inquiry* 30, no. 2 (Winter 2004): 225–48; Arthur Conan Doyle, "The Red-Headed League," in *The Complete Novels and Stories*, introduction by Loren Estleman (New York: Bantam Classic, 2003), 1:287; John Dewey, *Interest and Effort in Education* (Boston: Houghton Mifflin, 1913), 16–17.

26. Edgar Allan Poe, "The Man of the Crowd," in *Poetry and Tales*, ed. Patrick F. Quinn (New York: Library of America, 1984), 388; Poe, "Murders in the Rue Morgue," 400, 411; Moretti, "The Slaughterhouse of Literature," 218; Poe, review of "L. H. Sigourney—H. F. Gould—E. F. Ellet," 877. On the influence of A. W. Schlegel on Poe and especially the phrase "unity of interest," see Thomas S. Hansen and Burton R. Pollin, *The German Face of Edgar Allan Poe: A Study of Literary References in His Works* (Columbia, SC: Camden House, 1995), esp. 91–94. For circulation of Schlegel's phrase among English critics that Poe probably read, see Margaret Alterton, *The Origins of Poe's Critical Theory* (Iowa City: University of Iowa Press, 1925; repr., New York: Russell and Russell, 1965).

27. F. C. S. Schiller, *Logic for Use: An Introduction to the Voluntarist Theory of Knowledge* (New York: Harcourt, Brace, 1930), 80, 90–92, 94. For "clues to reality," see Schiller's contribution to F. C. S. Schiller, Bernard Bosanquet, and Hastings Rashdall, "Symposium: Can Logic Abstract from the Psychological Conditions of Thinking?," *Proceedings of the Aristotelian Society*, n.s., 6 (1905–1906): 235.

28. John Dewey, *Essays in Experimental Logic* (Chicago: University of Chicago Press, 1916), 6; Schiller, *Logic for Use*, 75, 79, 81; G. K. Chesterton, "A Defense of Detec-

tive Stories," in *The Defendant* (New York: Dodd, Mead, 1902), 121; Doyle, "Hound of the Baskervilles," in *Complete Novels and Stories*, 2:100.

29. Poe, "The Philosophy of Composition," 64, 65, 66, 67; "The Raven," 83; I take the phrase "intensity of interest" from the disposition of the narrator in Poe's "Berenice," in *Poetry and Tales*, ed. Patrick F. Quinn (New York: Library of America, 1984), 227.

30. Deirdre Wilson and Dan Sperber, "Relevance Theory," in *The Handbook of Pragmatics*, ed. Lawrence R. Horn and Gregory Ward (Oxford: Blackwell, 2004), 610; see also Cave, *Thinking with Literature*, 92–94; Terence Cave and Deirdre Wilson, eds., *Reading beyond the Code: Literature and Relevance Theory* (Oxford: Oxford University Press, 2018), 5.

31. See Wilson and Sperber, "Relevance Theory," 611; Sperber and Wilson, *Relevance: Communication and Cognition*, 2nd ed. (Oxford; Blackwell, 1995; first published 1986), 151–52.

32. Sperber and Wilson, *Relevance*, 153; Cave and Wilson, *Reading beyond the Code*, 5.

33. Sperber and Wilson, *Relevance*, 154; Cave and Wilson, *Reading beyond the Code*, 10. On "echoic utterances" and "poetic effects," see Sperber and Wilson, *Relevance*, 217–43. Also see Adrian Pilkington, *Poetic Effects: A Relevance Theory Perspective* (Amsterdam: John Benjamins, 2000). There is also Reuven Tsur, *Toward a Theory of Cognitive Poetics* (Brighton: Sussex Academic Press, 1992), and Ian MacKenzie, *Paradigms of Reading: Relevance Theory and Deconstruction* (London: Palgrave Macmillan, 2002).

34. Edgar Allan Poe, "The Raven," in *Poetry and Tales*, ed. Patrick F. Quinn (New York: Library of America, 1984), 84; Terence Cave, *Thinking with Literature*, 5, 93. Donald Davidson's term appears in "A Nice Derangement of Epitaphs," in *Truth and Interpretation: Perspectives on the Philosophy of Donald Davidson*, ed. Ernest Lepore (Oxford: Blackwell, 1986), 433–46. Cave qualifies that since Davidson did not think of the term in relation to relevance theory, this is a loose application of it. Steven Knapp's brief discussion of Sperber and Wilson's *Relevance*, as a response to Davidson—suggesting that relevance must be a factor in understanding the implications of metaphors in any particular context (and that Davidson's sense of metaphors as having no "definite cognitive content" does not take relevant meaning into account)—helps us see why Cave's application of Davidson is loose. Steven Knapp, *Literary Interest: The Limits of Anti-Formalism* (Cambridge, MA: Harvard University Press, 1993), 42–48.

35. The phrase "inference to the best explanation" derives from Gilbert H. Harman and corresponds to pragmatist Charles Sanders Peirce's concept of *abduction*, a term he coined. For Peirce, abduction amounts to an imaginative explanatory conjecture that may be tested later. Harman emphasizes instead the adequacy of inferences or conjectures based on the best account of the "relevant evidence." Gilbert H. Harman, *The Philosophical Review* 74, no. 1 (January 1965): 88–95. Terence Cave and Deirdre Wilson also use the phrase in *Reading beyond the Code*, 4. Paul Grimstad suggests that Poe's detective stories imply reasoning by way of conjectural leaps that are in the spirit of Peirce's theory of abduction later in the century; *The Edgar Allan Poe Review* 6, no. 2 (Fall 2005): 22–30. I think they are probably more in keeping with Harman's sense of the term, or else with William Whewell's theory of "colligation," as I suggested earlier and as David N. Stamos does as well. Also see essays comparing the real logical methods of Peirce with those of Dupin and Holmes in Umberto Eco and Thomas A. Sebeok, *The Sign of Three: Dupin, Holmes, Peirce* (Bloomington: Indiana University Press, 1988).

36. Poe, "The Philosophy of Composition," 70; Cave and Wilson, *Reading beyond the Code*, 4; Poe, "The Raven," 81, 84, 86; David Bohm, *Wholeness and the Implicate Order* (1980; London: Routledge Classics, 2002), 179, 188.

37. Poe, "The Philosophy of Composition," 60–62, 64–65; Doyle, "Hound of the Baskervilles," in *Complete Novels and Stories*, 2:27, 39.

38. Poe, "The Philosophy of Composition," 62; "The Rationale of Verse," in *Critical Theory: The Major Documents*, ed. Stuart Levine and Susan F. Levine (Urbana, IL: University of Illinois Press, 2009), 87; William Hogarth, *The Analysis of Beauty* (1753), ed. Ronald Paulson (Mineola, NY: Dover, 2015), 23–24; Ralph Waldo Emerson, "Beauty," in *The Collected Works of Ralph Waldo Emerson*, vol. 6, *The Conduct of Life*, ed. Douglas Emory Wilson, notes by Joseph Slater, introduction by Barbara L. Packer (Cambridge, MA: Belknap Press of Harvard University Press, 2003), 154; Ralph Waldo Emerson, "Thoughts on Art," *Dial* 1 (January 1841): 375.

39. Poe, "The Rationale of Verse," 82, 88; "The Poetic Principle," in *Critical Theory: The Major Documents*, ed. Stuart Levine and Susan F. Levine (Urbana, IL: University of Illinois Press, 2009), 183; "The Rationale of Verse," 87; Monroe C. Beardsley, *The Aesthetic Point of View: Selected Essays*, ed. Michael J. Wreen and Donald M. Callen (Ithaca, NY: Cornell University Press, 1982), 288–89; on Byron's "fyttes," see Jerome Christensen, *Lord Byron's Strength: Romantic Writing and Commercial Society* (Baltimore: Johns Hopkins University Press, 1993), 181.

40. See Cleanth Brooks, "Implications of an Organic Theory of Poetry," in *Literature and Belief: English Institute Essays, 1957*, ed. M. H. Abrams (New York: Columbia University Press, 1958), 53–79, and *The Well Wrought Urn: Studies in the Structure of Poetry* (1947; New York: Harcourt, Brace, and World, 1975); see also Lee Rust Brown, "Coleridge and the Prospect of the Whole," *Studies in Romanticism* 30, no. 2 (Summer 1991): 235–53; the phrase "source of interest" is from Poe's "The Philosophy of Composition," 60.

41. Poe, "The Philosophy of Composition," 67; "The Poetic Principle," 179; John Dewey, *Art as Experience*, in *The Collected Works of John Dewey*, ed. Jo Ann Boydston, *The Later Works, 1925–1953*, vol. 10, *1934*, ed. Harriet Furst Simon, introduction by Abraham Kaplan (Carbondale: Southern Illinois University Press, 2008), 57, 135, 198. Dewey mentions "The Raven" itself on pages 80–81; Laurence Buermeyer, *The Aesthetic Experience*, 2nd ed. (Merion, PA: Barnes Foundation Press, 1929), 82.

42. Edgar Allan Poe, letter to Phillip P. Cooke, August 9, 1846, in *The Collected Letters of Edgar Allan Poe*, vol. 1, *1824–1846*, ed. John Ward Ostrom, revised and corrected by Burton R. Pollin and Jeffrey A. Savoye (New York: Gordian Press, 2008), 596; review of *Ballad and Other Poems*, by Henry Wadsworth Longfellow, *Graham's Magazine*, April 1842, in *Essays and Reviews*, ed. G. R. Thompson (New York: Library of America, 1984), 691; review of "L. H. Sigourney—H. F. Gould—E. F. Ellet," in *Essays and Reviews*, ed. G. R. Thompson (New York: Library of America, 1984), 876–77; "Rufus Dawes: A Retrospective Criticism," *Graham's Magazine*, October 1842, in *Essays and Reviews*, ed. G. R. Thompson (New York: Library of America, 1984), esp. 493.

43. Poe, review of *Night and Morning: A Novel*, by Edward Bulwer Lytton, in *Graham's Magazine*, April 1841, in *Essays and Reviews*, ed. G. R. Thompson (New York: Library of America, 1984), 148–52.

44. Poe, "The American Drama," *American Whig Review* (August 1845), in *Essays*

and Reviews, ed. G. R. Thompson (New York: Library of America, 1984), 364–65, 367–68.

45. Poe, "The Philosophy of Composition," 66, 67, 69; William James, "The Stream of Consciousness," in *Psychology: Briefer Course*, in *Writings, 1878–1899*, ed. Gerald E. Myers (New York: Library of America, 1992), 159–60; John Dewey, speaking of James's "flights and perchings," in Dewey, *Art as Experience*, in *Collected Works, The Later Works, 1925–1953*, 10:62.

46. Poe, "The Philosophy of Composition," 63, 70; Poe, "The Raven," 85–86.

47. Poe, "The Philosophy of Composition," 64; I take the phrase "hang together" from Dewey (*Art as Experience*, in *Collected Works, The Later Works, 1925–1953*, 10:75) and elsewhere and will return to it later; Poe, "The Poetic Principle," 182.

Chapter 3

1. Journal entries from March to April 1847. Ralph Waldo Emerson, *The Journals and Miscellaneous Notebooks of Ralph Waldo Emerson*, vol. 10, *1847–1848*, ed. Merton M. Sealts Jr. (Cambridge, MA: Belknap Press of Harvard University Press, 1973) , 28–29, 34–35. The italics are the topic headings Emerson added for the purposes of indexing; see Lawrence Rosenwald, *Emerson and the Art of the Diary* (New York: Oxford University Press, 1988).

2. Ralph Waldo Emerson, "Introductory Lecture on the Times," in *The Collected Works of Ralph Waldo Emerson* (hereafter *CW*), vol. 1, *Nature, Addresses, and Lectures*, ed. Alfred R. Ferguson, introduction and notes by Robert E. Spiller (Cambridge, MA: Belknap Press of Harvard University Press, 1971), 183; Stanley Cavell, *This New Yet Unapproachable America: Lectures after Emerson and Wittgenstein*, the 1987 Frederick Ives Carpenter Lectures (Albuquerque, NM: Living Batch Press, 1989), 82; Ralph Waldo Emerson, "Art," in *CW*, vol. 2, *Essays: First Series*, ed. Alfred R. Ferguson and Jean Ferguson Carr, introduction and notes by Joseph Slater (Cambridge, MA: Belknap Press of Harvard University Press, 1979), 211–12; Ralph Waldo Emerson, "Genius," in *The Early Lectures of Ralph Waldo Emerson*, vol. 3, *1838–1842*, ed. Robert E. Spiller and Wallace E. Williams (Cambridge, MA: Belknap Press of Harvard University Press, 1972), 70, 80. The full line is "Genius grasps the pencil, and with sure audacity goes daring, daring on, new and incalculable ever, and the Soul attentive greets each stroke with entire welcome, and says, That is it: It is true; It is true." Emerson, "History," in *CW*, 2:10, 13; "Home," in *Early Lectures*, 3:29; Branka Arsić, *On Leaving: A Reading in Emerson* (Cambridge, MA: Harvard University Press, 2010), 50; "Natural History of Intellect," in *The Complete Works of Ralph Waldo Emerson*, vol. 12, *Natural History of Intellect and Other Papers*, ed. Edward W. Emerson (1893; Boston: Houghton, Mifflin, 1904), 40.

3. Ralph Waldo Emerson, "The American Scholar," in *CW*, vol. 1, *Nature, Addresses, and Lectures*, ed. Alfred R. Ferguson, introduction and notes by Robert E. Spiller (Cambridge, MA: Belknap Press of Harvard University Press, 1971), 53–54; see Maurice S. Lee, *Overwhelmed: Literature, Aesthetics, and the Nineteenth-Century Information Revolution* (Princeton, NJ: Princeton University Press, 2019), 39–56; and Cary Wolfe, "'The Eye Is the First Circle': Emerson's 'Romanticism,' Cavell's Skepticism, Luhmann's Modernity," in *The Other Emerson*, ed. Branka Arsić and Cary Wolfe (Minneapolis: University of Minnesota Press, 2010), 271–300; Emerson as quoted in Lee, *Overwhelmed*, 39.

"Relevance" is, of course, the key concept behind recent information science, and the algorithms for "retrieval" used by Google and all major search engines and databases. See, for example, Daniel Rosenberg, "Search," in *Information: A Historical Companion*, ed. Ann Blair, Paul Duguid, Anja-Silvia Goeing, and Anthony Grafton (Princeton, NJ: Princeton University Press, 2021), 259–84; "The Relevance of Algorithms," in *Media Technologies: Essays on Communication, Materiality, and Society*, ed. Tarleton Gillespie, Pablo J. Boczkowski, and Kirsten A. Foot (Cambridge, MA: MIT Press, 2014), 167–94; and Stefano Mizzaro, "Relevance: The Whole History," *Journal of the American Society for Information Science* 48, no. 9 (1997): 810–32.

4. Ralph Waldo Emerson, *The Journals and Miscellaneous Notebooks of Ralph Waldo Emerson*, vol. 11, *1848–1851*, ed. A. W. Plumstead and William H. Gilman (Cambridge, MA: Belknap Press of Harvard University Press, 1975), 271; Ralph Waldo Emerson, "Powers of the Mind" (1858), in *The Later Lectures of Ralph Waldo Emerson, 1843–1871*, vol. 2, *1855–1871*, ed. Ronald A. Bosco and Joel Myerson (Athens: University of Georgia Press, 2010), 69.

5. Ralph Waldo Emerson, "Experience," in *CW*, vol. 3, *Essays: Second Series*, ed. Alfred R. Ferguson and Jean Ferguson Carr, introduction and notes by Joseph Slater (Cambridge, MA: Belknap Press of Harvard University Press, 1983), 27; William James, "The Sentiment of Rationality," *The Will to Believe and Other Essays in Popular Philosophy*, in *Writings, 1878–1899*, ed. Gerald E. Myers (New York: Library of America, 1992), 519, 522–23; "Remarks on Spencer's Definition of Mind as Correspondence," *Journal of Speculative Philosophy* 12, no. 1 (January 1878): 17; also cited in Hilary Putnam, *Pragmatism: An Open Question* (Oxford: Blackwell, 1992), 17.

6. Emerson, *Nature*, in *CW*, 1:28; William James, *The Principles of Psychology* (1890; New York: Dover, 1950), 2:298; as reported by William Dean Howells in *Literary Friends and Acquaintance: A Personal Retrospect of American Authorship* (New York: Harper and Brothers, 1901), 63; Ralph Waldo Emerson, "Art," in *CW*, vol. 7, *Society and Solitude*, ed. Douglas Emory Wilson, introduction and notes by Ronald A. Bosco (Cambridge, MA: Belknap Press of Harvard University Press, 2007), 23; Alfred North Whitehead, *The Concept of Nature: The Tanner Lectures Delivered in Trinity College, November 1919* (Cambridge: Cambridge University Press, 1920), 29, 107; *Modes of Thought* (New York: Free Press, 1966; first published 1938 by Macmillan [New York]), 116; Isabelle Stengers, *Thinking with Whitehead: A Free and Wild Creation of Concepts*, trans. Michael Chase (Cambridge, MA: Harvard University Press, 2011), 67.

7. Emerson, "Experience," in *CW*, 3:28; Stengers, *Thinking with Whitehead*, 69.

8. Ralph Waldo Emerson, "The Poet," in *The Selected Lectures of Ralph Waldo Emerson*, ed. Ronald A. Bosco and Joel Myerson (Athens: University of Georgia Press, 2005), 91; "Experience," in *CW*, 3:44; "Natural History of Intellect," in *The Complete Works of Ralph Waldo Emerson*, 12:30, and from the chapter titled "Memory," *The Complete Works of Ralph Waldo Emerson*, 12:109; "Works and Days," in *CW*, 7:85, 86.

9. Emerson, "History," in *CW*, 2:13; "The Poet," in *CW*, 3:11; "Experience," in *CW*, 3:30; "The Poet," in *Selected Lectures*, 91–92; "Natural History of Intellect," in *The Complete Works of Ralph Waldo Emerson*, 12:39–41.

10. Emerson, "Intellect," *CW*, 2:194; "Works and Days," in *CW*, 7:85; "Beauty," in *CW*, vol. 6, *The Conduct of Life*, ed. Douglas Emory Wilson, notes by Joseph Slater, introduction by Barbara L. Packer (Cambridge, MA: Belknap Press of Harvard University Press, 2003), 162; "Poetry and Imagination," in *CW*, vol. 8, *Letters and Social Aims*, ed.

Joel Myerson, notes by Glen M. Johnson, introduction by Ronald A. Bosco (Cambridge, MA: Belknap Press of Harvard University Press, 2010), 6; "Works and Days," in *CW*, 7:91; John Dewey, "Experience, Nature and Art," in John Dewey, Albert C. Barnes, Laurence Buermeyer, Mary Mullen, and Violette de Mazia, *Art and Education: A Collection of Essays*, 3rd ed. (Merion, PA: Barnes Foundation Press, 1954; first published 1929 by the Barnes Foundation), 27 (the essay is adapted from material that would appear in *Experience and Nature* [1925]); Emerson, from the chapter "Memory," in *Natural History of Intellect*, in *The Complete Works of Ralph Waldo Emerson*, 12:91.

11. Emerson, "History," in *CW*, 2:14; "Art," in *CW*, 7:23.

12. Emerson, from the chapter "Memory," in *Natural History of Intellect*, in *The Complete Works of Ralph Waldo Emerson*, 12:101, 109; "Natural History of Intellect," 12:43; "Experience," in *CW*, 3:31; Stanley Cavell, *Emerson's Transcendental Etudes*, ed. David Justin Hodge (Stanford, CA: Stanford University Press, 2003), 118, 247.

13. Emerson, "Experience," in *CW*, 3:41; "History," in *CW*, 2:13; *Nature*, in *CW*, 1:44; "Works and Days," in *CW*, 7:89.

14. Dewey, "Experience, Nature and Art," 31; John Dewey, *Art as Experience*, in *The Collected Works of John Dewey*, ed. Jo Ann Boydston, *The Later Works, 1925–1953*, vol. 10, *1934*, ed. Harriet Furst Simon, introduction by Abraham Kaplan (Carbondale: Southern Illinois University Press, 2008), 270–71, 279; Emerson, "Love," in *CW*, 2:103; "Success," in *CW*, 7:153. In *Pragmatism*, James writes,

> The novelty soaks in; it stains the ancient mass; but it is also tinged by what absorbs it. Our past apperceives and co-operates; and in the new equilibrium in which each step forward in the process of learning terminates, it happens relatively seldom that the new fact is added *raw*. More usually it is embedded cooked, as one might say, or stewed down in the sauce of the old.
>
> New truths thus are resultants of new experiences and of old truths combined and mutually modifying one another. (William James, *Writings, 1902–1910*, ed. Bruce Kuklick [New York: Library of America 1987], 559–60)

15. Emerson, "Art," *CW*, 2:212; "Experience," *CW*, 3:32, 33. The phrase is from "Circles," in *CW*, vol. 2, *Essays: First Series*; see especially Stanley Cavell, "Finding as Founding: Taking Steps in Emerson's 'Experience,'" in *Emerson's Transcendental Etudes*, ed. David Justin Hodge (Stanford, CA: Stanford University Press, 2003), 110–40; Sharon Cameron, "The Way of Life by Abandonment: Emerson's Impersonal," *Critical Inquiry* 25, no. 1 (Autumn 1998): 1–31; Branka Arsić, *On Leaving: A Reading in Emerson* (Cambridge, MA: Harvard University Press, 2010), 21; Emerson, "Self-Reliance," in *CW*, 2:33; "Beauty," in *CW*, 6:155; "The Method of Nature," in *CW*, 1:124.

16. Emerson, "Experience," in *CW*, 3:29, 35, 39, 41; see Stanley Cavell, "Aversive Thinking: Emersonian Representations in Heidegger and Nietzsche," in *Emerson's Transcendental Etudes*, ed. David Justin Hodge (Stanford, CA: Stanford University Press, 2003), 146–47, and *Conditions Handsome and Unhandsome: The Constitution of Emersonian Perfectionism* (Chicago: University of Chicago Press, 1990).

17. Emerson, "Experience," in *CW*, 3:27, 30, 35, 44, 49.

18. Emerson, "Circles," in *CW*, 2:180.

19. Sianne Ngai, *Our Aesthetic Categories: Zany, Cute, Interesting* (Cambridge, MA: Harvard University Press, 2012), 120-21; Friedrich Schlegel, *On the Study of Greek*

Poetry, trans. Stuart Barnett (Albany: State University of New York Press, 2001), 19, 35; A. O. Lovejoy, "On the meaning of 'Romantic' in early German Romanticism: Part II," as quoted in Ngai, *Our Aesthetic Categories*, 121; Friedrich Schlegel, "Athenäum Fragments," in *German Aesthetic and Literary Criticism: The Romantic Ironists and Goethe*, ed. Kathleen M. Wheeler (Cambridge: Cambridge University Press, 1984), 47.

20. Hans-Georg Gadamer, "The Relevance of the Beautiful," in *The Relevance of the Beautiful and Other Essays*, trans. Nicholas Walker, ed. Robert Bernasconi (Cambridge: Cambridge University Press, 1986), 6, and see 3–11; G. W. F. Hegel, *Aesthetics: Lectures on Fine Arts*, 2 vols., trans. T. M. Knox (Oxford: Clarendon, 1975), 1:11. I am drawing on Susan Sontag here, whose argument resembles Danto's, *Against Interpretation and Other Essays* (New York: Picador, 1961), 3; Arthur C. Danto, *The Transfiguration of the Commonplace: A Philosophy of Art* (Cambridge, MA: Harvard University Press, 1981), 77.

21. Robert B. Pippin, *After the Beautiful: Hegel and the Philosophy of Pictorial Modernism* (Chicago: University of Chicago Press, 2014), 7–8; Gadamer, "Relevance of the Beautiful," 7.

22. Edgar Allan Poe, "The Philosophy of Composition," in *Critical Theory: The Major Documents*, ed. Stuart Levine and Susan F. Levine (Urbana: University of Illinois Press, 2009), 63; Ngai, *Our Aesthetic Categories*, 124; Friedrich Schlegel, from "Athenaeum Fragments," in *Philosophical Fragments*, trans. Peter Firchow (Minneapolis: University of Minnesota Press, 1991), 59; Pippin, *After the Beautiful*, 8; Hegel, *Aesthetics: Lectures on Fine Arts*, 1:11, and quoted in Pippin, 35.

23. Schlegel, *Study of Greek Poetry*, 35 and n47; Kathleen M. Wheeler introduction to *German Aesthetic and Literary Criticism*, 2; also quoted in Sianne Ngai, "Merely Interesting," *Critical Inquiry* 34, no. 4 (Summer 2008): 783; Friedrich Schlegel, from "Critical Fragments," in *Philosophical Fragments*, 10.

24. My source is Stanley M. Vogel, *German Literary Influences on the American Transcendentalists* (New Haven, CT: Yale University Press, 1955), 167–81. Emerson also owned a copy of Schlegel's *Philosophy of History* (London, 1835); see Walter Harding, *Emerson's Library* (Charlottesville: University Presses of Virginia, 1967), 241; Emerson, "History," in *CW*, 2:10; William Wordsworth, "Preface" (1802) to William Wordsworth and Samuel Taylor Coleridge, *Lyrical Ballads: 1798 and 1802* (Oxford: Oxford University Press, 2013), 96–97; see, for example, Samuel Taylor Coleridge, *Anima Poetae: From the Unpublished Note-Books of Samuel Taylor Coleridge* (London: William Heinemann, 1895), 168, and *Biographia Literaria*, in *The Collected Works of Samuel Taylor Coleridge*, ed. James Engell and W. Jackson Bate (Princeton, NJ: Princeton University Press, 1985), 7:31.

25. Stanley Cavell, *Emerson's Transcendental Etudes*, ed. David Justin Hodge (Stanford, CA: Stanford University Press, 2003), 36–37; *The Senses of Walden*, enl. ed. (Chicago: University of Chicago Press, 1992), 67, 102, 117; Cavell also quotes Wittgenstein, "Concepts . . . are the expression of our interest, and direct our interest," in *Emerson's Transcendental Etudes*, 217; Pippin, *After the Beautiful*, 14, 33–34; Ralph Waldo Emerson, *The Journals and Miscellaneous Notebooks of Ralph Waldo Emerson*, vol. 13, *1852–1855*, ed. Ralph H. Orth and Alfred R. Ferguson (Cambridge, MA: Belknap Press of Harvard University Press, 1977), 260: "In Art, we value the ideal, that is to say, nothing is interesting which is fixed, bounded, dead; but only that which streams with life, which is in act or endeavor to proceed, to reach somewhat beyond, &, all the better, if that be somewhat vast & divine."

26. Albert C. Barnes and Violette de Mazia, *The Art of Henri-Matisse* (New York: Charles Scribner's Sons, 1933), 2; Albert C. Barnes and Violette de Mazia, "Learning to See," in John Dewey, Albert C. Barnes, Laurence Buermeyer, Mary Mullen, and Violette de Mazia, *Art and Education: A Collection of Essays*, 3rd ed. (Merion, PA: Barnes Foundation Press, 1954; first published 1929 by the Barnes Foundation), 156–57; Stanley Cavell, *Pursuits of Happiness: The Hollywood Comedy of Remarriage* (Cambridge, MA: Harvard University Press, 1981), 10; Emerson, "Experience," in *CW*, 3:42; Dewey, *Art as Experience*, in *Collected Works, The Later Works, 1925–1953*, 10:258–59, 280; see also Thomas M. Alexander, *John Dewey's Theory of Art, Experience, and Nature: The Horizons of Feeling* (Albany: State University of New York Press, 1987), 226.

27. William James, *The Principles of Psychology* (1890; New York: Dover, 1950), 2:295.

28. Albert C. Barnes, "Plastic Form," in Dewey et al., *Art and Education*, 116; John Dewey, *Human Nature and Conduct: An Introduction to Social Psychology* (1922; New York: Modern Library, 1930), 191; Alfred Schutz as cited in Rodman B. Webb, *The Presence of the Past: John Dewey and Alfred Schutz on the Genesis and Organization of Experience* (Gainesville: University Presses of Florida, 1976), 75: "The ontological structure of the universe is imposed upon me and constitutes the frame of all possible spontaneous activity. Within this frame I have to find my bearings and I have to come to terms with its elements." Calvin Shrag as cited in Webb, *Presence of the Past*, 86; Albert C. Barnes, "The Roots of Art," in Dewey et al., *Art and Education*, 52.

29. John Dewey, *Interest and Effort in Education* (Boston: Houghton Mifflin, 1913), 17; *Art as Experience*, in *Collected Works, The Later Works, 1925–1953*, 10:190; Emerson, "The Divinity School Address," in *CW*, 1:92.

30. Sharon Cameron, "The Way of Life by Abandonment: Emerson's Impersonal," *Critical Inquiry* 25, no. 1 (Autumn 1998): 4, 5, 8, 10, 15, 26; Emerson, "The Over-Soul," in *CW*, 2:166; "Intellect," in *CW*, 2:194; "Self-Reliance," in *CW*, 2:40; "Compensation," in *CW*, 2:70; "Experience," in *CW*, 3:45–46.

31. Emerson, "Experience," in *CW*, 3:46; "Considerations by the Way," in *CW*, 6:147.

32. Emerson, *Nature*, in *CW*, 1:9; John Ruskin, *Modern Painters* (New York: John Wiley, 1862), vol. 1, part 2, sec. 1, chap. 2, p. 51; I am quoting William H. Gass here in his acceptance speech for the 2007 Truman Capote Award for Literary Criticism, "The Literary Miracle," in *Life Sentences: Literary Judgments and Accounts* (New York: Alfred A. Knopf, 2012), 3; Dewey, *Art as Experience*, in *Collected Works, The Later Works, 1925–1953*, 10:110; Cameron, "Way of Life by Abandonment," 19–20; Emerson, "Gifts," in *CW*, 3:94.

33. Emerson, *Nature*, in *CW*, 1:9–10.

34. Emerson, "The American Scholar," in *CW*, 1:60; "Intellect," in *CW*, 2:194, 198; "Spiritual Laws," in *CW*, 2:84.

35. Emerson, "Intellect," in *CW*, 2:194, 197–98; "Nominalist and Realist," in *CW*, 3:142; "Poetry and Imagination," in *CW*, 8:5–6; *Journals and Miscellaneous Notebooks of Ralph Waldo Emerson*, vol. 15, *1860–1866*, ed. Linda Allardt and David W. Hill (Cambridge, MA: Belknap Press of Harvard University Press, 1982), 96. In his discussion of Emerson's memory loss in the last decade of his life, Christopher Hanlon describes Emerson's "sense of amazement that anyone can ever remember anything." Much of Emerson's thinking on memory appears in the essays published as *Natural History of Intellect*, including "Natural History of Intellect" and "Memory" that I draw on throughout. Han-

lon provides an insightful account of the way these essays—based on Emerson's Harvard lecture series of 1870–1877 about how "the mind collects and re-collects"—were written while he was suffering from memory loss. Emerson needed the help of his daughter Ellen Tucker to prepare the lectures; she then pieced them together from his manuscripts and earlier writings for posthumous publication by Emerson's literary executor, James Elliot Cabot, and later by Edward Emerson, with Cabot's help; *Emerson's Memory Loss: Originality, Communality, and the Late Style* (New York: Oxford University Press, 2018), 31 and throughout. On the publication history of *Natural History of Intellect*, see also Nancy Craig Simmons, "Arranging the Sibylline Leaves: James Elliot Cabot's Work as Emerson's Literary Executor," *Studies in the American Renaissance* (1983): 335–89.

36. Emerson, "Natural History of Intellect," in *The Complete Works of Ralph Waldo Emerson*, 12:29–30; "Nominalist and Realist," in *CW*, 3:143; "Genius," *The Selected Lectures of Ralph Waldo Emerson*, ed. Ronald A. Bosco and Joel Myerson (Athens: University of Georgia Press, 2005), 75; "Intellect," in *CW*, 2:198. I am reminded throughout of Ross Posnock's remarkable discussion at the beginning of his book *Renunciation* of the long gap between the acquisition of his books—collected, sometimes for decades at a time, by habit and without much "reflective notice"—and the moments when they "had undergone a transformation." Those dusty books, there all along, suddenly struck him as just what he needed and, for all those years of half-conscious accumulation, "more than a serendipitous accident." They were "no longer inert objects but palpable presences," and he was not then "indifferent to reading them." Posnock thinks about his "thoughtless buying and deferred reading" in Emersonian terms: as a way of being drawn to things "without knowing how or why" at first and with the dawning of new meaning and value later. Ross Posnock, *Renunciation: Acts of Abandonment by Writers, Philosophers, and Artists* (Cambridge, MA: Harvard University Press, 2016), 1–3. Posnock's phrase "belated revelations" appears on page 7.

37. Emerson, "Natural History of Intellect," in *The Complete Works of Ralph Waldo Emerson*, 12:34–35, 41–42; Henry James, "Preface to *Roderick Hudson*," in *The Art of the Novel: Critical Prefaces by Henry James*, introduction by R. P. Blackmur (1934; Chicago: University of Chicago Press, 2011), 3, 9; Søren Kierkegaard, "Diary of the Seducer" (1843), in *Either/Or*, vol. 1, trans. David F. Swenson and Lillian Marvin Swenson with revisions by Howard A. Johnson (New York: Anchor Books, 1959), 341.

Chapter 4

1. William James, "On Some Mental Effects of the Earthquake" (1906), in *Essays* in *Writings, 1902–1910*, ed. Bruce Kuklick (New York: Library of America, 1987), 1215–18.

2. Alfred North Whitehead, *Modes of Thought* (New York: Free Press, 1966; first published 1938 by Macmillan [New York]), 116; James, "On Some Mental Effects," 1215–16; Jacques Barzun, *A Stroll with William James* (Chicago: University of Chicago Press, 1983), 269. Though ideas for the book date back to the moment James first identified himself with the term *pragmatism* in a lecture at Berkeley in 1898 (a term he credits to Charles Sanders Peirce), *Pragmatism: A New Name for Some Old Ways of Thinking* was published in 1907 based on lectures given at Stanford in 1906, then at Columbia University and in Boston in 1907.

3. William James, "On Some Omissions of Introspective Psychology," in *Essays in Psychology* (Cambridge, MA: Harvard University Press, 1983), 145, 160n6; also cited

in *The Principles of Psychology* (1890; New York: Dover, 1950), 1:478; "On a Certain Blindness in Human Beings," in *The Heart of William James*, ed. Robert Richardson (Cambridge, MA: Harvard University Press), 148–49; Ralph Waldo Emerson, "Genius," in *The Early Lectures of Ralph Waldo Emerson*, vol. 3, *1838–1842*, ed. Robert E. Spiller and Wallace E. Williams (Cambridge, MA: Belknap Press of Harvard University Press, 1972), 80; John Dewey, *Essays in Experimental Logic* (Chicago: University of Chicago Press, 1916), 6; James, "On Some Mental Effects," 1216.

4. James, "On Some Mental Effects," 1217–22.

5. James, "On Some Mental Effects," 1216; Alfred Schutz, *On Phenomenology and Social Relations: Selected Writings*, ed. Helmut R. Wagner (Chicago: University of Chicago Press, 1970), 68–69; see, for example, Henri Bergson, *Matter and Memory*, trans. Nancy Margaret Paul and W. Scott Palmer (New York: Zone Books, 1991), 173–74.

6. Wayne Wu, *Attention* (New York: Routledge, 2014), 10, 111, 140, 225. On this phenomenal quality of attention ("what it is like" to attend) and the idea of phenomenal states of consciousness more generally, see David Chalmers, *The Conscious Mind* (Oxford: Oxford University Press, 1996). Thomas Nagel famously asked, "What is it like to be a bat?" in an essay with this title, *Philosophical Review* 83 (October 1974), 435–56; see also Jonathan Kramnick, *Paper Minds: Literature and the Ecology of Consciousness* (Chicago: University of Chicago Press, 2018), 4.

7. On the history of the duck-rabbit, see, Peter Brugger, "One Hundred Years of an Ambiguous Figure: Happy Birthday, Duck/Rabbit!," *Perceptual and Motor Skills* 89, no. 3 (December 1999): 973–77; Joseph Jastrow, "The Mind's Eye," *Popular Science Monthly* 54 (January 1899): 299–312; *Fact and Fable in Psychology* (Boston: Houghton, Mifflin, 1900); Ludwig Wittgenstein, *Philosophical Investigations*, 3rd ed., trans. G. E. M. Anscomb (New York: Macmillan 1958), 193–96. For more on the phenomenology of a "figure" apprehended on a "background," see Maurice Merleau-Ponty, *Phenomenology of Perception*, trans. Colin Smith (1945; New York: Routledge, 2002), esp. 15–16. See also Eviatar Zerubavel, *Hidden in Plain Sight: The Social Structure of Irrelevance* (Oxford: Oxford University Press, 2015), 11–20.

8. Joseph Jastrow, *The Subconscious* (1905; Boston: Houghton, Mifflin, 1906), 3, 5–8. See also Jastrow and Charles Sanders Peirce's pioneering study of subliminal perception, "On Small Differences in Sensation," *Memoirs of the National Academy of Sciences* 3 (October 1884): 75–83.

9. Jastrow, *The Subconscious*, 8–9, 416n1.

10. Jastrow, *The Subconscious*, 14; Zerubavel, *Hidden in Plain Sight*, 10, 12, 16–17, 21.

11. Jastrow, *The Subconscious*, 352, 438–41, 447–48.

12. Edward Bradford Titchener, *Lectures on the Elementary Psychology of Feeling and Attention* (New York: Macmillan, 1908), 15, 186, 244, 251, 304; *A Text-Book of Psychology*, pt. 1, rev. ed. (1896; New York: Macmillan, 1909), 280, 298. For more on scientific experiments around 1900 involving attention and perception, see Jonathan Crary, *Suspensions of Perception: Attention, Spectacle, and Modern Culture* (Cambridge, MA: MIT Press, 1999), especially chapter 4.

13. Titchener, *Lectures* (New York: Macmillan, 1908), 220; *A Text-Book of Psychology*, 266–67, 276–77.

14. Titchener, *Lectures*, 305; Külpe as quoted in R. M. Ogden, "Oswald Külpe and the Würzburg School," *American Journal of Psychology* 64, no. 1 (January 1951): 16; Titchener, *A Text-Book of Psychology*, 267–68.

15. Titchener, *A Text-book of Psychology*, 268–69, 272–73, 276; Wu, *Attention*, 97, 125.

16. Titchener, *A Text-book of Psychology*, 186, 269, 270; James, *The Principles of Psychology*, 1:201.

17. Wayne Wu writes, "Attention is selection for action"; Wu, *Attention*, 9.

18. James, *The Principles of Psychology*, 1:403–4. For a long history of the problem of distraction, from Aristotle to Walter Benjamin, see Paul North's illuminating *The Problem of Distraction* (Stanford, CA: Stanford University Press, 2011); for a discussion of "distraction" and "cognitive overload" in the eighteenth century, see Natalie M. Phillips's equally wonderful *Distraction: Problems of Attention in Eighteenth-Century Literature* (Baltimore: Johns Hopkins University Press, 2016).

19. Wu, *Attention*, 92–93, 97.

20. James, *The Principles of Psychology*, 1:404–5, 409.

21. Wu, *Attention*, 233; James, *The Principles of Psychology*, 1:425–426; Ralph Waldo Emerson, "Spiritual Laws," in *The Collected Works of Ralph Waldo Emerson* (hereafter *CW*), vol. 2, *Essays: First Series*, ed. Alfred R. Ferguson and Jean Ferguson Carr, introduction and notes by Joseph Slater (Cambridge, MA: Belknap Press of Harvard University Press, 1979), 84.

22. James, *The Principles of Psychology*, 1:426; William James, "The Importance of Individuals," in *The Will to Believe and Other Essays in Popular Philosophy*, in *Writings, 1878–1899*, ed. Gerald E. Myers (New York: Library of America, 1992), 648.

23. James, *The Principles of Psychology*, 1:201, 258–60, 265, 402, 450; Hugo Münsterberg, *The Photoplay: A Psychological Study* (New York: D. Appleton, 1916), 85.

24. James, *The Principles of Psychology*, 1:259–260, 402, 407, 435, 583; Alfred North Whitehead, *Modes of Thought* (New York: Free Press, 1966; first published 1938 by Macmillan [New York]), 124.

25. William James, "The Spatial Quale," *Journal of Speculative Philosophy* 13, no. 1 (January 1879): 67; see, for example, John Dewey, *How We Think* (Boston: D. C. Heath, 1910).

26. Dewey, *Essays in Experimental Logic*, 6; John Dewey, *Logic: The Theory of Inquiry*, in *The Collected Works of John Dewey*, ed. Jo Ann Boydston, *The Later Works, 1925–1953*, vol. 12, *1938*, ed. Kathleen Poulos (Carbondale: Southern Illinois University Press, 2008), 72, 69 or 220; Alfred Schutz, *Reflections on the Problem of Relevance*, in *Collected Papers V. Phenomenology and the Social Sciences*, ed. Lester Embree (New York: Springer Sciences, 2011), 96.

27. James, *The Principles of Psychology*, 1:457–58.

28. William James, *Talks to Teachers on Psychology and to Students on Some of Life's Ideals*, in *Writings, 1878–1899*, ed. Gerald E. Myers (New York: Library of America, 1992), 774–75.

29. James, *Talks to Teachers*, 775; "The Hidden Self," in *The Heart of William James*, ed. Robert Richardson (Cambridge, MA: Harvard University Press, 2010), 79; James, *The Principles of Psychology*, 1:404, as cited in Robert D. Richardson, *William James in the Maelstrom of American Modernism: A Biography* (New York: Houghton, Mifflin, 2006), 430; Whitehead, *Modes of Thought*, 9.

30. James, *Talks to Teachers*, 768–77; the phrase "all consciousness tends to action" appears in James's table of contents, 712. *Talks to Teachers* is based on lectures James gave beginning in 1891, first in the new Department of Pedagogy at Harvard and later in

Colorado Springs, Buffalo, Chicago, Berkeley, and elsewhere. He follows a chapter on "Interest" with a chapter on "Attention." Kate Stanley includes a terrific discussion of James's pedagogical practices in *Practices of Surprise in American Literature after Emerson* (New York: Cambridge University Press, 2018). For Stanley, the pragmatist teacher works on "training our attention to notice and engage"; the classroom is where "certain kinds of perceptual preparation might facilitate rather than foreclose the experience of surprise," so that when students encounter something new, they may be receptive to it; Stanley, *Practices of Surprise*, 5, 52. For a recent discussion of how education can reshape our values by changing our patterns of attention, see Cathy N. Davidson, *Now You See It: How Technology and Brian Science Will Transform Schools and Business for the 21st Century* (New York: Penguin Books, 2011). Davidson asks, "How can what we know about attention help us change how we teach and learn?" (19).

31. James, *The Principles of Psychology*, 1:402, 403; Schutz, *Reflections on the Problem of Relevance*, in *Collected Papers V. Phenomenology and the Social Sciences*, 95; William James, "Are We Automata?," *Essays in Psychology* (Cambridge, MA: Harvard University Press, 1983), 46; William James, "The Sentiment of Rationality," in *The Will to Believe and Other Essays in Popular Philosophy*, in *Writings, 1878–1899*, ed. Gerald E. Myers (New York: Library of America, 1992), 519; John Dewey, *Psychology* (1887; 3rd. rev. ed. 1891), in *The Collected Works of John Dewey, The Early Works, 1882–1898*, vol. 2, *1887*, ed. Jo Ann Boydston and Fredson Bowers (Carbondale: Southern Illinois University Press, 1967), 19; John Dewey, *Experience and Nature*, in *The Collected Works of John Dewey*, ed. Jo Ann Boydston, *The Later Works, 1925–1953*, vol. 1, *1925*, ed. Patricia Baysinger and Barbara Levine (Carbondale: Southern Illinois University Press, 2008), 31. For more on James's response to Spencer, see Robert D. Richardson, *William James in the Maelstrom of American Modernism: A Biography* (Boston: Houghton, Mifflin, 2006), especially 183–90. For more on Dewey and "selection" and "selective emphasis," especially in light of Darwin, see Joan Richardson, *Pragmatism and American Experience: An Introduction* (New York: Cambridge University Press, 2014), esp. 105–9.

32. William James, "The Stream of Consciousness," in *Psychology: Briefer Course*, in *Writings, 1878–1899*, ed. Gerald E. Myers (New York: Library of America, 1992), 169; Dewey, *Experience and Nature*, 31; James, *The Principles of Psychology*, 2:295; James, "Are We Automata?," 46–47.

33. James, *The Principles of Psychology*, 1:424; Robert B. Brandom, *Perspectives on Pragmatism: Classical, Recent, and Contemporary* (Cambridge, MA; Harvard University Press, 2011), 5, 6, 8.

34. Whitehead, *Modes of Thought*, 123, 134–35, 147; *Process and Reality: An Essay in Cosmology*, ed. David Ray Griffin and Donald W. Sherburne (New York: Free Press, 1978; first published 1929 by Macmillan [New York]),190; *Essays in Science and Philosophy* (1947; New York: Greenwood, 1968), 77; Dewey, *Experience and Nature*, 218, 259.

35. James, *The Principles of Psychology*, 1:286, 288–289, 424; Richardson, *Pragmatism and American Experience*, 8; Richardson, *William James in the Maelstrom of American Modernism*, 4–5; George Eliot, *Middlemarch: A Study of Provincial Life*, ed. W. J. Harvey (New York: Penguin Books, 1965), 99, 170; from William James, *A Pluralistic Universe* (1909), as cited in Richardson, *William James in the Maelstrom of American Modernism*, 5.

36. Ralph Waldo Emerson, "Experience," in *CW*, vol. 3, *Essays: Second* Series, ed. Alfred R. Ferguson and Jean Ferguson Carr, introduction and notes by Joseph Slater

(Cambridge, MA: Belknap Press of Harvard University Press, 1983), 41, 32; in the essay "Beauty," Emerson cites Michelangelo as saying that beauty "is the purgation of superfluities," *CW*, vol. 6, *The Conduct of Life*, ed. Douglas Emory Wilson, notes by Joseph Slater, introduction by Barbara L. Packer (Cambridge, MA: Belknap Press of Harvard University Press, 2003), 157. Alfred Schutz, who also uses the sculptural metaphor in his book on relevance, says he is drawing on Leibniz who used the same metaphor to describe how experience brings ideas already existing to light, as a sculptor elicits a figure only hidden in the stone; see Schutz, *Reflections on the Problem of Relevance*, in *Collected Papers V. Phenomenology and the Social Sciences*, 95. James and Schutz both suggest that these forms, already there, are selected and brought out by pragmatic interest.

37. William James, *Pragmatism: A New Name for Some Old Ways of Thinking*, in *Writings, 1902–1910*, ed. Bruce Kuklick (New York: Library of America, 1987), 535; William James, *Essays in Psychology* (Cambridge, MA: Harvard University Press, 1983), 75; James, "Stream of Consciousness," 171; James, *The Principles of Psychology*, 1:287.

38. James, *The Principles of Psychology*, 1:287–88, 289; John Dewey, *Art as Experience*, in *The Collected Works of John Dewey*, ed. Jo Ann Boydston, *The Later Works, 1925–1953*, vol. 10, *1934*, ed. Harriet Furst Simon, introduction by Abraham Kaplan (Carbondale: Southern Illinois University Press, 2008), 73; Alfred Schutz, *On Phenomenology and Social Relations: Selected Writings*, ed. Helmut R. Wagner (Chicago: University of Chicago Press, 1970), 100; *Reflections on the Problem of Relevance*, in *Collected Papers V. Phenomenology and the Social Sciences*, 144–45; F. C. S. Schiller, *Logic for Use: An Introduction to the Voluntarist Theory of Knowledge* (New York: Harcourt, Brace, 1930), 78.

39. Brandom, *Perspectives on Pragmatism*, 4; see esp. the introduction, 1–34; see, for example, Immanuel Kant, *Kant's Prolegomena to Any Future Metaphysics*, ed. Paul Carus (Chicago: Open Court, 1949), 75; John Dewey, "The Theory of Emotion. (2) The Significance of Emotions," *Psychological Review* 2, no. 1 (January 1895): 23; Dewey's essay is largely a criticism of Darwin's *The Expression of the Emotions in Man and Animals* (1872); he takes the phrase "big, buzzing, blooming confusion" from a line in James's *Principles of Psychology*: "The baby, assailed by eyes, ears, nose, skin, and entrails at once, feels it all as one great blooming, buzzing confusion" (1:488).

40. See Emerson, "Experience," in *CW*, 3:35; "Self-Reliance," in *CW*, vol. 2, *Essays: First Series*, ed. Alfred R. Ferguson and Jean Ferguson Carr, introduction and notes by Joseph Slater (Cambridge, MA: Harvard University Press, 1979), 34; "Fate," in *CW*, 6:15; "Spiritual Laws," in *CW*, 2:83; "The Poet," in *CW*, 3:12; see also Emerson's "Perpetual Forces," *The Later Lectures of Ralph Waldo Emerson, 1843–1871. Volume 2: 1855–1871*, ed. Ronald A. Bosco and Joel Myerson (Athens: University of Georgia Press, 2001), 287–301; Stanley Cavell, "Emerson, Coleridge, Kant (Terms as Conditions)," *Emerson's Transcendental Etudes*, ed. David Justin Hodge (Stanford: Stanford University Press, 2003), 70; Robert B. Brandom, *Perspectives on Pragmatism: Classical, Recent, and Contemporary* (Cambridge, MA: Harvard University Press, 2011), 5.

41. Robert B. Brandom, *Perspectives on Pragmatism*, 8; Emerson, "The American Scholar," in *CW*, vol. 1, *Nature, Addresses, and Lectures*, ed. Alfred R. Ferguson, introduction and notes by Robert E. Spiller (Cambridge, MA: Belknap Press of Harvard University Press, 1971), 60; "The Transcendentalist," in *CW*, 1:203; "Natural History of Intellect," in *The Complete Works of Ralph Waldo Emerson*, vol. 12, *Natural History of Intellect and Other Papers*, ed. Edward W. Emerson (1893; Boston: Houghton, Mifflin,

1904), 40; "The Poet," in *CW*, 3:11. For more on how experimental psychology and ultimately pragmatism became new ways of addressing philosophical problems—about consciousness and the faculties of mind—that Kant first addressed, see Louis Menand, *The Metaphysical Club: A Story of Ideas in America* (New York: Farrar, Straus and Giroux, 2001), esp. 267–72. Menand writes, for example, that Wilhelm Wundt came to understand "that minds are capable of attending to only one thing at a time . . . and also that they are not just passive receivers of stimuli, not just blank slates. There is something 'in there,' some faculty of attention, that chooses its object. Minds select. Isn't that just what German philosophy since Kant had insisted? And now this faculty of attention (Kant had called it 'apperception') could be analyzed by empirical means" (269).

42. Emerson, "Spiritual Laws," in *CW*, 2:84. On James's annotations of Emerson and his process of indexing, see Robert D. Richardson, *William James in the Maelstrom of American Modernism: A Biography* (Boston: Houghton, Mifflin, 2006), 432–35; Susan Sontag, *As Consciousness Is Harnessed to Flesh: Journals and Notebooks, 1964–1980*, ed. David Rieff (New York: Picador, 2012), 219; William James, "Are We Automata?," in *Essays in Psychology* (Cambridge, MA: Harvard University Press, 1983), 46; Emerson, *Nature*, in *CW*, 1:38; Emerson, "Intellect," in *CW*, 2:194; Ross Posnock, *Renunciation: Acts of Abandonment by Writers, Philosophers, and Artists* (Cambridge, MA: Harvard University Press, 2016), 285; Alfred Schutz, *The Phenomenology of the Social World*, trans. George Walsh and Frederick Lehnert (Evanston, IL: Northwestern University Press, 1967), 250. On note taking and selective interest, see Lorraine Daston, "Taking Note(s)," *Isis* 95 (2004): 443–48, and Schutz on "marks" and "indications" in *On Phenomenology and Social Relations*, esp. 98–101; also, Nicholas Mathew's wonderful discussion of musical notation in "Interesting Haydn: On Attention's Materials," *Journal of American Musicological Society* 71.3 (2018): 655–701.

43. Schutz, *On Phenomenology and Social Relations*, 6; Ralph Waldo Emerson, "Nominalist and Realist," in *CW*, 3:142.

44. James acquired two volumes of Emerson's writings in 1871; on these markings and annotations, see Robert D. Richardson, *William James in the Maelstrom of American Modernism: A Biography* (Boston: Houghton, Mifflin, 2006), 435. For James's response to Bergson, see Richardson, 424–28; James on Emerson as quoted in Richardson, 202; Ralph Waldo Emerson, "Nominalist and Realist," in *CW*, 3:143: "Through solidest eternal things, the man finds his road, as if they did not subsist, and does not once suspect their being. As soon as he needs a new object, suddenly he beholds it, and no longer attempts to pass through it, but takes another way." See Alfred Schutz and Thomas Luckmann, *The Structures of the Life-World*, vol. 1, trans. Richard M. Zaner and H. Tristram Engelhardt Jr. (Evanston, IL: Northwestern University Press, 1973), 4; James, *The Principles of Psychology*, 2:313, 315. He is quoting from an earlier article, "Rationality, Activity, and Faith," *Princeton Review* (July 1882): 64–69.

45. Schutz, *Reflections on the Problem of Relevance*, ed. Richard M. Zaner (New Haven: Yale University Press, 1970), 3, 9–10. Zaner describes his efforts to edit the text in his Preface: "Among others of Schutz's papers and lectures was discovered the present manuscript. The original version was handwritten in English between August 1947 and August 1951, mainly during his infrequent vacations in Colorado. It was conceived as Part I of a five-part study and was to be entitled, *The World as Taken-For-Granted: Toward a Phenomenology of the Natural Attitude*. Part I bore the title, 'Preliminary Notes on the Problem of Relevance.' . . . The original text was in a handwritten form; a

typescript was also at hand, however . . . [It was decided] to tamper as little as possible with it and, retaining its original 'preliminary' flavor and style, merely to bring it into linguistically acceptable shape," viii. The text Zaner edited is included in Alfred Schutz, *Collected Papers V. Phenomenology and the Social Sciences*, ed. Lester Embree (New York: Springer Science, 2001), 93–199. Thomas Luckmann prepared an edition of Schutz's final work, *The Structures of the Life-World*, after he died in 1959, on the basis of Schutz's notes and written instructions; a large segment of that study is titled "The Problem of Relevance." See Alfred Schutz and Thomas Luckmann, *The Structures of the Life-World*, 2 vols., trans. Richard M. Zaner and H. Tristram Engelhardt Jr. (Evanston, IL: Northwestern University Press, 1973).

46. In his introduction, Zaner quotes a letter from Schutz's wife responding to his inquiry about the circumstances of writing the manuscript; Schutz, *Reflections on the Problem of Relevance*, ed. Richard M. Zaner (New Haven: Yale University Press, 1970), xxii–xxiii.

47. See, for example, Schutz, *On Phenomenology and Social Relations*, 59, 116. The volume collects and correlates passages from *The Phenomenology of the Social World* and from Schutz's scattered papers and essays. The first essay Schutz wrote in the US was "Phenomenology and the Social Sciences." See also Zaner, introduction to Schutz, *Reflections on the Problem of Relevance*, xi.

48. Schutz, *Reflections on the Problem of Relevance*, in *Collected Papers V. Phenomenology and the Social Sciences* (hereafter *CP*), 93–94, 96–100.

49. Schutz, *Reflections on the Problem of Relevance*, in *CP*, 97–98.

50. Schutz, in *CP*, 132.

51. Schutz, in *CP*, 102, 106–7.

52. Schutz, in *CP*, 95, 107–8, 132.

53. Schutz, in *CP*, 105, 119, 129.

54. Schutz, in *CP*, 109.

55. James, *The Principles of Psychology*, 2:287, 291, 293; Schutz, *On Phenomenology and Social Relations*, 57–59, 252, 253; see also, Wagner, introduction to Schutz, *On Phenomenology and Social Relations*, 6–7.

56. Schutz, *On Phenomenology and Social Relations*, 254–55.

57. Schutz, *Reflections on the Problem of Relevance*, in *CP*, 110, 153–54, 158–59, 162; Schutz turns to this same example of *Don Quixote*, a "voluminous book" that cannot be completed in one sitting, at other moments too; see, for example, Schutz and Luckmann, *Structures of the Life-World*, 1:132–33.

58. Schutz, *Reflections on the Problem of Relevance*, in *CP*, 150, 154, 168, 176.

59. Schutz, *On Phenomenology and Social Relations*, 304; *Reflections on the Problem of Relevance*, in *CP*, 151, 160; Emerson, "Spiritual Laws," in *CW*, 2:78.

60. Alfred Schutz, *On Phenomenology and Social Relations*, 74, 76, 113; Schutz, *Reflections on the Problem of Relevance*, in *CP*, 151; for Schutz on Heidegger, see, *Reflections on the Problem of Relevance*, in *CP*, 145 and 193.

61. Schutz, *On Phenomenology and Social Relations*, 245–48; Ralph Waldo Emerson, "Circles," in *CW*, 2:179, 181.

62. Ralph Waldo Emerson, "Experience," in *CW*, 3:48; Schutz, *On Phenomenology and Social Relations*, 82, 138; Eviatar Zerubavel, *Hidden in Plain Sight: The Social Structure of Irrelevance* (Oxford: Oxford University Press, 2015), 9–10, 52–53. See also Alfred

Schutz, "The Social World and the Theory of Social Action," *Social Research* 27, no. 2 (Summer 1960): 203–21.

63. Asia Friedman, *Blind to Sameness: Sexpectations and the Social Construction of Male and Female Bodies* (Chicago: University of Chicago Press, 2013), 23, as quoted in Zerubavel, *Hidden in Plain Sight*, 53; Schutz, *On Phenomenology and Social Relations*, 271. On the "leap from one province of meaning to another," and the feeling of "shock," see Schutz, *Reflections on the Problem of Relevance*, in *CP*, 96–98, 109, and 152–53, and on the "element of surprise," see 157. See also Rodman B. Webb, *The Presence of the Past: John Dewey and Alfred Schutz on the Genesis and Organization of Experience* (Gainesville: University Presses of Florida, 1976).

64. On the phrase, "until further notice," which Schutz uses throughout, see *Reflections on the Problem of Relevance*, in *CP*, 128 or 137.

Chapter 5

1. John Dewey, "Events and Meanings," in *The Collected Works of John Dewey*, ed. Jo Ann Boydston, *The Middle Works, 1899–1924*, vol. 13, *1921–1922*, ed. Barbara Levine (Carbondale: Southern Illinois University Press, 2008), 279.

2. From one of the newspaper reviews cited in Kathleen A. Foster, *Shipwreck! Winslow Homer and "The Life Line"* (New Haven, CT: Philadelphia Museum of Art in association with Yale University Press, 2012), 73, 75; William James, *The Principles of Psychology* (1890; New York: Dover, 1950), 1:404.

3. James, *Principles of Psychology*, 1:402–3; see John Wilmerding, "Winslow Homer's *Right and Left*," *Studies in the History of Art* 9 (1980): 68; Ralph Waldo Emerson, "Natural History of Intellect," in *The Complete Works of Ralph Waldo Emerson*, vol. 12, *Natural History of Intellect and Other Papers*, ed. Edward W. Emerson (1893; Boston: Houghton, Mifflin, 1904), 14; on Homer's books, see David Tatham, "Winslow Homer's Library," *American Art Journal* 9, no. 1 (May 1977): 92–98.

4. John Dewey, *Essays in Experimental Logic* (Chicago: University of Chicago Press, 1916), 6; see the Hugo Münsterberg chapter "Attention," in *The Photoplay: A Psychological Study* (1916; Mineola, NY: Dover, 1970), esp. 37–39 (the quote appears on 38); Emerson, "Art," in *The Collected Works of Ralph Waldo Emerson* (hereafter *CW*), vol. 2, *Essays: First Series*, ed. Alfred R. Ferguson and Jean Ferguson Carr, introduction and notes by Joseph Slater (Cambridge, MA: Belknap Press of Harvard University Press, 1979), 211.

5. Roland Barthes, *A Lover's Discourse: Fragments*, trans. Richard Howard (1978; New York: Hill and Wang, 2010), 230.

6. John Ruskin, *Praeterita*, ed. Francis O'Gorman (Oxford: Oxford University Press, 2012), 111, from a chapter first published in February 1886; *Modern Painters*, vol. 5, in *The Works of John Ruskin* (hereafter *WJR*), ed. Edward Tyas Cook and Alexander Wedderburn (London: George Allen, 1905), 7:215; *Modern Painters*, vol. 4, in *WJR*, 6:80.

7. Ruskin, *Modern Painters*, vol. 1, in *WJR*, 3:36–37; *Modern Painters*, vol. 2, in *WJR*, 4:240; *Praeterita*, 144; Ruskin, *Modern Painters*, vol. 5, in *WJR*, 7:209

8. Ruskin, *Modern Painters*, vol. 3, in *WJR*, 5:209–10; I'm referring back to my discussion of William James's "On Some Mental Effects of the Earthquake," (1906) in *Essays* in *Writings, 1902–1910*, ed. Bruce Kuklick (New York: Library of America, 1987).

9. Ruskin, *Modern Painters*, vol. 4, in *WJR*, 6:47; vol. 2, in *WJR*, 4:233, 249; vol. 1, in *WJR*, 3:199, 142; for the phrase "with love," see *Modern Painters*, vol. 1, in *WJR*, 3:143, for example, but Ruskin uses the phrase throughout; Ralph Waldo Emerson, "Love," in *CW*, 2:103, 104.

10. William James, "A World of Pure Experience," in *Essays in Radical Empiricism*, ed. Fredson Bowers and Ignas K. Skrupskelis, introduction by John J. McDermott (Cambridge, MA: Harvard University Press, 1976), 34; "On Some Omissions of Introspective Psychology," in *Essays in Psychology* (Cambridge, MA: Harvard University Press, 1983), 160; "On a Certain Blindness in Human Beings," in *The Heart of William James*, ed. Robert Richardson (Cambridge, MA: Harvard University Press, 2010), 148–49.

11. These halibut hooks, traditionally made by Native Americans in the Pacific Northwest, were popularized both as fishing tools and as art objects in the late nineteenth century. See, for example, *Descriptive Catalogues of the Collections Sent from the United States to the International Fisheries Exhibition*, London, 1883, in *Bulletin of the United States National Museum*, Department of the Interior (Washington: Smithsonian Institution, 1884), 922–24; see Alfred North Whitehead, *Process and Reality: An Essay in Cosmology* (1929), ed. David Ray Griffin and Donald W. Sherburne (New York: Free Press, 1978), 86 or 89.

12. Ruskin, *Modern Painters*, vol. 3, in *WJR*, 5:194, 209–10; vol. 5, in *WJR*, 7:263; E. D. Hirsch Jr., *Aims of Interpretation* (Chicago: University of Chicago Press, 1976), 146–47 (see also 45); John Dewey, *Experience and Nature*, in *The Collected Works of John Dewey*, ed. Jo Ann Boydston, *The Later Works, 1925–1953*, vol. 1, *1925*, ed. Patricia Baysinger and Barbara Levine (Carbondale: Southern Illinois University Press, 2008), 235. On Homer's *The Fog Warning*, see Paul Raymond Provost, "Winslow Homer's 'The Fog Warning': The Fisherman as Heroic Character," *American Art Journal* 22, no. 1 (Spring 1990): 20–27.

13. Alfred North Whitehead, *The Concept of Nature* (Cambridge, UK: Cambridge University Press, 1920), 177–78; Whitehead, *Process and Reality*, 62; Paul Rabinow, *The Accompaniment: Assembling the Contemporary* (Chicago: University of Chicago Press, 2011), 3; see also Martin Savransky, *The Adventure of Relevance: An Ethics of Social Inquiry*, foreword by Isabelle Stengers (London: Palgrave Macmillan, 2016), 17–19. In *Renunciation*, Ross Posnock wonderfully suggests that James's "reinstatement of the vague and inarticulate to its proper place in our mental life"—also the call to immerse ourselves in "phenomenal movement"—might be seen as a defense of his own early ambitions to become an artist and painter (a career he abandons). Painting is a "hands-on experience" committed, in James's words, to the making of "possibilities not yet in our present sight." *Renunciation: Acts of Abandonment by Writers, Philosophers, and Artists* (Cambridge, MA: Harvard University Press, 2016), 70–71.

14. Paul Rabinow, *Marking Time: On the Anthropology of the Contemporary* (Princeton, NJ: Princeton University Press, 2008), 29; Alfred Schutz, *On Phenomenology and Social Relations*, ed. Helmut R. Wagner (Chicago: University of Chicago Press, 1970), 218, 231–34. I take cues here from Michael Fried's sense of the German artist Adoph Menzel and the Danish philosopher Søren Kierkegaard as "nearly exact contemporaries" to suggest that Menzel may be read *through* Kierkegaard, though Menzel would not have read Kierkegaard, and that aspects of Menzel's art "invite understanding in terms analogous to those developed in certain early writings by Kierkegaard." See Fried, *Men-*

zel's Realism: Art and Embodiment in Nineteenth-Century Berlin (New Haven, CT: Yale University Press, 2002), 91–92.

15. See Foster, *Shipwreck!*, 46–58, 60; Jules D. Prown, "Winslow Homer in His Art," *Smithsonian Studies in American Art* 1, no. 1 (Spring 1987): 31–45. On figures of shipwrecks and spectators, especially the metaphorical use of shipwrecks by Pascal, Nietzsche, and Jacob Burckhardt to suggest the impossibility of disinterested spectators, see Hans Blumenberg, *Shipwreck with Spectator: Paradigm of a Metaphor for Existence* (Cambridge, MA: MIT Press, 1997). Blumenberg writes, "The metaphorics of embarkation includes the suggestion that living means already being on the high seas, where there is no outcome other than being saved or going down, and no possibility of abstention" (19).

16. John Dewey, *Art as Experience*, in *The Collected Works of John Dewey*, ed. Jo Ann Boydston, *The Later Works, 1925–1953*, vol. 10, *1934*, ed. Harriet Furst Simon, introduction by Abraham Kaplan (Carbondale: Southern Illinois University Press, 2008), 20–21, 47, 163; John Dewey, introduction to *Essays in Experimental Logic*, in *The Collected Works of John Dewey*, ed. Jo Ann Boydston, *The Middle Works, 1899–1924*, vol. 10, *1916–1917*, ed. Anne Sharpe (Carbondale: Southern Illinois University Press, 2008), 326; see also Thomas M. Alexander, *John Dewey's Theory of Art, Experience and Nature: The Horizons of Feeling* (Albany: State University of New York Press, 1987), 110, 204–5.

17. John Ruskin, *The Letters of John Ruskin*, ed. E. T. Cook and Alexander Wedderburn, vol. 1, *1827–1869* (London: George Allen, 1909), 446; Ruskin, *Modern Painters*, vol. 1, in *WJR*, 3:615, 625.

18. Michel Eugène Chevreul, *The Principles of Harmony and Contrast of Colours, and Their Applications to the Arts*, trans. Charles Martel (London: Longman, Brown, Green, and Longmans, 1855), for example, 121, 255, or 367; as quoted in John W. Beatty, "Recollections of an Intimate Friendship," in Lloyd Goodrich, *Winslow Homer* (New York: Macmillan, 1945), 223. For more on Homer and Chevreul, see Patricia Junker, "Expressions of Art and Life in *The Artist's Studio in an Afternoon Fog*," in *Winslow Homer in the 1890s: Prout's Neck Observed* (New York: Hudson Hills Press, 1990), 57–59.

19. Chevreul, *Principles of Harmony*, 121, 122, 256–257; as quoted in Foster, *Shipwreck!*, 68, 110n201.

20. William James, *Principles of Psychology*, 1:287; Dewey, *Art as Experience*, in *Collected Works, The Later Works*, 10:21.

21. Dewey, *Art as Experience*, in *Collected Works, The Later Works, 1925–1953*, 10:29, 42, 135; Alfred North Whitehead, *The Interpretation of Science: Selected Essays*, ed. Allison Heartz Johnson (Indianapolis: Bobbs-Merrill, 1961), 212; *Process and Reality*, 45; Dewey, *Essays in Experimental Logic* (Chicago: University of Chicago Press, 1916), 6; I derive the term from Dewey's *Art as Experience, Collected Works, The Later Works, 1925–1953*, vol. 10, esp. 143–44. See also, D. C. Mathur, "A Note on the Concept of 'Consummatory Experience' in Dewey's Aesthetics," *Journal of Philosophy* 63, no. 9 (April 1966): 225–31.

22. Ralph Waldo Emerson, *The Journals and Miscellaneous Notebooks of Ralph Waldo Emerson*, vol. 14, *1854–1861*, ed. Susan Sutton Smith and Harrison Hayford (Cambridge, MA: The Belknap Press of Harvard University Press, 1978), 179–80; Emerson, "Natural Method of Mental Philosophy, Lecture I: 'Country Life,'" in *The Later Lectures of Ralph Waldo Emerson: 1843–1871*, vol. 2, *1855–1871*, ed. Ronald A. Bosco and Joel Myerson (Athens: University of Georgia Press, 2010), 66.

23. See Gianluigi Guido, *The Salience of Marketing Stimuli: An Incongruity-Salience Hypothesis on Consumer Awareness* (Boston: Kluwer Academic, 2001); see Walter Pagel, *William Harvey's Biological Ideas: Selected Aspects and Historical Background* (Basel: S. Karger, 1967), 256, in reference to Harvey on the *punctum saliens* in *De generatione* (1662); Ralph Waldo Emerson, "Boston," in *The Complete Works of Ralph Waldo Emerson*, vol. 12, *Natural History of Intellect and Other Papers*, ed. Edward W. Emerson (1893; Boston: Houghton, Mifflin, 1904), 188; *Journals and Miscellaneous Notebooks of Ralph Waldo Emerson*, vol. 16, *1866–1882*, ed. Ronald A. Bosco and Glen M. Johnson (Cambridge, MA: The Belknap Press of Harvard University Press, 1982), 6.

24. Ralph Waldo Emerson, *The Journals and Miscellaneous Notebooks of Ralph Waldo Emerson*, vol. 10: *1847–1848*, ed. Merton M. Sealts Jr. (Cambridge, MA: Belknap Press of Harvard University Press, 1973), 141; Emerson, "Spiritual Laws," in *CW*, vol. 2, *Essays: First Series*, ed. Alfred R. Ferguson and Jean Ferguson Carr, introduction and notes by Joseph Slater (Cambridge: Belknap Press of Harvard University Press, 1979), 84; Emerson, "Natural History of Intellect," in *The Complete Works of Ralph Waldo Emerson*, 12:59.

25. Emerson, "Beauty," in *CW*, vol. 6, *The Conduct of Life*, ed. Douglas Emory Wilson, notes by Joseph Slater, introduction by Barbara L. Packer (Cambridge, MA: Belknap Press of Harvard University Press, 2003), 155; Emerson, "Plato; or the Philosopher," in *CW*, vol. 4, *Representative Men: Seven Lectures*, ed. Wallace E. Williams and Douglas Emory Wilson (Cambridge: Belknap Press of Harvard University Press, 1987), 31–32; Emerson, *Journals and Miscellaneous Notebooks*, 10:82.

26. See Steven Schwartzman, *The Words of Mathematics: An Etymological Dictionary of Mathematical Terms Used in English* (Washington, DC: Mathematical Association of America, 1994), 191–92; Emerson, "Natural History of Intellect," in *The Complete Works of Ralph Waldo Emerson*, 12:59.

27. Patricia Junker, "Expressions of Art and Life in *The Artist's Studio in an Afternoon Fog*," 57.

28. As quoted in Marc Simpson, "'You Must Wait, and Wait Patiently': Winslow Homer's Prout's Neck Marines," in *Weatherbeaten: Winslow Homer and Maine*, ed. Thomas A. Denenberg (New Haven, CT: Yale University Press, 2012), 96–97; John Durham Peters, *The Marvelous Clouds: Toward a Philosophy of Elemental Media* (Chicago: University of Chicago Press, 2015), 55; Whitehead, *Process and Reality*, 310; William James, "Human Immortality," in *Writings, 1878–1899*, ed. Gerald E. Myers (New York: Library of America, 1992), 1114–17n6, 1118. Erica Fretwell writes about Fechner's "wave" as a figure for states of consciousness in *Sensory Experiments: Psychophysics, Race, and the Aesthetics of Feeling* (Durham, NC: Duke University Press, 2020), 43.

29. Emerson, *Journals and Miscellaneous Notebooks*, 10:141; Emerson, "Natural History of Intellect," in *The Complete Works of Ralph Waldo Emerson*, 12:27–29; Emerson, *The Journals and Miscellaneous Notebooks of Ralph Waldo Emerson*, vol. 8, *1841–1843*, ed. William H. Gilpin and J. E. Parsons (Cambridge: Belknap Press of Harvard University Press, 1970), 70–71.

30. Alfred North Whitehead, *Modes of Thought* (New York: Free Press, 1966; first published 1938 by Macmillan [New York]), 116.

31. On the use of triangular forms in paintings, see Rebecca Zorach, *The Passionate Triangle* (Chicago: University of Chicago Press, 2011); Herman Melville, *Moby-Dick, or*

The Whale, ed. Harrison Hayford, Hershel Parker, and G. Thomas Tanselle (Evanston, IL: Northwestern University Press and The Newberry Library, 1988), 573; Emerson, "Spiritual Laws," in *CW*, 2:84.

32. Theodore E. Stebbins Jr., "Driftwood: Winslow Homer's Final Painting," *Magazine Antiques* 150, no. 1 (July 1996): 72, 75.

33. Walt Whitman, *Leaves of Grass* (1855), in *Complete Poetry and Collected Prose*, ed. Justin Kaplan (New York: Library of America, 1982), 47; Alfred Schutz, *Reflections on the Problem of Relevance*, in *Collected Papers V. Phenomenology and the Social Sciences*, ed. Lester Embree (New York: Springer Sciences, 2011), 113.

34. Charles Colbert, "Winslow Homer, Reluctant Modern," *Winterthur Portfolio* 38, no. 1 (Spring 2003): 50.

35. Thomas M. Alexander, describing Dewey's sense of an aesthetic experience as the moment when the "horizon of meaning," usually only "tacit" or in the background, comes to consciousness *as* an experience, in *John Dewey's Theory of Art*, 202; F. C. S. Schiller, from the chapter "Relevance," in *Logic for Use: An Introduction to the Voluntarist Theory of Knowledge* (New York: Harcourt, Brace, 1930), 78-79; William James, *The Principles of Psychology*, 1:256.

36. Alexander, *John Dewey's Theory of Art*, 202; John Dewey, *Experience and Nature*, in *Collected Works, The Later Works, 1925–1953*, 1:235, 238; Joseph Jastrow, *The Subconscious* (1905; Boston: Houghton, Mifflin, 1906), 8. On *Right and Left*, see John Wilmerding, "Winslow Homer's *Right and Left*," *Studies in the History of Art* 9 (1980): 59–85. I am quoting from page 85. On *Searchlight on Harbor Entrance, Santiago de Cuba*, see Nicolai Cikovsky Jr., "Homer around 1900," *Studies in the History of Art* 26 (1990): 133–54, esp. 150.

37. David Tatham, "Winslow Homer and the Sea," in *Winslow Homer in the 1890s: Prout's Neck Observed* (New York: Hudson Hills Press, 1990), 73–76. Maury's book, first published in 1855, became a best seller and went through eight editions in the United States and Britain. Homer may have attended Maury's lectures in Boston and his Lowell Lectures at Harvard in 1856. Maury is also cited at length in George Chaplin Child's *Benedicite: The Great Architect* (New York: G. P. Putnam and Sons, 1871), which Homer owned; inside his copy of Child's book, Homer pasted a print of a portrait of Maury. See Matthew Fontaine Maury, *The Physical Geography of the Sea* (New York: Harper and Brothers, 1855), 25–26, 34, 36–37.

38. In a letter from Homer to his art dealer, M. Knoedler, February 17, 1902, as cited in Randall C. Griffin, *Winslow Homer: An American Vision* (New York: Phaidon Press, 2006), 201, and Peter H. Wood, *Weathering the Storm: Inside Winslow Homer's "Gulf Stream"* (Athens: University of Georgia Press, 2004), 42; the critic is John Seelye in *New Republic* (January 1973), as quoted in Wood, *Weathering the Storm*, 42. See also Cikovsky, "Homer around 1900."

39. Matthew Fontaine Maury, *The Physical Geography of the Sea*, 28–29; William James, *Principles of Psychology*, I, on p. 70, for example, and in chapters 4 and 9 especially.

Chapter 6

1. Lawrence Venuti, introduction to Jacques Derrida, "What Is a 'Relevant' Translation?," trans. Lawrence Venuti, *Critical Inquiry* 27 (Winter 2001): 169–73. See Ernst-

August Gutt, *Translation and Relevance: Cognition and Context* (Oxford: Basil Blackwell, 1991).

2. Dan Sperber and Deirdre Wilson, *Relevance: Communication and Cognition*, 2nd ed. (Oxford: Blackwell, 1995; first published 1986), 59, 237–43. I am building on a familiar example from relevance theory discussed on page 239 and first discussed in Julia Jorgensen, George A. Miller, and Dan Sperber, "Test of the Mention Theory of Irony," *Journal of Experimental Psychology* 113, no. 1 (1984): 112–20; Deirdre Wilson and Dan Sperber, *Meaning and Relevance* (Cambridge: Cambridge University Press, 2012), 92–96, 123–45; Terence Cave and Deirdre Wilson, introduction to *Reading beyond the Code: Literature and Relevance Theory*, ed. Terence Cave and Deirdre Wilson (Oxford: Oxford University Press, 2018), 11–12, 196–98; Martin Davies, "Philosophy of Language," *The Blackwell Companion to Philosophy*, ed. Nicholas Bunnin and E. P. Tsui-James, 2nd ed. (Oxford: Blackwell, 2003), 132–39; Herbert H. Clark and Richard J. Gerrig, "On the Pretense Theory of Irony," *Irony in Language and Thought: A Cognitive Science Reader*, ed. Raymond W. Gibbs Jr. and Herbert L. Colston (New York: Taylor and Francis, 2007), 25–33.

3. Gutt, *Translation and Relevance*, 42–44; Terence Cave, *Thinking with Literature: Towards a Cognitive Criticism* (Oxford: Oxford University Press, 2016), 26–28, 110–14; Sperber and Wilson, *Relevance*, 49.

4. Billy Clark, *Relevance Theory* (Cambridge: Cambridge University Press, 2013), 48; Sperber and Wilson, *Relevance*, 32–35; Paul Grice, *Studies in the Way of Words* (Cambridge, MA: Harvard University Press, 1991), 22–57. Grice inspired later work in linguistic pragmatics by trying to explain how we make inferences about what speakers are communicating indirectly and by distinguishing between "what is said" by an utterance and what Grice called its "implicatures." For Grice, understanding "implicatures" always involves context but also a certain amount of intuition on the part of listeners. Sperber and Wilson build on Grice's ideas about how cognition works in communication for their "theory of relevance." See also Dan Sperber and Deirdre Wilson, "Pragmatics," *Cognition* 10 (1981): 281–86.

5. Cave and Wilson, introduction to *Reading beyond the Code*, 3, 4, 10; Deirdre Wilson, "Relevance Theory and Literary Interpretation," in Cave and Wilson, *Reading beyond the Code*, 194; Deirdre Wilson and Dan Sperber, "Relevance Theory," in *The Handbook of Pragmatics*, ed. Laurence R. Horn and Gregory Ward (Oxford: Blackwell, 2006), 608.

6. Sperber and Wilson, *Relevance*, 33, 103, 152, 183, 217.

7. Sperber and Wilson, *Relevance*, 49; Clark, *Relevance Theory*, 7.

8. Sperber and Wilson, *Relevance*, 142, 264–266; Wilson and Sperber, *Meaning and Relevance*, 176. In *Conceptual Relevance* (Amsterdam: B. R. Grüner, 1989), Joseph Grünfeld, building on critics Ian Hacking and N. R. Hanson, writes that "we notice things only when we have expectations that will make them seem interesting" (110).

9. Sperber and Wilson, *Relevance*, 265–66; Deirdre Wilson and Dan Sperber, "Pragmatics and Time," in *Relevance Theory: Applications and Implications*, ed. Robyn Carston and Seiji Uchida (Amsterdam: John Benjamins, 1998), 8; Wilson and Sperber, *Meaning and Relevance*, 176.

10. Sperber and Wilson, *Relevance*, 109, 118, 265. See also my discussion in chapter 4 of Schutz's very similar ideas about relevance, cognitive processing, and the phenomenology of time.

11. Gutt, *Translation and Relevance*, 41; Sperber and Wilson, *Relevance*, 203, 219; on "background," 137–38 or 209–11, 214–17.

12. Sperber and Wilson, *Relevance*, 218, 224; see also p. 192 on "clues"; Gutt, *Translation and Relevance*, 128; Cave, *Thinking with Literature*, 38, 91.

13. Stanley Cavell, "Aesthetic Problems of Modern Philosophy," in *Philosophy in America*, ed. Max Black (Ithaca, NY: Cornell University Press, 1965); reprinted in Stanley Cavell, *Must We Mean What We Say?* (Cambridge: Cambridge University Press, 1976), 73–96; John R. Searle, *Expression and Meaning: Studies in the Theory of Speech Acts* (New York: Cambridge University Press, 1979), 94–95; see also Adrian Pilkington, *Poetic Effects: A Relevance Theory Perspective* (Philadelphia: John Benjamins, 2000), 94–95; William Shakespeare, *Romeo and Juliet*, in *The Arden Shakespeare Complete Works*, ed. Richard Proudfoot, Ann Thompson, and David Scott Kastan (Walton-on-Thames: Thomas Nelson, 1998), 2.2.2–3; Alastair Fowler, "A New Theory of Communication," *London Review of Books*, March 20, 1989, 16–17. See also Raphael Lyne, "Relevance across History," in Cave and Wilson, *Reading beyond the Code*, 40.

14. Terence Cave, *Thinking with Literature: Towards a Cognitive Criticism*, 142; John Dewey, *Art as Experience*, in *The Collected Works of John Dewey*, ed. Jo Ann Boydston, *The Later Works, 1925–1953*, vol. 10, *1934*, ed. Harriet Furst Simon, introduction by Abraham Kaplan (Carbondale: Southern Illinois University Press, 2008), 246; Terence Cave and Deirdre Wilson, preface to Cave and Wilson, *Reading beyond the Code*, v.

15. Gutt, *Translation and Relevance*, 10, 41, 53, 74, 127.

16. Gutt, *Translation and Relevance*, 56–57, 130; William Frawley, review of *Translation and Relevance: Cognition and Context*, by Ernst-August Gutt, *Journal of Linguistics* 28, no. 2 (September 1992), 517.

17. Gutt, *Translation and Relevance*, 102–6. Gutt is discussing Robert M. Adams's discussion of C. K. Scott-Moncrieff's translation of Stendhal's *Le rouge et le noir*.

18. Jacques Derrida, "What Is a 'Relevant' Translation?," trans. Lawrence Venuti, *Critical Inquiry* 27 (Winter 2001): 176–78, 181–82.

19. Derrida, 177–78.

20. Derrida, 179, 181–83.

21. Derrida, 194–97.

22. Philippe Büttgen, "Aufheben," in *Dictionary of Untranslatables: A Philosophical Lexicon*, ed. Barbara Cassin, trans. Steven Rendall, Christian Hubert, Jeffrey Mehlman, Nathanael Stein, and Michael Syrotinski (Princeton, NJ: Princeton University Press, 2014), 71–75; see "Sublation" in Glenn Alexander Magee, *The Hegel Dictionary* (New York: Continuum, 2010), 236; and Michael Inwood, *A Hegel Dictionary* (Cambridge, MA: Blackwell's, 1992), 283–85; G. W. F. Hegel, *Science of Logic*, in Stephen Houlgate, *The Opening of Hegel's "Logic": From Being to Infinity* (West Lafayette: Purdue University Press, 2006), 201; Derrida, "What Is a 'Relevant' Translation?," 196.

23. Derrida, "What Is a 'Relevant' Translation?," 196, 198; Büttgen, "Aufheben," 74; Jacques Derrida, "What Is a 'Relevant' Translation?," 117, 196–97, 199–200.

24. Alfred Schutz, *On Phenomenology and Social Relations: Selected Writings*, ed. Helmut R. Wagner (Chicago: University of Chicago Press, 1970), 90, 97, or 106; Friedrich Nietzsche, *The Gay Science*, ed. Bernard Williams, trans. Josefine Nauckhoff (Cambridge: Cambridge University Press, 2001), 83.

Chapter 7

1. Alfred North Whitehead, *Process and Reality: An Essay in Cosmology*, ed. David Ray Griffin and Donald W. Sherburne (New York: Free Press, 1978; first published 1929 by Macmillan [New York]), 15–16, 27, 32, 45, 105, 189, 257; Louis Menand, *The Metaphysical Club: A Story of Ideas in America* (New York: Farrar, Straus and Giroux, 2001), 369.

2. Whitehead, *Process and Reality*, 15, 23, 47, 86, 105, 185, 244, 280, 344, 346; Isabelle Stengers, *Thinking with Whitehead: A Free and Wild Creation of Concepts*, trans. Michael Chase (Cambridge, MA: Harvard University Press, 2011), 421; Alfred North Whitehead, *The Interpretation of Science: Selected Essays*, ed. Allison Heartz Johnson (Indianapolis: Bobbs-Merrill, 1961), 212.

3. Whitehead, *Process and Reality*, 16, 32, 41, 46, 50, 62, 87, 185–86; Alfred North Whitehead, *Modes of Thought* (New York: Free Press, 1966; first published 1938 by Macmillan [New York]), 74.

4. Whitehead, *Process and Reality*, 32, 46, 48, 79, 185–187, 278, 344, 351; Whitehead describes the "envisagement of the realm of all eternal objects" in *Science and the Modern World* (1925; New York: Macmillan, 1948), 154. "Also," he says, "in the nature of the eternal activity there must stand an envisagement of all values to be obtained by a real togetherness of eternal objects, as envisaged in ideal situations" (154); Stengers, *Thinking with Whitehead*, 455, 477; Alfred North Whitehead, "Immortality," in *Science and Philosophy* (New York: Philosophical Library, 1948), 85; Whitehead, *Modes of Thought*, 79; for more on this kind of "speculation" in Whitehead, see Nicholas Gaskill and A. J. Nocek, "Introduction: An Adventure of Thought" in *The Lure of Whitehead*, ed. Nicholas Gaskill and A. J. Nocek (Minneapolis: University of Minnesota Press, 2014), 11–40.

5. Whitehead, *Modes of Thought*, 100, 102; *Process and Reality*, 16, 40, 210, 252, 280, 351.

6. Stengers, *Thinking with Whitehead*, 358, 421; Whitehead, *Process and Reality*, 86–87, 268, 278, 280; William Lapoujade, *William James: Empiricism and Pragmatism*, trans. Thomas Lamarre (Durham, NC: Duke University Press, 2020), 57.

7. Stengers, *Thinking with Whitehead*, 358, 447, 484, italics added; Whitehead, *Process and Reality*, 345–347; W. H. Auden, *A Certain World*, in *The Complete Works of W. H. Auden*, vol. 6, *1969–1973*, ed. by Edward Mendelson (Princeton, NJ: Princeton University Press), 235; Walter Benjamin, *Illuminations*, trans. Harry Zohn, ed. Hannah Arendt (New York: Schocken Books, 1968), 134. Benjamin is quoting Nicolas Malebranche and speaking of Franz Kafka.

8. Whitehead, *Process and Reality*, 213, 339; Alfred Schutz, *On Phenomenology and Social Relations: Selected Writings*, ed. Helmut R. Wagner (Chicago: University of Chicago Press, 1970), 40; Lapoujade, *William James*, 17, 57; John Dewey, *Art as Experience*, in *The Collected Works of John Dewey*, ed. Jo Ann Boydston, *The Later Works, 1925–1953*, vol. 10, *1934*, ed. Harriet Furst Simon, introduction by Abraham Kaplan (Carbondale: Southern Illinois University Press, 2008), 48.

9. William James to Oliver Wendell Holmes Jr., May 15, 1868, *The Correspondence of William James*, vol. 4, *1856–1877*, ed. Ignas K. Skrupskelis and Elizabeth M. Berkeley (Charlottesville: University of Virginia Press, 1995), 303; John Dewey, *A Common Faith*, in *The Collected Works of John Dewey*, ed. Jo Ann Boydston, *The Later Works, 1925–1953*, vol. 9: *1933–1934*, ed. Anne Sharpe (Carbondale, IL: Southern Illinois University Press, 2008), 13, 29, 30, 34. See Joan Richardson for a nuanced discussion of James's project

to "widen the field of search for God" and to redescribe "God" and religious thought as an accommodation of preexisting elements and thoughts to the "varieties" of new experiences, where they are given new meaning; *Pragmatism and American Experience: An Introduction* (New York: Cambridge University Press, 2014), esp. 37–40.

10. Dewey, *A Common Faith*, in *Collected Works, The Later Works, 1925–1953*, 9:36; *Art as Experience*, in *Collected Works, The Later Works, 1925–1953*, 10: 48; George Santayana, *Interpretations of Poetry and Religion* (1900), ed. William G. Holzberger and Herman J. Saatkamp Jr. (Cambridge, MA: MIT Press, 1989), 47; Whitehead, *Process and Reality*, 105.

11. William James, *The Varieties of Religious Experience*, in *Writings: 1902–1910*, ed. Bruce Kuklick (New York: Library of America, 1987), 190; James, *Pragmatism: A New Name for Some Old Ways of Thinking*, in *Writings: 1902–1910*, ed. Bruce Kuklick (New York: Library of America, 1987), 567; Ralph Waldo Emerson, "Natural History of Intellect," in *The Complete Works of Ralph Waldo Emerson*, vol. 12, *Natural History of Intellect and Other Papers*, ed. Edward W. Emerson (1893; Boston: Houghton, Mifflin, 1904), 43; from the manuscript for Gladys Thayer's "Reminiscences," Archives of American Art, Smithsonian, as quoted in Nelson C. White, *Abbott H. Thayer: Painter and Naturalist* (1951; repr., Hartford: Connecticut Printers, 1967), 194; Letter from Abbott Thayer to Mr. Chesterton, April 17, 1907, as quoted in Susan Hobbs, "Nature into Art: The Landscapes of Abbott Handerson Thayer," *The American Art Journal* 14.3 (Summer 1982): 18–19, 19n49, 33–35. On Thayer's replica of Daniel Chester French's bust of Emerson, see Hobbs, "Nature into Art," 18–19 and White, *Abbott H. Thayer*, 95; at Thayer's home, "Emerson seemed almost a presiding genius" (White, 95). Ralph Waldo Emerson, "Spiritual Laws," in *The Collected Works of Ralph Waldo Emerson* (hereafter *CW*), vol. 2, *Essays: First Series*, ed. Alfred R. Ferguson and Jean Ferguson Carr, introduction and notes by Joseph Slater (Cambridge, MA: Belknap Press of Harvard University Press, 1979), 84. On Thayer's interest in Emerson's "Spiritual Laws" (which he called "my Bible"), see Hobbs, 19n49 and White, 37.

12. Ralph Waldo Emerson, "Nominalist and Realist," in *CW*, vol. 3, *Essays: Second Series*, ed. Alfred R. Ferguson and Jean Ferguson Carr, introduction and notes by Joseph Slater (Cambridge, MA: Belknap Press of Harvard University Press, 1983), 140, 142; Ralph Waldo Emerson, "Natural History of Intellect," in *The Complete Works of Ralph Waldo Emerson*, 12:27–28; Ralph Waldo Emerson, "Intellect," in *CW*, vol. 2, *Essays: First Series*, 194, 198.

13. The critic William Howe Downes on Thayer's *Angel* when it was shown at the Museum of Fine Arts in Boston in 1888, as quoted in Richard Murray, "Abbott Thayer's 'Stevenson Memorial,'" *American Art* 13, no. 2 (Summer 1999): 8; Thayer in a letter to Emma Beach, May 8, 1902, as quoted in Kristin Schwain, *Signs of Grace: Religion and American Art in the Gilded Age* (Ithaca, NY: Cornell University Press, 2008), 121; Gladys Thayer, from the manuscript for her "Reminiscences," as quoted in Hobbs, "Nature into Art," 32; Homer Saint-Gaudens, "Abbott H. Thayer," *Critic and Literary World* 46, no. 5 (1905): 423, as quoted in Schwain, *Signs of Grace*, 126.

14. William James, *The Principles of Psychology* (1890; New York: Dover, 1950), 1:243; Thayer to Rockwell Kent, as quoted in Ross Anderson, *Abbott Handerson Thayer* (Syracuse, NY: Everson Museum of Art, 1982), 71.

15. Whitehead, *Process and Reality*, 15, 185; William James, "On Some Omissions of Introspective Psychology," in *Essays in Psychology* (Cambridge, MA: Harvard University

Press, 1983), 157–159, 160n6, 164. Thayer refused to explain his angels to critics except to say that they "symbolize an exalted atmosphere," as quoted in Richard Murray, "Abbott Thayer's 'Stevenson Memorial,'" 3. For more on Thayer's angels, see Kevin M. Murphy, *"Not Theories but Revelations": The Art and Science of Abbott Handerson Thayer* (Williamstown, MA: Williams College Museum of Art, 2016).

16. Thayer is writing to Royal Cortissoz, an art historian and the art critic for the *New York Herald Tribune*, as quoted in the introductory note to *Abbott H. Thayer Memorial Exhibition* (New York: The Metropolitan Museum of Art, 1922), xvi.

17. Alexander Nemerov, "Vanishing Americans: Abbott Thayer, Theodore Roosevelt, and the Attraction of Camouflage," *American Art* 11, no. 2 (Summer 1997): 51; Murphy, *"Not Theories but Revelations,"* 79; see also 60–87; Ross Anderson, *Abbott Handerson Thayer*, 121; Hannah Rose Shell, *Hide and Seek: Camouflage, Photography, and the Media of Reconnaissance* (New York: Zone Books, 2012), 59–62; E. B. Titchener, review of *An Arraignment of the Theories of Mimicry and Warning Colors* and *Concealing Coloration in the Animal Kingdom: An Exposition of the Laws of Disguise through Color and Pattern*, by Abbott H. Thayer, in *American Journal of Psychology* 21, no. 3 (July 1910): 504.

18. Gerald Handerson Thayer, with Abbott Handerson Thayer, *Concealing-Coloration in the Animal Kingdom: An Exposition of the Laws of Disguise through Color and Pattern: Being a Summary of Abbott H. Thayer's Discoveries* (New York: Macmillan, 1909), 4, 7, 88, 153–55, 185, 244.

19. Titchener, review of *Arraignment of the Theories of Mimicry*, 500; Thayer and Thayer, *Concealing-Coloration in the Animal Kingdom*, 19, 35, 38, 39, 93; Thayer discounts theories of animals mimicking their natural surroundings, suggesting that the "notion of resemblance" does not properly capture the evolutionary effect of making the animal disappear: "Mimicry makes an animal appear to be some other thing, whereas this newly discovered law makes him cease to appear to exist at all. The spectator seems to see right through the space really occupied by an opaque animal"; see Thayer, "The Law Which Underlies Protective Coloration," *The Auk* 13 (April 1896), 126, as quoted in Shell, *Hide and Seek*, 29; while relying on evolutionary theories, Thayer was nonetheless challenged by scientists for discounting sexual selection as a plausible cause for animal coloration; see Murphy, *"Not Theories but Revelations,"* esp. 82.

20. Thayer and Thayer, *Concealing-Coloration in the Animal Kingdom*, 15, 19, 38–39, 150, 153, 168, 179; Thayer calls some of his illustrations "hole-picturing"; Jno. H. Sage, "Fourteenth Congress of the American Ornithologists' Union," *Auk* 14, no. 1 (January 1897): 85.

21. Thayer and Thayer, *Concealing-Coloration in the Animal Kingdom*, 3; Thayer, "The Titanic's Fate in a New Light: Abbott Thayer Tells Why Icebergs Are Invisible at Night," *New York Tribune* (February 15, 1914): 11, as quoted in Murphy, *"Not Theories but Revelations,"* 102; William James, *The Principles of Psychology*, 1:585.

22. On the *Titanic* and Thayer's theory of icebergs, see Thayer, "Titanic's Fate in a New Light," 11 and Murphy, *"Not Theories but Revelations,"* 101–4; Thayer as quoted in Murphy, 104; Shell, *Hide and Seek*, 72, and 71–74; see also Thayer to Sargent as quoted in Murphy, *"Not Theories but Revelations,"* 92–96.

23. See Shell, *Hide and Seek*, 73; Murphy, *"Not Theories but Revelations,"* 96, 99–100.

24. Ralph Waldo Emerson, "Monadnoc," in *Collected Poems and Translations* (New York: Library of America, 1994), 50, 59; Schwain, *Signs of Grace*, 111; Thayer's draft of a

letter to potential buyers as quoted in White, *Abbott H. Thayer*, 142; see also Anderson, *Abbott Handerson Thayer*, 107–8.

25. Murphy, *"Not Theories but Revelations,"* 51; *Abbott H. Thayer Memorial Exhibition* (New York: Metropolitan Museum of Art, 1922), xvi; Elizabeth Lee, "Therapeutic Beauty: Abbott Thayer, Antimodernism, and the Fear of Disease," *American Art* 18, no. 3 (Fall 2004): 42; see also Nemerov, "Vanishing Americans," and Schwain, *Signs of Grace*; Erin Kinhart and Jayna Josefson, "Why Abbott Thayer and His Family Slept Outside during a Polar Vortex," *Archives of American Art Blog, Smithsonian Magazine*, January 2, 2018, https://www.smithsonianmag.com/blogs/archives-american-art/2018/01/02/extreme-sleeping-thayer-family-outdoor-sleeping-huts/.

26. Nemerov, "Vanishing Americans," 56; *Abbott H. Thayer Memorial Exhibition*, xviii; Dewey, *Art as Experience*, in *Collected Works, The Later Works, 1925–1953*, 10:278; Laurence Buermeyer, *The Aesthetic Experience*, 2nd ed. (Merion, PA: Barnes Foundation Press, 1929), 17; Emerson, "Intellect," in *CW*, vol. 2, *Essays: First Series*, 194; "Natural History of Intellect," in *Complete Works of Ralph Waldo Emerson*, 12:91; "The American Scholar," in *CW*, vol. 1, *Nature, Addresses, and Lectures*, ed. Alfred R. Ferguson, introduction and notes by Robert E. Spiller (Cambridge, MA: Belknap Press of Harvard University Press, 1971), 60.

27. Gladys Thayer as quoted in White, *Abbott H. Thayer*, 192–193; Ralph Waldo Emerson, "Self-Reliance," in *CW*, vol. 2, *Essays: First Series*, ed. Alfred R. Ferguson and Jean Ferguson Carr, introduction and notes by Joseph Slater (Cambridge, MA: Belknap Press of Harvard University Press, 1979), 30; Stanley Cavell, *Emerson's Transcendental Etudes*, ed. David Justin Hodge (Stanford, CA: Stanford University Press, 2003), 27–30.

28. Lapoujade, *William James*, 57; Emerson, "Intellect," in *CW*, 2:198.

Chapter 8

1. As quoted in Dewey F. Mosby, *Across Continents and Cultures: The Art and Life of Henry Ossawa Tanner* (Kansas City: Nelson-Atkins Museum of Art, 1995), 31; Alain Locke, *Negro Art: Past and Present* (Washington, DC: Associates in Negro Folk Education, 1936), 22; see also Alain Locke, "The Legacy of the Ancestral Arts," in *The New Negro*, ed. Alain Locke, introduction by Arnold Rampersad (1925; New York: Atheneum, 1992), 264–66, and discussion in Alan C. Braddock, "Christian Cosmopolitanism: Henry Ossawa Tanner and the Beginning of the End of Race," in *Henry Ossawa Tanner: Modern Spirit*, ed. Anna O. Marley (Philadelphia: Pennsylvania Academy of Fine Arts and University of California Press, 2012), 140–41; from a review in the *Philadelphia Daily Evening Telegraph* as quoted in Marcia M. Matthews, *Henry Ossawa Tanner: American Artist* (Chicago: University of Chicago Press, 1969), 70.

2. Alain Locke, "The Concept of Race as Applied to Social Culture," in *The Works of Alain Locke* (hereafter *WAL*), ed. Charles Molesworth (New York: Oxford University Press, 2012), 275; John Dewey, "Introduction: Reconstruction as Seen Twenty-Five Years Later," *Reconstruction in Philosophy*, enl. edition (Boston: Beach Press, 1948; reprint Mineola, NY: Dover, 2004; first published 1920 by Henry Holt [New York]), iv–v; Booker T. Washington, *Up from Slavery: An Autobiography* (1901; New York: Dover, 1995).

3. Alain Locke, "Negro Youth Speaks," in *The New Negro*, ed. Alain Locke, introduction by Arnold Rampersad (1925; New York: Atheneum, 1992), 48.

4. Locke, 48, 50; Alain Locke, "The New Negro," in *The New Negro*, ed. Alain Locke, introduction by Arnold Rampersad (1925; New York: Atheneum, 1992), 3–4. Locke, "The Concept of Race as Applied to Social Culture," 270. Locke describes a "mission of revitalizing Negro life today through the revival and rediscovery of its heroic past" in a speech on the anniversary of Frederick Douglass's escape from slavery, "Frederick Douglass's 'Life and Times,'" in *The Works of Alain Locke*, ed. Charles Molesworth (New York: Oxford University Press, 2012), 321.

5. Alain Locke, "The Legacy of the Ancestral Arts," in *WAL*, 191; Alain Locke, "A Functional View of Value Ultimates," in *WAL*, 485; Alain Locke, "Negro Youth Speaks," 48; Alain Locke, "Émile Verhaeren," in *WAL*, 33; W. E. B. Du Bois, "The New Negro," *Crisis* 31 (1926), as quoted in Ross Posnock, *Color and Culture: Black Writers and the Making of the Modern Intellectual* (Cambridge, MA: Harvard University Press, 1998), 144; "President Harding and Social Equality," *Writings* (New York: Library of America, 1986), 1189; "Criteria of Negro Art," *Writings* (New York: Library of America, 1986), 1000; Alain Locke, "Art or Propaganda?," in *WAL*, 219; see also Leonard Harris, "The Great Debate: W. E. B. Du Bois vs. Alain Locke on the Aesthetic," *Philosophia Africana* 7, no. 1 (March 2004): 15–39.

6. Henry James to H. G. Wells, July 10, 1915, in Henry James, *A Life in Letters*, ed. Philip Horne (New York: Penguin Books, 1999), 555; Locke, "Functional View of Value Ultimates," 484. For an account of W. James's influence on Locke at Oxford and beyond, see Ross Posnock, *Color and Culture*, esp. 189–96.

7. John Dewey's eulogy for F. C. S. Schiller delivered at the New School for Social Research, November 28, 1937, in Allen Shields, "F. C. S. Schiller: An Unpublished Memorial by John Dewey," *Transactions of the Charles S. Peirce Society* 3, no. 2 (Fall 1967), 51–54; Locke on Schiller as quoted in Jeffrey C. Stewart, *The New Negro: The Life of Alain Locke* (Oxford: Oxford University Press, 2018), 153.

8. Locke, "Values and Imperatives," in *WAL*, 452–53, 455–57.

9. Locke, 454–55; "Value," in *WAL*, 465.

10. Locke, "Values and Imperatives," 454–56; "Value," 466–68; Ralph Barton Perry, *General Theory of Value: Its Meaning and Basic Principles Construed in Terms of Interest* (1926; Cambridge, MA: Harvard University Press, 1950), 213, and the three chapters titled "Modes of Interest"; see also *Realms of Value: A Critique of Human Civilization* (Cambridge, MA: Harvard University Press, 1954).

11. Locke, "Value," 468, 474; "Values and Imperatives," 462–63; "Functional View of Value Ultimates," 477.

12. Locke, "Functional View of Value Ultimates," 479.

13. Locke, "Value," 473, 475; F. C. S. Schiller, *Logic for Use: An Introduction to the Voluntarist Theory of Knowledge* (New York: Harcourt, Brace, 1930), 77, 79; Locke, "Concept of Race as Applied to Social Culture," 274.

14. Locke, "Value," 475; Paul W. Taylor, *Normative Discourse: A Modern Study in General Theory of Value Using the Technique and Approach of Contemporary Philosophical Analysis* (Englewood Cliffs, NJ: Prentice-Hall, 1961), 155–56; Leonard Harris, "Rendering the Text," in *The Philosophy of Alain Locke: Harlem Renaissance and Beyond*, ed. Leonard Harris (Philadelphia: Temple University Press, 1989), 19; Locke, "Functional View of Value Ultimates," 481, 479; "Concept of Race as Applied to Social Culture," 269.

15. Locke, "Values and Imperatives," 456–57, 46–62; "Functional View of Value Ultimates," 479, 484.

16. John Dewey, *Experience and Nature*, in *The Collected Works of John Dewey*,

ed. Jo Ann Boydston, *The Later Works, 1925–1953*, vol. 1, *1925*, ed. Patricia Baysinger and Barbara Levine (Carbondale: Southern Illinois University Press, 2008), 296–99; "expansion and emancipation of values" is Dewey's term, 305; Locke, "Concept of Race as Applied to Social Culture," 270; "Functional View of Value Ultimates," 485; "Value," 474; Alain Locke, "Self Criticism: The Third Dimension in Culture," in *WAL*, 489.

17. Dewey, *Experience and Nature*, 259; Charles Molesworth, introduction to *WAL*, xxxi; Alain Locke, "Value and Imperatives," in *WAL*, 463, 464.

18. Contemporary reviewers on the painting as quoted in Kristin Schwain, *Signs of Grace: Religion and American Art in the Gilded Age* (Ithaca, NY: Cornell University Press, 2008), 46, 66; Henry James, *The Art of the Novel: Critical Prefaces by Henry James*, introduction by R. P. Blackmur (1934; Chicago: University of Chicago Press, 2011), 257.

19. Jesse Ossawa Tanner, introduction to *Henry Ossawa Tanner: American Artist*, by Marcia M. Matthews (Chicago: University of Chicago Press, 1969), xii.

20. See Marcus Bruce, *Henry Ossawa Tanner: A Spiritual Biography* (New York: Crossroad, 2002), 120; Laurence Buermeyer, *The Aesthetic Experience*, 2nd ed. (Merion, PA: Barnes Foundation Press, 1929), 155.

21. Henry Ossawa Tanner, "Story of an Artist's Life," *World's Work* 18 (July 1909): 11774; Albert C. Barnes and Violette de Mazia, *The Art of Henri-Matisse* (New York: Charles Scribner's Sons, 1933), 31.

22. Marcus Bruce quotes from Hebrews 11:1 to describe each Tanner work as "the assurance of things hoped for, the conviction of things not seen," in *Henry Ossawa Tanner*, 13; Oscar L. Joseph, "Henry O. Tanner's Religious Paintings," *Epworth Herald*, March 6, 1909, as quoted in Robert Cozzolino, "'I Invited the Christ Spirit to Manifest in Me': Tanner and Symbolism," in *Henry Ossawa Tanner: Modern Spirit* (Philadelphia: Pennsylvania Academy of Fine Arts and University of California Press, 2012), 123; Tanner, "Story of an Artist's Life," 11774.

23. Locke, "Functional View of Value Ultimates," 484–85; "The New Negro," 4; Monroe C. Beardsley, "The Creation of Art," in *The Aesthetic Point of View: Selected Essays*, ed. Michael J. Wreen and Donald M. Callen (Ithaca, NY: Cornell University Press, 1982), 259; Jesse Ossawa Tanner in a letter to Tanner's biographer Marcia M. Matthews as quoted in Cozzolino, "'I Invited the Christ Spirit to Manifest in Me,'" 120.

24. From Hale Woodruff's interview with Tanner in 1928, "My Meeting with Henry O. Tanner," *The Crisis* 77, no. 1 (January 1970), 11; Alain Locke, "Émile Verhaeren," in *WAL*, 33.

25. John Dewey, *Art as Experience*, in *The Collected Works of John Dewey*, ed. Jo Ann Boydston, *The Later Works, 1925–1953*, vol. 10, *1934*, ed. Harriet Furst Simon, introduction by Abraham Kaplan (Carbondale: Southern Illinois University Press, 2008), 73; Alfred North Whitehead, *Science and the Modern World* (1925; New York: Macmillan, 1948), 286–87.

26. Eviatar Zerubavel, *Hidden in Plain Sight: The Social Structure of Irrelevance* (Oxford: Oxford University Press, 2015), 52, 63; Albert C. Barnes and Violette de Mazia, "Expression and Form," in John Dewey, Albert C. Barnes, Laurence Buermeyer, Mary Mullen, and Violette de Mazia, *Art and Education: A Collection of Essays*, 3rd ed. (Merion, PA: Barnes Foundation Press, 1954; first published 1929 by the Barnes Foundation), 176; Alfred North Whitehead, *Modes of Thought* (New York: Free Press, 1966; first published 1938 by Macmillan [New York]), 102.

27. Zerubavel, *Hidden in Plain Sight*, 28, 57; Zerubavel writes, "What we consider relevant and therefore tend to notice also varies across different settings and social occa-

sions within the same society" (57); Charles Derber, *The Pursuit of Attention: Power and Ego in Everyday Life*, 2nd ed. (New York: Oxford University Press, 2000), 15, and Erving Goffman, *Forms of Talk* (Philadelphia: University of Pennsylvania Press, 1981), 132, as quoted in Zerubavel, 28; see also Eviatar Zerubavel, *The Fine Line: Making Distinctions in Everyday Life* (New York: Free Press, 1991) and Alfred Schutz, *The Phenomenology of the Social World*, trans. George Walsh and Frederick Lehnert (Evanston, IL: Northwestern University Press, 1967).

28. Alfred Schutz, *On Phenomenology and Social Relations: Selected Writings*, ed. Helmut R. Wagner (Chicago: University of Chicago Press, 1970), 43, 114–17, 159, 209; Henry David Thoreau, "A Plea for Captain John Brown," in *Collected Essays and Poems*, ed. Elizabeth Hall Witherell (New York: Library of America, 2001), 407; Robert B. Pippin, *After the Beautiful: Hegel and the Philosophy of Pictorial Modernism* (Chicago: University of Chicago Press, 2014), 97; Henry David Thoreau, "Civil Disobedience," in *Collected Essays and Poems*, 206, 212; for more on "recognition," see Axel Honneth, *The Struggle for Recognition: The Moral Grammar of Social Conflicts* (Cambridge, MA: MIT Press, 1995), and Charles Taylor, "The Politics of Recognition," in *Multiculturalism and "The Politics of Recognition": An Essay with Commentary*, ed. Amy Gutmann (Princeton, NJ: Princeton University Press, 1992), 25–73; Locke, "Value," 465; Locke describes the philosophical work of "reconstruction" in his essays on value—see, for example, "Values and Imperatives," 464.

29. W. S. Scarborough, "Henry Ossian [*sic*] Tanner," *Southern Workman* 31 (December 1902): 666, as quoted in Dewey F. Mosby, *Across Continents and Cultures: The Art and Life of Henry Ossawa Tanner* (Kansas City: Nelson-Atkins Museum of Art, 1995), 40; Frederick Douglass, "Speech at the Thirty-Third Anniversary of the Jerry Rescue," Syracuse, 1884, as quoted in David W. Blight, "'For Something beyond the Battlefield': Frederick Douglass and the Struggle for the Memory of the Civil War," *Journal of American History* 75, no. 4 (March 1989): 1177. For background on the painting, see Anna O. Marley, introduction to *Henry Ossawa Tanner: Modern Spirit*, ed. Anna O. Marley (Philadelphia: Pennsylvania Academy of Fine Arts and University of California Press, 2012), 28–29; Marc Simpson, "*The Resurrection of Lazarus* from the *Quartier Latin* to the Musée du Luxembourg," in Marley, *Henry Ossawa Tanner*, 69–78; on Tanner's self-portrait as Lazarus, see Cozzolino, "'I Invited the Christ Spirit to Manifest in Me,'" 119.

30. F. C. S. Schiller, *Logic for Use: An Introduction to the Voluntarist Theory of Knowledge* (New York: Harcourt, Brace, 1930), 80; Ernest D. Mason on Locke in his essay "Black Art and the Configurations of Experience: The Philosophy of the Black Aesthetic," *College Language Association Journal* 27, no. 1 (September 1983): 3; William James, *A Pluralistic Universe*, in *Writings, 1902–1910*, ed. Bruce Kuklick (New York: Library of America, 1987), 813.

31. John Dewey, *Reconstruction in Philosophy*, in *The Collected Works of John Dewey*, ed. Jo Ann Boydston, *The Middle Works, 1899–1924*, vol. 12, *1920*, ed. Bridget A. Walsh (Carbondale: Southern Illinois University Press, 2008), 166; from reviews of the painting as cited in Kristin Schwain, *Signs of Grace: Religion and American Art in the Gilded Age* (Ithaca, NY: Cornell University Press, 2008), 45–46.

32. See Locke, "Concept of Race as Applied to Culture," 270, 272; Nancy Fraser, "Another Pragmatism: Alain Locke, Critical 'Race' Theory, and the Politics of Culture," in *The Critical Pragmatism of Alain Locke: A Reader on Value Theory, Aesthetics, Community, Culture, Race, and Education*, ed. Leonard Harris (Lanham, MD: Rowman

and Littlefield, 1999), 15; Alain Locke, "Race Contacts and Inter-racial Relations: A Study in the Theory and Practice of Race," in *WAL*, 256–58; Locke's five lectures on race delivered at Howard University in 1916 as cited in Fraser, "Another Pragmatism," 16; Locke, "The New Negro," 11, 14; Cedric Robinson, "A Critique of W. E. B. Du Bois' *Black Reconstruction*," *Black Scholar* 8, no. 7 (May 1977): 46.

33. Locke, "The New Negro," 8–9, 14.

34. Locke, "Concept of Race as Applied to Social Culture," 269, 274; "Negro Youth Speaks," 47. For more on "race" in Locke, freed of biologism and put to the "advantage" of a group, see Ross Posnock, *Color and Culture: Black Writers and the Making of the Modern Intellectual* (Cambridge, MA: Harvard University Press, 1998), esp. 197–200.

35. Locke, "Values and Imperatives," 462; Dewey, *Art as Experience*, in *Collected Works, The Later Works, 1925–1953*, 10:179, 261, 269.

36. Locke, "Functional View of Value Ultimates," 485; Dewey, *Art as Experience*, in *Collected Works, The Later Works, 1925–1953*, 10:66, 270 (on this experience as a "reconstruction" of past experience, see 59, 276); Locke, "Values and Imperatives," 456; Mason, "Black Art and the Configurations of Experience," 3.

37. Alain Locke, "Forward: Frederick Douglass's 'Life and Times,'" in *WAL*, 321; "Race Contacts and Inter-racial Relations," 258; Henry James, preface to *The Golden Bowl* in *The Art of the Novel: Critical Prefaces*, introduction by R. P. Blackmur (1934; Chicago: University of Chicago Press, 2011), 339–40; Albert C. Barnes and Violette de Mazia, *The Art of Henri-Matisse* (New York: Charles Scribner's Sons, 1933), 31.

38. Locke, "The New Negro," 6; see also Alain Locke, "The Legacy of the Ancestral Arts," and Albert C. Barnes, "Negro Art and America," in *The New Negro*, ed. Alain Locke, introduction by Arnold Rampersad (1925; New York: Atheneum, 1992), 254–68 and 19–25; on Barnes's collection of African American and African art and on his educational outreach and relationship to the Harlem Renaissance, see Mary Ann Meyers, *Art, Education, and African-American Culture: Albert Barnes and the Science of Philanthropy* (2004; New York: Routledge, 2017); on Locke's relationship to Barnes, see also Jeffrey C. Stewart, *The New Negro: The Life of Alain Locke* (New York: Oxford University Press, 2018), 420–39.

39. As quoted in Judith F. Dolkart, "To See as the Artist Sees: Albert C. Barnes and the Experiment in Education," in *The Barnes Foundation: Masterworks*, by Judith F. Dolkart and Martha Lucy (New York: Skira Rizzoli and The Barnes Foundation, 2012), 25, 26.

40. Barnes in a letter to the American painter Stuart Davis, as quoted in Dolkart, "To See as the Artist Sees," 26; Locke, "Values and Imperatives," 456.

41. The essay is adapted from Dewey's *Experience and Nature* and was reprinted in a collection of essays published by Barnes. John Dewey, "Experience, Nature and Art," in John Dewey, Albert C. Barnes, Laurence Buermeyer, Mary Mullen, and Violette de Mazia, *Art and Education: A Collection of Essays*, 3rd ed. (Merion, PA: Barnes Foundation Press, 1954; first published 1929 by the Barnes Foundation), 26; Albert C. Barnes, *The Art in Painting* (1925; Merion, PA: Barnes Foundation Press, 1990), 5, 7, 10, 12; Mary Mullen, "Problems Encountered in Art Education," in Dewey et al., *Art and Education*, 255; Albert C. Barnes, "The Problem of Appreciation," in Dewey et al., *Art and Education*, 47; Albert C. Barnes and Violette de Mazia, "Expression and Form," in Dewey et al., *Art and Education*, 163.

42. Barnes, *The Art in Painting*, 5, 7; Albert C. Barnes and Violette de Mazia,

"Method," in Dewey et al., *Art and Education*, 13, 15; Albert C. Barnes, "The Roots of Art," in Dewey et al., *Art and Education*, 53; John Dewey, "Experience, Nature and Art," in Dewey et al., *Art and Education*, 27.

43. Barnes and de Mazia, "Method," 13; on "academicism," see Barnes, *The Art in Painting*, 4–5; Laurence Buermeyer, "Art as Creative," in Dewey et al., *Art and Education*, 63.

44. See Richard J. Wattenmaker, *American Paintings and Works on Paper in the Barnes Foundation* (New Haven, CT: The Barnes Foundation and Yale University Press, 2010), 305–10; Barnes, *The Art in Painting*, 470; Horace Pippin, "How I Paint," in *Horace Pippin, American Modern*, by Anne Monahan (New Haven, CT: Yale University Press, 2020), 210; John Dewey, "Experience, Nature and Art," in Dewey et al., *Art and Education*, 31.

45. This third version is the one I am citing here. Countee Cullen, "Heritage," in *Color* (New York: Harper and Brothers, 1925), as reprinted in *The Portable Harlem Renaissance Reader*, ed. David Levering Lewis (New York: Viking, 1994), 244–47; also see, Countee Cullen, "Heritage," in *The New Negro*, ed. Alain Locke, introduction by Arnold Rampersad (1925; New York: Atheneum, 1992), 250–53.

46. On homosexual desire latent in the poem, see Jeremy Braddock, "The Poetics of Conjecture: Countee Cullen's Subversive Exemplarity," *Callaloo* 25, no. 4 (Autumn 2002), 1260–68.

47. Dewey, *Art as Experience*, in *Collected Works, The Later Works, 1925–1953*, 10:260; on the attempt and failure to repress the African past in the poem, see Walter Benn Michaels, *Our America: Nativism, Modernism, and Pluralism* (Durham, NC: Duke University Press, 1995), 123–24.

48. Isabelle Stengers, *Thinking with Whitehead: A Free and Wild Creation of Concepts*, trans Michael Chase (Cambridge, MA: Harvard University Press, 2011), 18; I will say more later about the sense of relevance as an "adventure" in F. C. S. Schiller, Dewey, Whitehead, and others. Almost no one speaks of relevance in these decades without describing it as an adventure, including Whitehead in *Process and Reality*, *Modes of Thought*, and also, though more implicitly, *Adventures of Ideas* (New York: Macmillan, 1933); Martin Savransky, *The Adventure of Relevance: An Ethics of Social Inquiry*, foreword by Isabelle Stengers (London: Palgrave Macmillan, 2016), 40; Dewey, *Art as Experience*, in *Collected Works, The Later Works, 1925–1953*, 10:271.

49. Alain Locke, "Negro Youth Speaks," 48; Dewey, *Art as Experience*, in *Collected Works, The Later Works, 1925–1953*, 10:66–67.

Chapter 9

1. James McNeill Whistler, *The Gentle Art of Making Enemies* (London: W. Heinemann, 1892), 128; J. A. McNeill Whistler, *Whistler v. Ruskin: Art & Art Critics* (London: Chatto and Windus, 1878), 10.

2. Robyn Asleson, *Albert Moore* (London: Phaidon Press, 2000), 87; also see Asleson's terrific catalog on the geometry and patterning of the painting (85–87) and on Moore's use of fifth-century Greek vase painting as a model (69); as quoted in William Sharp, *Dante Gabriel Rossetti: A Record and a Study* (London: Macmillan, 1882), 236.

3. C. L. Hamblin, *Fallacies* (London: Methuen, 1970), 136; on Richard Whately, see 168–75; Raymie E. McKerrow, "Whately and the Study of Fallacious Reasoning," in

Historical Foundations of Informal Logic, ed. Douglas Walton and Alan Brinton (Aldershot: Ashgate, 1997), 99–113; James Van Evra, "Richard Whately and Logical Theory," in *Handbook of the History of Logic*, ed. Dov M. Gabbay and John Woods, vol. 4, *British Logic in the Nineteenth Century* (Oxford: Elsevier, 2008), 75–91; John Stuart Mill, "On Fallacies," in *A System of Logic, Ratiocinative and Inductive*, ed. J. M. Robson, in *Collected Works of John Stuart Mill*, vol. 8 (Toronto: University of Toronto Press, 1974), 739; Augustus de Morgan, *Formal Logic: or, The Calculus of Inference, Necessary and Probable* (1847), ed. A. E. Taylor (London: Open Court, 1926), 276; Jeremy Bentham, *The Book of Fallacies: From Unfinished Papers of Jeremy Bentham*, ed. Peregrine Bingham (London: John and H. L. Hunt, 1824), 2.

4. Bentham, *The Book of Fallacies*, 2, 213. Some of Bentham's work on fallacies appeared earlier in "Traité de sophisms politiques," in *Tactiques des assemblées législatives*, a two-volume recension of the work, translated and published by Étienne Louis Dumont in 1816.

5. John Locke, *An Essay Concerning Human Understanding* (1689), ed. Roger Woolhouse (New York: Penguin Books, 1997), 606; see also Isaac Watts's *Logick: Or, The Right Use of Reason in the Enquiry after Truth, with a Variety of Rules to Guard against Error, in the Affairs of Religion and Human Life, as well as in the Sciences* (1725). For more on Locke, Watts, and others, see Douglas Walton and Alan Brinton, eds., *Historical Foundations of Informal Logic* (Aldershot: Ashgate, 1997). There was also Thomas Browne's catalog of errors in thinking in *Pseudodoxia Epidemica: or, Enquiries into very many received tenants and commonly presumed truths* (1646), influenced by Bacon. Later, Charles Lamb, responsible for popularizing Browne in the nineteenth century, drew on his work on "vulgar errors" for his own series of essays, *Popular Fallacies*, published in the *New Monthly Magazine* from January to September 1826; see Charles Lamb, *The Essays of Elia and the Last Essays of Elia* (London: Oxford University Press, 1969), 363–96.

6. Mill, "On Fallacies," in *A System of Logic*, 8:736, 739; D. Vance Smith, "Fallacy: Close Reading and the Beginning of Philosophy," *Representations* 140 (Fall 2017): 32, 35; on William of Sherwood and other logicians in the Latin Middle Ages who discuss Aristotle's logical texts, see Alan R. Perreiah, "Forms of Argumentation in Medieval Dialect," in Walton and Brinton, *Historical Foundations of Informal Logic*, 51–66. The expression "some beautiful appearance" derives from the French Academy dictionary's 1694 definition of *sophism*; Michel Dufour suggests that "the stress put on an appearance that is at the root of the deception makes this definition very close to the definition of a paralogism in Aristotle's *On Sophistical Refutations*," in "Old and New Fallacies in Port-Royal Logic," *Argumentation* 33 (February 2019): 254; Terence Cave, *Recognitions: A Study in Poetics* (1988; Oxford: Oxford University Press, 2002), 43.

7. Richard Whately, *Elements of Logic* (London: J. Mawman, 1826), 141, 187; Hamblin, *Fallacies*, 31. As late as 1970, Hamblin still could write, "there has never yet been a book on fallacies; never, that is, a book-length study of the subject as a whole, or of incorrect reasoning in its own right rather than as an afterthought or adjunct to something else" (10). He also writes, "We have no *theory* of fallacy at all, in the sense in which we have theories of correct reasoning or inference. . . . In some respects, as I shall argue later, we are in the position of the medieval logicians before the twelfth century; we have lost the doctrine of fallacy and need to rediscover it" (11).

8. Alfred Sidgwick, *Fallacies: A View of Logic from the Practical Side* (London: Kegan Paul, Trench, 1883), 182; Bentham, *The Book of Fallacies*, 195.

9. See Fred Wilson, "The Logic of John Stuart Mill," in Gabbay and Woods, *Handbook of the History of Logic*, 2:229–81; see also R. F. McRae, introduction to Mill, *A System of Logic*, 7:xxi-xlviii.

10. Eric White, *Kaironomia: On the Will-to-Invent* (1987), as cited in John Poulakos, "The Logic of Greek Sophistry," in Walton and Brinton, *Historical Foundations of Informal Logic*, 18; Barbara Cassin, *Sophistical Practice: Toward a Consistent Relativism* (New York: Fordham University Press, 2014), 30.

11. Cassin, *Sophistical Practice*, 6, 27, 79, 89, 92–93, 97; F. C. S. Schiller, *Our Human Truths* (New York: Columbia University Press, 1939), 312. Schiller is referring to a famous saying by John Pentland Mahaffy, a classicist at Trinity College, Dublin. An "Irish bull" is an incongruent, paradoxical, or logically absurd statement that appears at first to make sense, with "bull" meaning "deceit" or "trickery" and the Irish epithet added later.

12. F. C. S. Schiller, *Logic for Use: An Introduction to the Voluntarist Theory of Knowledge* (New York: Harcourt, Brace, 1930), 75–76, 83.

13. Schiller, 79.

14. Schiller, *Our Human Truths*, 181, 182; F. C. S. Schiller, *Studies in Humanism* (London: Macmillan, 1907), 13; *Humanism: Philosophical Essays* (London: Macmillan, 1903), xvii. For more on the connections between Schiller's humanism and Protagoras's sophistical thought, see Steven Mailloux, "Introduction: Sophistry and Rhetorical Pragmatism," in *Rhetoric, Sophistry, Pragmatism*, ed. Steven Mailloux (Cambridge: Cambridge University Press, 1995), 1–32; Schiller, *Logic for Use*, 17, 80; Cassin, *Sophistical Practice*, 21.

15. See Jill Vance Buroker, "The Port-Royal Semantics of Terms," *Synthese* 96, no.3 (September 1993): 455–75; Dufour, "Old and New Fallacies," 241–67; Gary Hatfield, "Attention in Early Scientific Psychology," in *Visual Attention*, ed. Richard D. Wright (New York: Oxford University Press, 1998), 7.

16. Bentham, *The Book of Fallacies*, 2, 4, 6, 21, 74, 131–33, 209–10, 359.

17. See *Journal of the House of Representatives of the United States, 1841–1842* (February 5, 1842): 1696; "Summary of Politics: Proceedings in Parliament," *Cobbett's Weekly Political Register* 11 (February 14, 1807): 232–33. See also, William Cobbett, *Rural Rides* (1853; London: J. M. Dent and Sons, 1924), 2:309–10.

18. Bentham, *The Book of Fallacies*, 359, 370.

19. Alex Stein, "The Refoundation of Evidence Law," *Canadian Journal of Law and Jurisprudence* 9, no. 2 (July 1996): 279–342, with the quote on 280; John H. Langbein, "Historical Foundations of the Law of Evidence: A View from the Ryder Sources," *Columbia Law Review* 96 (1996): 1168–1202, with the quote on 1200; John H. Wigmore, "Required Numbers of Witnesses: A Brief History of the Numerical System in England," *Harvard Law Review* 15, no. 2 (June 1901): 83–108. On the history of Anglo-American evidence law from Bentham to Wigmore, see William Twining, "The Rationalist Tradition of Evidence Scholarship," in *Rethinking Evidence: Exploratory Essays*, 2nd ed. (Cambridge: Cambridge University Press, 2009), 35–98.

20. Jeremy Bentham, *Rationale of Judicial Evidence, Specially Applied to English Practice*, (London: Hunt and Clarke, 1827), 1:128, 164, 282, 290, 430, 440, 447, 456; Jeremy Bentham, *A Treatise on Judicial Evidence, Extracted from the Manuscripts of Jeremy Bentham by M. Dumont* (London: J. W. Paget, 1825), 333; W. D. Evans as cited in Langbein, "Historical Foundations of the Law of Evidence," 1200; John Henry Wigmore,

A Treatise on the System of Evidence in Trials at Common Law (Boston: Little, Brown, 1904), 1:91; see also, Alexander M. Burrill, *A Treatise on the Nature, Principles and Rules of Circumstantial Evidence, Especially That of the Presumptive Kind, in Criminal Cases* (New York: J. S. Voorhies, 1856).

21. James Fitzjames Stephen, *An Introduction to the Indian Evidence Act: The Principles of Judicial Evidence*, as quoted in J. L. Montrose, "Basic Concepts of the Law of Evidence" (1954), *Law Quarterly Review* 70, in *Evidence and Proof*, ed. William Twining and Alex Stein (New York: New York University Press Reference Collection, 1992), 350, and see Montrose on "extra-legality"; James Fitzjames Stephen, *A Digest of the Law of Evidence* (London: Macmillan, 1876), 4, 13, 136.

22. James Bradley Thayer, *A Preliminary Treatise on Evidence at the Common Law*, pt. 2: *Other Preliminary Topics* (Boston: Little, Brown, 1898), 264–65, 268–69, 270–71, 273–74; Montrose, "Basic Concepts of the Law of Evidence," 358, 374. On Thayer's view that the law "furnishes no test of relevancy" and on relevant evidence as a logical determination, see Twining, "Rationalist Tradition of Evidence Scholarship," 61–63. In *The Science of the Law* (New York: D. Appleton and Company, 1885), 296, Sheldon Amos writes, "The process of ascertaining what are the facts which one party alleges, and the other denies, and of separating them from facts either admitted by both parties or wholly irrelevant to the true issue, is one which needs, indeed, the general supervision of a judicial officer, but does not call for the active interposition of a court of justice. How many facts are relevant to the issue in any given case may be a difficult question to answer, and much injustice may follow from a rash or precipitate judgment in the matter. Much must depend upon the subject-matter of the suit, and the actual complication of the affairs which have led to it."

23. John Henry Wigmore, *The Principles of Judicial Proof, As Given by Logic, Psychology, and General Experience and Illustrated by Judicial Trials* (Boston: Little, Brown, 1913), 4, 748; see also, *A Students' Textbook of the Law of Evidence* (Brooklyn, NY: Foundation Press, 1935); Jean Goodwin, "Wigmore's Chart Method," *Informal Logic* 20, no. 3 (2000): 223–43; William Twining, "Taking Facts Seriously," *Journal of Legal Education* 34, no. 1 (March 1984): 22–42; *Theories of Evidence: Bentham and Wigmore* (London: Weidenfeld and Nicolson, 1985).

24. F. C. S. Schiller, *Our Human Truths*, 23, 293–95; Schiller, *Logic for Use*, 78, 81, 90–91, 93.

25. Schiller, *Logic for Use*, 77–79, 82, 146; *Our Human Truths*, 292–293.

26. Alain Locke, "Value," *The Works of Alain Locke*, ed. Charles Molesworth (New York: Oxford University Press, 2012), 470.

27. John Dewey, *Essays in Experimental Logic* (Chicago: University of Chicago Press, 1916), 13–14, 196, 243, 348, 361; Alfred North Whitehead, *Process and Reality: An Essay in Cosmology*, ed. David Ray Griffin and Donald W. Sherburne (New York: Free Press, 1978; first published 1929 by Macmillan [New York]), 186, 280. Paul W. Taylor's work on "normative values" and "rules of relevance" credits Ralph Barton Perry, C. I. Lewis, and other theorists of value as influences, but it especially credits studies in "informal logic": "My greatest philosophical debt is to those philosophers who have carried out in recent years careful analytic investigations of 'informal logic' in the more restricted areas of moral, aesthetic, political, and religious discourse." He claims his book is "the first fullscale attempt to use the 'informal logic' approach in a general theory of value"; *Normative Discourse* (Englewood Cliffs, NJ: Prentice-Hall, 1961), xi.

28. Dewey, *Essays in Experimental Logic*, 58–59.

29. Dewey, 353, 358; *How We Think* (Boston: D. C. Heath, 1910), 57; *Essays in Experimental Logic*, 78; I am quoting George Santayana here on logic and propositions in *The Realm of Essence* (New York: Scribner's, 1927), 105; Ralph Waldo Emerson, "Natural History of Intellect," in *The Complete Works of Ralph Waldo Emerson*, vol. 12, *Natural History of Intellect and Other Papers*, ed. Edward W. Emerson (1893; Boston: Houghton, Mifflin, 1904), 13; Locke, "Value," 471.

30. Schiller, *Logic for Use*, 88; Alain Locke, "Race Contacts and Inter-racial Relations: A Study in the Theory and Practice of Race," in *The Works of Alain Locke*, ed. Charles Molesworth (New York: Oxford University Press, 2012), 257; Cassin, *Sophistical Practice*, 97, 119, 135.

31. Hannah Arendt, "Truth and Politics," in *Between Past and Future: Eight Exercises in Political Thought*, ed. Jerome Kohn (1954; New York: Penguin Books, 1977), 255; "What Is Authority?," in *Between Past and Future*, 113, 95; *The Human Condition* (Chicago: University of Chicago Press, 1958), 3, 50–52. See also Barbara Cassin's wonderful discussion of Arendt and sophistical thought in *Sophistical Practice*, 164–88.

32. Schiller, *Our Human Truths*, 286; *Logic for Use*, 93; William James, *Pragmatism*, in *Writings, 1902–1910*, ed. Bruce Kuklick (New York: Library of America, 1987), 586–87; John Dewey, *Experience and Nature*, in *The Collected Works of John Dewey*, ed. Jo Ann Boydston, *The Later Works, 1925–1953*, vol. 1, *1925*, ed. Patricia Baysinger and Barbara Levine (Carbondale: Southern Illinois University Press, 2008), 32; F. C. S. Schiller, "Relevance," *Mind* 82 (April 1912): 158–59.

33. Schiller, *Logic for Use*, 77, 93; Schiller, "Relevance," 156.

34. Robyn Asleson, *Albert Moore* (London: Phaidon Press, 2000), 130.

35. I. A. Richards, *Practical Criticism: A Study of Literary Judgment* (1929; New York: Harcourt, Brace, 1954), 188; Henry James, preface to *The Spoils of Poynton*, in *The Art of the Novel: Critical Prefaces by Henry James*, introduction by R. P. Blackmur (1934; Chicago: University of Chicago Press, 2011), 119.

36. Paul Ricoeur, "Narrative and Hermeneutics," in *Essays on Aesthetics: Perspectives on the Work of Monroe C. Beardsley*, ed. John Fisher (Philadelphia: Temple University Press, 1983), 153–54.

37. Alfred North Whitehead, *Modes of Thought* (New York: Free Press, 1966; first published 1938 by Macmillan [New York]), 57; Laurence Perrine, *The Art of Total Relevance* (Rowley, MA: Newbury House, 1976), 3, 30–31; David Bohm, *Wholeness and the Implicate Order* (1980; London: Routledge Classics, 2002), 187–88.

38. Richards, *Practical Criticism*, 11–12, 15–17, 235, 246, 302.

39. Richards, 241–42, 259, 268. The symposium with F. C. S. Schiller, Bertrand Russell, and Harold Henry Joachim took place at Oxford in September 1920 and was published as "The Meaning of 'Meaning,'" in the journal *Mind* that same year ["The Meaning of 'Meaning': A Symposium," *Mind* 29, no. 116 (October 1920): 395–414]; see, John Paul Russo, *I. A. Richards: His Life and Work* (Baltimore: The Johns Hopkins University Press, 1989), 65, 704n6; F. C. S. Schiller, "The Meaning of 'Meaning,'" in *F. C. S. Schiller on Pragmatism and Humanism: Selected Writings 1891–1939*, ed. John R. Shook and Hugh P. McDonald (Amherst, NY: Humanity Books, 2008), 601–2.

40. W. K. Wimsatt, *The Verbal Icon: Studies in the Meaning of Poetry* (1954; Lexington: University Press of Kentucky, 1982), xiii, xv, 4, 86; W. K. Wimsatt and Monroe C. Beardsley, "The Intentional Fallacy" (1946), in Wimsatt, *The Verbal Icon*, 18; W. K.

Wimsatt and Monroe C. Beardsley, “The Affective Fallacy” (1946), in Wimsatt, *The Verbal Icon*, 38.

41. Monroe C. Beardsley, *Practical Logic* (Englewood Cliffs, NJ: Prentice-Hall, 1950), x–xii, xiv–xv, 124–25, 140–43. See also, Monroe C. Beardsley, *Thinking Straight: A Guide for Readers and Writers* (New York: Prentice-Hall, 1950), esp. 124–25.

42. Monroe C. Beardsley, *Aesthetics: Problems in the Philosophy of Criticism* (1958; Indianapolis: Hackett, 1981), 86, 88, 96, 101, 129–30, 132, 147, 375, 436, 492, 533, 543, 563.

43. Beardsley, 129, 144–45, 168, 196, 208, 220, 236, 253, 351, 386, 387, 527–28, 554, 563; see also George Dickie, *Evaluating Art* (Philadelphia: Temple University Press, 1988), 56–58; John Dewey, *Art as Experience*, in *The Collected Works of John Dewey*, ed. Jo Ann Boydston, *The Later Works, 1925–1953*, vol. 10, *1934*, ed. Harriet Furst Simon, introduction by Abraham Kaplan (Carbondale: Southern Illinois University Press, 2008), 263; Ricoeur, “Narrative and Hermeneutics,” 149.

44. Monroe C. Beardsley, *The Aesthetic Point of View: Selected Essays*, ed. Michael J. Wreen and Donald M. Callen (Ithaca, NY: Cornell University Press, 1982), 212, 341; *Aesthetics*, 563. Beardsley is alluding to a line at the end of Walter Pater’s *The Renaissance: Studies in Art and Poetry* (1873).

45. Richard Green Moulton, *Shakespeare as a Dramatic Artist* (Oxford: Clarendon, 1885), 2, 6, 7.

46. Richard Green Moulton, *The Modern Study of Literature: An Introduction to Literary Theory and Interpretation* (Chicago: University of Chicago Press, 1915), 49, 74, 97, 228, 272, 289–95, 331–32, 349.

47. Edgar Allan Poe, “How to Write a Blackwood Article,” in *Poetry and Tales*, ed. Patrick F. Quinn (New York: Library of America, 1984), 286.

48. Dewey, *Art as Experience*, in *Collected Works*, *The Later Works, 1925–1953*, 10:144–45.

49. Wimsatt, *The Verbal Icon*, 231; I am referring here to the title of Cleanth Brooks’s book *The Well Wrought Urn: Studies in the Structure of Poetry* based on Keats’s “Ode on a Grecian Urn.” It is another example of a New Critical work that asks us to read a poem as if it is “self-contained.”

50. Terence Cave, *Recognitions: A Study in Poetics* (1988; Oxford, UK: Oxford University Press, 2002), 1–4, 37–46, and throughout.

51. Henry James, *The Golden Bowl* (1904), introduction by Gore Vidal, notes by Patricia Crick (New York: Penguin Classics, 1987), 104, 116, 118, 292, 440. I am taking the phrases “as if it were important” and “signally attaching proposition” from James’s preface to *The Ambassadors*, with more on this in a moment; see *The Art of the Novel: Critical Prefaces by Henry James*, introduction by R. P. Blackmur (1934; Chicago: University of Chicago Press, 2011), 324.

52. James, *The Golden Bowl*, 214, 274, 334–35, 338, 346, 354, 356, 432, 437, 440.

53. James, 286, 362, 431, 434–35, 440, 455; Henry James, *The Art of the Novel*, 13–15, 30, 65, 302.

54. Henry James, *The Golden Bowl*, 190–92, 245, 271, 401, 423–25, 430, 447, 573–74, 580; James, *Art of the Novel*, 15–16, 157–58, 262–63.

55. Henry James, *The Ambassadors* (1903), ed. Harry Levin (New York: Penguin Books, 1986), 452, 457–59, 461–62, 467–68.

56. James, *Art of the Novel*, 3, 16, 308, 314, 339; *The Ambassadors*, 39, 73, 114, 122, 129, 215, 426, 466, 497, 512. The phrase “leaving no touch of experience irrelevant” is from

Henry James, *The American Scene*, in *Collected Travel Writings: Great Britain and America*, ed. Richard Howard (New York: Library of America, 1993), 359.

57. James, *The Ambassadors*, 40, 452; James, *Art of the Novel*, 311–12, 314.

58. James, *Art of the Novel*, 322–24.

59. James, *Art of the Novel*, 44, 119, 323–24; *The Ambassadors*, 48, 59, 184, 306, 313. I discussed Emerson on "smelling salts" and salience in chapter 3.

Chapter 10

1. As quoted in Terry Pinkard, *Hegel: A Biography* (Cambridge: Cambridge University Press, 2000), 242. See also G. W. F. Hegel, "Aphorisms from the Wastebook," *Miscellaneous Writings of G. W. F. Hegel*, ed. Jon Stewart (Evanston, IL: Northwestern University Press, 2002), 247; Immanuel Kant, *The Jäsche Logic*, in *Lectures on Logic*, as quoted in Rudolf A. Makkreel, *Orientation and Judgment in Hermeneutics* (Chicago: University of Chicago Press, 2015), 79.

2. As quoted in Frederic Hudson, *Journalism in the United States, from 1690 to 1872* (New York: Harper and Brothers, 1873), xviii; as quoted in Menahem Blondheim, *News over the Wires: The Telegraph and the Flow of Public Information in America, 1844–1897* (Cambridge: Harvard University Press, 1994), 29; "The Mission of the Newspaper," *Springfield Republican*, January 4, 1851, reprinted in *Voices of the Past: Key Documents in the History of American Journalism*, ed. Calder M. Pickett (Columbus: Grid, 1977), 109; James Parton, *The Life of Horace Greeley* (Boston: James R. Osgood, 1872), 104; Georg Wilhelm Friedrich Hegel, *Lectures on the Philosophy of World History: Introduction*, trans. H. B. Nisbet (Cambridge: Cambridge University Press, 1975), 135; James Parton, "James Gordon Bennett and The New York Herald," in *Famous Americans of Recent Times* (1867; Boston: Houghton, Mifflin, 1897), 265; Schelling in a letter to Hegel, Jan. 5, 1795, as quoted in Susan Buck-Morss, "Hegel and Haiti," *Critical Inquiry* 26, no. 4 (Summer 2000): 852n97; Susan Buck-Morss, *Hegel, Haiti, and Universal History* (Pittsburgh: University of Pittsburgh Press, 2009), 115; George Lunt, "The Uses and Abuses of the Press," in *Three Eras of New England and Other Addresses, with Papers Critical and Biographical* (Boston: Ticknor and Fields, 1857), 68, 80.

3. From Hegel's lectures on the history of philosophy, as quoted in Stephen Houlgate, *An Introduction to Hegel: Freedom, Truth and History*, 2nd ed. (Malden, MA: Blackwell, 2005), 9; Parton, "James Gordon Bennett and The New York Herald," 264. This is the English motto on the title page of the German-language journal *Minerva*, founded in the 1790s; see Buck-Morss, *Hegel, Haiti, and Universal History*, 44. On Hegel's sense of "self-consciousness" as the "new shape" of knowledge, see Horst Althaus, *Hegel: An Intellectual Biography*, trans. Michael Tarsh (Cambridge: Polity, 2000), 99–100 and G. W. F. Hegel, *Phenomenology of Spirit*, trans. A. V. Miller (Oxford: Oxford University Press, 1977), esp. 104–5.

4. Robert E. Park, "The Natural History of the Newspaper," in *On Social Control and Collective Behavior: Selected Papers*, ed. Ralph H. Turner (Chicago: University of Chicago Press, 1967), 99–100; "An Autobiographical Note" (1944) and from his diary, as quoted in Fred H. Matthews, *The Quest for an American Sociology: Robert E. Park and the Chicago School* (Montreal: McGill-Queen's University Press, 1977), 31; Dewey writing to William James, June 3, 1891, as quoted in Matthews, *Quest for an American Sociology*, 22; William James, "The Sentiment of Rationality," in *The Will to Believe and*

Other Essays in Popular Philosophy, in *Writings, 1878–1899*, ed. Gerald E. Myers (New York: Library of America, 1992), 518–519; Robert E. Park, "News as a Form of Knowledge," in *On Social Control and Collective Behavior*, 41–42, 50.

5. Immanuel Kant, "What Does It Mean to Orient Oneself in Thinking?" (1786), in *Religion and Rational Theology*, trans. and ed. Allen W. Wood (Cambridge: Cambridge University Press, 1996), 8–11

6. William James, *Pragmatism*, in *Writings, 1902–1910*, ed. Bruce Kuklick (New York: Library of America, 1987), 510, 603; Joan Richardson, *Pragmatism and American Experience: An Introduction* (New York: Cambridge University Press, 2014), 51; Richard Shusterman, *Pragmatist Aesthetics: Living Beauty, Rethinking Art*, 2nd ed. (Lanham, MD: Rowman and Littlefield, 2000), xiii, 127. Ross Posnock, *Renunciation: Acts of Abandonment by Writers, Philosophers, and Artists* (Cambridge, MA: Harvard University Press, 2016), 310.

7. John Dewey, *Essays in Experimental Logic* (Chicago: University of Chicago Press, 1916), 4, 9; John Dewey, "What Does Pragmatism Mean by Practical?," *Journal of Philosophy, Psychology and Scientific Methods* 5, no. 4 (February 13, 1908): 96; Albert C. Barnes and Violette de Mazia, after Dewey, on the beginnings of artistic, or any, expression, "Expression and Form," in John Dewey, Albert C. Barnes, Laurence Buermeyer, Mary Mullen, and Violette de Mazia, *Art and Education: A Collection of Essays*, 3rd ed. (Merion, PA: Barnes Foundation Press, 1954; first published 1929 by the Barnes Foundation), 165; John Dewey, *Art as Experience*, in *The Collected Works of John Dewey*, ed. Jo Ann Boydston, *The Later Works, 1925–1953*, vol. 10, *1934*, ed. Harriet Furst Simon, introduction by Abraham Kaplan (Carbondale: Southern Illinois University Press, 2008), 64; Alfred North Whitehead, *The Function of Reason* (Princeton, NJ: Princeton University Press, 1929), 51.

8. Park, "News as a Form of Knowledge," 51; Washington Irving, "Rip Van Winkle" (1819), *The Sketch Book of Geoffrey Crayon, Gent.*, in *History, Tales, Sketches*, ed. James W. Tuttleton (New York: Library of America, 1983), 772; Henry David Thoreau, *Walden; or, Life in the Woods* (1854), ed. Robert F. Sayre (New York: Library of America, 1985), 356; Henry David Thoreau, *A Week on the Concord and Merrimack Rivers* (1849), ed. Robert F. Sayre (New York: Library of America, 1985), 251, 293; Henry David Thoreau, "Life without Principle" (1863), in *Collected Essays and Poems*, ed. Elizabeth Hall Witherell (New York: Library of America, 2001), 360; Charles A. Dana, *The Art of Newspaper Making: Three Lectures* (New York: D. Appleton, 1895), 60; Parton, "James Gordon Bennett and The New York Herald," 263; George Lunt, "The Uses and Abuses of the Press," 68; Park, "The Natural History of the Newspaper," 108; from an editorial on January 4, 1851, quoted in George S. Merriam, *The Life and Times of Samuel Bowles* (New York: Century, 1885), 1:98. See also, John Nerone, "Newspapers and the Public Sphere," in *A History of the Book in America*, vol. 3, *The Industrial Book, 1840–1880*, ed. Scott E. Casper, Jeffrey D. Groves, Stephen W. Nissenbaum, and Michael Winship (Chapel Hill: University of North Carolina Press, 2007), 203–48; Hazel Dicken-Garcia, *Journalistic Standards in Nineteenth-Century America* (Madison: University of Wisconsin Press, 1989); Michael Schudson, *Discovering the News: A Social History of American Newspapers* (New York: Basic Books, 1973); Menahem Blondheim, *News over the Wires: The Telegraph and the Flow of Public Information in America, 1844–1897*.

9. Benedict Anderson, *Imagined Communities: Reflections on the Origin and Spread of Nationalism*, rev. ed. (New York: Verso, 1991), 35; Henry David Thoreau, *Cape Cod*

(1865), ed. Robert F. Sayre (New York: Library of America, 1985), 946; "NEWS," *Providence Patriot, Columbian Phenix*, September 10, 1814. See also David M. Henkin, *City Reading: Written Words and Public Spaces in Antebellum New York* (New York: Columbia University Press, 1998).

10. Marilyn R. Brown, *Degas and the Business of Art: "A Cotton Office in New Orleans"* (University Park: College Art Association and Pennsylvania State University Press, 1994), 70–80, on Zola and other critical responses to the painting; the critic Alfred de Lostalot, as quoted on 71; quoted in Christopher Benfey, *Degas in New Orleans: Encounters in the Creole World of Kate Chopin and George Washington Cable* (Berkeley: University of California Press, 1997), 155, 157; Zola actually described the painting as "halfway between a seascape and a plate from an illustrated journal," as quoted in Brown, *Degas and the Business of Art*, 70. On the dissolution and liquidation of the family business, the announcement in the *Daily Picayune*, and the suggestion that René De Gas might be depicted here "perusing the fatal announcement," see Brown, 32–33.

11. Benfey, *Degas in New Orleans*, 166; Charles Baudelaire as quoted in Benfey, 158. On the shift in printing from cotton paper to paper made from wood pulp, see AJ Valente, "Changes in Print Paper During the 19th Century," in *Charleston Conference Proceedings 2010*, ed. Katina Strauch, Beth R. Bernhardt, and Leah H. Hinds (Charleston, SC: Against the Grain, 2011), 182–87.

12. Robert E. Park, "Succession, An Ecological Concept" (1936), in *On Social Control and Collective Behavior*, 85–94; "News as a Form of Knowledge," 50; Dewey on the philosophy behind *Thought News*, his collaboration with Park, as quoted in Matthews, *Quest for an American Sociology*, 28.

13. See Michael Fried, "Orientation in Painting: Casper David Friedrich," in *Another Light: Jacques-Louis David to Thomas Demand* (New Haven, CT: Yale University Press, 2014), esp. 146; John Dewey, *Leibniz's New Essays Concerning the Human Understanding: A Critical Exposition* (Chicago: Scott, Foresman, 1902), 21–22; see also Scott R. Stroud, "John Dewey, Kenneth Burke, and the Role of Orientation in Rhetoric," in *Trained Capacities: John Dewey, Rhetoric, and Democratic Practice*, ed. Brian Jackson and Gregory Clark (Columbia, SC: University of South Carolina Press, 2014), 51, and throughout, 47–64.

14. Matthews, *Quest for an American Sociology*, 31–33, 48; William James, "On a Certain Blindness in Human Beings," in *The Heart of William James*, ed. Robert Richardson (Cambridge, MA; Harvard University Press, 2010), 148–49, 158–60.

15. Walt Whitman, *The Journalism: The Collected Writings of Walt Whitman*, ed. Herbert Bergman (New York: Peter Lang, 1998–2003), 1:xxv–xxvi, 402; Walt Whitman, "open letter" to Emerson, August 1856, in *Leaves of Grass and Other Writings*, ed. Michael Moon (New York: Norton, 2002), 640; "Song of Myself" (1891–92), in *Leaves of Grass*, 39, 77; preface to *Leaves of* Grass (1855) in *Leaves of Grass*, 633; "A Song of Joys," in *Leaves of Grass*, 152; Dana, *Art of Newspaper Making*, 12; Ed Folsom, "What We're Still Learning about the 1855 *Leaves of Grass* 150 Years Later," in *Leaves of Grass: The Sesquicentennial Essays*, ed. Susan Belasco, Ed Folsom, and Kenneth Price (Lincoln: University of Nebraska Press, 2007), 16; Whitman to Horace Traubel, as quoted in Folsom, 10; Whitman, "The Press—Its Future," *Brooklyn Daily Times*, July 31, 1857, as quoted in Douglas A. Noverr and Jason Stacy, "Introduction: Walt Whitman's Journalism Career in New York and Brooklyn," in *Walt Whitman's Selected Journalism*, ed. Douglas A. Noverr and Jason Stacy (Iowa City: University of Iowa Press, 2015), xxx;

Whitman, *Specimen Days*, in *Poetry and Prose*, ed. Justin Kaplan (New York: Library of America, 1982), 706, 711–12, 896; John Dewey, *Psychology* (1887; 3rd. rev. ed. 1891), in *The Collected Works of John Dewey*, *The Early Works, 1882–1898*, vol. 2, *1887*, ed. Jo Ann Boydston and Fredson Bowers (Carbondale: Southern Illinois University Press, 1967), 119. See also Alan Trachtenberg, "Whitman's Lesson of the City," in *Breaking Bounds: Whitman and American Cultural Studies*, ed. Betsy Erkkila and Jay Grossman (New York: Oxford University Press, 1996), 163–73.

16. Robert E. Park, "Morale and the News," in *On Social Control and Collective Behavior*, 261; "News as a Form of Knowledge," 33–34, 36–37, 39, 40–41; Hugo Münsterberg, *The Photoplay: A Psychology Study* (New York: D. Appleton, 1916), 88-89; Richardson, *Pragmatism and American Experience*, 54; Park, "News as a Form of Knowledge," 41-42. In *The Bias of Communication*, Harold A. Innis emphasizes "the importance of communication in determining 'things to which we attend,'" suggesting also "that changes in communication will follow changes in 'the things to which we attend.'" Innis writes that his essays on mass communication and media are reflections prompted by a question that James Ten Broeke, a philosophy professor at McMaster University, used to ask: "Why do we attend to the things to which we attend?" *The Bias of Communication* (1951), 2nd ed., intro. by Alexander John Watson (Toronto: University of Toronto Press, 2012), xliii.

17. Edmond Duranty, *The New Painting* (1876), as quoted in Brown, *Degas and the Business of Art*, 77; Park, "News as a Form of Knowledge," 34, 36, 47. Of course what Park identifies as the function of the newspaper since the nineteenth century might be seen as anticipating our contemporary information economy, with its search engines and algorithms optimized to sort through too much information for "relevance"; see, for example, Daniel Rosenberg, "Search," in *Information: A Historical Companion*, ed. Ann Blair, Paul Duguid, Anja-Silvia Goeing, and Anthony Grafton (Princeton, NJ: Princeton University Press, 2021), 259–84.

18. Frank Kermode, *The Sense of an Ending: Studies in the Theory of Fiction*, rev. ed. (1966; New York: Oxford University Press, 2000), 56.

19. Kevin G. Barnhurst and John Nerone, *The Form of News: A History* (New York: Guilford, 2001), 75; also called "seizing the points," see James Grant, *The Newspaper Press: Its Origin Progress—and Present Position* (Lindon: Tinsley Brothers, 1871), 2:121, 145; Park, "The Natural History of the Newspaper," 112. On changes in the appearance of newspapers, also see, for example, Kevin G. Barnhurst, *News as Art*, in Journalism Monographs 130 (Columbia, SC: Association for Education in Journalism and Mass Communication, 1991); John E. Allen, *Newspaper Makeup* (New York: Harper and Brothers, 1936); Allen Hutt, *The Changing Newspaper: Typographical Trends in Britain and America, 1622–1972* (London: Gordon Fraser, 1973); Helen Ogden Mahin, *The Development and Significance of the Newspaper Headline* (Ann Arbor, MI: George Wahr, 1924); Robert E. Garst and Theodore M. Bernstein, *Headlines and Deadlines: A Manual for Copy Editors*, 4th ed. (New York: Columbia University Press, 1982); Herbert Bruckner, *The Changing American Newspaper* (New York: Columbia University Press, 1937); Menahem Blondheim, *News Over the Wires: The Telegraph and the Flow of Public Information in America, 1844–1897*. See also Daniel Dor, "On Newspaper Headlines as Relevance Optimizers," *Journal of Pragmatics* 35, no. 5 (May 2003): 695–721.

20. On Degas's practice of revising compositions over many years, see, for example, Elizabeth Steele, "The Evolution of *Dancers at the Barre*: A Technical Study," in *Degas's*

Dancers at the Barre: Point and Counterpoint, ed. Elizabeth Rathbone and Elizabeth Steele (Washington, DC: The Phillips Collection, distributed by Yale University Press, 2011), 57–70; Rilke as quoted in Lillian Schacherl, *Edgar Degas: Dancers and Nudes* (New York: Prestel, 1997), 30. On Degas's interest in Darwin, see Richard Kendall, "Monet and the Monkeys: The Impressionist Encounter with Darwinism," in *Endless Forms: Charles Darwin, Natural Science and the Visual Arts*, ed. Diana Donald and Jane Munro (New Haven, CT: Yale Center for British Art and Yale University Press, 2009), 302–8; Douglas Druick, "Framing the *Little Dancer Aged Fourteen*," in Richard Kendall, *Degas and the Little Dancer* (New Haven, CT: Yale University Press, 1998), 77–96; and Harvey Buchanan, "Edgar Degas and Ludovic Lepic: An Impressionist Friendship," *Cleveland Studies in the History of Art* 2 (1997): 32–121.

21. Rosalind Kraus, "Grids," *October* 9 (Summer 1979): 55.

Index

Page numbers in italics refer to illustrations; the term "art" can apply to literature, poetry, and music as well as visual arts.